Sexuality in Austria

Contemporary Austrian Studies, Volume 15

Günter Bischof,
Anton Pelinka,
and
Dagmar Herzog
editors

Transaction Publishers
New Brunswick (U.S.A.) and London (U.K.)

Library of Congress Catalog Number: 2006051105
ISBN: 1-4128-0606-2; 978-1-4128-0606-0
Printed in the United States of America

Library of Congress Cataloging-in-Publication Data

Sexuality in Austria / Günter Bischof, Anton Pelinka, Josef Köstlbauer, editors.
    p. cm. -- (Contemporary Austrian studies ; v. 15)
    Includes index.
    ISBN 1-4128-0606-2 (alk. paper)
    1. Sex--Austria--History--20th century. I. Bischof, Günter, 1953-
II. Pelinka, Anton, 1941- III. Köstlbauer, Josef, 1976-

HQ18.A9S48 2007
306.709436--dc22

2006051105

Sexuality in Austria

Contemporary Austrian Studies

Sponsored by the University of New Orleans and Universität Innsbruck

Publication of this volume has been made possible through one time generous post-Hurricane Katrina grants by the Austrian Ministry of Science and Research as well as the Austrian Ministry of Foreign Affairs through the Austrian Cultural Forum in New York. The Austrian Marshall Plan Anniversary Foundation in Vienna has also supported the production of this volume. Metropolitan College at the University of New Orleans and the *Auslandsamt* of the University of Innsbruck have provided additional financial support. The University of Chicago Press has granted permission to reprint David Luft's lead essay.

Table of Contents

ANNUAL REVIEW

PREFACE

The Fifteenth Anniversary Issue
and the Stormy Season

Of all the fifteen issues of *Contemporary Austrian Studies*, this one was the most challenging to prepare for publication. I call it the emotional roller-coaster volume. The idea was born three years ago during a visit to Michigan State University in East Lansing, Michigan. There I first envisioned and discussed with Dagmar Herzog, who had just finished a monograph on sexuality in postwar Germany, the possibility of an issue on "Sexuality in Austria." In a follow-up lunch meeting with Dagmar in an Arlington, Virginia, hotel during the annual meeting of the German Studies Association, we conceptualized the volume and drew up a list of names of scholars to be invited to contribute to this volume. Most of those contacted eagerly agreed to write essays; a few were hesitant and turned us down. Some agreed and did not deliver. Others joined late in the game when the volume was already conceptualized and sent us excellent work from their ongoing research projects. First and foremost, we are grateful to our contributors for helping us to make this volume a special one.

This "fifteenth anniversary issue" is a special one for a number of reasons. The essays were due by the end of 2005 in the midst of the aftermath of a devastating natural catastrophe in the Crescent City and along the Louisiana Gulf Coast. On August 29, Hurricane Katrina hit New Orleans; its 20 to 30-foot water surges broke the floodwalls of canals and inundated 80 percent of the city. A month later, Hurricane Rita hit the coast of western Louisiana and finished off what Katrina had left standing. The University of New Orleans (UNO), home of CenterAustria where *CAS* is produced, experienced some flooding and wind damage, but suffered the most devastation from some 2,500 storm survivors, who, abandoned and without food and water, went on looting binges throughout the campus. UNO staged an astounding comeback. It was *the only* university in the Crescent City that resumed classes in the fall. On 10 October, five weeks "post-Katrina" (the new way time is being measured in the Crescent City) on a satellite campus in the suburbs, 7,000 students resumed their studies with online courses; another 1,000 were taught in regular classrooms by a faculty that had been scattered across the continent only weeks before. In mid-January, some 750 students graduated, many of them as a result of UNO's gargantuan effort to salvage the fall term. Chancellor Timothy Ryan and his vice-chancellors and deans came together a few days after Katrina hit and were determined to have a fall term and to re-launch the university in spite of the 100 million dollars in damages the facilities had suffered, including a brand new business college that had opened its doors barely a month before Katrina. Clearly, there were institutional responses that upstaged FEMA, the laggard and disoriented federal agency whose failure became symptomatic of the disastrous governmental response to this unprecedented catastrophe.

Katrina scattered the CenterAustria staff, too, far and wide. Gertraud Griessner, who manages the Center on a daily basis, relocated with her family to Seattle, Washington, for the fall term to place her kids in school. She returned in December to her Mid-City home that had escaped flooding by mere inches. Margaret Davidson, the resident director of our "Academic Year Abroad" program in Innsbruck, saw her apartment in Slidell badly damaged. Living an hour southwest of New Orleans, I was lucky to reside in the least mangled parish of coastal Louisiana and to find my home still standing and undamaged. My family returned to Larose after a two-day evacuation "vacation" to Hot Springs, Arkansas. Ten days after the storm, I began commuting to Baton Rouge, teaching for the fall semester at Louisiana State University. Jennifer Shimek, our devoted long-time copy editor at Loyola University in New Orleans, relocated to her parents' house in Erie, Pennsylvania, and returned by October to find that her new Uptown home had escaped flooding, too. The annual dissertation fellow at UNO, financed through the Austrian Ministry of Education, Culture, and Science, decided she had had enough of the stormy Gulf Coast and returned to Vienna two weeks after Katrina. Part of the job of the "Ministry Fellow" is to help with the daily production chores of *CAS*: maintaining contact with and tracking the manuscripts of some twenty-five contributors. In mid-September, I asked Josef Köstlbauer, the 2004/05 Ministry Fellow who had done a marvelous job with the production of volume XIV, whether he would resume his former duties "long distance," for he had returned to Austria. He spontaneously and graciously agreed to do so from his Lower Austrian domicile where he was finishing his dissertation on Atlantic history. Now he was engaging in what can be called "electronic Atlanticism." A one-time special grant from the Ministry of Education, Arts, and Sciences in Vienna helped us to pay him modestly for his services. Our devoted partners, Anton Pelinka, Franz Mathis, and Ellen Palli in Innsbruck, Austria, gave us moral support when we needed it most. When I first visited UNO on 3 October, I saw a battered campus where the clean-up work was already in full swing. The CenterAustria offices were left eerily untouched by the storm with a flyer for a 1 September lunchtime lecture still flapping on the office door. With electricity and air conditioning returning, the mustiness evaporated, and the mold never had a chance to spread as it did in the devastated Lakeview neighborhoods next to the UNO campus. We still had our files and could resume work, if only from a distance, for the state's "mold Nazis" kept the campus inaccessible until December.

My scheduled early October trip to the annual German Studies Association meeting in Milwaukee, Wisconsin, had to be cancelled. The Messner, Bauer/Huber, and Judson papers were first presented in a panel at the GSA and commented on by Dagmar Herzog; they were much improved as a result. Dagmar had just moved her family to Princeton, New Jersey, to assume a new senior appointment at the Graduate Center, City University of New York. To her great credit, she worked even harder as this volume's guest editor to keep the timelines on track, to assist with the editing of papers, and to ensure the timely publication of this volume. The topical essays are a tribute to her consummate knowledge of the subject matter and her unmatched professionalism. *CAS* may well be one of the very few programs at UNO that was challenged by Katrina, yet continued on its regular path uninterrupted. Without efficient electronic communication, of course, the volume could have never been published. Multiple daily e-mail exchanges between the editorial staff, production staff, and the authors saved us.

This fifteenth anniversary issue is also special since it is Anton Pelinka's last one as co-editor. Anton is retiring from the University of Innsbruck after a 30-plus year career at the end of the summer semester 2006. He will assume his new role as distinguished professor at Central European University in Budapest, Hungary, in the fall of 2006, before this volume will be out. Anton Pelinka has been a congenial partner through a long fifteen-year history of launching *CAS* and making it one of the two premier journals in Austrian Studies in North America. He is a scholar with phenomenal contacts around the world in the social sciences. His networking skills have been crucial in ensuring that *CAS* would be a wide-open interdisciplinary social sciences journal. It is this broad interdisciplinary focus which has given *CAS* its imprint and character from the very beginning. After many issues on comparative politics, sociology, economics, and historical subjects, for the first time we venture into the complex world of mentalities and social habits with this issue. We hope to continue with this focus, too, next to our tradi-

4 Contemporary Austrian Studies

tional interdisciplinary social sciences approach. We wish Anton Pelinka all the best in Budapest and thank him for him many years of highly professional cooperation. We will miss him and hope to see him often as a contributor to *CAS*. Given the challenges we have faced over the years, he is probably as surprised as I am that *CAS* is still going strong.

Fritz Plasser, one of Austria's foremost political scientists and pollsters from the University of Innsbruck, will be Anton's successor as the "Innsbruck co-editor" starting with volume XVI. He will put his immediate imprint on *CAS* with a volume that will reflect his interest in "The Changing Austrian Voter." Our UNO staff is looking forward to working with him.

Dagmar Herzog's far-ranging introductory essay sets the stage for our topical essays on sexuality. The FORUM on the big Austrian anniversary year 2005 makes this issue special as well. After a ROUND-TABLE on "The Historiography and Memory of the Austrian Occupation (1945-1955)" in volume XIV (2006), we are now following up with a FORUM on the "Memory Year 2005." The Republic of Austria celebrated a blizzard of commemorations in the *"Gedenkjahr"* 2005 and declared it also a year of "thoughtful reflection" (*"Gedankenjahr"*) on the country's recent past. Among the major anniversaries were the sixtieth anniversary of Austria's liberation at the end of World War II and the beginning of the Austrian Second Republic on 27 April 1945; the fiftieth anniversary of the Austrian State Treaty signed on 15 May 1955; and the tenth anniversary of Austria joining the European Union in 1995. One need not go as far as the ornery German philosopher Peter Sloterdijk did recently, when he blasted the popularizing Austrian anniversary culture in staging Freud's 150th birthday and Mozart's 250th birthday in 2006 as a "shameless assassination by trivialization" (*"unverschämtes Trivialisierungsattentat"*; "Gedenkjahre als Attentate," *Kurier*, 6 May 2005). The three review essays in this FORUM approach the 2005 anniversary year from different angles. *Katharina Wegan* questions the staging of the State Treaty celebrations in 1995 and before and looks at Austrian memory culture on this signal historic event. *Günter Bischof* analyzes some of the major historical exhibits and the genre of catalogues coming with these extravaganza historical shows. He asks whether these events constituted a "surfeit of memory" and how these "public productions of the past" (Lucy Noakes) might have shaped Austrian national and regional identities, as museums in Austria and elsewhere function as "powerful sites of cultural transmission and public education" (Noakes), producing hegemonic national grand narratives of the past. *Peter Berger* reviews a number of history books that were timed to be published in the "memory year" in order to ride the wave of public interest in contemporary history. This is our contribution to the 2005 *"Gedanken-*

jahr," namely to reflect on the Austrian historical memory cult with a critical distance in contrast to the government's very conscious central staging of the memory year and the political speeches oozing with self-congratulatory pieties.

In the end, then, we want to express our customary thanks to those who have made this volume possible. This year, our sincere gratitude is coupled with a profound feeling of respect and deep indebtedness to those who have supported us twice as hard with their moral contributions and symbolic gestures to New Orleans, UNO, and CenterAustria's recovery. For their hard work and unflagging support, my deepest debt goes to Dagmar Herzog, who has served as a model guest editor, and Josef Köstlbauer, who so kindly agreed to resume his duties as assistant editor, even if he would go unpaid. Franz Eder at the University of Vienna has given us valuable advice early on in the conceptualization of this volume. Jennifer Shimek performed her duties on difficult "Germano-English" syntax and diction with her usual professional skills and cheerful disposition. At UNO, Gertraud Griessner, Beryl Gauthier, and Dean Robert Dupont lent a helping hand when it was needed. In spite of an exceedingly difficult financial situation at UNO, Dean Dupont never hesitated to encourage me to go forward with this volume. In Innsbruck, Ellen Palli typeset the volume with her customary professional acumen in desktop publishing. Anton Pelinka and Franz Mathis gave assistance when needed.

Special thanks go to our publisher, Transaction, and to its founder, Irving Louis Horowitz, and his wife Mary Curtis, now the CEO of the company. Horowitz contacted me soon after Katrina and offered to do whatever was necessary to keep *CAS* going. With two Austrian series and a marketing/distribution agreement with StudienVerlag in Innsbruck, Transaction has now become the premier publisher in Austrian Studies in North America. It has taken fifteen years to get to this point, and Horowitz shares our pride in producing top-notch Austrian Studies scholarship in his house. Cheryl Orson has worked hard as the Transaction editor of this volume.

Finally, our financial supporters, who make the publication of *CAS* possible in the first place, deserve our deepest appreciation. The leadership of Austrian cultural diplomacy in the Federal Ministry of Foreign Affairs, (formerly) on Vienna's *Ballhausplatz*, has supported *Contemporary Austrian Studies* unstintingly from its beginning, when Peter Marboe in 1991 extended the initial grant for publishing this series. His present successor, Ambassador Emil Brix, has been no less supportive and enthusiastic about our trans-Atlantic publishing venture. Next to the general subsidy towards the publication of every volume, Brix spontaneously offered a one-time "post-Katrina" grant to ensure the continued appearance of *CAS*. He could not have honored our work in promoting the international dimension of Austrian Studies in a more timely fashion. No one has been more supportive over many years than Ernst Aichinger at the Austrian Cultural Forum (ACF) in New York. Ever since his first tour in New York, when it was still called the "Austrian Cultural Institute," and back in Vienna, Aichinger has been our most persistent backer in the Foreign Ministry and has given of his time unsparingly. ACF's current director, Christoph Thun-Hohenstein, has extended his blessing to our venture as well. In the Austrian Ministry of Education, Arts, and Science, our strongest backer has been Josef Leidenfrost, who has always pleaded our case with his superiors. He is even known to have read the volumes! Barbara Weitgruber has blessed us with her support, too. This year, Alois Söhn and Gottfried Prinz extended a one-time special post-Katrina grant as had Ambassador Brix to assist us with financing our editorial staff. The Austrian Marshall Plan Anniversary Foundation in Vienna through its very generous support of CenterAustria activities has been backing the publication of this journal, too. Special thanks to its executive directors, Wolfgang Stoiber and Eugen Stark, are overdue. Their aid and friendship during a trying time of loss in the traumatized Crescent City is our blessing—we treasure it much more than they could ever imagine. The University of New Orleans and the Leopold Franzens University of Innsbruck are supporting *CAS* by continuing to pay our salaries and, thus, helping to secure our livelihoods, not a given these days in post-Katrina New Orleans when universities have to cut their budgets—due to the loss of students—by tens of millions of dollars.

Günter Bischof

Larose, Lafourche Parish in Coastal Louisiana, May 2006

I. TOPICAL ESSAYS

Sexuality in Twentieth-Century Austria: An Introduction

Dagmar Herzog

The twentieth century was, in many ways, the century of sexuality. No prior era in European history was as strongly defined by issues relating to sex. On the one hand, sex became ever more central to individual identity. The growing interest—and success—in controlling fertility changed heterosexual experiences, albeit in often contradictory ways (as newly heightened expectations of pleasure, especially for women, collided with the challenges posed by contraceptive strategies). At the same time, the growing professionalization of research into sex—in dialectical interaction with the self-representations of sexual minorities—generated an intensifying preoccupation with questions of sexual orientation. Ordinary people increasingly understood and represented themselves not only as beings with sexual identities, but also as beings with sexual *rights*—whether to privacy or to public attention, to "normal" functioning or to the transgression of norms perceived as illegitimate, to intensity of experience or to safety from sexual harm. Sex was also increasingly expected to be the main adhesive in marital partnerships, as the practice of prostitution declined while rates of premarital intercourse with a future spouse rose, and as the years of marriage themselves were imagined as a site for continuously renewed romance, desire, and fulfillment.

On the other hand, sexual matters also acquired growing political salience. In the course of the twentieth century, sexuality became a prime arena of often virulent social and cultural conflict, a key element in processes of secularization and religious renewal, a main motor of commercial development, a constant theme in highbrow art and low-brow advertising alike, and a locus of increasing government-citizen negotiation (whether in courtrooms, classrooms, military brothels, government-funded maternal welfare or marital guidance clinics, or

street demonstrations). In a constantly reconfigured combination of
stimulus and regulation, prohibition and exposure, norm-expounding and
obsessed detailing of deviance, liberalizing and repressive impulses
together worked to make conflicts over sexual matters consequential for
politics writ large.

This amplified significance of sexuality, and its ever-spreading
intersections with almost all other domains of existence, has to do—and
this is difficult to express, but crucial for our comprehension—with the
intrinsic complexity of sexual matters. One need only think of the vital
role of sexual scandal in making newspaper reading a mass and not just
an elite phenomenon in the 1900s-1920s (Is voyeurism itself a sexual
act?), the saturation of anti-Semitic rhetoric with sexual innuendo and
the role of this sexualized rhetoric in making persecution of Jews seem
morally acceptable in the 1930s-1940s (Is there a libidinal element in
cruelty?), or the inseparability of antiwar protest from efforts at sexual
liberation in the 1960s-1970s (How can we make sense of this moment
when so many human beings sincerely believed that making more love
could also profoundly change the world?), to recognize the poverty and
inadequacy of the theoretical language and conceptual frameworks
available to us. Yet, for all of the diffuseness and elusiveness of the
terms, looking back on the twentieth century as a whole from the
vantage point of the twenty-first, we can also recognize that over the
course of that century something like a semi-coherent entity—a complex
of physiological and emotional impulses and sensations, acts and
ideals—took shape and was designated as "sexuality" in the collective
imaginary.

Is the era of sexuality now behind us? Experts on sexuality disagree,
and prophecies are notoriously wrong. However, a proliferating number
of surveys and analyses, in scholarly publications and pop culture
venues alike, indicates that a cluster of new developments are occurring
that are changing fundamental assumptions about what sexuality is and
how it is experienced. One strand of analysis emphasizes the impact of
psychopharmacology (from Prozac and Zoloft to Viagra and Cialis) in
changing human beings' relationship to their own and each others'
bodies. Others point to the proliferation of Internet porn and cybersex
and diagnose what they see as a trend toward the "onanization" of
sexuality.[1] Yet others seek to make sense of the notable conjunction of
a hypersexualization of visual culture and fashion with a pronounced
drop (as study after study—also, apparently, in Austria—shows) in
many human beings' levels of interest in sex.[2] Scholars also call attention to the greater pleasure people appear to be finding in exhibitionist
self-styling and experiencing themselves as objects of desire than in the
actual physiological sensation of orgasm itself; these scholars also note

a trend toward attempting to make sexual encounters more time-efficient, squeezed as they are into overstressed, multitasking lives. All these phenomena together are often conceptualized under the rubric of a "neosexual revolution."[3] Yet another strand of analysis focuses on an entirely different (though, one suspects, not entirely unrelated) phenomenon: the utter centrality of sexual matters in the ascendance of militant Islam and, thus, also to the culture clashes now raging across Western European nations. Secular Europeans have revealed themselves to be rather unprepared to defend the sexual values they claim to hold dear without resorting to racist language.[4]

What is the place of Austria in this tumultuous and complicated history? Austria provides an especially important laboratory for exploring all the broader themes of the history of sexuality in the twentieth-century West. Austria, after all, was home to both Sigmund Freud and Adolf Hitler.

At the very beginning of the twentieth century, as the contributions by David Luft and Scott Spector note, Vienna was already known as the city of sex. This was true even as, and however paradoxically, Vienna was also considered a traditionally-minded, provincial backwater run by a conservative, bourgeois elite. What was it about this Habsburg empire hothouse of ennui and enervation that also made it a center of explosively productive aesthetic and philosophical experimentation, and that generated such a rich proliferation of theorizing about the nature of sexual drives, orientations, and obsessions? By the 1920s, Vienna was capital to a much smaller country, run by socialists, and—as Maria Mesner's article demonstrates—was also home to some of the earliest sex reform clinics anywhere in the world. The motivations of the founders of these clinics ran the gamut from fantasies of eugenic perfectibility to empowerment of the poor to greater sensual enjoyment and control over their own fertility. In these early decades of the twentieth century, both under imperial and then under socialist auspices, Vienna was understood as a main hub of cultural production in the wider orbit of German culture. (When conservative Italian Catholics, for instance, in the 1920s condemned Germans as sexually obsessed, they certainly were referring to Vienna as much as to Berlin.)[5] Yet it is precisely the combination of similarities *and* differences between German and Austrian developments in the decades that followed that makes Austrian history such a valuable site for testing the strengths and weaknesses of many of our standard assumptions about causation and periodization in the history of sexuality.

The history of sexuality in Austria is just beginning to come out from the shadow of the history of sexuality in Germany, a history into or under which is has too long been merged or subsumed. Groundbreaking work on Austrian sexuality specifically has been undertaken by Ingrid Bauer, Matti Bunzl, Franz Eder, and Maria Mesner.[6] All four are also represented in this volume with new work. What this volume seeks to bring into focus, however, are *both* the unusual and the more broadly resonant aspects of Austrian sexual history. For instance, as Ingrid Bauer and Renate Huber's comprehensive co-written article on Austrian women's numerous—voluntary and involuntary—sexual encounters with the American, British, French, and Soviet military occupiers in the 1950s makes clear, as does Franz Eder's analysis of the media-mediated diffusion of sex-affirmative values in the Austrian populace from the 1930s to the 1960s (despite and yet also because of the successive interventions of Nazis, postwar conservatives, and consumerism-enjoining liberalizers), developments in Austria echoed those in Nazi and then West Germany, but also took their own distinctive course. This resulted in part from the at once more tradition-bound and claustro-phobic quality of postwar Austrian culture (including the long-unchallenged political influence of the Catholic Church). It was due as well to the relative lack of international scrutiny experienced by Austrians in the initial four postwar decades (which, for complicated reasons, caused the realm of sexuality to be much less a site for coming to terms with the Nazi past than it would be in the continuously morally monitored case of West Germany).[7]

Austria's insularity and the long delay in its confrontation of its national past, in turn, provide at least a partial explanation for the often surprisingly crude and aggressive expressions of both homophobia and anti-foreigner racism which the final three contributions analyze. Matti Bunzl's essay on the key factors facilitating the rise of queer visibility and the precipitous subsequent decline of homophobia in the 1990s offers an optimistic interpretation of the unexpected benefits of Austria's incorporation into the European Union and of the political elites' desire to present Austria as a beacon of sophisticated cosmopolitanism. Pieter Judson tells a less hopeful story about the all-too-easy resurgence of fantastically muddled and histrionic homophobic notions in the midst of a 2004 scandal over child pornography and consensual homosexuality at a Catholic seminary in St. Pölten, and Julia Woesthoff reveals a similar dynamic in her reading of the sensationalist media coverage surrounding the restriction of immigrants' abilities to marry Austrians in a law passed in January 2006. Inchoate but intensely held notions of love as the only acceptable basis for any marriage coexist with hyper-ventilating tales of immigrant men who pay for "fictitious marriages" to drug-addicted Austrian prostitutes or hapless single mothers. Crucially, all three of these essays reveal just how many *other* political and cultural issues are getting processed when Austrians argue with one another over sex, love, and marriage—from Austria's international status to the tensions between reform-minded and authoritarian-traditionalist Catholics to the challenges both of integrating immigrants and of regulating their entry.

It is specifically this continual dual function of sexuality in the twentieth century—the way it serves as a transmission belt for wider cultural conflicts even as it is itself being produced and reproduced as an intelligible domain—that weaves its way through all of the contributions to this volume. David Luft's meditative opening contribution—an excerpt from his book, *Eros and Inwardness*, a historically situated, nuanced interpretation of the works of Otto Weininger, Robert Musil, and Heimito von Doderer—revisits the much-debated phenomenon of *fin-de-siècle* Viennese culture's remarkable density of sex-related aesthetic and philosophical productivity. Other scholars—like Carl Schorske, Stephen Beller, and Sander Gilman—have stressed intergenerational tensions, the prominent role of Jewish intellectuals in the city's cultural life or, conversely, the power and pervasiveness of anti-Semitism in their speculative assessments.[8] Luft, by contrast, emphasizes the crisis of the male ego at the onset of the modern era. On the one hand, reflecting on heterosexual relations was a way to think through a wider sense of alienation and anxiety prompted by the collapse of liberal political and cultural confidence and to navigate the challenges of nihilism and irrationalism, as well as the tensions between scientific materialism, morality, and metaphysics. Writing about sexuality offered opportunities for pondering a more general feeling of "uncertainty about the reality and coherence of the self."[9] On the other hand, while Austrian feminism was still in its infancy at the turn of the century and posed hardly any threat to the power of men, Luft concludes that male writers of the era were very much preoccupied with the perceived threat of female sexuality and their own reactions to it.

Turning from the select circles of now canonized writers, Scott Spector directs our attention to the less well heeled, "ordinary" working-class people of Vienna, in particular the readers of the newly expanding tabloid press, as well as the underworld of streetwalkers and working-class homosexuals so often sensationally rendered in these new periodicals. Many scholars have sought to respond to Michel Foucault's challenge to make sense of the dialogic dynamic by which the very same juridical and medical professional discourses which stigmatized same-sex desiring individuals in the late nineteenth and early twentieth centuries also served as a catalyst and framework for those individuals to define themselves and "talk back" on their own behalf.[10] Yet—aside from court records, with their own inherent biases—we rarely have sources which permit us to understand the intricacies of this, as Spector phrases it, "feedback loop of pathologization and potentially liberating sexual identity" from the point of view of working-class subjects. A riveting series of letters to the editor of the Viennese *Kriminal-Zeitung* in 1907 forms the basis of Spector's intriguing analysis of one such feedback loop: a wide-ranging repartee between the paper and readers over the nature and origins of homosexuality, the incidence of homosexuality in Viennese culture both high and low, the prevalence of cafés and other watering holes with a queer clientele, and the value (or not) of reforming or abolishing Paragraph 129 (b), which criminalized same-sex activity. While recognizing that letter writers were most likely not always telling the truth about their own identities and social location, Spector nonetheless mines the evidence for fascinating insights into how queer subjects in this historical moment phrased their challenges to heteronormativity and represented themselves, as well as into the ways that sexual scandal magnetized public attention and produced new conceptions of sexuality in the process.

Maria Mesner's contribution on 1920s Vienna analyzes another site of interaction between members of the working class and educated professionals: marital and sex advice clinics. The 1920s are a crucial decade in the history of sexuality not least because these years mark the transition from an era of popular searching for new ways of understanding sex—a kind of pressure from below—and a novel interest on the part of the state and local governments to intervene in the realm of sex, to be responsive to popular longings, but also to channel and redirect them in ways we can, in retrospect, see were actually highly normative. Mesner reconstructs for us the phenomenon of self-appointed activists who sought to meet their clients' needs but also to define them (albeit in a striking diversity of ways). She also reads the evidence against the grain to assess the kinds of concerns that clients brought to the counseling centers and to identify the instances when they were at cross-purposes with the motivations of the activists. Mesner has especially important things to say about eugenics and the tentacles of "bio-power"—even as she also documents working-class individuals' far greater interest in controlling fertility than in improving the "quality" of their offspring. In juxtaposing evidence of activists' and clients' concerns, Mesner is able to give us glimpses of contemporaries' changing assumptions about the very nature of corporeality. She evokes powerfully the perceptions of contemporaries about the damaged state of women's bodies, the misery and conflict and "neurosis" within couples over sex, and male anxieties and "scruples" around masturbation and potency.

Franz Eder takes up the story where Mesner leaves off, and he emphasizes the striking continuities in popular sexual values between the 1930s and 1960s, despite the regime changes due to the Anschluß, the defeat of National Socialism, the decade of military occupation and Cold War, and then the growing independence of Austria. One of Eder's great strengths has to do with his sophisticated understanding of the ideological work of the media. He helpfully directs our attention not just to the content of images and texts, but also to the strategies of address employed, and to the many invitations provided by the media to aspire, to compare, to define, to imagine. He also usefully insists on seeing the diffusion of ideologies not as a one-way street between government and populace, or media and populace, but as a continuously interactive and multisite process in which reception also involves adaptation, intensification, reaction, relay, and reinterpretation. Contradictions within discourses and intersections between discourses often strengthen rather than undermine their impact. The value of this more expansive understanding of both media and ideology for furthering our understanding of such elusive but central topics in the history of sexuality as the nature of desire can hardly be overestimated. For example, as Eder explores, it is crucial that although National Socialist imagery and texts certainly insisted on the health, beauty, and strength of the Nazi sexual vision as a contrast to the decadent "Jewish" sensuality of the interwar period, from the populace's perspective the message received and put into lived practice was one of "positive sexualization." As Eder notes, the idealized images of the naked body, as internalized fantasies, could intensify both anticipation and the sensations of actual encounters. Conversely, to make the matter even more complicated, the republication of images labeled disgusting and degenerate could just as well have served as fantasy supports, despite or, perhaps, even because of the negative rhetoric accompanying them. Similarly, Eder reads the cacophonous, mutually competing but simultaneously mutually reinforcing rhetorics of Christian conservatism, consumerism-inciting sexualization of advertising and magazine reportage, and Kinsey-emulating statistics and analysis as *together* accelerating popular "expertise" and the focus on sexuality in the postwar decades—all long before the so-called Sexual Revolution occurred.

Deepening our understanding of the complex transformations in popular mores in the occupation decade of 1945-1955, Ingrid Bauer and Renate Huber put the sexual experiences of Austrian women at the center of their comprehensive and analytically revelatory assessment of the "romantic triangle" between these women and the foreign soldiers and Austrian men rivaling for their attention. Their main aim has been to systematize, for the first time ever, what is known about the contrasting experiences in the British, French, U.S., and Soviet zones, and also to consider how the issue of "race" played out with respect to

Moroccans in the French army, African-American GIs, and "Asian" Soviets. But the relevance of their contribution goes far beyond the empirical. Particularly illuminating are Bauer and Huber's insights into the intricate overlapping of the ever-evolving present with the Nazi and wartime past, as what happened during the war was continually referenced and reinterpreted in the aftermath of defeat; once again, it becomes clear how sexual relations can offer a site for processing a whole range of matters seemingly unrelated to sex. At the same time, more than any other contribution, this essay captures a remarkable sense of female sexual agency, self-assertiveness, and inventiveness. It also conveys, both through the inclusion of evocative quotes and through the authors' thoughtful and theoretically informed reflections, a great deal about the complexity of emotions brought to transnational sexual encounters: the inextricability of erotic attraction from such matters as the physicality of music or cleanliness; the powerful appeal of self-confidence or nonchalance, but also the fundamental role of material assets and power itself in making (some) men appealing to (many) women; as well as the acute pain and longing to connect with long-lost fathers expressed by some children of occupation relationships many decades later.

Matti Bunzl and Pieter Judson's essays on homophobia throw the "positive sexualization" accruing to heterosexuality in the postwar decades into sharp relief. As Matti Bunzl's prior work has documented, postwar Austrian prosecution of homosexuality was exceptionally harsh. Austria was one of the few Western European nations which criminalized lesbianism as well as male homosexuality, with the result that lesbianism in the postwar period was nearly invisible to outsiders, and male homosexual networks and meeting spaces were clandestine and constantly vulnerable. Multi-year prison sentences were standard until the liberalization of the law in 1971 (over 13,000 convictions since 1945), and ongoing systemic homophobia and new legal strictures explicitly limiting queer associational life and media visibility until well into the 1990s made for a two-decade time lag in the advent of gay and lesbian liberalization in comparison with the United States, France, or West Germany. The pressures to perform heterosexuality (for instance, by entering into "fake" marriages) were pervasive; the Catholic Church was unabashed in insisting on the maintenance of criminalization and social abjection; and the Socialist party was hardly committed to providing much of a contrasting legal agenda.[11] It is against this background that the enormous benefits to gays and lesbians of Austria's entry into the supra-national context of the European Union in 1995, the exuberant manifestations of queer pride in the Rainbow Parade of 1996, and the subsequent embrace of queers as symbols of Austria's newfound suave trendiness are especially remarkable. Comfort with, even celebration of, queerness, became *the* marker of Austrian maturity and chic. Pieter Judson's cautionary tale about the sex scandals at the archconservative St. Pölten seminary in the summer of 2004, however, although also hilarious in his particularly acerbic rendition, is a sobering reminder that the newly acquired status of *Vorzeige*-queers and the diminishment in reported feelings of homophobia in national surveys has not correlated with an ability on either the media or the public's part to think very tolerantly, or even very clearly, about sexual orientation and "deviance." A series of incidents—child pornography found on seminary computers, a suicide, a photograph of adult seminarians kissing at a Christmas party, an accusation that the director of the seminary had engaged in homosexual behavior—fused in the public's mind into composite proof of the Catholic Church's malfeasance. Consensual adult homosexuality was merged willy-nilly into widespread anxieties over what was assumed to be a priestly predilection for pedophilia or at least the abuse of teacher-student power disparities. Centuries-old anticlerical reflexes linking the celibacy requirement with sexual abnormality were updated for the era of the Internet and obsession with child sexuality; media sensationalism rerouted legitimate concerns about clergy child abuse of both boys and girls and Catholic hierarchy cover-ups into a full-fledged "homo-panic" that invited leering voyeurism and outraged hysteria by turns. The rather incoherent reassertions of heteronormative fantasies provided by letters to the editor in the wake of the scandals—from "everyone should have a healthy sex life. Get rid of celibacy" to "a priest with a family would have a greater sense of responsibility" to "a married priest with a good woman who can support him [. . .] that would be a good model"— reveal yet again, albeit from a different angle than that analyzed by Eder, just how much ideologies operate via inchoate assumptions as much as through any direct purveyance of information or analyses.

Julia Woesthoff's article takes the story up to the very present, as the human rights-securing European Union described by Bunzl turns also into "Fortress Europe" attempting to stem the tide of illegal immigration. Woesthoff sorts out the conflicting evidence from the media spin. What she finds is that in the past decade the number of binational marriages has risen to almost one in four of all Austrian marriages; within the same time span, the public preoccupation with the possibility of "fictitious" marriages (that is, marriages for the sole purpose of facilitating the foreign partner's immigration) has increased exponentially, as have government efforts to respond with legal strictures and monitoring strategies. Anywhere from one quarter to one third of all binational marriages each year are considered to be "under suspicion."

Yet, as Woesthoff unravels the story, it becomes clear that media hype, as in Judson's tale, is crucial to the rerouting of the public's concerns. While at least 40 percent of the binational marriages are between Austrian men and foreign (often Eastern European) women, these couplings merit little attention. Instead, there is a profusion of headlines and chatter over the 60 percent of binational marriages entered into by Austrian women. Many of these are to Turkish men, or men coming from the countries of the former Yugoslavia. While activist groups that seek to assist these women advance the slogan that "marriage is not a crime," or tend to see these women as motivated either by love pure and simple or by a desire to "rescue" their partners from deportation, the government and the media are more inclined to see desperation or conniving for easy money as the motivations. Ultimately, as Woesthoff notes, what is actually revealed is a strenuous attempt to ward off the reality that unquestioned assumptions about marriage are under siege from so many sources—from the prevalence of divorce to heterosexual cohabitation to the pressure to recognize same-sex unions; the incessant talk about binational marriages as somehow not based on "true love" reveals the already-existing and ever-widening disconnects between sex, affection, and marriage as an institution which also bestows legal privileges.

Where does this leave us? Whatever the remainder of the twenty-first century will hold in store for us, there is no question that this is a good moment to inquire into the intricacies of sexuality in the twentieth. There are many areas which deserve far more research. One of these is the phenomenon of long-term popular acceptance of illegitimate births in some regions of Austria, a phenomenon which reaches back into the nineteenth century, even as its character has changed over the course of the twentieth.[12] Another (and related) area worthy of systematic study has to do with what might be called "sex tourism" within Austria—the prevalence of short-term consensual affairs between skiing (or hiking) tourists and locals, already in the 1950s-1960s. Two further topics which need differentiated and sustained analysis involve the history of prostitution within Austria (though also now, in the post-communist era, the prostitution traffic reaching across the border into the Czech Republic), and the other kind of sex tourism—the phenomenon of Austrian men traveling further abroad to have sex-for-pay, first to Thailand in the 1960s-1970s, and then to South America and the Caribbean in the 1980s-1990s.

A very different topic with substantial ramifications for the comparative history of religion as well has to do with the peculiarities of the history of the Catholic Church in Austria. One dimension that needs much further research is the gap between church influence on politics and popular secularization; many Austrians are nominally affiliated with the church and depend on it for the celebration of life-cycle events such as baptisms, marriages, and funerals, but certainly do not orient themselves to its teachings.[13] This phenomenon varies considerably by region within Austria.[14] Its evolution needs to be periodized and described far more carefully. In this context, it will be especially important to consider the unique features of fascism in Austria as well. Because of its overlap with authoritarian Catholicism, Austro-fascism had perhaps more similarity to the fascisms in Spain, Romania, Italy, Slovakia, Croatia, and Vichy France than to German Nazism.[15] The potential consequences of this difference for sexual politics in Nazi Austria, and its militarily occupied aftermath, have yet to be carefully specified.

It would be good as well to know more about the sex radical activists trying to advance the Sexual Revolution in Austria in the 1960s-1970s. From Maria Mesner's work on the history of feminism and the campaign for abortion rights, we know how much activists "looked across the border" to West Germany and France for orientation on strategy and for opportunities to pressure the Austrian government to keep pace with international developments.[16] But we know far less both about the internal dynamics among sex radicals and about their relationships to the populace as a whole and to the media. The history of the Sexual Revolution in West Germany suggests just how crucial the voyeuristic fascination with *other* people's sexual experimentations was in advancing liberalized sexual values—and ultimately in the liberalization of sex-related law.[17] It is also possible that the history of sexuality in Switzerland will offer a better comparative vantage point for making sense of Austria; there, too, we find a gradual loosening of popular mores without political fanfare in the earlier postwar decades, then a countercultural youth rebellion delayed until the 1980s.[18]

Finally, as almost all the essays gathered in this volume suggest, albeit in completely different ways, the relationship between sexuality and the media in the twentieth-century West is one of the most important theoretical and empirical problems facing us. The whole phenomenon of "sex as spectator sport" has yet to be understood as a profoundly political factor (fostering as it does *both* identificatory and emancipatory *and* punitive and reactionary impulses with respect to sex itself) and simultaneously offering the site for battling over a multitude of other social and cultural conflicts. A glance at the current crisis over sexual freedoms in the United States—the demand for teen celibacy, the assault on contraception for the unwed, the virulent attacks on same-sex marriage, the efforts to cast aspersions on condom effectiveness, the hysteria over Internet pornography—indicates just how potent a weapon this spectator sport has become for political and religious conservatives. One can only hope that Europe will continue to pursue a more generous path.

Notes

1. Alexander Schuller cited in Rüdiger Lautmann et al., "Germany," in *The Continuum Complete International Encyclopedia of Sexuality*, ed. Robert Francoeur et al. (New York: Continuum, 2003).

2. Ernest Borneman, "Hat es eine sexuelle Befreiung gegeben? Oder: Der Verfall des sexuellen Begehrens 1960-1990," in *Sexualität in ausgewählten sozialwissenschaftlichen Perspektiven* ed. Wolfgang Dür et al. (Vienna: Institut für Soziologie, 1997), 127: "A large number of doctors, sex therapists and marital counselors [. . .] have reported, in short, about the death of sexual desire and sexual satisfaction in the rich countries of the first world. The sexual doldrums extend so far that one could describe contemporary Austria as a two-thirds society, in which one third states that it is sexually inactive." Note as well, however, the most recent news brought by a (Pfizer-funded) Global Sex Satisfaction study: After a world-spanning survey of more than 27,000 adults between the ages of 40 and 80, University of Chicago researchers found that the Austrians were, overall, the ones "most satisfied with their sex lives." See "Global Sex Survey: Satisfied in the West," NPR, July 12, 2006, http://www.npr.org.

3. Volkmar Sigusch, *Neosexualitäten: Über den kulturellen Wandel von Liebe und Perversion* (Frankfurt: Campus, 2005).

4. See, on France, the Netherlands, and Germany, Joan Scott, "Symptomatic Politics: The Banning of Islamic Head Scarves in French Public Schools," *French Politics, Culture, and Society* 23.3 (Winter 2005): 106-28; "Integration auf Niederländisch: Der Holland-Test der eisernen Rita," *Spiegel Online* 14 March 2006; "Die Gesinnungsprüfung," *taz*, 4 January 2006, 3.

5. Bruno P.F. Wanrooij, "The History of Sexuality in Italy (1860-1945)," in *Gender, Family and Sexuality: The Private Sphere in Italy, 1860-1945*, ed. Perry Willson (New York: Palgrave Macmillan, 2004), 177.

6. See especially Ingrid Bauer, "'Austria's Prestige Dragged into the Dirt'? The 'GI-Brides' and Postwar Austrian Society (1945-1955)," *Contemporary Austrian Studies*, vol. 6, *Women in Austria*, ed. Günter Bischof et al. (New Brunswick, NJ: Transaction, 1998), 41-55; Matti Bunzl, *Symptoms of Modernity: Jews and Queers in Late Twentieth-Century Vienna* (Berkeley: Univ. of California P, 2004); Franz X. Eder, *Kultur der Begierde: Eine Geschichte der Sexualität* (Munich: Beck, 2002); Franz X. Eder, "Sexual Cultures in Germany and Austria, 1700-2000," in *Sexual Cultures in Europe: National Histories*, ed. Franz Eder et al. (Manchester, 1999); Maria Mesner, "Political Culture and the Abortion Conflict: A Comparison of Austria and the United States," in *From World War to Waldheim: Culture and Politics in Austria and the United States*, ed. David F. Good and Ruth Wodak (New York: Berghahn Books, 1999), 187-209; Maria Mesner, "Auf dem Weg zur Fristenlösung: Eine Reform mit Hindernissen," in *Frauen in Bewegung—Frauen in der SPÖ*, ed. Irmtraut Karlsson (Vienna: Löcker, 1998), 83-112; Maria Mesner, "Vom Paragraph 144 zum Paragraph 97: Eine Reform mit Hindernissen," in *Beharrlichkeit, Anpassung und Widerstand: Die Sozialdemokratische Frauenorganisation und ausgewählte Bereiche sozialdemokratischer Frauenpolitik, 1945-1990*, ed. Dr. Karl Renner Institut (Vienna: Dr. Karl Renner Institut, 1993), 377-513. On the history of sexuality in Austria specifically, see additionally Helmut Gruber, *Red Vienna: Experiment in Working-Class Culture, 1919-1934* (Oxford: Oxford UP, 1991); Claudia

Schoppmann, *Verbotene Verhältnisse: Frauenliebe, 1938-1945* (Berlin: Querverlag, 1999); Erika Thurner, "Die stabile Innenseite der Politik: Geschlechterbeziehungen und Rollenverhalten," in *Österreich in den Fünfzigern*, ed. Thomas Albrich et al. (Vienna: Österreichischer StudienVerlag, 1995), 53-117; Wolfgang Dür, "Liebe ohne Zeit: Zufällige Intimsysteme und die moderne Gesellschaft," in *Neue Geschichten der Sexualität: Beispiele aus Ostasien und Zentraleuropa, 1700-2000*, ed. Franz X. Eder and Sabine Frühstück (Vienna: Turia & Kant, 2000), 279-302; Christine Zerzer, "Sexuelles Verhalten österreichischer Schüler," in *Jugendsexualität: Forschungsergebnisse einer Untersuchung an über 2000 Schülern in Österreich*, ed. Rudolf Weiss (Innsbruck: Univ. Verlag Wagner, 1978), 55-71; and Verein für erzählte Lebensgeschichte, ed., *Ich weiss über die Liebe gar nicht viel: Waldviertler Frauen erzählen über Heirat, Liebe, Sexualität und Aufklärung* (Vitis, 1990).

7. See Dagmar Herzog, *Sex after Fascism: Memory and Morality in Twentieth-Century Germany* (Princeton: Princeton UP, 2005).

8. Carl Schorske, *Fin-de-Siècle Vienna: Politics and Culture* (New York: Vintage, 1981); Steven Beller, *Vienna and the Jews, 1867-1938: A Cultural History* (Cambridge: Cambridge UP, 1989); Sander Gilman, *Freud, Race, and Gender* (Princeton: Princeton UP, 1993). On these books and the terms of debate, see also Matti Bunzl's review of Harry Oosterhuis' *Stepchildren of Nature* in "Sexual Modernity as Subject and Object," *Modernism/ Modernity* 9.1 (2002): 170-71.

9. David Luft, *Eros and Inwardness in Vienna: Weininger, Musil, Doderer* (Chicago: Univ. of Chicago P, 2003), 21.

10. Especially impressive formulations of this challenge and its rich interpretive implications can be found in Harry Oosterhuis, *Stepchildren of Nature: Krafft-Ebing, Psychiatry, and the Making of Sexual Identity* (Chicago: Univ. of Chicago P, 2000); as well as in George Chauncey, "From Sexual Inversion to Homosexuality: The Changing Medical Conceptualization of Female 'Deviance,'" in *Passion and Power: Sexuality in History*, ed. Kathy Peiss and Christina Simmons (Philadelphia: Temple, 1989), 87-117; and Jens Rydström, *Sinners and Citizens: Bestiality and Homosexuality in Sweden, 1880-1950* (Chicago: Univ. of Chicago P, 2003).

11. Bunzl, *Symptoms of Modernity*. See also my review in *Contemporary Austrian Studies*, vol. 14, *Austrian Foreign Policy in Historical Context*, ed. Günter Bischof et al. (New Brunswick, NJ: Transaction, 2005), 394-400.

12. See in this context the remarks about some regions of Austria having the highest illegitimacy rates in the world in Hans Harmsen, "Mittel zur Geburtenregelung in der Gesetzgebung des Staates," in *Sexualität und Verbrechen*, ed. Fritz Bauer et al. (Frankfurt: Fischer, 1963), 175.

13. The Nazi newspaper *Das schwarze Korps* was already commenting on the gulf in Austria between church attendance and orientation to church teachings on birth control in the 1930s. See "Österreich erwache!" *Das schwarze Korps*, 25 Feb. 1937, 6.

14. See "Austria." *About, Inc.* <http://atheism.about.com/library/world/AJ/bl_Austria Index.htm> (accessed 15 May 2006).

15. Mark Mazower, *Dark Continent: Europe's Twentieth Century* (New York: Vintage, 1998), 31-32; cf. Herzog, *Sex after Fascism*, 42-55, 103-07.

16. Mesner, "Vom Paragraph 144 zum Paragraph 97," 441-42.

17. See in this context Herzog, *Sex after Fascism*, 141-52; and Dagmar Herzog, "Sexuality in the Postwar West," *Journal of Modern History* 78 (March 2006): 144-71.

18. See Jean-Daniel Blanc and Christine Luchsinger, eds., *Achtung: Die fünfziger Jahre. Annäherung an eine widersprüchliche Zeit* (Zurich: Chronos, 1994); and Heinz Nigg, ed., *Wir wollen alles und zwar Subito! Die achtziger Jugendunruhen in der Schweiz und ihre Folgen* (Zurich: Limmat, 2001). What requires more research, for Switzerland as for Austria, is the interrelationship between homegrown radical impulses and those emerging from the German and wider European 1968.

Thinking about Sexuality and Gender in Vienna*

David S. Luft

> Sexual feeling is really the root of all ethics,
> and no doubt of aestheticism and religion.
>
> Richard von Krafft-Ebing,
> *Psychopathia Sexualis* (1886)

We are unknown to ourselves, we men of knowledge . . .
Friedrich Nietzsche, *Genealogy of Morals* (1887)
There is general agreement about the importance of Vienna in the 1890s as an historical location for thinking about sexuality. Austrian writers, physicians, and painters of the 1890s have attracted considerable attention for their interest in sexuality, in sexual behavior, and in sexual convention, but also for their emphasis on the power and threat of femininity for men. In the early twentieth century, Viennese writers were acknowledged within the wider sphere of German culture for their distinctive preoccupation with sexuality:

> In all areas, Austrians—poets, novelists, psychologists, cultural critics—transmitted to their German audience their obsession with decadence and their attempt to come to terms with eros: Sigmund Freud, Hugo von Hofmannsthal, Karl Kraus, and Arthur Schnitzler had as many readers in Berlin, Munich, and Frankfurt as they had in Vienna—perhaps more.[1]

At the same time, the emphasis on sexuality and gender in Vienna after 1900 was often a way of addressing other issues. As Edward Timms puts it, in "turn-of-the-century Vienna sexuality became the 'symbolic

---

* Except for minor changes, this essay follows the text of David S. Luft, *Eros and Inwardness in Vienna: Weininger, Musil, Doderer* (Chicago: Univ. of Chicago P, 2003), 36-42, 202-05.

territory' where the fundamental issues of the age were debated: the crisis of individual identity, the conflicts between reason and irrationalism, between domination and subservience."[2]

In relation to Europe and the wider realm of German culture, there was little to set Vienna apart in 1900, whether in bourgeois social convention or in thinking about sexuality and gender. The sexual conventions of the upper *Bürgertum* conformed, for the most part, to European standards—from prostitution to proper marriage—and the social realities of sexuality and gender in Vienna offered little to challenge nineteenth-century assumptions. Thinking about sexuality and gender in Vienna before 1900 was not fundamentally different from such thinking elsewhere in Europe and in the United States. The men who wrote about sexuality in Austria, whether for medical journals or for the theater, generally shared the values and perceptions of educated European men in the late nineteenth century. Freud had not yet published his views on sexuality and gender, nor had Karl Kraus published his attack on the Austrian legal system and his defense of sexual freedom. Except for hints of psychoanalysis in the work of Josef Breuer and Freud in the 1890s, medicalized discourse about sexuality and gender in Vienna was still firmly embedded in the European norms of the nineteenth century.

Both social convention and scientific research in liberal Vienna set out from the assumption of deep and fundamental differences between men and women.[3] The polarity of gender was a European-wide phenomenon in the nineteenth century, although in Vienna conventions of cavalier grace and style, learned by bourgeois sons in their year of military service, may actually have exaggerated perceptions of this polarity common to European culture as a whole. In terms of our contemporary discourse about gender, a great deal still remained concealed under the word *Geschlecht*, which meant both "sex" and "gender" and which was the conventional German prefix for "sexual," to say nothing of its associations with everything from grammar to species. Ordinary language routinely blurred these issues in much the same way that the word "sex" does in English: that is, a discussion of sex was a discussion of gender.[4] In much the same way, Austrian literature drew on conventional European stereotypes about women, sexuality, and love.[5] But the issues were not yet formulated in ways that became familiar in the late twentieth century. For example, there was no clear distinction in the 1890s between "sex" and "gender," but most physicians and a majority of other writers matter-of-factly assumed fundamental and more or less bipolar differences between men and women. The realities of sexual pleasure (let alone some norm or average experience) are one area in which the limits of historical knowledge become conspicuous. Scholars are not even in rough agreement about the realities of sexual life in bourgeois marriage, to say nothing of its national variations.[6] For the Victorian world of England and the United States, Steven Marcus' view of repression and the woman is often cited, but Peter Gay has argued that reality was less repressive and that the woman was more involved in sexual experience than has often been supposed.[7]

The men who wrote about sexuality and gender in Vienna were all strongly influenced by the tensions within the liberal tradition on these issues. The great nineteenth-century liberal, John Stuart Mill (1806-1873), wrote one of the classic statements on women's emancipation, but liberalism also belonged to the conventions of *bürgerlich* life in the nineteenth century. The emancipatory tradition of liberal humanism and individualism influenced early feminism and brought a large number of men into the women's movement, yet the University of Vienna did not make a place for women as matriculated students until 1897 in the sciences and the humanities (philosophy faculty) and until 1900 in medicine.[8] As in Germany, Austrian bourgeois liberal goals of emancipation raised the "woman-question", and bourgeois emancipation through education was allied with liberalism and the cultural sciences at the university. At the same time, women's emancipation conflicted with bourgeois notions of the family, and very little had changed by the 1890s.[9] Although Liberalism was the leading advocate of women's rights in nineteenth-century Austria, most liberal men assumed the limitations of reproduction, family, and the management of the house. These ways of thinking were informed by the powerful realities of disease, unwanted children, and death in childbirth.[10]

Mill had great influence on liberal Vienna in almost every respect, but *The Subjection of Women* (1869) seems to have found little resonance among liberals. Despite widespread admiration for Mill, the Viennese high *Bürgertum* did no better with the theme of women than other European liberal elites in the late nineteenth century. The ambivalence of Austrian liberalism on the woman question is perhaps most evident in Theodor Gomperz (1832-1912), whose credentials as a liberal and as Mill's translator are not in doubt.[11] Although Gomperz was one of the most prominent men in the women's movement, he seems to have had difficulty appreciating Mill's essay on women. Mill's wish to extend liberal conceptions of humanity and education to women met with incomprehension even from Gomperz, who regarded higher education and professional life as suitable for women only in exceptional cases, but not as relevant to the majority of women.

Ernest Jones recounts Freud's perceptions of his own views on women in reference to Freud's 1880 translation of Mill. Freud regarded

Mill as "perhaps the man of the century who best managed to free himself from the domination of customary prejudices":

> On the other hand—and that always goes together with it—he lacked in many matters the sense of the absurd; for example, in that of female emancipation and in the woman's question altogether. I recollect that in the essay I translated a prominent argument was that a married woman could earn as much as her husband. We surely agree that the management of a house, the care and bringing up of children, demands the whole of a human being and almost excludes any earning, even if a simplified household relieve her of dusting, cleaning, cooking, etc. He had simply forgotten all that, like everything else concerning the relationship between the sexes. That is altogether a point with Mill where one simply cannot find him human.[12]

Although many readers will be inclined to think of this passage as a commentary on Freud, it represented the enlightened view of an educated young man from the Viennese liberal *Bürgertum* in 1883. In the context of bourgeois conventions about the family and the management of a house, Mill's views seemed simply "inhuman"—and utterly out of touch with the realities of social and biological life. For Austrian liberals, the principal obstacles to Mill's kind of feminism were reproduction and the family, and Freud reacted much like other liberals such as Gomperz or Eduard von Bauernfeld (1802-1890). This view allowed for exceptions, but not for fundamental changes in social life.

A more extreme opposition to feminism came from a German scholar whose views were familiar in Vienna around the turn of the century. P.J. Möbius (1853-1907) emphasized the biological obstacles to equality and contended that the average woman would never be capable of intellectual or professional life, or at least not for a very long time to come.[13] Möbius argued that intellectual differences between men and women were grounded in biological differences. He believed that average differences between men and women in his own time were evident and considerable, and that, in spite of individual exceptions, talk of equality injured society because it injured women and the best conditions for reproduction. He rejected the "American wisdom" that women should enter the workplace, and he argued that women were needed in the home. Möbius represented one way in which the biological reduction could be used to justify gendered roles in society, whereas Mill offered the most eloquent nineteenth-century application of the emancipatory tradition within the liberal movement.

The principal advances of women's rights in Austria before 1900 coincided with the achievements of Josephinism and liberalism. The Code of Civil Law of 1812 gave women rights of property and inheritance. In these and other respects, Austrian women were actually better endowed with legal rights than women in other European countries. The February Constitution of 1861 granted women who were large property owners the right to vote in Lower Austria, and progressive reform of public schools in 1869 allowed women a larger role in education. In the last third of the nineteenth century, the main goals of the women's movement in Austria were equal employment and equal opportunity in secondary education, but the movements for suffrage and women's rights were weak.[14] The women's movement was at an early stage in Vienna in 1900, involving a small number of key figures and supported mainly by socialists and liberals, as well as a variety of writers and philosophers.[15] Women in Austria began to contribute to this public discussion at the end of the nineteenth century. Most significant in intellectual terms were Irma von Troll-Borostyáni (1847-1912), Grete Meisel-Hess (1879-1922), and Rosa Mayreder (1858-1938), though only Troll-Borostyáni had much impact before the turn of the century. Mayreder, intellectually the most interesting representative of the women's movement at the turn of the century, did not publish her most important work until after 1900.

The intellectual world of liberal Vienna was almost exclusively male. The most conspicuous exceptions to this generalization—Marie von Ebner Eschenbach (1830-1916) and Josephine von Wertheim-stein—recall the elevated social status of the exceptions and confirm the impression that the public world of culture was largely shaped by men. This tendency to acknowledge exceptions appears in the granting of an honorary doctorate to Eschenbach, one of liberal Vienna's finest writers, in 1900, the year that women were first permitted to matriculate in medicine at the University of Vienna.[16] Thus, public discourse about sexuality and gender in liberal Vienna was dominated by men, both in medicalized discourse about sexuality and in literary portrayals of sexual life. Austrian feminism in the early twentieth century did not constitute a very significant threat to the power of men. As with much of feminism in Germany, the emphasis was on valuing motherhood and feminine qualities within the larger context of the family and patriarchy. Certainly Austrian intellectuals such as the young Otto Weininger were not confronted with a movement comparable to the Anglo-American suffrage movement.

The issue of concern for male writers in Vienna around 1900 seems not to have been the strength of the feminist movement, which was still in its early stages, but the power of femininity and female sexuality over men, or put differently, the uncertainty and confusion of men as they encountered their own feelings and sexuality. The power, intensity, and threat of sexuality were apparent in the paintings of Gustav Klimt, and the hypocrisy and destructiveness of the social conventions surrounding sexuality in bourgeois Vienna were most evident in the stories and plays of Schnitzler. The social conventions of sexuality seemed obviously unsatisfactory (whether seen through the eyes of Schnitzler, Weininger, Kraus, or Mayreder), and Freud's early attempts to give some order to the realm of the feelings were still virtually unknown among educated people. In the stylized decade of the 1890s, women were both idealized as decorations and demonized as threats to reason.[17] Women and the feminine served as symbols of kitsch and escape from reality, but they were also threats to masculine rationalism.

In Austria, as in other European countries at the turn of the century, medicine and literature did the most to shape discourse about sexuality. Medicine was strongly influenced by a scientific materialism that ordinarily took for granted great differences between men and women and sought to impose conventional conceptions of sexuality and gender. Within this context, a few writers were beginning to work toward a more modern notion of sexuality.[18] Medical research on sexuality was important in Vienna, especially work on the psychopathology of sexual life and childhood sexuality, but this was not distinct from other work in Europe and the United States in its attitudes toward women, children, and masturbation. Freud had very little influence within the medical profession, and even he did not publish his first important work on sexuality (in relation to the general nature of neurosis) until 1905 in *Three Essays on the Theory of Sexuality*. Freud had still not met Schnitzler, whose plays offered realistic portrayals of the sexual customs of *fin-de-siècle* Vienna.

Literature was at once the medium for the culture's clichés about gender identity and the location for tentative attempts to understand human irrationality and the links between passion and social convention. Viennese modernism was preoccupied with sexuality—and in Arthur Schnitzler, Viennese literature produced an important social critic of European stature. Carl Schorske characterizes Schnitzler as describing "the social matrix in which so much of twentieth-century subjectivism took form: the disintegrating moral aesthetic culture of *fin-de-siècle* Vienna"; moreover, Schorske describes Young Vienna as a movement that "challenged the moralistic stance of nineteenth century literature in favor of sociological truth and psychological—especially sexual —openness."[19] Although there were only very minor personal and intellectual connections between Freud and literary Vienna, Michael Worbs argues that the concerns of nineteenth-century psychiatry and Austrian literature converged in an introspective *Nervenkunst*: both psychoanalysis and Young Vienna developed psychological, inward visions out of the naturalism and positivism of the late nineteenth century. The most striking similarities are between Freud and Schnitzler, whom Freud regarded as his *Doppelgänger* (double), but the other writers of Young Vienna had little interest in psychoanalysis, and Hugo von Hofmannsthal regarded the founder of psychoanalysis as "'an absolute mediocrity.'"[20]

The most dramatic development in thinking about sexuality in the 1890s came in *Studies on Hysteria* (1895) by Freud and Joseph Breuer, particularly in their emphases on the significance of internal processes, the rationality of apparently irrational feelings and behaviors, and the role of transference in the relationship between the patient and the physician.[21] These new ways of thinking emerged out of the mainstream of psychiatric research on hysteria in France and Austria, and all of this work was available to students of physiology and psychology at the turn of the century such as Weininger. But these developments in the medical profession were influenced very little, if at all, by the literary and artistic movements of the 1890s. Freud's *Interpretation of Dreams* appeared in 1900, but it had only slight impact at the outset, especially in comparison with the work of his younger contemporary, Otto Weininger.[22] Indeed, Sander Gilman emphasizes both Weininger's influence on Freud's thinking between 1903 and 1910 and Weininger's significance as a summation of late nineteenth-century thought.[23]

Weininger attempted both to clarify what his culture meant by "masculine" and "feminine" and to distinguish these notions from actual individual men and women, and his work offers insight into the gendered values of male, liberal culture in Vienna around 1900. Weininger's book draws attention to the significance of gender and sexuality as a way of thinking about central problems in philosophy for Viennese intellectuals after 1900. The theme of sexuality and gender provided these writers with ways to think about science, modern society, and resistance to modernity in the German-speaking culture of Central Europe, but without the customary emphasis on German nationalism. In the creative minds of Vienna after 1900, sexuality and gender became metaphors for thinking out human experience in the wake of scientific materialism and philosophical irrationalism. It was in this context that Weininger's radical critique of sexuality and gender appeared, a critique which adopted the grammar of gender to interpret the central philosophical issues of modern culture in the aftermath of positivism and the work of Friedrich Nietzsche.

Notes

1. Peter Gay, *Weimar Culture* (New York: Harper and Row, 1968), 7.

2. Edward Timms, *Karl Kraus: Apocalyptic Satirist* (New Haven, CT: Yale UP, 1986), 28. Jacques Le Rider argues in *Modernity and Crises of Identity: Culture and Society in fin-de-siècle Vienna*, trans. Rosemary Morris (New York: Continuum, 1993) that Viennese modernism must be understood in terms of the triangle of sexuality, Jewishness, and identity. See also Nike Wagner, *Geist und Geschlecht: Karl Kraus und die Erotik der Wiener Moderne* (Frankfurt am Main: Suhrkamp, 1982), 39: "Im 'Weib' haben die ikonographische und der literarische Symbolismus und Jugendstil ihr Hauptthema gefunden." On the fascination of the themes of sexuality and femininity for the male writers of liberal Vienna, see Karlheinz Rossbacher, *Literatur und Liberalismus: Zur Kultur der Ringstrassenzeit in Wien* (Vienna: J & V, 1992), 319 ff.

3. See Thomas Laqueur, *Making Sex: Body and Gender from the Greeks to Freud* (Cambridge, MA: Harvard UP, 1990). Laqueur is particularly interested in the decision of nineteenth-century scientists and physicians to emphasize the differences between men and women rather than the similarities.

4. See Joan Wallach Scott's discussion of the polarity of gender in her *Gender and the Politics of History* (New York: Columbia UP, 1988), 7: Fixed oppositions conceal the heterogeneity of either category, the extent to which terms presented as oppositional are interdependent—that is, derive their meaning from internally established contrast rather than from some inherent or pure antithesis. Furthermore, the interdependence is usually hierarchical, with one term dominant, prior, and visible, the opposite subordinate, secondary, and often absent or invisible. Yet precisely through this arrangement, the second term is present and central because required for the definition of the first. Otto Weininger is both an example of the problem of these fixed oppositions and an attempt to make it conscious and address it. Most discussions of Weininger have not sufficiently emphasized the problems raised by translation.

5. On male projection and stereotypes, see Sander L. Gilman, "Male Stereotypes of Female Sexuality in *Fin-de-siècle* Vienna," in *Difference and Pathology: Stereotypes of Sexuality, Race, and Madness* (Ithaca, NY: Cornell UP, 1985), 37-58.

6. See Priscilla Smith Robertson, *An Experience of Women: Pattern and Change in Nineteenth-Century Europe* (Philadelphia: Temple UP, 1982) and George L. Mosse, *Nationalism and Sexuality: Middle-Class Morality and Sexual Norms in Modern Europe* (Madison: Univ. of Wisconsin P, 1985).

7. Steven Marcus, *The Other Victorians: A Study of Sexuality and Pornography in Mid-Nineteenth-century England* (New York: Basic, 1974). Marcus cites William Acton: "I should say that the majority of women (happily for them) are not very much troubled with sexual feeling of any kind" (31). In *The Education of the Senses*, see Peter Gay's critique of the view that women in the nineteenth century were not very sexual. See also Michel Foucault's critique of "the repressive hypothesis" in *The History of Sexuality, Vol. 1: An Introduction*, trans. Robert Hurley (New York: Pantheon, 1978).

8. Women were first permitted to attend lectures as auditors in 1878. The study of law, the customary path to political power, was not open to women until 1919, a year after women were allowed to vote. See Richard Meister, *Geschichte der Wiener Universität* (Vienna: L. Auer, 1934), 58-62.

9. See Ute Frevert, *Women in German History: From Bourgeois Emancipation to Sexual Liberation*, trans. Stuart McKinnon-Evans (Oxford: Berg, 1989); and Waltraud Heindl and Marina Tichy, ed., *Durch Erkennthis zu Freiheit und Glück. . .* (Vienna, 1900), 9. Austrian scholars still depend heavily on work that deals with Germany in this period, and Eve Nyaradi Dvorak argues that scholarly developments in women's studies over

the past two or three decades have hardly touched the study of Austrian women. See David Good, Margarete Grandner, and Mary Jo Maynes, eds., *Austrian Women in the Nineteenth and Twentieth Centuries* (Providence, RI: Berghahan, 1996), xi. On German feminism, see Ann Taylor Allen, *Feminism and Motherhood in Germany, 1800-1914* (New Brunswick, NJ: Rutgers UP, 1991). Liberal, *bürgerlich* culture emphasized notions of the free personality and the professions that were strongly oriented to a certain kind of masculine type and an emphasis on a particular style of rationalism. Only a few (whether men or women) had thought of applying these values to women before 1900. On the masculine coding of liberal individualism, see Brigitte Spreitzer, *Texturen: Die österreichische Moderne der Frauen* (Vienna: Passagen, 1999).

10. Few recall that Freud's early work on neurosis focused on his attempts to help married couples deal with the neurotic consequences of coitus interruptus. The realities of sexual and family life should be kept in mind before judging values too ahistorically. In the 1890s, the views of intellectuals about sexuality were bounded by fears of syphilis and prejudices about homosexuality and marriage. On Freud's views in the 1890s, see *The Complete Letters of Sigmund Freud to Wilhelm Fliess, 1887-1904*, trans. and ed. Jeffrey Moussaieff Masson (Cambridge, MA: Harvard UP, 1985).

11. Rossbacher, *Literatur und Liberalismus*, 322-32.

12. Ernest Jones, *The Life and Work of Sigmund Freud* (New York: Basic, 1953), 176. The idea of a man concerning himself with running a household was apparently inconceivable to a member of the Austrian liberal *Bürgertum* in the late nineteenth century. "In [Mill's] whole presentation it never emerges that women are different beings—we will not say lesser, rather the opposite from men. He finds the suppression of women an analogy to that of negroes. Any girl, even without a suffrage or legal competence, whose hand a man kisses and for whose love he is prepared to dare all, could have set him right." The main point for Freud, at the age of twenty-seven, seems to have been that women do not belong in the harsh, competitive world of earning a livelihood. See John Stuart Mill, *Ueber Frauenemancipation; Plato; Arbeiterfrage; Socialismus*, trans. Siegmund Freud (Leipzig: Fues's Verlag [R. Reisland], 1880).

13. P.J. Möbius, *Über den physiologischen Schwachsinn des Weibes* (Halle: Marhold, 1905), 5. For Möbius, *Schwachsinn* meant less than normal intelligence, and he argued that the woman was in virtually all respects inferior in capacity to the man.

14. See Marianne Hainisch, "Die Geschichte der Frauenbewegung in Österreich," in *Handbuch der Frauenbewegung,* ed. Helene Lange und Gertraud Bäumer, part 1: *Die Geschichte der Frauenbewegung in den Kulturländern* (Berlin: W. Moeser, 1901), 167-88. On elementary and secondary education and teachers, see James C. Albisetti, *Schooling German Girls and Women* (Princeton, NJ: Princeton UP, 1988).

15. See Harriet Anderson, *Utopian Feminism: Women's Movements in Fin-de-siècle Vienna* (New Haven, CT: Yale UP, 1992). The word *Feministin* was not widely used until 1914; before that, the word *Feminist* had referred to men who supported the movement (see pages 9-10).

16. Rossbacher, *Literatur und Liberalismus*, 366. On the place of women in scholarship on Viennese modernism, see Lisa Fischer, "Weibliche Kreativität—Oder warum assoziieren Männer Fäden mit Spinnen?" in *Die Wiener Jahrhundertwende*, ed. Jürgen Nautz and Richard Vahrenkamp (Vienna: Böhlau, 1993), 144-58.

17. See Bram Dijkstra, *Idols of Perversity: Fantasies of Feminine Evil in Fin-de-siècle Culture* (New York: Oxford UP, 1986).

18. Paul Robinson, *The Modernization of Sex: Havelock Ellis, Alfred Kinsey, William Masters, and Virginia Johnson* (New York: Harper and Row, 1976). Robinson finds in the years between 1890 and 1910 "a major transformation in sexuality," and he points out that the pioneer modernists—Edward Carpenter, Albert Moll, Auguste Forel, Ivan Bloch, and Magnus Hirschfield—are "now largely forgotten" (2). Although Freud is the best-remembered figure from this period, Robinson argues that it was Havelock Ellis who contributed most to a distinctively modern sexual ethos, which was characterized by new attitudes toward female sexuality and toward "apparently deviant forms of sexuality" (3). For a different, partly Foucauldian, view of these questions, see Lawrence Birken, *Consuming Desire: Sexual Science and the Emergence of a Culture of Abundance, 1871-1914* (Ithaca, NY: Cornell UP, 1988). See *The History of Sexuality*, vol. 1, for Foucault's account of the nineteenth century in terms of "the transformation of sex into discourse" (61) and "the production of sexuality rather than the repression of sex" (114).

19. Carl E. Schorske, *Fin-de-siècle Vienna: Politics and Culture* (New York: Knopf, 1980), 15, 212.

20. Michael Worbs, *Nervenkunst: Literatur und Psychoanalyse im Wien der Jahrhundertwende* (Frankfurt am Main: Europäische Verlagsanstalt, 1983), 267.

21. Josef Breuer and Sigmund Freud, *Studies in Hysteria* in *The Standard Edition*, vol. 2. Freud did not work out his view of gender until the First World War. On the asymmetry of Freud's view of gender, see Judith Van Herik, *Freud on Femininity and Faith* (Berkeley, CA: Univ. of California P, 1982). I make no attempt here to offer an independent history of what sexuality is. See Jeffrey Weeks, *Sexuality* (New York: Tavistock, 1983): a history of sexuality is "a history without a proper subject" (21); and Michel Foucault's discussion of sexuality as "a historical construct" in *A History of Sexuality*, 105.

22. Freud was not well known even in Vienna before 1900; the Wednesday night meetings and the psychoanalytic movement came only later.

23. See Sander L. Gilman, *The Jew's Body* (London: Routledge, 1991), 133.

The Wrath of the "Countess Merviola": Tabloid Exposé and the Emergence of Homosexual Subjects in Vienna in 1907

Scott Spector

Esteemed Editor,

As you read these lines I do procede to pass among the living alas not in Vienna. For reasons I cannot furthermore put forward I must depart Austria's metropole for indeterminant time. I undertake to the Orient, and as I have the frontiers of the monarchy behind me shall I permit myself to forward you an image of my person. I am ever much more placably inclined toward you since you have made indeed a halfway generus judgement about us unlucky warm ones in your last issue and I offer you the well-meaning advise change your tactick completely and place your self completely to our side and thousands of sincerely meant thanks from warm hearts will prove to you what a good work you have done. Fight with us on our side against the stupid prejudice of the world that cannot grasp that there are warm ones and who are at the mercy of a miserable penal code demanding ruthless procedings over and above we already unlucky creatures. There is no aquired pederasty, we thousands who call ourselves "warm" are all born bourdened with this defect and no great luminery, of the medical arts and least of all the state attorny can cure us. Since it is impossible for me to speak to all like inclined so I appeal right here and now to all your warm hearts, purchase or subscrib to the *Kriminal Zeitung* in your own interests and right try to find other buyers in your circles That way finally for once the people will be enlightened about us, When I was just very small, I felt the need in me to get involved in talk only with gentlemen and I engaged socially with my own playmates as little as possible, wheras I was in fact happy when I was only in proximaty of a man. And as it was for me so has it gone for the thousands of others. For the acceptance of these lines in your valued paper in most polite thanks I remain

Your Countess Merviola[1]

Sexuality in Austrian history has already been recognized as an important topic, not only by Austrian historians. Pride of place has been given to the extraordinary contributions emerging out of Vienna, without doubt a prime center of the emergence of discourses on sexuality from Richard von Krafft-Ebing to Sigmund Freud, as well as others far afield from the city's prestigious medical institutions. Cultural histories of *"fin-de-siècle* Vienna" remind us of the innovations in modernist art and literature that betray the city's presumed affinity for the sensual.[2] If this apparent consensus about a seething erotic metropolis seems to brush against the grain of other images of a staid, constrained, and relatively sleepy capital city in this period, that merely proves the rules we have taken either from Freud (the only apparent contradiction of placid exteriors and unconscious life), or from Michel Foucault (the presumption of repression and acting-out of sexuality are of the same piece).

It is not surprising that this broad attention to turn-of-the-century Vienna's contributions to the "superstructure" of sexuality studies, from medical science to art and literature, should be accompanied by a relative lack of discussion of popular sexuality in the same place and time. The textual traces of sexual science, legal proscription, art, and literature always grant a historiographical advantage to these fields that sexuality as it was experienced by subjects at the time is not likely to obtain. Yet studies of the empire to the north and its capital city have yielded much more in terms of sexual association, political activity for sexual emancipation, the sex trade, and more.[3] In sex as in fascism, *fin-de-siècle* Austria seems to offer the theory to the German Reich's practice.

The problem goes deeper than this, though. The historian of sexuality must return to Foucault, whose *History of Sexuality* has been a towering, but also puzzling, presence in this field.[4] As people most often note, the first short volume of this work did expose the ruse of the "repressive hypothesis," whereby society's claim of its own sexual repression provided an alibi for the seemingly endless production of discourse on sex; it also revealed the "perpetual spirals of power and pleasure" inherent in the disciplines of sexuality this unleashed.[5] Less understood and less discussed is the thesis, core to the first volume but less elaborated than the other points, that the emergence of sexuality is also, and even primarily, about a transition in the way subjects understand themselves. The disciplining discourses of the *Scientia sexualis* are not instruments of a singular power restraining a free erotic spirit, but (famously), "Power is everywhere, not because it is all-embracing, but because it comes from everywhere"—sexual subjects are hailed in the same instant as the disciplinary discourses that seem to emerge to contain them.[6] If Foucault spends very little time on these sexual subjectivities in comparison with the disciplinary discourses, it is for strategic reasons specific to the needs of the period in which he was writing. He does importantly suggest that, for instance, "homosexuality began to speak on its own behalf" using the language provided by such discourses.[7] He calls this a "reverse discourse," but it is the same one, and hence more of an extension of his previous discussion than a turn to sexual subjectivity.

The relations between professional discourse and subjects' self-understandings are complex, but not too obscure to be charted. The marvelous archive of Krafft-Ebing, only recently obtained and catalogued by the Wellcome Trust and made generally available to researchers, demonstrates this in an unprecedented way.[8] In it, we find stacks of case studies and notes, many by Krafft-Ebing and many more sent in by physicians from across Europe, and above all the letters sent directly by individuals in their own words.[9] Their own words—but whose words? These are the very letters quoted throughout Krafft-Ebing's encyclopedic *Psychopathia sexualis*, and added as the editions became thicker and thicker; at the same time, the letters confess the revelation entailed by reading that same or other works of sexual science, as if the encounter with this "disciplinary discourse" were nothing less than a first encounter with oneself. The breathtaking recursivity of discourse—the feedback loop of pathologization and potentially liberating sexual identity—is nowhere so compact as in these cartons.

For the purposes of the present essay, we can bypass the loaded judgment of whether this moment made hapless victims or empowered agents of the sexual subjects it produced.[10] More can nonetheless be done to explore articulations of sexual subjectivity and to place it historically. One serious limitation, familiar to social historians in other fields, arises with the question of class background. The contributors to Krafft-Ebing's future archive were overwhelmingly bourgeois or upper-class. The term "homosexual" emerged in the 1860s, and what was coming to be thought of as human sexuality was being organized in new legal and scientific categories through the last third of the nineteenth century. Yet, most of the population of Austria and all other European countries remained insulated from these professional discourses. This was deliberate. The caution taken to protect these potentially volatile languages from a general public is apparent in everything from the use of Latin in Krafft-Ebing's own text to police surveillance of scholarly lectures on sexual subjects.[11]

The vehicle through which a general public in Germany and Austria became familiar with these discourses on sexuality was scandal. The first decade of the twentieth century was punctuated by sensational reports involving male homosexual public figures, leading to a general cultural awareness of homosexuality and the existence of modern homosexuals in a way that had not occurred before. The Oscar Wilde trials in England in 1895 foreshadowed these scandals and this consciousness, but only vaguely. For Germans, the biggest sex scandal of the decade would be in Imperial Germany, where Maximilian Harden's suggestions about the perverse sexualities of members of the Kaiser's closest advisory circle would shake press, public, and regime (the "Harden-Eulenburg affair"). In 1907, at the height of the scandal, a Catholic organ in Austria declared that the events were typical of Protestant morality, and that Catholic Austria would surely be immune.[12] Not so, suggested the *Oesterreichische Kriminal-Zeitung,* a relatively new publication that had even more recently changed hands and taken a more sensationalist approach to the reportage of criminality in Austria. "Could such a homosexual trial like the recent Prussian one be possible in our own Vienna, dear reader? Sadly not just one, but thousands, and in all social classes up to the highest."[13] The journalist ventured that Austria, with its unenlightened approach to what were now being recognized as in-born pathologies, was, if anything, more vulnerable than Prussia. He was thus able to link recently minted medical and socio-scientific discourses on the homosexual to matters of broad public concern, indeed with the intention to provoke and to exploit broad public concern for the purpose of selling newspapers. The reference to social class, in particular the identification of deviant sexuality within "even the highest social circles," would prove to be a recurrent theme in the first exposés on an emerging homosexual shadow society in Central Europe. The Harden-Eulenburg scandal in a most general sense accomplished all this as well, by linking the homosexual to public concern via the focus on class power and homosexual conspiracy.

Clearly, the Harden-Eulenburg scandal, by its sheer magnitude, did more to bring the reality of actually existing homosexuals into broad public view than all previous prosecutions of Paragraph 175 in Germany and 129(b) in Austria and progressive political efforts to reform them combined. The affair was complex in its discursive effects, but for our purposes here, suffice it to say that the affair was at once a culmination, an effect, and a further motor of growing awareness of a homosexual subculture and the suspicion of the sinister social and political implications of such a sub-group.[14] It is well-known that public attention to the issue of homosexuality seemed at first a hopeful sign to Magnus Hirschfeld and other members of the Scientific-Humanitarian Committee (for the repeal of Paragraph 175), but that the actual effects of the attention with regard to those efforts were dismal.[15] In any event, the word "homosexual" and the notions it evoked of both actual persons and unspeakable acts in one's very midst were suddenly present from 1907 on in a way they had not been before.

In Vienna, as indicated above, the Harden-Eulenburg affair seemed at once so distant—so German, so Prussian—and at the same time, it could not help but raise questions about the possible existence of such activity in Vienna. Austrian echoes of the scandal provide a glimpse into the way questions of sexuality, society, and politics were played out in the Habsburg Empire, but they performed another, unanticipated function: in bringing homosexuality to public consciousness through the vehicle of political scandal in a neighboring country, a platform for discourse was created that could support the discourse of homosexuals themselves. Journalistic sensationalism, like medical and juridical discourses on homosexuality, subjected people engaging in sex with others of their gender to new forms of stigmatization and persecution and at the same time played a key role in the historical process leading to the emergence of homosexual subjectivities and group identities. It is neither a matter of deciding whether these emancipations-qua-stigmatizations were ultimately "positive" or "negative" developments, nor whether less predominant disciplinary discourses on same-sex desire (say literary or aesthetic ones) would have proven "more" liberating.[16] Neither do historians have to choose between narratives of gay or queer subjects resisting stigmatizing images of themselves, or colluding in the production of those images, or appropriating and instrumentalizing their own marginalization. All of these were from the start features of the process Foucault described in the *History of Sexuality*. What he left for other historians to do was to track how the process actually operated— the moment of sexual subject-formation is described, but not demonstrated in his work (and others' after him) in the way that the emergence of stigmatizing discourses has been charted. The case of an exposé and editorial campaign and reader responses to it in a single Austrian tabloid newspaper is offered here as a peculiar but telling example of two things: first, how the discourse of scandal can be seen alongside and linked to the disciplinary discourses on sexuality that have received the most attention, namely the medical and juridical discourses; and second, *how* homosexual subjects emerged qua subjects, how models of self-identity were confected out of the complex cooperation of discursive collusion and queer resistance.[17]

The *Oesterreichische Kriminal-Zeitung* released its first weekly issue on 1 April 1907.[18] Ferdinand Lebzelter, former head police commissioner of Vienna, was editor. On the basis of its lead program article and the first several issues, one gets a clear image of enlightened law enforcement, where largely modern and educated judges, police, and public are seen to be held hostage to an antiquated ("barbaric," "medieval") penal code.[19] Vowing to expose corruption and pursue enlightened reform, the paper offered different ongoing rubrics on penal reform, forensic advances, and also, more incidentally, glimpses of an exotic netherworld of crime, prostitution, and so forth corresponding to certain genres of urban life.[20]

The financial success of the newspaper seems to have been insecure, and it changed hands after a six-week run; the former commissioner tendered his polite resignation two weeks later, and the following issue was already markedly more provocative than before; it was also the first of many issues to be censored. By the tenth issue (20 June 1907), the big shift to tabloid journalism is apparent, with the bold headline *"Sensationeller Inhalt!"* ("Sensational Content!") emblazoned on the cover. By August, the word "illustrated" was added to the title, and the paper resembled other European "illustrated criminal" and/or "detective" newspapers. In the wake of the Riehl affair involving police corruption and the regulation of prostitution, the newspaper turned its focus to prostitution and, more incidentally, to pederasty.[21] Whole districts, declared more than one article, are plagued by masses of promenading little ladies and their procurers, often endangering the general public. Respectable women cannot even go out after 10:00 anymore. Police are at once scandalous in their behavior toward girls and powerless to stem the tide. The image, then, was of a criminal/sexual underworld run amok and threatening to consume the city. "Beyond uncontrolled trollops, the most attention is earned by their procurers as well as the ever more self-confident pederasts and their gathering places," declared one story, reminding readers that the ever-growing perverse subcultures of Vienna are also part of this picture and promising to report on this in future articles in order to "orient" the public.[22] This at first ancillary interest turned out to be a goldmine for the paper, and clearly the key to its potential success as well as to its eventual demise. Weekly reports on "pederasty" were accompanied by an ever-growing set of letters to the editor spurred on by the articles; soon the heavy hand of the censor intervened.[23] By September, circulation had reached an unprecedented 20,000 copies, which would become 30,000 by the end of the year.

In keeping with its enlightened crusader self-image, the paper took an editorial stance in favor of the reform of Paragraph 129(b) on the basis of natural inclination and threat of blackmail, and at the same time, it reproduced that blackmail by consistently denouncing individual cafés and meeting places. It chided the police for turning a blind eye to this underground activity and called for a crackdown to eliminate the scourge and for arrests of the pederasts as well as their blackmailers. The proposed penal reform concerned the reclassification of homosexual inclination as a disease and the forced internment of the afflicted in mental institutions.[24] In the earliest articles, cafés frequented by homosexuals were explicitly named, but the owners of these establishments were not blamed. It was even suggested that they were oblivious to the function of their businesses as gay haunts, because the "contrary sexual elements are so fantastically organized that they leave no external clue and behave as normally as possible."[25] The editors promised a campaign not against these pub and café owners, but against "pederasty" as such, to stem the tide of immorality sweeping Vienna.

While the references to the homosexual life of the city were merely tangential elements of the long article on prostitution, they elicited an immediate and unexpected response in the form of impassioned and angry anonymous letters to the editor from homosexual quarters. Once those letters were published and the pederasty series had begun, the pages of letters to the editor expanded, becoming an exhibition of perversity with as much sensational power as the reports themselves. The flurry of response from the homosexual street, as it were, cued the editors of the newspaper that they were onto something; for several weeks, they printed the letters unedited, until finally, under great pressure of the authorities, eliminating anonymous and outrageous contributions. The original spate of letters, however, while hardly an unproblematic source, is nonetheless a unique case where the responses of homosexual men to the initial public representations of them and their sexuality are preserved.

The issue following the original prostitution article included the first run of letters, the sensational potential of which was at once recognized by the editors. Calling attention to the section with such subtitles as "Letter-Threat of a Passive Pederast," the newspaper was more than willing to put the most hostile attacks on its own reportage on display. They printed (or claimed to print) the letters in full and unedited, including spelling and grammatical errors that betrayed the contributors' class backgrounds. The threatening letter to which the editors refer was signed by one "Countess Merviola," whose letter, according to the newspaper, was received on "trollop paper," stinking of disgusting perfume. The letter reads:

> It is incredible to us the way you in your scandal sheet treat those of us who are unhappy victims by our very nature. Do you really think that the state attorney is the most appropriate expert to cure us? You find yourself in great error if you think we "warm brothers" belong in the "black house" of the Josefstadt. Every single judgment against one of our number is a horrible error of justice.[26]

In tune with much of the conventional description of homosexuality at the time, this reader depicted himself and his kind as "unhappy victims" of their own sexuality, who could not be helped by further persecution by journalistic trash and state intervention. The effect on each convicted "warm one" is never the reversal of homosexuality, but the contrary, for "he becomes freer and more open in his outlook because he feels himself a martyr and is also treated as such by his sexual compatriots who number many thousands just here in Vienna [...]".[27]

A community of "martyred" homosexuals is, thus, a direct consequence of persecution and prosecution. The "threat" of this letter is contained, in part, in the suggestion that an attack on homosexuality will have the effect of galvanizing a community of homosexuals—thousands of them in Vienna—hidden so far even to themselves. This was an exaggerated restatement of the newspaper's own sensational discourse, which sought to make visible a social problem its readers were not even aware existed. Merviola's threat continued, making use of a more nefarious suggestion of the newspaper, that the pederast "community" included elements of great wealth and power:

> Among us we have men of resounding name who are decorated with high recognitions and offices by the State of Austria [...] That would look quite fine if the most honored carriers of state recognition, aristocrats from the oldest lines, millionaires and the chiefs of the most significant major firms suddenly lost all their offices and prizes and had to move to the so-called grey house [...].[28]

"Countess Merviola" continued to describe her own personal presence, grace, and power in the most inflated and florid terms, then promising that the newspaper will receive a warning of a more official nature from the "Central Direction of the 'Warm League.'"[29]

Interestingly, the particular threat made to the newspaper was directly related to the homophobic conspiracy fantasy suggested in the offending article. The paper was able to pick up on this:

> They speak completely openly about the central office of a pederasts' league, and the gentlemen comport themselves with such self-conscious arrogance that one begins to suspect that the Viennese pederasts must enjoy some particularly highly placed protection, a protection that places them above the law. If such were not the case, these people would surely not speak so freely and openly, without any shame, about their deviations—deviations that are prosecuted as crimes under law.[30]

While the lower-class Merviola's threat was that members of Vienna's elite would be brought down along with common homosexuals, perhaps outed by the latter, the newspaper implied here and elsewhere that the toleration of the homosexual underworld was facilitated by the influence of powerful pederasts in Vienna.

The newspaper continued its pederasty series and expanded the section of letters to the editor, ostensibly in the interests of bringing the presence and aggressive stance of the inverts to the attention of the authorities. One such letter uses the ingenious strategy of asking the editor to put himself in this "unhappy place" and imagine he would be institutionalized for his own sexuality. But sympathy is not the only strategy employed by the readers. A particularly combative letter from a bold contributor reads:

Brainless individual!
In your trash rag, hopefully soon to vanish from the surface of the earth, you demonstrate very well what a godforsaken numbskull you are to judge people about whom every physician and half-thinking layman understands are not to be liable in the slightest, since they are totally innocent [...].[31]

This description merely reiterated the newspaper's own position as well as that of Merviola, but here the condition given by nature is not marked as either "sick" or "unhappy," simply "innocent." Guilt in the letter is reserved for the newspaper editors, who cause only harm and to what purpose, wonders the reader, "I can imagine that all your nonsense is based entirely on blackmail, and to reach your goal you do not shy from desiring to attract denouncers who belong in prison along with *you*."[32] Indeed, it seems the writer had more than instinct at hand, as the series did, in fact, lead not only to heavy censorship, but eventually to a blackmail case and secession of publication.[33] The articles contained denunciations, to be sure, but not so many as the letters to the editor—a point to which I will return. Another raving letter comes from the Countess Merviola, whose most intimate friend, "Princess Louse," has sent a letter to the *Kriminal-Zeitung* revealing Merviola's "intimate secrets," which, he warns, must not be published:

Alas, hear me well, woe to you if you betray the secret proceedings of my residence; I will hereby declare war on you until one of us or the other falls to ruin. You will soon be made to feel how dangerous and powerful an opponent you have in me [...] Since your disgusting nose cannot fancy my fine perfumed letter so I will not forward any more perfumed luxury letter paper. Please be so kind as to avoid the term "trollop paper" in future as I am a highly respectable lady and, therefore, my letter paper has not earned this expression.[34]

The drama unfolding among such characters as the Countess Merviola, the Princess Louse von ***, the "Black Pearl," and the editors was a display that made other readers cringe. These others described themselves as physicians (unlikely, suggests the newspaper), or otherwise well-educated professionals, competing with what they see as a group of street tramps for representation of their sexual inclination.

One such reader, this one writing under the name "Lady Camellia," sharply attacked the newspaper campaign and the suggestion that homosexuality is a "so-called 'vice,'" whose victims belong in institutions.[35] Using the argument known from both the liberal camp of Hirschfeld and associates of the *Jahrbücher für sexuelle Zwischenstufen* (*Yearbook for Intermediary Forms*) as well as the conservative camp of Adolf Brand, Benedict Friedländer, and the *Gemeinschaft der Eigenen*, "Lady Camellia" reminded the editors that this policy would have landed in asylums figures of historical greatness from Socrates and Plato to Frederick the Great and Grillparzer.[36] The letter is more original in its suggestion that homosexuality offered an alternative to the man-woman love relationship that exceeded the latter in nobility, describing his own six-year relationship with a certain officer, in which relationship ruled "purest harmony," full acceptance from his esteemed family, and which nonetheless allowed for a sexual freedom no wife would suffer. "Merviola" and other readers, while unhalting in their attacks on the campaign, nonetheless included certain apologetics in their arguments, admitting homosexuality to be a "defect," an "unhappy predisposition," or even a "vice." The difference between these self-representations may be seen to correspond to the split between the Hirschfeld and Brand camps; the latter, explicitly misogynist and elitist, was at the same time less likely to concede to social assumptions of sexual abnormality, defect, or inferiority.[37] Whether describing themselves (or in the third person, the "unlucky/unhappy ones") as burdened or not, whether aggressive or placating, rationalist or outrageous, the insistence on natural sexuality rang through the letters to the editor, in ways that sometimes implicated the sexuality of the editors themselves—imagine it were you who were sent to an asylum to be healed of your own desire, suggest two different contributors.[38] In the same early August 1907 issue, the newspaper clarified (in fact revised) its editorial position on the issue of Paragraph 129(b) of the Austrian penal code, proposing that it be amended to exempt "in-born pederasty," which should be handled medically and not criminally.[39]

It is in this context that the original "threatening pederast," Merviola, sent the more conciliatory letter quoted in full at the beginning of this article. The initial lines of the letter simply reinforce the impression of an aggressively narcissistic author left by the earlier correspondence, but the tone rapidly changes, as the letter becomes a kind of negotiation. Merviola is more "placably inclined" toward the editor in light of the "halfway generous judgement" represented by the proposed exemption, and invites the newspaper to change strategy and "place yourself completely to our side" in a struggle with an ignorant outside world that does not recognize the double-burden of unlucky (or unhappy) souls stricken both by same-sex desire and the threat of criminal prosecution for the pursuit of their natural sexuality. The appeal connecting a medical claim of in-born sexual inclination to a juridical reform in the form of decriminalization is familiar—it is a linkage, in fact, that was made by homosexual emancipators even before the medical discourse on sexuality formally emerged.[40] Merviola both reproduces and contests this medico-juridical discourse in presenting the empirical evidence of personal experience: there is no such thing as acquired pederasty, it is rather in-born in all cases, and medical and legal experts cannot do anything to change it. The plea that the *Kriminal-Zeitung* fight on the side of those so inclined—in fact, the whole letter—is an indication that Merviola recognizes in the newspaper the voice of another, and competing, authoritative discourse. Recognition of the tabloid's commercial motivations for the pederasty series is implicit in Merviola's strategy to win it over, as he solicits homosexual readers to support the paper by subscribing *en masse*.[41]

It would be an excessive claim to romanticize these few weeks of pages of readers' letters as a nascent public sphere of homosexual community, or the responses contained within them as queer declarations of an autonomous and legitimate sexual identity. The forum offered by the newspaper in fact produced more intra-group conflict than it did a united front against heterosexual persecution. Each week's letters to the editor were filled with denunciations, listings of establishments missed by the newspaper articles, and even specific names of persons seen at such establishments or loitering in public parks and toilets. Even Lady Camellia's proud attack on heterosexual arrogance ended with the complaint that male homosexuals were singled out in the articles, and the demand that the newspaper "open the eyes of the public" to "feminine love," naming locales where they gather, and suggesting, as had been suggested about the society of male homosexuals, that they were particularly powerful as a social group. Another letter writer, signing himself as "One Too," named a series of notorious homosexuals and a long list of commercial establishments tolerating them.[42] A later respondent may well have been right that "One Too" was probably "None at All," or rather, that the nascent public sphere improvised in the forum paralleled that on the streets, including not only inverts but their blackmailers as well. Some of these letters may also have been drafted by the café proprietors themselves, denouncing their own competition. More likely than this is that many of the letters written ostensibly by sympathetic heterosexual readers or even physicians were indeed by homosexuals, and this possibility was not lost on the editors.

From our contemporary perspective, the most outrageous and inflammatory of the letters correspond in many ways to a queer critique

of heteronormativity, conceding to the homophobic assumptions of
queer difference—even a difference ranging from "perversity" to lasci-
viousness—and extolling these as potential virtues in the face of a hypocritical general culture. Other letters, corresponding more clearly to the
agenda of the liberal homosexual emancipation movement, stress the
normality of presumed abnormal sexual orientation, pointing out (often
citing Magnus Hirschfeld's own research) that perverse practices occur
in homosexual and in heterosexual men in similar proportions. As one
reader argued, how could he be "healed" of a drive that was natural to
him, and does not even the suggestion that it require healing imply a
certain brutality? With an eloquent defense of his sexuality that at the
same time implicitly marginalized Merviola and her cohort, this precur-
sor of a familiar position signed himself simply, "Rita."

Finally, the *Kriminal-Zeitung*'s "pederasty" series was met by a
response by "the homosexual community" in the form of a didactic and
polite protest by the Vienna chapter of the Scientific-Humanitarian
Committee. In their controlled and only slightly patronizing letter, the
Committee was selective in what it chose to discuss with regard to the
scandalous articles. First, it clarified that the term "pederasty" itself,
meaning boy-love, was not a synonym for homosexuality, which in its
adult and consensual form was not a perversion, as such. Second, it was
an in-born inclination and, therefore, could not lead to recruitment of
other men of normal sexuality. Finally, the committee representatives
politely suggested that homosexuality was not technically a form of
insanity, and, therefore, decriminalization, as the Committee had long
campaigned, would be a more appropriate solution than institutionalization. To this missive was attached a friendly note from the central
Scientific-Humanitarian Committee signed by Dr. Magnus Hirschfeld,
in which suggestions for reading up on the subject were offered. This
tame intervention sealed the exchange briefly offered in the letters-to-
the-editor section, or was at least the newspaper's excuse to do so; in
response, they promised not to print anymore anonymous letters.

There is much more to be culled from these pages of the *Kriminal-
Zeitung*, which must be contextualized within other contemporary
discourses on sexual identity, social class, and a modern moral order.
The particular facet of the letters-to-the-editor highlighted here is the
pugnacious acceptance of a marginal identity and a declaration of war
against the hegemonic norms of heterosexuality. More needs to be said
about this aspect, too. Clearly, when they began their "pederasty
campaign," the editors of the *Kriminal-Zeitung* had no idea that the
"pederasts" themselves would object to it in this aggressive and, to their
ears, unapologetic way. At each point, they were able to turn this to their
own advantage, incorporating every response into their own picture of

43

a pathological clique endangering the general society. Just as clearly, letter-writers often resorted to the same language of pathologization in use in the inflammatory articles themselves. In some ways, the newspaper's aggressive campaign simply bumped into the obstacle of actually existing homosexuals—but did its campaign have an influence on the ways in which individuals defended themselves, how they thought about their own sexualities? This seems perhaps too grand a claim, even if the campaign brought the Viennese community into public view in a way that was never the case before. Yet these articulations did not emerge merely in reply to the *Kriminal-Zeitung* and its exposés, but to a couple of short decades of representations of homosexual identity, group identity, and sexual behavior. Self-understandings of homosexuals were in some sense hailed by such representations, including those in sensational news reports.[43] However complicit with the normative ideologies to which they responded, the aggressive self-defenses printed in this newspaper—along with countless, unvocalized such responses to medical, juridical, and sensational discourses on male-to-male sex—can be seen as constitutive elements of early twentieth-century male homosexual subjectivity.

Notes

1. *Illustrierte Oesterreichische Kriminal-Zeitung* [Vienna] vol. 1., no. 20 (2 September 1907): 8. The source is a letter to the editor of a sensationalist tabloid in response to an exposé and editorial series on homosexuality in Vienna, as will be discussed below. The original contains grammatical and spelling errors, along with the stilted prose that I have attempted to capture in the translation. The newspaper claimed to publish the letters unedited.

2. Carl Schorske's classic volume provides not only the prime example, but a canon of relevant figures including Sigmund Freud, Arthur Schnitzler, Gustav Klimt, and Oskar Kokoshka; see Carl Schorske, *Fin-de-Siècle Vienna: Politics and Culture* (New York: Knopf, 1980). More recent work recovers Otto Weininger, Lou Andreas Salomé, Robert Musil, Egon Schiele, and others.

3. While Austria-Hungary produced its own early sexuality theorist and advocate for homosexual emancipation, Károly Maria Kertbeny (Karl Maria Benkert) at the same time as Hanover's Karl Heinrich Ulrichs was writing, the latter's work was more conscious of the relationship of the legal project to a social movement. Cf. Jean-Claude Féray and Manfred Herzer, "Homosexual Studies and Politics in the 19th Century: Karl Maria Kertbeny," *Journal of Homosexuality* 19.1 (1990): 23-47. Attempts to repeal Paragraph 129(b) of the Austrian Penal Code never reached the formal and organized levels of the German "Scientific-Humanitarian Committee," and its rival homophile movement of *Die Eigenen* was specifically identified with the German Empire and German nationalism. Studies of these social and cultural phenomena as well as others, such as youth culture, are more common in German studies than in Austrian history.

4. Michel Foucault, *The History of Sexuality*, 3 vols., trans. Robert Hurley (New York: Random House, 1978-1986).

5. Michel Foucault, *History of Sexuality: Volume I, An Introduction* (New York: Random House, 1978), 45.

6. Ibid., 93.

7. Ibid., 101.

8. PP-KEB, Western Manuscripts and Archives, Wellcome Library for the History and Understanding of Medicine [WLHUM] (London). The material in the archive is not exclusively or specifically Austrian, or even German-language, although there is a general Central European predominance.

9. PP-KEB/A-C, WLHUM. This material was studied by Harry Oosterhuis while held in the private Krafft-Ebing family archive in Graz. Oosterhuis' thesis, while explicitly anti-Foucauldian in some respects and according to his own understanding, does much to expose the circuits connecting the emergent medical discourse on sexuality to sexual subjectivity. See Harry Oosterhuis, *Stepchildren of Nature: Krafft-Ebing, Psychiatry, and the Making of Sexual Identity* (Chicago: Univ. of Chicago P, 2000).

10. Laura Doan and Chris Waters, in their introduction to the section "Homosexualities" in a reader of translated documents of sexual science, concisely represent this dispute in relation to the legacy of sexology. See Doan and Waters in Lucy Bland and Laura Doan, eds., *Sexology Uncensored: The Documents of Sexual Science* (Chicago: Univ. of Chicago P, 1998), 41. Oosterhuis' major dispute with Foucault and Foucauldians is not merely that they underemphasize the way that the designation of perversions unleashed emancipatory potential for sexually marginal individuals; he believes that sexual science (at least in the foundational project of Krafft-Ebing) was liberal and emancipatory in its very impulse. See Oosterhuis, *Stepchildren*, 2-14.

11. Richard von Krafft-Ebing, *Psychopathia sexualis*, repr. (Munich: Mattes & Seitz, 1997). Beyond the title itself, all readers of Krafft-Ebing know that in all descriptions of any sexual acts whatsoever he lapsed into Latin. The efforts of sexual enlighteners seeking to educate the public and to purge the scourge of venereal disease and other ills were consistently challenged by criminal and vice police concerned about the lectures' potential pornographic content. The composition of the audience (which should be male and bourgeois) and the academic qualifications of the speaker were important criteria. See, e.g., Brandenburgisches Landeshauptarchiv [frmrly Potsdam] [BLHA] 16927/2, Hirschfeld, Magnus, Bericht über die Tätigkeit 1902-1912 (this material has now been moved to the Landesarchiv, Berlin).

12. Cited in "Ein homosexuellenprozess in Wien?" *Oesterreichische Kriminal-Zeitung. Wochenblatt für öffentliches Leben, Kriminal- und Polizeiwesen* [later called *Illustrierte Oesterreichische Kriminal-Zeitung*, see fn. 1, hereafter *Kriminal-Zeitung*] [Vienna], vol. 1, no. 32 (25 November 1907): 4.

13. Ibid., 5.

14. The historical literature on the affair is formidable, but a very incisive treatment is to be found in Isabel V. Hull, "Kaiser Wilhelm II and the 'Liebenberg Circle,'" in *Kaiser Wilhelm II: New Interpretations, The Corfu Papers*, ed. John C. G. Röhl (Cambridge, U.K.: Cambridge UP, 1982), 193-220, or idem, *The Entourage of Kaiser Wilhelm II, 1888-1918* (New York: Cambridge UP, 1982), 45-145.

15. See e.g. James Steakley, *The Homosexual Emancipation Movement in Germany* (New York: Arno, 1975), and Charlotte Wolff, *Magnus Hirschfeld: Portrait of a Pioneer in Sexology* (London: Quartet Books, 1986), 65-85.

16. Newspaper discourses have not generally been included in historiographical critiques of the linkage between expert (medico-juridical) discourses and homosexual emancipation movements. The kind of counter-factual historical hypotheses of which I am thinking is well exemplified by Gilles Barbedette and Michel Carassou in *Paris Gay 1925* (Paris: Presses de la Renaissance, 1981), where it is speculated that the origins of the modern homosexual emancipation movement in a German model dominated by "men of science" condemned it to a "psychiatric trap" that would have been "thwarted" by the contemporary French movement, which was led by literary figures. See Andrew Hewitt, *Political Inversions: Homosexuality, Fascism, & the Modernist Imaginary* (Stanford, CA: Stanford UP, 1996), 130. The translations in quotes here are Hewitt's.

17. Didier Eribon has recently tried to extrapolate on this aspect of homosexual identity formation in D. Eribon, tr. Michael Lucey, *Insult and the Making of the Gay Self* (Durham, NC: Duke UP, 2004).

18. *Kriminal-Zeitung*, vol. 1, no. 1 (1 April 1907).

19. "Zur Reform des österreichischen Strafgesetzes." Ibid., 3.

20. "Programmartikel." Ibid., 1.

21. See e.g. "Kinderspital und Nachtcafé" and "Prostitution und Polizei," *Kriminal-Zeitung*, vol. 1, no. 14 (18 July 1907): 1-4; "Die Prostitution in Wien," *Kriminal-Zeitung*, vol. 1, no. 19 (26 August 1907): 4-5; such reports would appear in every issue around this time.

22. "Die Prostitution in Wien," *Kriminal-Zeitung*, vol. 1, no. 16 (5 August 1907): 4-5.

23. See e.g. *Kriminal-Zeitung*, vol. 1, nos. 16-20 (5 August 1907-2 September 1907) for the escalation from the initial references to the existence of a male same-sex erotic subculture in Vienna to the regular "Pederasty" series, the letters to the editor pages, and a two-part exposé on a gay café entitled "A Night Among Loving Men," *Kriminal-Zeitung* vol. 1, no. 19 (26 August 1907): 5-6 and no. 20 (2 September 1907): 7-8. The newspaper's attention to the homosexual underworld of Vienna was among its most important editorial decisions, contributing not only to the massive increase in circulation, but to the regular censorship of the weekly, and, finally, to the prosecution of its editors and forced cessation of publication.

24. See "Päderastie," *Kriminal-Zeitung*, vol. 1, no 18 (19 August 1907), 6-7.

25. Ibid., 6.

26. *Kriminal-Zeitung*, v. 1, no. 18: 7.

27. Ibid.

28. Ibid.

29. Ibid.

30. *Kriminal-Zeitung*, vol. 1, no. 19 (26 August 1907), 6.

31. Ibid., 7.

32. Ibid.

33. The newspaper itself presented a brief (and obviously biased) report on the threats to revoke its license, see "Sittlichkeitskoller," *Kriminal-Zeitung*, vol. 1, no. 23 (27 September 1907), 2. All issues from late September forward were heavily censored, including not only the letters to the editor and the "Pederasty" series articles, but also editorials on policy and scientific articles concerning homosexuality. State records are incomplete, but leave traces of state prosecution of the editors on charges of extortion, leading to forced cessation of publication. See Österreichisches Staatsarchiv (Verwal-

tungsarchiv), Allgemeine Reihc, Ministerium des Innern, 1907 Präsidiale Index Z: Zeitschriften: Wiener Schmutz-Presse; s.a. 1907 Materien-Index Z: Zeitungsnotizen: Kriminalzeitung.

34. *Kriminal-Zeitung*, vol. 1, no. 19 (26 August 1907), 7.

35. *Kriminal-Zeitung*, vol. 1, no. 20 (2 September 1907), 8.

36. On the Gemeinschaft der Eigenen, see esp. Marita Keilson-Lauritz, *Die Geschichte der eigenen Geschichte: Literatur und Literaturkritik in den Anfängen der Schwulenbewegung am Beispiel des Jahrbuchs für sexuelle Zwischenstufen und der Zeitschrift Der Eigene* (Berlin: Rosa Winkel, 1997), and Harry Oosterhuis and Hubert Kennedy, *Homosexuality and Male Bonding in Pre-Nazi Germany: The Youth Movement, the Gay Movement, and Male Bonding Before Hitler's Rise, Original Transcripts from Der Eigene, The First Gay Journal in the World* (New York: Haworth, 1991).

37. The literature on these "two traditions" of the early homosexual emancipation movement has matured enough to already be enjoying revision. See esp. Harry Oosterhuis, "Homosexual Emancipation in Germany before 1933: Two Traditions," *Homosexuality and Male Bonding*, 1-28; Andrew Hewitt, *Political Inversions*, 79-170.

38. Cf. *Kriminal-Zeitung*, vol. 1, no. 19 (26 August 1907), 7.

39. Ibid., 6. The editors took this to be Krafft-Ebing's own position.

40. It was the Hanoverian jurist Karl Heinrich Ulrichs who made the claim for innate homosexuality the foundation for an argument against the criminalization of same-sex acts. The first of his pamphlets on the subject was published in 1864, at least a half-decade before what is taken to be the first example of the formally medical discourse by Carl Westphal. See Karl Heinrich Ulrichs, *Forschungen über das Räthsel der mannmännlichen Liebe*, vol. 1, *Vindex* (1864), repr. Ed. Hubert Kennedy, Bibliothek rosa Winkel 7 (Berlin: Rosa Winkel, 1994); and Carl Friedrich Otto Westphal, "Die conträre Sexualempfindung, Symptom eines neuropathischen (psychopathischen) Zustandes," *Archiv für Psychiatrie und Nervenkrankheiten* vol. 2, no. 1 (1869): 73-108. Foucault famously cited the occasion of this publication as the "date of birth" of the "psychological, psychiatric, medical category of homosexuality" (*History of Sexuality* 43), and there is some degree of consensus on this point, although David M. Halperin helpfully clarifies the distinction between the discourse on erotic orientation and that of "homosexuality" as such; see his *How to Do the History of Homosexuality* (Chicago: Univ. of Chicago P, 2002): 193, n. 61.

41. This is perhaps the best place to address the methodological problem of the authenticity of the letters, which naturally cannot be verified. In spite of the editors' claims to reproduce these reader letters unedited, it can never be clear how selective they were with their publication and whether or not letters were fabricated entirely. In light of the absence of any similar sources before this point—the novelty of the whole genre of authorship that Merviola, Rita, Mme. Louse et al. represent—it is safe to assume the contributions were not wholly invented, but rather exploited for their sensational value. Still, a clause such as the one at issue here, where a reader openly solicits broader readership, could have been confected by profit-motivated editors. None of this would compromise the argument put forth here, since even invented fragments would have been designed to conform to the conventions quickly established in the rush of reader responses. The discourses analyzed here are so densely recursive that the question of individual authorship moves to the background in some sense.

42. *Kriminal-Zeitung* vol. 1, no. 20 (2 September 1907), 8.

43. Reflection on this relationship relies upon an understanding of ideology and the subject inherited from Althusser, see Louis Althusser, "Ideology and Ideological State Apparatuses (Notes towards an Investigation)," *Lenin and Philosophy and other Essays*, trans. Ben Brewster (New York: Monthly Review, 1971), 127-86, see esp. 174, 173-83 for this notion of hailing or interpellation.

Educating Reasonable Lovers: Sex Counseling in Austria in the First Half of the Twentieth Century

Maria Mesner

During interwar years of the 1920s, Vienna witnessed the foundation of a new kind of health service, with the city of Vienna taking lead by opening its "Health Advice Center for Engaged Couples" (*Gesundheitliche Beratungsstelle für Ehewerber*) in the town hall on the first of June 1922. A group called *Bund gegen den Mutterschaftszwang* (League against Forced Motherhood) followed only a few months later, on 2 November 1922, with its first advice center (*Frauenschutz-Beratungsstelle*) in Vienna's sixth district. Finally at the end of December 1928, psychoanalyst Wilhelm Reich and physician Marie Frischauf founded a "Socialist Society for Sex Counseling and Research" (*Sozialistische Gesellschaft für Sexualberatung und Sexualforschung*), its members soon opening six centers for sex counseling.

Even though the Viennese *Gesundheitliche Beratungsstelle* boasted it was the first of its kind in Europe, sex counseling centers were common in many European cities during the interwar era. For example, in 1928 the first advice center for marital problems (*Beratungsstelle für Ehefragen*) was founded in Zurich.[1] Similar institutions spread all over Germany during the Weimar Republic.[2] At about the same time in New York City, Margaret Sanger fought the police searching her centers while she simultaneously struggled to get recognition from the medical authorities for her birth control activities.

The Viennese advice centers had one feature in common with a range of advice centers emerging at about the same time in other parts of Europe: they supported sexual reform and implicitly advocated new regimes of the body. Their inspiration was an idea of "progress," and they wanted to see its principles being established in human sexuality and/or procreation. Their activities aimed at life, for they wanted to affect its reproduction.

In the introduction to his *History of Sexuality*, French philosopher Michel Foucault maintained that in the early eighteenth century, at the start of modernity, life itself entered the realm of history. The phenomena of life became part of a new "bio-power" and of new political techniques. Thereby life and its creation were subjected to the control of knowledge and seized by the new power technique. The responsibility for life opened the access to the body for the power.[3]

A continuum of apparatuses emerged as markers and effects of the bio-power; they administered life, procreation and health, for "[s]uch a power has to qualify, measure, appraise, and hierarchize" in order to lay down a norm—descriptively as well as normatively. "A normalizing society is the historical outcome of a technology of power centered at life."[4]

This article attempts to identify the goals of the people who founded and ran the advice centers and thereby participated in the production of Foucault's bio-power. Moreover, it seeks to uncover the tenets inspiring their endeavors, their aims, and their goals. Furthermore, it looks at the bodies these activities addressed and produced: As Foucault has pointed out, it must be stressed that destructive as well as constructive aspects of power have to be kept in mind. Discourses and normative practices, as effects of power, frame a subject, but also produce it, making its existence possible. That is not to say that bodies would not exist without bio-power. However, the way people think and talk about their corporeality, the meanings they assign to bodily representations and phenomena, how they (re-)produce corporeality and respective norms in everyday life is defined by the culture of which they are part.

In the volume *Rationale Beziehungen*, Dagmar Reese, Eve Hosenhaft, Carola Sachse, and Tilla Siegel applied the notion of rationalization to describe gender relations in the twentieth century.[5] The evidence presented here supports this concept, but also clearly shows that there was not one single rationalization. The sexual advice initiatives were part of that rationalization process, but developed different concepts on how gender relations and human procreation should be (re-)structured in a "progressive," that is, rational, way.

Historical Context

Information on sexuality, especially on how to prevent unwanted pregnancies, had circulated in society before the 1920s.[6] At the turn of the twentieth century, itinerant preachers of sexual knowledge had already attracted large audiences in many European capitals. Literature intended to offer sexual advice had been spread widely.[7] However, sexual advice centers developed—in Europe and in North America—

only after World War I, this being the first war perceived as a "total war" by the societies affected by it. Apart from individual human tragedy, the war caused serious ruptures in the social and cultural framework of the societies involved. Modern wars are social situations which foster highly polarized gender stereotypes: a male front line is opposed to a female home front.[8] Those metaphors correspond to a strict gendering of individual war experience. However, at the same time, World War I disrupted the dichotomous balance of the gender system, for women entered spheres formerly defined as exclusively male, but which now lay deserted while the men were at war. The men's return after the war's end caused conflict and irritation, not only but specifically in gender relations.

Furthermore, the defeat of the Habsburg Empire created a general crisis in the Austrian successor state, resulting in the decline of the influence of former authorities, especially the imperial dynasty, the Catholic Church, the army, and the state bureaucracy. Industrialization had lured many people, especially women, away from the patriarchal sphere of the rural farm economy, to work in more impersonal factories. All these ruptures, leaving many contemporaries unsure and sometimes aggressive,[9] can be interpreted as a fundamental crisis of manhood. This was reflected on an individual level by the destabilization of private relations and a general unease becoming visible, for example, in the fact that less people decided to have children. Margaret and Patrick Higgonet assume that World War I caused only a temporary disturbance of gender relations followed by a fast restoration after the end of the war.[10] However, from my point of view, the rapid spread of sexual advice centers and sexual reform movements after World War I were signs of a permanent rupture in the normative basis of gender relations, which, as far as Austria is concerned, was settled only after World War II, in the 1950s.[11]

The norms and regulations which had hitherto defined the social framework and cultural meaning of sexuality and procreation had already been challenged at the turn of the century with World War I only enhancing the pressure. After the war, previously held sexual regulations kept losing their validity. The sexual advice initiatives can be seen as attempts to replace those withering norms that were mostly inspired by Catholicism with new ones. However, the three different groups I am going to introduce represent three different sets of norms. They advocated differing meanings of gendered bodies as embodiments of sexual and procreative potentials. Those groups had also very different ideas about the social conditions they envisioned as a framework for sexuality and procreation and about the mutual relationship between those two. Despite their differences, all groups had at least one intention in common: they wanted to make their concepts hegemonic within society, wanted to establish them as commonly accepted truth. Therefore, at the center of the story which follows there are three different truths on how gendered bodies ought to behave when it comes to sexuality and procreation.

The Historical Evidence
The *Gesundheitliche Beratungsstelle für Ehewerber*

All social relations were subject to public welfare, every step in human life was to be kept under surveillance. Finally also the unborn, even those who were not begotten yet, were included into this circumspection.[12]

These are the words Karl Kautsky, medical director of the *Beratungsstelle*, used when looking back at the time when his bureau was established by a resolution of the Viennese city council on 3 March 1922. Indeed, the net of welfare measures and institutions established by the city of Vienna after the election victory of the Social Democratic Workers' Party (SDAP) in 1919 was comprehensive—at least as far as the intentions of its creators were concerned.[13] Apart from the *Eheberatungsstelle*, a range of institutions aimed at life in a Foucaultian sense emerged. In 1930, advice centers for pregnant women were founded, thirteen pre-existing advice centers for mothers were significantly extended, and kindergartens were also built for very small preschool-age children. If the latter showed alleged problematic behavior, they were sent to a *Kinderübernahmsstelle* (child transfer center) and a *Zentralkinderheim* (central foster home).[14] School medical services, advice centers, and clinics for people with tuberculosis or sexually transmitted deceases (STDs) were established. This dense framework of institutions was permeated by an economic paradigm: human resources ought to be used economically, not wasted, and therefore only "minimal variations" (*Minusvarianten*) should be tolerated. Julius Tandler, city councilor for welfare, youth, and health from 1920 to 1932 and initiator of the *Beratungsstellen*, laid down the principles of his welfare policies in many speeches and articles. He divided public expenses into productive and unproductive ones, the former having to outnumber the latter. The notion of waste, which was opposed to rational efficiency, should—according to Tandler— also be applied to human reproduction. Eugenically inspired morals were set against a nature perceived as primitive, irrational, and lavish. Therefore, *Minusvarianten* were not only wasteful in respect to welfare expenses, but also in respect to procreative acts. In my analysis, I will concentrate on the *Eheberatungsstellen*, for they aimed directly at human procreation and are, therefore, comparable to other sexual advice centers.

During World War I, Tandler had already published on war-related negative eugenic selection because "in a state life is not a private matter, neither is health."[15] In his estimation, material postwar reconstruction should be paralleled by a reconstruction of the so-called "organic capital" of the state and the city of Vienna. At least in that period, Tandler's ambition and his trust in administrative feasibility seemed nearly without limits. With the words "I am convinced, that these things are manageable, as not only STDs but also a range of mental abnormalities can preclude somebody from procreation. Without any sentimentalities we have to state our right to safeguard the fate of our descendants,"[16] Tandler justified his support for obligatory medical marriage consents in December 1921. When the city government finally abandoned its plan to introduce obligatory marriage consents, it was on pragmatic, not ethical, grounds; coercive measures could easily be avoided by those concerned, for the Viennese government could only introduce them in Vienna, not in nearby Lower Austria, which was governed by Christian Social Party (CSP) Catholics.

When the *Eheberatungsstelle* opened its doors on 1 June 1922, Tandler and the director of the new public service, the physician Karl Kautsky, who shared Tandler's eugenic beliefs,[17] saw this as an experiment regarding whether or not people would appreciate eugenic counseling. According to the "Instructions for People Getting Married" (*Merkblatt für Eheschließende*) and a "Regulation for the Consulting Physician" (*Dienstvorschrift für den beratenden Arzt*)—both issued by the public health center (*Gesundheitsamt*)—the main part of the consultation and basis of its results was an extensive interview of both the engaged man and woman as well as of their practitioners. The inquiry included questions about chronic and other diseases (including, for example, STDs, mental diseases, epilepsy, gout, diabetes), disabilities (including those within the client's families and encompassing deafness, color-blindness, and the like), alcohol or any other drug addiction of the client or of his or her family member(s), hysteria or "signs of degeneration and significant deformities" or "congenital abnormalities." On the basis of this information and other possibly required examinations, the consulting physician offered his opinion on the applicants' "aptitude for marriage," becoming thereby the only authoritative expert for human reproduction.[18]

However, the *Eheberatungsstelle*'s development did not meet the expectations and hopes of its founders. In 1921, Julius Tandler had envisioned ten thousand people looking for advice.[19] In 1929, the year with the highest number of clients, city statistics counted only 892.[20] The needs and expectations the clients expressed also differed from what had been expected. The advice center's director, Kautsky, soon admitted that the consultations concerned all fields of sexual hygiene, the audience being not only people who wanted to get married or married couples. Kautsky now claimed that "marriage guidance counselors have to be knowledgeable in all details of contraception and have to teach people if they wish."[21] This offers one of the scarce glimpses at the "applicants," the clients of the *Eheberatungsstelle*: Obviously, they were not driven by "procreative responsibility," but by the urge to control their fertility. By the way, the high demand for contraceptive knowledge in interwar Vienna can also be deduced from the large audiences that Max Hodann's public lectures attracted. "More than a thousand young people" came on 16 December 1928 to hear and to see the renowned author of sex advice literature and founder of a sex advice center in Berlin.[22] Presumably, these obviously very needed services affected the everyday practice of the municipal *Eheberatungsstelle* and caused its primary intentions to shift.

Everyday practice also had its impact on Kautsky's view on the realization of the clinic's initial intentions. After five years in this position, he challenged the medical monopoly of procreation by complaining about the lack of psychoanalytical advice. As—according to Kautsky— he could only offer uncertain prognosis, the decision about getting married had to be left "to the daring and the temperament of the spouses,"[23] a statement that can be interpreted as a withdrawal from previous fantasies of power and control.

However, as far as can be judged on the basis of very scarce evidence, the practice of the *Eheberatungsstelle* remained ambiguous until its (temporary) closing in 1934. On the one hand, there is some indication that the eugenic intentions were put into perspective and that the involved physicians distanced themselves from the bureaucratic attempt to control the procreative potentials of the citizens. On the other hand, in one of his reports Kautsky mentioned a close cooperation between his office and public institutions for people who suffered from STDs, tuberculosis, or alcoholism and for advice centers for pregnant women. Obviously, municipal authorities frequently consulted the *Eheberatungsstelle* before issuing dispensations necessary for the re-marriage of divorcees. Most significantly, welfare officers were asked to refer all people to the *Eheberatungsstelle* who wanted to get married and whose fitness for marriage (that is, procreation) seemed doubtful.[24] This provision had the potential for totalitarian control—if the strictly voluntary character of a visit to the *Eheberatungsstelle* (which Kautsky kept stressing) was ever abolished.

Analyzing body images and normative attitudes prevailing in the *Eheberatungsstelle*, one concept becomes very clear: those who sought advice were—as subjects and as bodies—imagined within the framework of the postwar reconstruction of "organic capital." Therefore, sexuality was not a private matter, nor a matter of personal pleasure, but part of a manufacturing process which society had the right and the duty to control. In Foucaultian words, the procreative behavior was "socialized."[25] Human fertility should be either fostered or prevented. Through the notion of "transmission" of (possibly negative) traits, every individual became responsible for the social body, for the entire "organic capital." Therefore, sexual activity was situated at the intersection between the individual and society/population/the people/*Volk*. This relation is the linchpin for the attempt at disciplining adults. Its aim was the heterosexual couple. A revision of gender norms was not at stake. Thus those who wanted to get married seem in a paradoxical way sexless or unspecific in terms of gender, "Marriage [is] an institution, which enables the reproduction of humankind, i.e. positive procreation by efficient selection and legally as well as materially protected breeding."[26] It was considered crucial that this entity function well because "[t]he health of the spouses is more important for the working of a marriage than money and assets."[27] The spouses were supposed to fulfill their "breeding" duties within marriage with an efficiency and rationality enhanced by social control. The bi-polar gender roles were legitimized in a pre-social, unquestionable, and categorical way. Men should take part in the procreation process and be the main wage earners; women were responsible for the rest of the reproduction process. That supports Gottfried Pirhofer and Reinhard Sieder's description of the official life model of Red Vienna, "the nuclear working-class family as a norm."[28] However, the implementation of this model was not at the core of the *Eheberatungsstelle*; its main goal was the acceptance of an economic-rational concept of human (re-)production. Because the politicians in Vienna refrained from force in order to bring people to marriage counseling, they had to hope for self-control and self-discipline. The *Eheberatungsstelle* aimed at the production of self-controlling subjects who voluntarily pushed forward the project of rational manufacturing of humans. According to Karl Kautsky, these intentions were thwarted by "the indifference of the bulk of the population,"[29] a kind of passive resistance. It can be seen as a bitter historical irony that it was coercion and violence which made similar National Socialist attempts so much more "efficient."

The *Frauenschutz-Beratungsstelle*

The journal *Sexual-Reform: Journal für Sexualreform und Neo-malthusianismus* announced in its January 1923 issue that the *Bund gegen den Mutterschaftszwang* (Association against Forced Motherhood) had established an advice center open every Tuesday and Thursday from 5 to 6 p.m. "Every poor woman (or girl), who wants to use protection [*pessary*]" would be referred to a doctor who would examine her and fit a pessary free of charge. If she needed further consultations, she would get them at reduced fees, and the *Bund* would cover the difference. Better-off members could turn to the *Bund* to get a list of physicians. The counseling was anonymous; only births were recorded. The *Bund* also lobbied for free access to abortion, however—in order to avoid prosecution—stated in its journal frequently that questions about abortion could not be answered.

As already made clear by the subtitle of its journal, the *Bund* supported contraception out of neo-Malthusian reasoning; it also expressed this in statements like, "Children are protected from privation [. . .] if they are left unborn."[30] According to the *Bund*'s founder, Johann Ferch, a declining birthrate was a sign of release from the disastrous consequences of "overpopulation" including lack of housing, unemployment, hunger, the madness of megalopolis.[31] "The future belongs to the doctrine of quality—as a product of reason and morality. The doctrine of quality makes birth control necessary."[32]

Sole speaker of the *Bund* which was renamed the *Bund für Geburtenkontrolle* (Association for Birth Control) in 1925 was also Johann Ferch, printer and author of love stories. According to his wife, Betty, in 1926 four advice centers existed in Vienna;[33] in 1928 there were seven and an additional twelve at other places in Austria.[34] Therefore, it can be assumed that, apart from Betty and Johann Ferch, a whole group of people must have been involved. But hardly any information can be found in the records. Betty Ferch mentions forty socially-minded physicians with whom she cooperated as the administrator of the advice centers in Vienna. Mostly women volunteered to work in the advice centers; therefore, the centers were run at low costs. It is impossible to tell how many people turned to the centers in Vienna for advice. In a letter to Margaret Sanger, Betty Ferch pointed out that in 1932 1,709 women came to the advice centers all over Austria, while another 3,400 wrote letters and received the information they requested via mail.[35] The end of the Austrian republic in 1933/34 also caused the closing down of the *Beratungsstellen*. Betty Ferch, as the chairwoman of the *Bund*, proposed its dissolution at the meeting of 25 January 1934 because, as she argued, the restrictions on the freedom of assembly, which had been imposed after the dissolution of the parliament in March 1933, made the

Beratungsstellen's work too difficult.[36] Presumably that was also the end of the advice centers because no further archival traces can be found after this date.

The *Bund*'s activities were funded by private donations collected during Johann Ferch's public lectures, which attracted—at least according to information in the *Sexual-Reform*—a large audience. Furthermore, a slide show produced by Johann Ferch was publicly shown for money. The *Bund* attached great importance to public relations. Johann Ferch was obviously a very skilled communicator and was able to extend his network to many countries. For example, his reputation was high among those involved with the birth control movement in the United States.

The *Bund* was very ambivalent toward the eugenic movement within the SDAP. In some respects, both shared a common political interest, especially when the liberalization of the abortion ban was at stake.[37] Activists of the *Bund* had close relations to some people in Social Democratic organizations. Johann Ferch, for example, wrote articles for the Social Democratic journal *Die Frau*.[38] The *Arbeiterkrankenkasse* (workers' health insurance) supported the *Bund* in its early days by letting it use its building. However, the *Bund*'s journal often polemically criticized Tandler's *Eheberatungsstelle* and Viennese welfare policies in general, attributing to them "the emptiness of Austrian welfare misinformation."[39]

Coming to the significant characteristics of the *Frauenschutz-Beratungsstellen* and their activists, it is important to note that they maintained their independence of political parties—which was unusual within Austrian political culture. Instead, they trusted in private organizations and attached high value to voluntary service and lobbying activities. These features are evocative of the U.S. model, the white middle-class birth control movement with its figurehead Margaret Sanger. In the *Bund*'s rhetoric, women were the only addressees of the counseling (again a reminder of Sanger's clinics); a plan to establish an advice center for men was announced publicly in 1931,[40] but no traces of such a clinic exist in the archival sources. Women were presented as responsible for physical and social reproduction; their maltreated bodies were described as signs of exploitation and strain by frequent births and inexpert abortions. Poor women were seen as victims "of a sordid social order based on the meanest egotism" who were subjected to the yoke of "coerced motherhood" by "male ignorance." Therefore, "[t]he mother and woman, the female, must not be the unprotected game of thoughtlessness, of suffering and devastation of the body anymore."[41] Whereas society and its "organic capital" were at the core of the concepts of the municipal *Eheberatungsstelle*, the *Bund*'s aim was happy marriages through birth control promising an ideal future, "Children coming from loving and understanding marriages living under the sign of birth control will create a different mankind."[42] The *Bund*'s advice centers promised "economically safe homes, a marriage liberated from unbearable misery, quarrel and fight, and a satisfying sex-life, no longer unnatural and distorted from fear."[43]

Therefore, the *Bund* advocated ideas which anticipated U.S. family planning concepts prevailing in Europe only after World War II. Unlike Tandler's concepts which, in the name of an abstract community, demanded responsible behavior from individuals and, therefore, called for his/her subordination to a common weal, the *Bund* held out the prospect of individual happiness and domestic bliss if people behaved correctly, that is, followed the *Bund*'s suggestions: children born with less siblings and, therefore, raised with more emotional and material investment would become happier adults.

The Advice Centers of the *Sozialistische Gesellschaft für Sexualberatung und Sexualforschung*

With the approval of the Society's statute—filed by Marie Frischauf and Wilhelm Reich—by the city authorities of Vienna in December 1928, the advice centers were established. According to this statute, the Society had three main goals: counseling in cases of sexual conflict, information on "hygiene as well as disclosure of and fight against shortcomings of existing institutions," and research on sex.[44] Therefore, the Society established "advice centers for workers and employees" (*Beratungsstellen für Arbeiter und Angestellte*), organized public lectures, collected statistical data, and published an academic series, *Schriften der sozialistischen Gesellschaft für Sexualberatung und Sexualforschung*.

At the end of January 1929, the communist newspaper *Rote Fahne* (*Red Flag*) announced the opening of six centers located in private apartments and medical practices in which counseling should take place "on the basis of scientific, especially psycho-analytic research. Counseling includes psychic and somatic examination as well as the provision of results."[45] Each advice center was open to everybody two hours per day.[46] One consultation took about half an hour; in the first eighteen months after the opening, 700 people had turned to the centers for advice.[47] In addition, 7,000 people had come to public lectures.[48]

In the course of 1930, the counseling activities were restructured. The new list shows the range of fields of interest: Marie Frischauf and Isidor Fassler gave advice on contraception and STDs, Frischauf only accepting female clients. Reich and Anny Angel were in charge of consultations on sexual conflicts and neurosis; Lia Swarowsky and Edith

Buxbaum specialized in the counseling of children and young people; Eduard Fliegel, the only jurist among the medical experts, provided information on legal matters.[49] It remains unclear if the Society's advice centers survived Reich's move to Berlin in the fall of 1930, as no records can be found after 1931.

Conclusions in respect to the clients and the counseling itself can be drawn from Reich's publication of detailed statistical evidence. He described the clients as "poor blue- and white-collar workers," only about 30 percent of whom could be helped in "one or more consultations." Most of them had turned to the centers because of "scruples about masturbation, slight virility problems, slight sexual conflicts" or because they needed information on contraception. Usually they were recommended a pessary in combination with spermicidal jelly."[50] According to Reich, 70 percent of the clients were "neurotic to an extent which made it impossible to provide help without thorough psychotherapeutic treatment."[51] Reich was very pessimistic concerning these cases, given "the factual impossibility to provide only a small share of the patients with an appropriate treatment."[52] He called it an illusion to believe "that a solution of the problem was possible within bourgeois society, taking into account the inadequacy of existing institutions, the masses of people who suffered, the continuous production of neurosis and disorders of sex-life by the education common in average families." Moreover, Reich asserted, "If there is nothing left to say for the physician, the socialist has to take his place." Reich pointed out that he himself had succeeded several times "in getting such workers [he was not able to help as a doctor, M.M.] interested in party activities."[53]

Analyzing sexual and procreative norms as well as body concepts, Reich's comprehensive pathology of lived sexuality seems striking. According to him, 50 percent of all men and 70 percent of all women showed signs of neurosis. About half of the men, but at least 90 percent of all women, suffered from "temporary impotence or disorders in their ability to experience sexual pleasure during intercourse."[54] Reich blamed bourgeois sexuality and marriage ethics—accepting sexual activity only in order to procreate children within the context of marriage or else demanding abstinence—for the "endemic disease of neurosis" which "the proletariat faced helpless," whereas well-off people could have their problems taken care of by private doctors.[55]

Reich's views on "correct" sexuality were framed in an inseparable intertwining of rhetoric of emancipation on the one hand and authoritative instructions on the other. Sexual activity should be liberated from bourgeois sexual repression and be, therefore, regular, joyful, satisfying, and—as unspoken as obvious—heterosexual as well as oriented towards orgasm. Sexual activities deviating from this scheme were derogatorily calling "neurotic." According to Reich, homosexuals were "sick people," having experienced "a developmental disorder in respect to the opposite sex."[56] At first glance, the subject's urge to act out his or her "natural" sexual drive is not gendered. However, a closer analysis shows that especially unsatisfied (proletarian) men needed to be liberated. Therefore, "female frigidity is one of the most prominent causes for the fact that many marriages become unhappy so quickly."[57] Consequently, women, whom Reich finds to suffer more from the effects of sexual repression and the demand for abstinence than men, should be helped on the road to "normal" sexual excitability.

Reich's considerations were oriented towards liberation of sexuality resulting in sexual pleasure. Although—according to his own testimony—working closely together with the municipal *Eheberatungsstelle*, he criticized eugenicists and people concerned with population development, "All the eagerness and care about welfare and non-extinction of mankind forgets about human beings. [...] It is desirable that all the biologists and population politicians immerse themselves in the concept of awarding pleasure [Freud's *Lustprämie*, M.M.[58]] to ensure procreation."[59] Reich, on the other hand, insisted on this concept of awarding pleasure so much that it evolved into a norm, one that perhaps not everybody regarded as pleasurable.

Conclusions

Undoubtedly, the three sexual counseling initiatives presented here differ greatly as far as their concepts of society and societal utopias in general and procreation in particular are concerned. Nowadays, Tandler's eugenically inspired vision of society is—keeping in mind the National Socialist "use" of similar concepts—much more disturbing than the basically bourgeois model of families living in perfectly planned harmony propagated by the Ferchs, the latter being surpassed by the radicalism of Wilhelm Reich's social utopia.

Furthermore, the different concepts went down very different roads after the respective institutions had been closed down in the early 1930s. After the consolidation of the authoritarian *Ständestaat*, the municipal *Eheberatungsstelle* was re-opened in June 1935. Its new director, Albert Niedermeyer, a theologian, jurist, and physician, advocated Catholic eugenics.[60] Unlike his Social Democratic predecessors, he rejected "artificial contraception" and—in accordance with Catholic moral theology—accepted only abstinence as a means of birth control. Niedermeyer saw marriage counseling within a national Austrian framework, considering "his" *Eheberatungsstelle* at least in retrospect "an important mental bulwark for the defense of the 'bastion Austria.'"[61]Although

60 Contemporary Austrian Studies

Niedermeyer published in abundance on marriage counseling in general and on the *Eheberatungsstelle* in particular, no information on the everyday practice of the consultations can be found, neither in his publications, nor in the records of the city of Vienna. After the Anschluss, the *Eheberatungsstelle* was closed once and for all. After World War II, the eugenic pre-war concepts were de-legitimized together with their last advocates, the National Socialists. It took until the mid-1970s to pick up the thread and to incorporate "genetic family counseling" in major university clinics in Austria.[62]

Reich's *Beratungsstellen* had already vanished before the end of the First Austrian Republic, the *Ständestaat* and the Third Reich scattering all traditions and continuities that might have been left in the practices of a few individual physicians. They did not turn up again until the students' movement of the late 1960s and early 1970s rediscovered Reich's ideas about the relationship between political emancipation and sexual liberation.[63]

As already mentioned, the Ferchs' *Frauenschutz-Beratungsstellen* were in strategy and ideology close to the U.S. family planning movement. However, unlike in the United States after World War II, family planning did not become a major endeavor in postwar Austria. Although no research has been done on the topic, it is safe to assume that sexual counseling was occasionally part of "family counseling" in parishes and cities or part of doctor-patient conversations. But sexual counseling did not become institutionalized before the foundation of the Austrian Society for Family Planning emerged in 1966. One can only speculate on the reasons for this Austrian difference from U.S. or German developments. National Socialism had destroyed liberal and secular— and especially Jewish—milieus, leaving a conservative Catholicism dominating Austrian public discourse and policies at least into the 1960s. Austrian Social Democracy, which during the interwar era had advocated sexual reform as part of its comprehensive political project, was weakened by intellectual and personnel loss from genocide and expulsion. Furthermore, party elites prioritized political cooperation with the Catholic conservative party at the expense of liberalization and secularization.

Despite different developments and histories, the sexual counseling initiatives presented in this paper have some conspicuous features in common. First, they aimed at the substitution of the hitherto existing authorities for sexual ethics, priests and jurists, by (mental or somatic) health professionals. The medical paradigm of scientific truth competed with the Catholic Church's claim to divine truth. The physician provided access to safe contraceptives by examining the patients, writing a prescription, and instructing people in the contraceptive's use.[64]

Second, it seems remarkable that the target of all initiatives was the (heterosexual) couple as an entity. The gender relations within that entity were not at stake. If one takes into account that it was exactly gender relations which were shaken by social change and the impact of World War I, this neglect can be interpreted as an attempt to affirm and/or to reconstruct the ideal of the couple. However, this attempt at restoration stands in stark contrast to the rhetoric of radical change used by the social reform movements of the interwar era.

Third, in stark contrast to foreign counterparts, like for example Weimar Germany or the U.S., none of the counseling initiatives involved feminist movements: There only is scarce evidence, that connections between the Social democratic women's organization and the Ferchs' *Frauenschutz-Beratungsstellen* existed: Johann Ferch was invited to talk about birth control on occasion of the annual meetings of the organization and its newspaper ran ads for the Ferchs' advice centers. However, unlike feminists in Weimar Germany or in the U.S., the respective Austrian protagonists made no traceable effort to get involved with policies and everyday practice of counseling initiatives. There is no evidence that feminists of any political affiliation played a significant role in birth control movements in interwar Austria.

I started from the assumption that a serious de-legitimization of until then powerful institutions of social regulation and production of meaning was the reason for the concurrent emergence of sexual reform movements and sexual counseling institutions in the 1920s. Indeed, the initiatives I mentioned turned against Austria's prevailing sexual ethics, related laws, and rules of public rhetoric influenced and coined by the Catholic hierarchy. The city of Vienna's *Eheberatungsstelle* set its project of an economically planned manufacturing of human beings—embedded in a rationally and comprehensively planned society—against the divine imperative. The *Bund* advocated a modernization of the couple within the bourgeois family model based on mutual love, respect, and fulfillment; the *Frauenschutz-Beratungsstellen* attempted to transfer this middle-class norm to the working classes. Wilhelm Reich finally outlined a liberated, sexually active proletarian able to shed his or her formerly repressed sexuality which had been suppressed by capitalism.

Because these social visions addressed working class people in particular and offered them access to knowledge hitherto mostly unavailable, they were personally empowering. The separation of sexual activity from procreation, which was strictly rejected by Catholic ethics, opened up new space for individuals. However, the empowering implications of the interwar sexual reform movements were closely interwoven with their normative strategies in an ambiguous and vexing way. This ambiguity is—in a historical perspective—typical for interwar sexual counseling. It can and should neither be dissolved nor neglected, but has to be taken into account as an essential aspect of all these initiatives, referring once again to the Janus-faced—productive and restrictive—potentials of norms.

Notes

1. *Blätter für das Wohlfahrtswesen* 26: 106.

2. Kristine von Soden, *Die Sexualberatungsstellen der Weimarer Republik, 1919-1933* (Berlin: Henrich, 1988).

3. Michel Foucault, *The History of Sexuality: An Introduction*, vol. 1 (New York: Vintage Books, 1990).

4. Ibid., 144.

5. "Einleitung," in *Rationale Beziehungen? Geschlechterverhältnisse im Rationalisierungsprozeß*, ed. Dagmar Reese et al. (Frankfurt am Main: Suhrkamp, 1993), 7-16.

6. See, for example, Robert Jütte, *Lust ohne Last. Geschichte der Empfängnisverhütung von der Antike bis zur Gegenwart* (Munich: C. H. Beck, 2003); John M. Riddle, *Eve's Herbs: A History of Contraception and Abortion in the West* (Cambridge, MA: Harvard UP, 1997).

7. For Vienna, see Britta McEwen, "Viennese Sexual Knowledge as Science and Social Reform Movement, 1900-1934," Ph.D. diss., University of California at Los Angeles, 2003.

8. Margaret Randolph Higonnet et al., "Introduction," in *Behind the Lines: Gender and Two World Wars*, ed. Margaret Randolph Higonnet et al. (New Haven, CT: Yale UP, 1987), 1-17.

9. Reinhard Sieder, "Zur alltäglichen Praxis der Wiener Arbeiterschaft im ersten Drittel des 20. Jahrhunderts," Ph.D. diss., University of Vienna, 1988.

10. Margaret R. Higonnet and Patick L.R. Higonnet, "The Double Helix," in Higonnet et al., *Behind the Lines*, 34.

11. In contrast, Margaret R. Higonnet and Patrick L.R. Higonnet maintain that the disturbance was only temporary and was settled soon after the war ("The Double Helix," 34).

12. Karl Kautsky, "Die Eheberatung im Dienste der Wohlfahrtspflege," *Blätter für das Wohlfahrtswesen der Stadt Wien* 24/248 (1925): 26.

13. Doris Byer, *Rassenhygiene und Wohlfahrtspflege: Zur Entstehung eines sozialdemokratischen Machtdispositivs in Österreich bis 1934* (Frankfurt: Campus, 1988).

14. Gudrun Wolfgruber, "Kinder- und Jugendfürsorge im roten Wien zwischen sozialer Kontrolle und Hilfe; dargestellt am Beispiel der Kindesabnahmen," Ph.D. diss., University of Vienna, 1996.

15. Julius Tandler, "Krieg und Bevölkerung," *Wiener klinische Wochenschrift* 29 (1916): 450.

16. Session 21 December 1921, Gemeinderat, Wiener Stadt- und Landesarchiv, 1481.

17. Karl Sablik, *Julius Tandler, Mediziner und Sozialreformer: Eine Biographie* (Vienna: Schendl, 1983), 278.

18. *Das neue Wien: Städtewerk herausgegeben unter offizieller Mitwirkung der Gemeinde Wien*, vol. 2 (Vienna, 1927), 578, 571.

19. Session 21 December 1921, *Gemeinderat*, 1481.

20. *Statistisches Jahrbuch der Stadt Wien für das Jahr 1929*, Neue Folge, vol. 2 (Vienna, 1930), 59.

21. Karl Kautsky, "Fünf Jahre öffentliche Eheberatung," *Blätter für das Wohlfahrtswesen* 27/265 (1928): 23.

22. *Arbeiter-Zeitung*, 18 December 1928, p. 4.

23. Kautsky, "Fünf Jahre," 24.

24. Karl Kautsky, "Die Eheberatungsstelle der Gemeinde Wien," *Blätter für das Wohlfahrtswesen* 29/282 (1930): 309.

25. Foucault, *History of Sexuality*, 104.

26. Julius Tandler, *Ehe und Bevölkerungspolitik* (Vienna: Perles, 1924), 1.

27. *Das neue Wien*, 578.

28. Gottfried Pirhofer and Reinhard Sieder, "Zur Konstitution der Arbeiterfamilie im Roten Wien: Familienpolitik, Kulturreform, Alltag und Ästhetik," in *Historische Familienforschung*, ed. Michael Mitterauer and Reinhard Sieder (Frankfurt am Main: Suhrkamp, 1982), 326-68.

29. Kautsky, "Fünf Jahre," 24.

30. Joh[ann]. Ferch, *Die Unterbrechung der Schwangerschaft* (Vienna: Verlag Sexualreform), 6.

31. Joh[ann]. Ferch, *Geburtenregelung* (Leipzig: Parthenon, 1929), 37, 57.

32. Ferch, *Unterbrechung*, 4f.

33. Betty Ferch, "A Chain of Clinics," *Birth Control Review* (Jan. 1926): 21.

34. *Birth Control Review* August 1928: 289.

35. Betty Ferch to Margaret Sanger, 15 Sept. 1933, Margaret Sanger Papers, Microfilm, Series III, subseries 1—Correspondence, Library of Congress, Washington, D. C.

36. Karin Lehner, *Verpönte Eingriffe: Sozialdemokratische Reformbestrebungen zu den Abtreibungsbestimmungen der Zwischenkriegszeit* (Vienna: Picus, 1989), 39.

37. Ibid., 36f.

38. Martha Eckl, "Körperkultur und proletarische 'Weiblichkeit' 1918-1934: Eine Untersuchung am Beispiel der Frauenzeitschriften der sozialdemokratischen Arbeiterpartei Deutsch-Österreichs," Ph.D. diss., University of Vienna, 1986.

39. *Sexual-Reform* 14.4: 1.

40. *Die Unzufriedene* 9/40, 5.

41. *Sexual-Reform* 13.4: 1.

42. Ibid.

43. Ferch, *Unterbrechung*, 11.

44. Statute cit. in. Karl Fallend, *Wilhelm Reich in Wien: Psychoanalyse und Politik* (Vienna: Geyer Edition, 1988), 116.

45. §4 of the statute cit. in Ibid.

46. Ursula Kubes, "'Moderne Nervositäten' und die Anfänge der Psychoanalyse" in *Aufbruch und Untergang: Österreichische Kultur zwischen 1918 und 1938*, ed. Franz Kadrnoska (Vienna: Europaverlag, 1981), 274.

47. Wilhelm Reich, "Die Sexualnot der werktätigen Massen und die Schwierigkeiten der Sexualreform," in *Sexualnot und Sexualreform. Verhandlungen der Weltliga für Sexualreform. IV. Kongress*, ed Josef K. Friedjung et al. (Vienna: Elbmühl-Verlag, 1931), 78.

48. Wilhelm Reich, "The Socialistic Society for Sexual Advice and Sexual Research," in *The Practice of Contraception: An International Symposium and Survey*, ed. Margaret Sanger and Hannah M. Stone (Baltimore: Williams & Wilkins, 1931), 271.

49. Fallend, *Wilhelm Reich*, 122.

50. Marie Frischauf and Annie Reich, *Ist Abtreibung schädlich?* (Vienna: Münster-Verlag, 1930), 38.

51. Wilhelm Reich, "Erfahrungen und Probleme der Sexualberatungsstellen für Arbeiter und Angestellte in Wien," *Der sozialistische Arzt* 5 (1929): 98.

52. Ibid., 100.

53. Ibid., 102.

54. Reich, "Sexualnot," 78.

55. Reich, "Erfahrungen und Probleme," 101.

56. Wilhelm Reich, *Sexualerregung und Sexualbefriedigung* (Vienna: Münster-Verlag, 1929), 59.

57. Ibid., 25.

58. Apart from Reich's approach, Freudian ideas on sexuality had no traceable impact on the interwar sexual reform activists' reasoning in Vienna; Tandler's initiative was interested more in population policies than in individual development. The Ferchs—although relying on university-trained physicians but without formal higher education themselves—were influenced mainly by neo-Malthusian ideas; under that umbrella, collective and individual well-being were conflated.

59. Wilhelm Reich, "Der Koitus und die Geschlechter" *Zeitschrift für Sexualwissenschaft* 8 (1922): 352.

60. Monika Löscher, "'Der gesunden Vernunft nicht zuwider': Katholizismus und Eugenik in Österreich vor 1938," in *Wert des Lebens: Gedenken—lernen—begreifen. Begleitpublikation zur Ausstellung des Landes OÖ in Schloss Hartheim 2003* (Linz: Trauner Verlag, 2003), 47-53.

61. Albert Niedermeyer, *Wahn, Wissenschaft und Wahrheit: Lebenserinnerungen eines Arztes* (Innsbruck: Tyrolia, 1956), 332.

62. Maria Andrea Wolf, "Eugenisierung der Mutterschaft. Wissenschaftsdiskurse zur Neuordnung der Reproduktion am Beispiel Österreich 1900-2000," Ph.D. diss., University of Innbruck, 2004.

63. See Dagmar Herzog, *Sex after Fascism: Memory and Morality in Twentieth-Century Germany* (Princeton, NJ: Princeton UP, 2005), 158pp.

64. It is remarkable that the few female counselors involved were more critical of the medical monopoly and of the dependence of (female) users. Whereas the medical position remains unquestioned in the statements of male speakers, Annie Reich as well as Marie Frischauf pleaded for contraceptives which could be used without needing a doctor. The evidence is too fragmentary, to draw more far-reaching conclusions.

Sexual Encounters across (Former) Enemy Boderlines

Ingrid Bauer and Renate Huber

The connections between war, occupation, and sexuality are ambiguous and complex, and hence are frequently suppressed. This is particularly true with regard to World War II and its aftermath, not least because of the ways that war was associated with such intensely and emotionally fraught matters of extreme violence, military and ideological defeat, collaboration, and treason.

This paper examines the personal and sexual relationships between Austrian women and soldiers of the Allied Occupation Forces which represented a significant phenomenon in postwar Austria. The broad spectrum of such erotic liaisons ranged from so-called "prostitution in order to survive," to flirtations, to love affairs, and to thousands of marriages. The dark underside of these postwar relationships was rape, professional prostitution, and the stigmatization of "occupation children."

Looking at all four occupation zones—U.S., Soviet, French, and British—generates a long overdue synthesis of what until now appeared only independently in published research on the topic. Discussed in the context of the history of sexuality in the twentieth century, these findings are embedded in discourses on interculturality and the paradigm of self/other.

Chocolate of All Things . . . Atmospheric Vibrations

Es war heut' mittag gegen zwei,
da kam am Stadtplatz ich vorbei. /
Plötzlich sah ich, daß ein Mädchen um die Straßenecke bog,
wie ein süßer kleiner Vogel über's Straßenasphalt flog /
Und zumal sie wirklich hübsch war, noch nicht alt und nicht zu jung,
war es klar, daß ich ihr folgte in dem neubelebten Schwung. /
Also ging es durch das Städtchen, viele Straßen ab und auf,

mit den Augen auf dem Mädchen, mit den Beinen Dauerlauf. /
Doch in Anbetracht der Zeit,
war der Weg mir doch zu weit. /
Und ich sprach sie einfach an,
ob sie mir nicht sagen kann,
was mich brennend interessiert,
ob der Weg zum Friedhof führt. /
Darauf eisigkaltes Schweigen wie ein scharfer Peitschenhieb,
Näschen hoch—auf einmal Lächeln, an der Ecke hielt ein Jeep. /
„Hallo Blondy" oder ähnlich, und das Mädchen stieg hinein,
und ich stand nun, wie gewöhnlich, auf der Straße ganz allein. /
War ein trauriges Erlebnis
und ich kam zu dem Ergebnis,
daß man ohne Schokolade—
wie ein Bettler dasteht—schade.[1]

Under "normal" circumstances, this pretty awkward poem about a failed flirtation, published in a letter to the editor of the *Pinzgauer und Pongauer Zeitung*, a local newspaper, could appear as a rather banal everyday story. However, it certainly did not in the postwar setting of March 1947. Just two "code words" within this poem—"jeep" and the Americanized name "Blondy" for the courted woman—made it absolutely clear to each and every reader that this local male letter writer was harshly criticizing relationships between Austrian women and soldiers of the Allied Occupation Forces. The writer concluded his poem with the implication that men courting local women would need to be supplied with the rare new "currency" of chocolate; otherwise, their love would remain unrequited.[2]

The writer clearly perceived himself as a victim, as the loser in an erotic ménage à trois. Within this dynamic triangle, the local women recognized the value of their own competitive advantages considering occupation soldiers' erotic needs. They obviously seized this opportunity, thereby evidently intensifying the feelings of "local boys" that they stood no chance. Without stating it explicitly, the letter writer expressed a strong feeling of uneasiness and insecurity caused by the double rivalry with the occupiers on a national/military as well as on a sexual level, a rivalry which for German and Austrian men finally turned into a double defeat as both soldiers *and* as men.[3]

A few days later, a female letter writer responded with a poem full of sparkling wit and irony. By reminding the readers of the affairs soldiers of the *Wehrmacht* had in many of the countries (in particular in northern and western Europe)[4] which had been occupied by the forces of the Third Reich, she opened the discursive field from another angle.

In so doing, she discussed a topic about which silence was kept, not only immediately after the war, but until very recently:[5]

Armer Schelm, ich hätt' beinahe Tränen der Ergriffenheit
Deinem Reinfall mit der „Blondy" und dem schnöden Jeep geweiht./
Zeiten sind das, nicht zu sagen! Schröcklich, diese Unmoral!
Anders wars doch in den Tagen an der sonnigen Loire. /
Mit Yvonne daselbst spazierte man beglückt dort Arm in Arm.
Daß bekannt sie war als Circe, nahm ihr nichts von ihrem Charme. /
Weiter nördlich an der Schelde, an der Maas, am Niederrhein,
hieß sie Rosje oder Nelle—und Du wollt'st sie gar nicht frei'n. /
Ebenso in Trondheim Sigrid, und Dagmar in Kopenhagen.
(Viele Strophen hätt' dies Lied …) Alles Liebe!—sozusagen. /
Griechenland und oh Italia. Ach, ihr wußtet zu verwöhnen!
Unvergleichlich eure Weine, unvergessen eure Schönen! /
Bändevoll ließ sich noch schwärmen, was sich hier und dort getan. /
Ach wie werden sie sich härmen um den flotten Don Juan! /
Denn oh weh, er kehrt nicht wieder. Sucht bescheiden nun sein Glück
nur bei Gretchen treu und bieder, die er einstens ließ zurück. /
Doch was hat denn schon Bestand heutzutags im Weltgetriebe.
Dieser läßt sein Vaterland, den anderen verläßt die Liebe. /
Der Versuchung freche Tücke
nicht mehr mit Juwelen zielt, sondern mit Schokoladenstücken! /
Oh Verderbtheit unsrer Tage, die so Teuflisches ersinnt!
Ausgerechnet Schokolade, die so mild im Mund zerrinnt! /
Gegen manches herbe Leid, half schon Selbstgefälligkeit. /
Man weist entrüstet auf die Schande, die man stets von weitem floh
und spricht das fromme altgekannte: „Doch Gott sei Dank, ich bin
nicht so!"[6]

Once more, stories of local men's flirtations are told, but this time under different premises. The stories in this poem took place during the war, when the now defeated men were still powerful, victorious soldiers of the *Wehrmacht* occupying foreign places in half of Europe. In contrast to the first letter, this letter's stories told of successful erotic adventures: the "smart Don Juan" happily promenading "arm in arm" with his respective "conquests" in France, Belgium, the Netherlands, Norway, Denmark, Italy, or Greece.

The female author with a winking eye tackled the "complacency" and the double standards of the defeated home comers who were presently full of self-pity and lamented the behavior of women at home. By taking up the motif of "chocolate as currency" introduced in the first letter, the author asked in a rather sneering way how could the postwar world only be so "depraved" to bring something so "devilish" like "chocolate" into play, "… chocolate of all things which so sweetly melts away in the mouth … ."[7] At this point, there might also be a kind of female contentment in enjoying the sweet pleasures of an erotic affair which was actually considered to be immoral, even though it may be as fleeting a thing as the taste of chocolate.

Both letters to the editor reveal the extent to which occupation, apart from the military/political aspect, also always contains a sexual dimension. This element found expression in love relationships as well as in prostitution (an implied suspicion in both letters), and in sexual violence (which both writers ignored).

The discourse within these poems also mirrors manifold-- and indeed often also contradictory-- experiences and atmospheric settings regarding the desired gender order, its gender-specific demands and categorizations, and its extremely nationalized connotations in times of war and occupation. The intertwining of occupation, nation, and gender roles[8] turned love relationships between women and "foreign" soldiers into a subject to regard with disapproval, a form of love which stood outside the norms. This was the case regardless of whether the occupation happened before or after the end of the war, even though the respective political contexts were completely different.[9]

To be more precise, however, the sexuality of the victorious soldier in the foreign country was not primarily under scrutiny, but the sexual behavior of women in general was scrutinized because of their specific role within their respective nation as "symbolic bearers of the collectivity's identity and honor."[10] Thus, in contrast to the sexual activities of men, the cultural role of women as "national embodiments" and correspondingly their sexual morals gained eminent public significance in particular against the backdrop of victory and defeat at the end of World War II.

Compared to (West) Germany, the situation in Austria after the capitulation of the Third Reich seems to have been even more complex regarding the intertwinement of occupation, nation, and gender roles. Therefore, sexual relationships between Austrian women and soldiers of the Allied occupation forces gained added significance, too.

Austria was not only a defeated nation. Unlike Germany, it was just beginning the process of becoming a nation at all. As in all European postwar societies, the construction of national political myths was part of the identity-building strategies of the political elites. The Allied occupation would become a central event in the production of such myths in Austria. In retrospect, the stories made up in this discursive field are tied to the Austrian success story: the saga of how the young republic freed itself from "foreign rule." Within this national narrative, the position of the victim, Austria, combines with paternalistic rhetoric to present a helpless country, caught in the web of history, innocently confronted with foreign powers. This rhetoric dates back to the founding fathers of the Second Republic and has strongly determined the self-perception of the Austrian people.[11] Through this myth, the seventeen years of the occupation period became anchored in the Austrian national memory as an epoch of continuous subjection to "foreign sovereigns," which began in 1938 with the occupation of Hitler's Germany and ended only when the last Allied soldier left Austria in 1955.[12]

Perceiving themselves as victims, the Austrian elites tried to get rid of the Allied occupation forces more intensively than did their German counterparts, though there might have been a further reason involved here. While the foundation of the Federal Republic of Germany already in 1949 precluded the Red Army's influence on this Western country, the occupation setting in Austria included the Soviet element (and the threat it appeared to pose) until the signing of the State Treaty in 1955.

Thus, the analysis of sexual relationships of local "Blondies" (and "Gretchens") with foreign "Don Juans"—to remain in the contemporary diction of the poems—in the specific postwar context of Austria promises possibly richer and even more conflictual variations of inter-cultural encounters as in other national settings.[13] After all, relationships with members of the Allied occupation forces as "foreign sovereigns" were in a particular way burdened with national meaning.

Who's Got the Power? Love under "Regulation"

If and how occupation soldiers were allowed to get in touch with Austrians was regulated in different ways in the four occupation zones. The Soviets at first did not impose any restrictions on contact with the Austrian people. Only after a while did they enact a general prohibition of marriage, a ban that was only lifted under exceptional circumstances. Fathers of illegitimate children were posted away from Austria.[14] In the postwar period, especially as the Cold War progressed, Austrian women, but also members of the Red Army themselves, could become condemned because of their relationships because "pillow talk" could quickly become "counter-revolutionary spying."[15] Such suspicions could result in kidnapping and placement in a labor camp for women. For the Soviet soldiers, too, the consequences could be severe.

In the American and British zones, however, a strict non-fraternization rule initially existed, and any private contact was forbidden. Soldiers were not allowed to visit local women at their homes or to take them out to a restaurant or a dance, or even to go for a walk or to have a drink with them.[16] This rigorous restriction was loosened by the summer of 1945 and was completely abolished in the fall. Later on, the ban on marriages was also abolished. The negative image of such marriages remained, though, in particular because of the pressure of the (female) public's opinion in the soldiers' countries of origin. Furthermore, British and U.S. authorities installed numerous legal and bureaucratic hurdles to prevent those marriages, including, among other things, a certain waiting period for the British,[17] and character references and the confirmation of the political harmlessness with regards to National Socialism for the brides of American GIs.[18]

Only French and Moroccan soldiers (as part of the French occupation forces) had no regulations regarding contact with the locals. This was true from the very beginning of the occupation because France considered Austria to be a "friendly," not a "defeated" nation.[19]

In all four occupation zones, higher military ranks and civil servants were allowed to bring their families to Austria.[20] This measure may be interpreted as a kind of counterstrategy of the Allied occupation forces designed to limit liaisons and marriages between Austrian women and occupation soldiers.

Despite all the above-mentioned regulations, a manifold network of relationships proved constitutive for all four zones from the very beginning. Fellowships, friendships, and, at a very early stage, erotic and love relationships were established between foreign soldiers and the local people.

This fact raises the questions, "How was that possible? How did these first gaps within the fraternizing restrictions and within the friend-or-foe schemata developed in wartime come into being?"

These relationships indeed emerged from the proximity of soldiers and Austrians within the daily routine of the occupation. The practical needs of the occupation forces like washing clothes, ironing, mending, and so forth, as well as later cultural activities like concerts and plays, made contacts possible. Relationships also began in bars, cafés, and dance halls. Further opportunities for contact arose out of employment of locals in the shops, offices, and canteens of the Allied authorities.[21]

Likewise, local women's need for protection and the desire to leave behind the "emotional homelessness"[22] experienced during the war favored the emergence of relationships early in the occupation period. So, too, did existing material hierarchies. In particular, children, and later on (male and female) adults as well, got in touch with the occupation soldiers not least because of this attraction. These also were first strategies of redistribution invented by local people.

"Prostitution in order to survive" as a specific form of a sexual contact and as a kind of economic marriage of convenience began to emerge, too. But even such relationships could not simply be reduced to the deal of sex for food. The fact of having survived as well as the hunger for life and the desire to make up for lost time were thoroughly tied up with these strategies. It was, therefore, not merely a question of material incentives; rather, the attractiveness of the foreign soldiers had many different facets.

On the other hand, even within the most romantic relationships the material realities of a destroyed country, in which the supply networks for energy and goods had collapsed,[23] could not be ignored. Thus the question remains whether material power—especially in cases where the gender-specific differences in social chances are huge—is not generally a substantial component of male attractiveness. "He was like a magnet for me. A dashing guy, communicative, courteous. And all American soldiers had money; they could spoil you as a woman," recalls a female witness of the times.[24]

Soldiers' Attractiveness

In May 1945, there were some 700,000 Allied—therefore foreign— soldiers in Austria. At the end of the year, their number was roughly cut in half and broken down as 180,000 Soviet, 75,000 British, 70,000 U.S. American, and 40,000 French members of the army.[25]

This reality got the gender relations all flustered because the Allied troops met with a community of want and need within a postwar society which was dominated by women. This domination was due to the fact that 240,000 Austrian soldiers of the *Wehrmacht* did not return from the front lines, not to mention the victims of political and racial persecution. Half a million Austrian men were put into prisoner of war camps, some of them imprisoned for years. And those who returned not only physically disabled, but above all psychically traumatized and damaged in their masculinity can numerically not be grasped.[26]

The extreme lack of local males was accompanied by the presence of occupation troops which represented a potential of men in the prime of their lives who were particularly "starved for women."[27] According to the recollections of numerous female contemporaries, these victorious occupation soldiers particularly impressed them because of their un- damaged, healthy good looks and their nonchalance. It was a question of "intact" men, without war injuries, who demonstrated calmness and success at the same time. For example, the actress Anneliese Uhlig, who was twenty-seven years old in 1945, found employment in the U.S. Army department called "European artists in charge of the American troops" a short time after the end of the war. "Like many others," she felt attracted by the nonchalance, the coolness, and the undamaged quality of the victors, "Why are they only so impertinently healthy, so young, so tall, and why do they have such wonderful teeth? How often they smile!" That is the way she remembers her first impressions at that time. In her autobiography, she notes that in accordance with the "excited fooling around of the first postwar months" she also got engaged in a relationship with an occupation soldier.[28] The carefree manner of the Allied soldiers further increased when the combat troops of the immediate postwar period were replaced by occupation troops. The U.S. soldiers, for instance, were often very young and away from home for the first time in their lives.

"And suddenly, there was music in the air"[29] was another lasting impression. "There still is a little pop song of those days I remember. For us, these things were completely new: pop songs, tango, all those things we did not know at that time. We only knew round dances, and we all wore *Juppen* [traditional dresses], and you couldn't dance the modern way in a *Juppe*."[30] That is how a woman, born in 1921, from the rural *Bregenzer Wald* in Vorarlberg recalled striking encounters with the new world brought by the French occupation force. She did not forget to add, "I do not really want to say that I am suffering today [… laughing …], but today I am sorry that I did not learn the modern dances at that time."[31] A woman from Graz in Styria of about the same age apparently did learn the new dances: "Quickstep, foxtrot, tango, all the figures ... you have no idea how pleasantly the British could dance […] and that music, that was unique!"[32] In her memory, the general enthusiasm among girls about the dances organized by the British soldiers becomes clearly visible.

The fascination with the jazz music brought by the American GIs is legendary, too.[33] Without a doubt, such previously unknown, but exciting music correlated with a new experience of life in a demanding postwar daily routine.

Likewise, the Soviet soldiers were very fond of dancing, as remembered by another, at that time still very young, woman. In the *Mühlviertel* in Upper Austria, evening dances took place "where the Russians and a lot of girls were. […] The Russians were so glad to dance. They were so pleased when the girls came for the dance."[34]

A female contemporary who experienced the end of the war in the French occupation zone in Tyrol explains why women were attracted to occupation soldiers. There was "an unsatisfied need" of women, namely of "women whose husbands were in the war or had been killed, young women. Or, they [the women] returned from the Labor Service, or from duty as a news transmission helper. And then they were back at home again, and foreign troops arrived, and there was music again ...."[35] As in all other zones, the hunger for life apparently was tremendous. In contemporaries' accounts, memories of that hunger for life are frequently stored in bright, happy images of music and dance.

After years of the self-isolation of the *"Volksgemeinschaft,"*[36] the contact with foreign soldiers also stood for a new openness, for variety, and new possibilities, as well as for the end of a specific kind of pressures to which many, even though not all,[37] women felt themselves to have been exposed in the National Socialist era.[38] In particular within the first postwar months, which were characterized by an incredible mobility of people because of the consequences of war and occupation, of flight and expulsion,[39] there had been slightly different conditions for such encounters. People had been occupied by worries about how to survive in a setting of want and need. The social control within this society on the move, therefore, was possibly less rigid than in more stable periods. Furthermore, the war had—as already mentioned—changed the order of desires and hungers so that, for instance, "respectability,"[40] which had become established as *the* core virtue of women by the bourgeois education model in the nineteenth and twentieth centuries, lost importance, at least for a short while.[41]

Another shift, namely the transition from a masculinity conceptualised as "hard" toward one conceived of as "soft,"[42] was to have an even deeper impact on the postwar societies. Confronted with total defeat and the no less than total disgrace of everything military, the former soldiers of the *Wehrmacht* had to face a radical biographical break at the end of the war. National Socialism's "hard" concept of a "hegemonic masculinity,"[43] which during wartime was "the actual guarantor" of the soldiers' masculinity,[44] vanished as a model with the capitulation and the obligation to take off the uniforms. The result was a deep uneasiness of men in particular.[45]

Ironically, it was not least the uniform of the occupation soldiers which was part of their attraction. The appeal of a uniform was in no way felt only by women who intended to "fraternize," as is shown in the following statement of a woman born in the early 1920s in Vorarlberg, who revealed pretty openly her sympathies for National Socialism: "Look, a soldier, each soldier, is basically attractive. Often a uniform makes a difference." Her friend of about the same age continued by pointing out the whole ambivalence of the situation: "A uniform does make a difference, and one was young, but one knew that, basically, that was our enemy."[46]

The continuous propaganda in the period of National Socialism, including especially newspaper caricatures, set the tone in making each of the enemies look ridiculous. A tried and tested method was to dispute the enemy's masculinity either by effeminating his whole society or by drawing the picture of mannish women as "poor" substitutes for the lack of "real" men.[47] Only shortly afterwards, the former and seemingly emasculated enemies took over and almost paradoxically became the attractive winners, not least also because of their *different* masculinity.

But how were these cross-cultural encounters perceived by local women? Furthermore, which attributes were ascribed to the different nationalities of the occupation soldiers in their roles as men and especially as potential lovers? The recollections of female contemporaries offer insight into this question. A British soldier in Graz impressed an—at that time—still very young girl by his almost movie-star-like behavior and appearance. "… The effect was the following: we had nothing after the war, and then there comes such a nice-smelling man, he was so good-looking, everything was so …, I do not know, so noble, when he was in the bathroom. The cigarettes did smell so nice and he was singing in the bathroom. It was like being in a movie."[48] The British were commonly considered to be "gallant soldiers." They had the reputation of being attentive, elegant, and they also had a worldly, sophisticated air—all desirable attributes which could fall on fertile ground among local women who were burdened with anxieties about survival.[49]

The image of the French soldiers was similar to that of the British, but nevertheless slightly different. They were described as "charmers," but also as "discrete"—and, therefore, possibly a bit immoral—, as "elegant" and "smelling of lavender." A Frenchman, it was said, "did have a different fire compared to an Austrian," and Frenchmen also were "good-looking men." They were associated with the image of a Mediterranean type, Latin lover. Thus, the general tenor was that the French knew better how to court women's favor than the local men did.[50]

The attributes women associated with the Moroccan soldiers, however, were more emotionally charged and ranged from perceiving of them as a (sexual) threat to regarding them as fascinating exotic strangers. At this latter end of the scale, they got labeled as "hot-blooded" and "good lovers." Their earth-colored uniforms in combination with the bright white turbans apparently had an "erotic effect" on women. Apart from being highly virile, however, they also were seen as behaving like children.[51]

The dichotomy between black and white soldiers within the U.S. Army was perceived in a quite similar way in the American occupation zone. Yet the range of women's imaginations concerning the U.S. American "black man" was even broader.[52] The numerous relationships between Austrian women and African-American occupation soldiers were remarkable in the sense that they violated deep-seated racial taboos. They also seem to have contained a rebellious element,[53] not least of all towards the racist ideology of National Socialism, in which the construct of "black cannibals" had been integral.

On a general level, the American GIs were perceived as "good milk cows" and as "Santa Clauses in the jeep."[54] Aside from this extremely widespread image, there was also the perception of Americans as "a completely different breed of people." For instance, it was very strange for locals to see adult men reading Mickey Mouse comic books.[55] Another contemporary noticed that "they were simply more carefree, they were not so handicapped."[56] A woman born in 1931, who married a member of the U.S. Army in 1954 and today lives in the United States, identified "one huge difference: the American men were more gallant, not so—today one would say—macho." Her husband "never ever made a big fuss about helping a bit in the household," and he found it by no means extraordinary to push a baby carriage when they started to live together in the States.[57]

A similar story was told by a woman from Graz in the British zone who still was a child at the end of the war, "There were fathers in uniform, in shorts and socks, and they were pushing baby carriages. I believe that at that time no one had ever seen any other father with a baby carriage in Austria, just the Englishmen in Graz."[58] It seems that local women, regardless of their age, found it exciting to get to know other possible gender orders, like the ones mentioned here, which apparently already had started to spread within the Anglo-Saxon societies.

The Soviets, for many reasons—which included the troops' rapes of women and homecomers' stories about the prisoner of war camps in Siberia and material shortages—did not hold the same appeal as members of the other occupation armies did. Only their position of power as the victors gained them respect, though not trust.[59] The complex situation of the immediate postwar period, however, created complicated and differing realities. To the liberated, Soviet, female forced laborers who still stayed in postwar Austria as Displaced Persons, the soldiers of the Red Army could very well have been attractive. There were early and continuous contacts. The women themselves could bring an important know-how into these postwar relationships with their Soviet compatriots: they had established a certain knowledge of the German language which was for the soldiers a useful aid on foreign soil, in particular with regards to the acquisition of services. Local studies have demonstrated that in the Soviet occupation zone members of the armed forces and the local people established a barter system.[60]

High-ranking Soviet officers in particular had local contacts, especially with women. In stories, the Soviet officer often appears as a friend and protector.[61] Thus, in contrast to the uncivilized, brutal Russian soldier, the "guardian" is "usually a high-ranking officer, a German-speaking, educated 'refined' man, who in civilian life may be a teacher or a student," or—as is mentioned in stories of rural women—, an ho-

nest elderly farmer who has a family at home and knows about the difficulties of the local people. Often it is remembered that the "Russian"
protectors brought "sugar for the children and other scarce foodstuffs."[62]
The Soviet officers, in fact, had a wider range of economic possibilities
than the ordinary soldiers.[63]

The image of the Soviet troops as a whole remained very negative.
Therefore, locals' disapproval of relationships with occupation soldiers
might have been even more prevalent in the Soviet zone than in the
others. This probably also has to do with the existing negative stereotype
of the "ugly Mongolian" within the "Russian" army. Nevertheless,
despite such images, relationships did occur between members of the
Red Army—officers as well as ordinary soldiers—and Austrian women.[64]

Simplistic clichés like those of the "Red Army Soldier chasing
women" and the "GI surrounded by the *Fräuleins*" ignore such
nuances.[65] In any case, the erotic attraction between soldiers and local
women could over and over again suspend such stereotypes, even
though the postwar reality frequently caught up with such lovers, as
demonstrated by the following example. The Austrian Ingeborg W. met
Iwan P. in bomb-scarred postwar Vienna: "How and when, I can't tell
anymore. He wasn't high-ranking; he was somewhat ordinary. But good-
looking. And obliging. He was a smart guy, with lovely teeth. I took to
him straightaway."[66] For the at that time 17-year-old girl, it became the
romance of her life. She met the Soviet soldier very often. Because of
her good knowledge of the Russian language, she got a job as a
telephone operator in the Soviet administration of Vienna, which was "a
wonderful advancement for a girl who had to drop out of school at the
age of fourteen and who had to work hard in a bombed-out metal goods
factory because of the war." The couple made plans to marry. Ingeborg
W. was ready to move to the Soviet Union. The soldier informed his
mother, and she gave her blessing to the marriage. Why, then, Iwan P.
suddenly disappeared from the face of the earth, became clear to her
only years later. The Soviet soldier had formally asked the father of the
bride for the hand of his daughter. The father, though, tried to ward off
the marriage by making up a story, saying, "Ingeborg has venereal
disease. Didn't you know —?"

The number of such relationships certainly was not small, judging
by the number of "occupation children" who had a Soviet soldier as
father.[67]

Finally, the attractiveness of the foreign soldiers also correlated
with their material power. According to a newspaper article, the Americans had been the absolutely best remunerated soldiers.[68] Also, the
British soldiers were apparently very well provided with goods,[69]

whereas the pay and provisions of the French soldiers appeared to be less generous,[70] and that of the Soviet soldiers was the lowest.[71]

Women's Attractiveness

The reasons – looking at the situation the other way around – that occupation soldiers found Austrian women attractive were not completely identical, however. The recollections of an Austrian male who was a young teen during the occupation period offers some interesting insight into this:

> The first approach was almost familiar. I was also asked by a GI whether my mother could do his washing and ironing. But it was not really that much a question of washing shirts. He simply wanted to speak to somebody. And of course, there was also the matter of chasing girls. That took place on all levels, from romantic down to venal love. I was frequently asked whether I had a sister.[72]

In these few sentences, the essence of the key elements of the women's attractiveness is already revealed. In short, it was about domestic, communicative, and sexual "services."

For the occupation soldiers, outsourcing all duties which were commonly considered to be the duties of a housewife like cooking, washing, ironing, and so forth, was undoubtedly appealing. Usually such services were paid by wages in kind like food cans, coffee, sugar, bread, cigarettes, and other rare commodities.

Another important reason for the soldiers to make contact with local women was the soldiers' need for communication. "It was really noticeable that the soldiers actively sought out contact with us, of their own accord," remembered the above mentioned teenager. After experiencing a chaotic time full of exciting and traumatic experiences far away from home, many soldiers were longing for "normalcy," for a familiar social setting. Hence they sometimes sought out familial affiliations. So it was also the quality of motherliness which made women attractive for them.

And, of course, there was the search for sex, too, which as was mentioned above, "took place on all levels, from romantic down to venal love." Also at play was the element of violence within the "sexist tradition" that saw "women as spoils of war and trophy of the winner" and has been for so long a constituent feature of making war.[73] We will return to this aspect later.

How closely all the different layers could be linked together becomes obvious in the following memory of a young girl in the French occupation zone in Vorarlberg:

"And then mum did the washing for Achmed who was colored. But
he was nice. He brought us soap and meat and cans for the washing.
He was extremely nice. He always called mum 'mummy'. This
Achmed never ever did anything wrong. Only when they got
alcohol—then it became critical. You know, the Muslims are not used
to alcohol."[74]

When the factor of alcohol was involved, fights for the favor of
women repeatedly broke out in pubs, especially in rural regions. The
Soviets in particular were considered to be drunkards who easily lost
control when under the influence of alcohol: "When men in Russian
uniforms were there, clashes quite often took place. Our young boys did
not let them get away with anything, either, when the Russians went for
the girls."[75]

It seems that after the end of the war a need to let one's hair down
existed. Or, to put it in less dramatic terms, there apparently was a
certain necessity for a "vacation" after the demanding years of the war.
Thus it is not surprising that, for instance, French occupation officers
frequently remember their occupation duty in Austria as quite a relaxing
period "in between" the Second World War and the Indochina War, in
which they served only a couple of years later.[76] In this sense, the occupation setting also allowed the mostly relatively young soldiers—for
example, the majority of the U.S. occupation forces were "boys"
between eighteen and twenty-two years of age[77]—to experiment and to
gather sexual experiences.

"[—T]he lads with the sunburnt blondes were fulfilling their dreams
[—]," writes U.S. historian Stephen E. Ambrose of the prevailing spirit
of the period. In his book *Band of Brothers*, he bluntly describes the
soldiers' dreams which came true at that time, "[I]n Austria, where the
women were cleaner, fairer, better built, and more willing than in any
other part of Europe, the GIs had a field day."[78]

The early and high number of contacts caused nervousness in the
U.S. American and British public.[79] "Do the *Fräuleins* Change Our
Joe?" asked the U.S. magazine *Newsweek* in December 1945. Under this
headline, the possible negative political influence of German and
Austrian women on the GIs stationed in the former "enemy countries"
was discussed. But the magazine's correspondent calmed the public's
fears, saying that in fact the GIs' running after the women was merely
a question of boredom, "nothing else."[80]

Apparently boredom was not the only reason for these relationships;
something else was at least as important, namely the difference between
American and European women.[81] The attractiveness of Austrian women
to U.S. soldiers was repeatedly debated in the contemporary press at

home and abroad. The tenor of the discussion from the U.S. point of view was that Austrian women, as well as other European women, were more adaptable and devoted than U.S. American women. The latter would insist on "having a big say in all matters" and on "becoming engineers, architects, and presidents of banks," whereas the former would "first of all marry, get pregnant, and—just as far as the circumstances allow—create a sweet home."[82] An article with the heading "Gretchen against an American Girl" deduced, "The modesty and the simplicity of the average European woman, her gratitude for little, her devotion for nothing, and in particular her bright partnership in terms of love were the powerful impressions which were taken back home by the GI."[83]

The Variety and Quantity of Relationships
The spectrum of erotic encounters was broad. It ranged from flirtations, to relationships for now and then to short-term relationships lasting for a summer or for the period of the soldier's stationing, up to several thousand marriages.[84] Furthermore, each form of professional and casual prostitution existed as well as the already mentioned phenomenon of "prostitution in order to survive" with its time-specific logic to secure supplies, for food provisioning had completely broken down after the war. Nobody could live on the hunger rations handed out on food rationing cards. In order to survive, it was, therefore, absolutely necessary to locate or generate further resources, for example by hoarding, exchange deals, and illicit trade—or through a relationship with an occupation soldier. "To have an American means to experience security and to escape hunger," a village chronicle in the U.S. zone very pragmatically informed readers about this "'female way' to secure food."[85] Frequently, whole families lived on these returns. What made Austrian men—in particular soldiers returning home from war— outraged was considered by many women to be an art of survival: "The time was that dreadful. You have to imagine not getting anything for years, no coffee, no … Frankly, one was actually dying for all that. It was just as a glimmer of hope to get to know an American soldier. I only condemned it when a woman had today this and tomorrow that guy …" That is the way one contemporary female witness specified the mores of female survival[86]
Such survival-oriented moral standards were also applied in other occupation zones, as the following example under the extreme conditions of a municipal house in Vienna in the first postwar days shows. Women were in the cellar while the Russians did the cooking upstairs. The young girls there pretended to have venereal disease and, therefore,

were left in peace, whereas a sixty-year-old woman was "taken" by the Russians apparently almost every evening. Even though it was not explicitly expressed, reading between the lines of the memory from one of these young girls, one may conclude that this sixty-year-old woman contributed in a considerable way to providing the people in the cellar with food. Central to her memory is not pity for the older woman because of what was, essentially, rape, but gratitude because of the suddenly plentiful supply of available food:[87] "It is unimaginable what that's like, what all goes on, when one is in desperate want. And then suddenly we got loads of saucepans full of the most wonderful things. Stews, all with meat, nourishing food, all the things we needed. [...] for two weeks, in any event, we stayed in the cellar, then we slowly could go upstairs again."[88]

It is difficult to grasp the dimensions of occupation relationships quantitatively because numbers can be gleaned from sources only indirectly. An example is the approximate number of children that resulted from such relationships. An Austrian newspaper from the year 1955 speaks of approximately 8,000 children of soldiers who were born between 1946 and 1953.[89] The number of unreported cases is estimated to be about 20,000 children.[90] Even when only taking into account the official numbers of these children—namely some 5,000 for the U.S. zone, some 2,000 for the British, some thousands for the Soviet and some hundreds for the French zone[91]— the significance of these sexual relationships across (former) enemy borderlines is obvious.

However, it seems that the significance of such relationships diminished considerably in the course of the occupation period. On the one hand, the number of occupation soldiers decreased significantly. On the other hand, on the side of the Austrian women, the pressure to survive was slowly replaced by normalization.

In the first years after the war, the proximity of soldiers to civilians caused by the daily routine of occupation—not least due to the private housing of soldiers—favored relationships. Later on, the Allied troops were living in a kind of parallel society with their own camps, schools, PX shops, leisure-time activities, and so forth.[92] For example, according to a local employee of French occupation troops, in the public swimming area in Bregenz at the Lake of Constance a separate area for French officers and their families was apparently established.[93] The common ground between the locals and the occupation forces vanished more and more, as did the opportunities for contact.

In order to estimate the number of occupation relationships, it is useful to look at those cases which resulted in marriage. In June 1946, newspapers were already reporting the first transport of "American war-brides" leaving Austria for the United States. This took place at the earliest possible moment,[94] for as already mentioned, marriages between Austrian women and U.S. soldiers were only allowed from 1946 onward. On top of a strict control procedure, a waiting period of ninety days existed.[95] Until the beginning of the year 1947, 462 applications for marriages with Austrian women arrived in the headquarters of the United States Forces Austria. At that time, 168 applicants had already received permission to marry.[96]

The willingness to marry after having known each other for only a short time apparently was high in all occupation zones immediately after the war. In the French zone, for instance, there is evidence for marriages already taking place in the first half of 1946.[97]

All in all, the number of the marriages between Austrian women and members of the occupation forces is an estimated 4,000 to 5,000 unions. However, quite some marriages might have escaped the notice of the Austrian registry offices, since officials of the occupation forces were also allowed to conduct marriage ceremonies.[98]

Apparently, the spread of the marriage phenomenon differed noticeably between the zones. This leads to the conclusion that the legal standards as well as the number of occupation soldiers present, but very probably also the attractiveness of a grooms-to-be, were dissimilar. It could almost be considered a side issue in the French zone, for there were less than 200 marriages in Vorarlberg,[99] and for Tyrol there are no concrete numbers.[100] In contrast, in the U.S. zone already until the end of the year 1948, more than 2,000 Austrian women got married to members of the U.S. American army.[101]

It becomes even more evident how imposing the U.S. soldiers were as a factor on the marriage market when statistically analyzing the documents in the Salzburg registry office which was the center of the U.S. occupation zone in Austria. In the decade after 1945, 1,200 of all women with Austrian nationality who got married in the city of Salzburg, or 10 percent of the total number, married a bridegroom from the United States. The number apparently got so high that a special column, "USA Brides," was introduced in these documents.[102]

Marriage ads often specifically asked for an American who was keen to get married. For example, one ad read, "Young Austrian lady, twenty-seven, brunette, speaks English and French fluently, own apartment, would like to marry an educated, good-hearted American in good position. Under 'Looking for Happiness 26.054' to the publisher."[103]

The Dark Underside

The connection of war, occupation, and sexuality was—as already mentioned at the beginning—ambivalent and also packed with violence. The dark underside of the Allied occupation reality of Austria revealed itself most clearly in the acts of sexual violence committed by Soviet soldiers during the first weeks of occupation. The shock which the wave of rapes committed by the Red Army in 1945 caused is still remembered by the Austrian people. However, reliable information on the actual dimensions of these violations is unavailable as is data on its geographical extent. Contemporary sources mention approximately 80,000 rapes in the area of Vienna and Lower Austria.[104] According to official reports, there were some further 10,000 cases in Styria which initially also was occupied by the Soviet Army.[105] Studies conducted by historians point out the difficulties in quantifying the amount of these postwar rapes due both to the number of unreported cases and to the exaggerations of the number of cases promoted for ideological, namely anti-communist, reasons. However, what numbers cannot relate is the omnipresence of the threat and the "feeling of sheer terror of the women facing acts of violence committed by the approaching Soviet soldiers everywhere." This terror was calculatedly stirred up by the National Socialists in the last days of the war.[106] The Austrian historian Marianne Baumgartner comments, "Just the threat and fear of sexual assault already represent an act of sexual violence; they force women to overexert their energies in repulsing it and in developing effective counterstrategies."[107]

The spectrum of such counterstrategies was huge. It ranged from taking refuge in all sorts of hiding places, to disguising as old and/or ugly people, to faking infectious (venereal) diseases and/or menstruation. The latter apparently was a quite effective way to get rid of Soviet soldiers, for they were known for their deep fear of menstrual blood.[108] A frequently used strategy, especially in a rural context, also was to avert harassment by offering food. This strategy was in particular employed by elderly women in order to give the younger women a chance to disappear from view of the "Russians".[109] Even in the situation of a rape itself, women tried to engage the harasser in conversation, or to fake suffering from tuberculosis, syphilis, or similar ailments. So "a continuous game of cat and mouse"[110] between Soviet occupiers and the female population was part of the occupation's daily routine.

Although there were rapes reported not only in the Soviet occupation zone, but also in the zones occupied by the Western allies,[111] these were not a widespread occurrence. Rapes in these zones were isolated cases, but exact numbers do not exist in these zones either.

The hierarchy of power between winners and the defeated people tends to blur the boundary between compulsory and voluntary engagement in women's relationships with occupation soldiers. Furthermore, because of the material asymmetries, such occupation relationships for women always involved a "balancing act between the anticipated freedom from survival worries and real subjection under the new protectors."[112] Quite often, occupation contacts for the concerned women led to their social isolation. This was particularly true for young women who were left with an illegitimate child while their lovers were rotated back home, or for women who got caught up in the maelstrom of casual prostitution because of their contacts with occupation soldiers.

Prostitution, regardless whether it was professional or casual, was a further facet of the occupation's dark underside. In particular, in the neighborhood of the military quarters as well as next to the clubs, bars, dance halls, and cafés frequented by military personnel, that phenomenon appeared which seems almost always to belong as a matter of course to the men's club atmosphere of the army.

The author Max Frisch recorded the following impressions in his diary after observing the dynamics in a coffee house in postwar Vienna in January 1948:

Amerikanische Soldaten treffen ihre Mädel. Täglich zwischen sieben und acht. Sie kommen herein, lassen die Mädchen stehen, indem sie untereinander plaudern, die Hände in den Hosentaschen, die Mützen in der Stirn. Die Mädchen wissen nicht recht, ob sie sich setzen sollen oder wie; sie wagen nicht, etwas zu bestellen. Alles andere als Kokotten von Welt. Arme kleine Bummerl, die man sich als Näherinnen denken kann, als Zimmermädchen, denen der Lohn nicht reicht wie den meisten. [...] Die Burschen, die ihre Beine von sich spreizen, in das rote Polster gelehnt, das etwas zerschlissene, sie haben schon in der Messe gegessen; sie rauchen nur noch wortlos, während die kleinen Mädchen sich stärken.[113]

Frisch's sensitive gaze, which does not overlook the male consumer who "buys" his female booty with the arrogance of the winner, is exceptional. According to traditional moral standards, critics' entire contempt usually focuses exclusively on the women.[114]

Even though prostitution did exist in all occupation zones, it seems that in the U.S. zone it reached exceptional dimensions. The day when the soldiers received their pay, the number of the prostitutes present doubled, as complaints in police reports and chronicles of the time show. A Salzburg newspaper harshly critizised "these girls" coming from Vienna and other regions, who would hang around the American military bases "like a swarm of locusts" waiting for their chance.[115]

The term "prostitution" was—as notes historian Siegfried Mattl—
"interpreted in an extremely broad way by the administration and police
and cannot unconditionally be put on the same level with real 'prostitution' for money or gifts. Even being present in specific bars or at entertainment events outside the norms might be sufficient for arousing
suspicion and for getting picked up."[116] It was a widespread reality of
that time that the public almost automatically linked sexuality and
prostitution. Even love relationships and occupation marriages were
often seen in this light.

According to the public authorities, prostitution in all its varieties
represented the main reason for the rising number of venereal diseases,
apart from the rapes immediately after the end of the war and the
infections caused by returning *Wehrmacht* soldiers.

In fact, venereal diseases had become a major problem in the
postwar period. In 1946, experts estimated the monthly increase of the
venereal diseases in Austria at 3,500 up to 4,000 cases.[117] Therefore, in
all four occupation zones, preventive information campaigns were
launched by both occupation and local authorities. Sometimes even quite
harsh countermeasures were taken,[118] as in the Soviet zone where
Austrian women who were proven to have infected Soviet soldiers were
condemned in front of a military tribunal.[119] In the French zone in
Vorarlberg, women could be summoned to the public health center just
on suspicion or on denunciation, as happened to a female contemporary.[120]

The public campaigns of the local authorities which were supported
by the print media stemmed not only from an understandable medical
and social concern, but were also fuelled by other motives. The carefree
attitude towards sexual relationships exhibited by a minority of girls and
young women represented an attack on traditional and culturally deeply
rooted images of women.[121]

"Unfaithfulness" of Women as a Crime against
the "National Honor":
Perceptions of "Condemned" Love

In the postwar period, relationships between Austrian women and
members of the occupation forces became a central topic. These
relations were usually seen in an ambivalent or even hostile way. The
relationships themselves were not seldom a release for tensions and
conflicts arising in everyday life. At the same time, the public attached
an overriding importance to them. This disapproval is not least
evidenced by an abundance of stigmatizing terms which in the end were
all variations on the principal appellation of "occupation whore." The

dimensions and the vehemence of the disapproval were by no means proportionate to the real number of the contacts.[122]

It was in particular the homecoming soldiers who felt provoked. For personal and ideological reasons, they could not or did not want to come to terms with the fact of relationships between local women and the former enemy. The homecomers were marked by war, defeat, and imprisonment. Now they felt they had been defeated by the victorious Allied soldiers on a sexual level, too. "The Yanks had an easy time of it," recalled a veteran who had survived Stalingrad although he had been severely wounded, in an oral history interview. "Even as men, they were far superior to our soldiers, who returned hungry and emaciated from the POW camps," he remembered. He took recourse to a Darwinian explanation, "Of course, that's the way it is in nature, too. When the bucks fight it out, the doe goes to the winner." This permitted him to remain pragmatic about this competitive struggle.[123] Embedding his own traumatic experiences within a scenario seemingly governed by natural laws imbued them with some sort of sense.

In order to deal better with the threat to their own masculinity, others even took up more violent strategies such as describing women who had contacts with occupation soldiers in degrading terms as "whores of the Russians, the Yanks, the Frenchmen, or the Englishmen." Women could quickly find themselves exposed to such an accusation not only in their private environment, but also in public, for example through leaflets and posters. In February 1946 in Dornbirn (Vorarlberg), such a poster said, "Many an Austrian woman is whoring around with foreigners in the most shameless way. We know all about it.[. . .] They [the foreigners] needed five years to defeat the German soldier, but they could get some Austrian women in only five minutes."[124]

Also in many letters to the editor, raw aggression and threats of physical violence were articulated repeatedly, such as demands for "corporal punishment for these good-for-nothing broads" or "forced labor camps" for "occupation brides."[125] In a letter to the editor in the British zone, the "suggestion" was made that these "shameless girls" should be kept out of all professional positions in the public sector where they would block jobs for "decent homecomers, women and girls": "Should we, with our hard-earned pennies, arrange for this scum an undeserved, beautiful life free from any cares? No and once more no!"[126]

Catholic spokespeople regained powerful authority in postwar Austrian discourse not least because of the longing for stability of the local population after the chaotic war period.[127] The Church also engaged in aggressive processes of exclusion. Women who were suspected of having a relationship with an occupation soldier could easily get "punished." The Catholic Church still exercised tremendous power regarding control of sexual morals. In this context, a female contemporary in Vorarlberg remembers a neighbor of hers who went to the Holy Communion at Easter wearing a lot of makeup and, therefore, did not receive Communion. Even today, the contemporary witness still recalls her "bright red, passing by the people. The priest did not give her the Host because she wore so much makeup. Later, she married this Frenchman, and she became very happy with him ... . But at that time people were so petty."[128]

The acts of exclusion did not end with just verbal aggression, threats, and symbolic stigmatizations; violent encroachments occurred over and over again. There are records from the U.S., the British, and the French zones about women getting their hair cut as a punishment. In these "kangaroo courts,"[129] not only homecoming soldiers were involved, but in particular young boys who formed real haircutter gangs. This phenomenon apparently turned out to be so significant that the commanders of the Allied occupation troops felt compelled to declare their views on the problem. For instance, a British commander-in-chief addressed the matter in a radio commentary, while the British army newspaper, *The Oak*, wrote:

> About Leoben one can see large posters, issued by Welfar, of course, advertising the local attractions—well, most of them anyway! Imagine our surprise when, recently, a few rather unfriendly posters appeared, threatening to cut off the hair of any local female population who walked out with British Soldiers. My! How this non-fraternization spreads! The result was rather amazing—so many girls turned up at the Garrison Dance that large numbers had to be turned away, owing to lack of room.[130]

By definition, the relationship triangle[131] of Austrian women, Austrian men, and Allied soldiers was emotionally packed, especially in the first years after the end of the war. But rivalries as well as discussions of the "betrayal by the women" occurred during the whole period of the occupation.

In such private and public reactions to the occupation relationships, a huge number of old and new streams of different emotions and mentalities flowed together. These included the already mentioned frustration as well as feelings of sexual inferiority plaguing the homecomers; the already previously existing xenophobia which became further racially charged by National Socialism and, therefore, in particular turned against the "completely foreign" lover: the black GI, the Moroccan soldier, the "ugly Mongolian"; the thinking of male teenagers, particularly in rural regions, in terms of protecting their "hunting grounds" due to their fear of the threat to the local relationship market; social envy regarding the material possibilities associated with a relationship to an Allied soldier; Catholic morals which condemned each illegitimate liaison as whoring; and the emerging Austrian patriotism of the political elites who considered occupation relationships as a stain on Austrian honor.[132]

Last but not least, fears concerning changes of the social position of women existed. A remarkably pointed example appeared in a Church publication bemoaning the fact that "nowadays, many girls take up the search for a man themselves, instead of permitting themselves to be sought." It formulated even more pointed views on the subject of the breakdown of traditional gender hierarchies, "How many women would still concede to the man the right to have the final word when it comes down to it?"[133]

Let's Go Back to (Sex) Business as Usual? – Or How to Grasp this "Postwar Chapter" within a History of Sexuality

"Wars are," as notes Christine Eifler, "drastic social incidents whose consequences are by no means closed with their ending."[134] The reshaping of the gender differences can even increase rather intensely during a transition period from wartime to peacetime.[135] In the context of the presence of foreign liberators/occupiers, this process becomes even more complex and conflict-laden since this situation creates many opportunities for crossing borderlines.

So, what was the actual position of local women (and, consequently, also of local men) within this transition period? What was exceptional about this situation with regards to sexuality?

Obviously, the years of the war and its aftermath brought for women, and not only those in Austria, more independence. Women were removed from men's sphere of control. By taking over the duties of the men, into which they were forced due to the war, many of them also claimed liberties which were usually left to men, such as that of sexual choice.[136] And, of course, an occupation relationship meant the "choice of a partner who offended against the criteria of most possible authorities" as well as a choice in defiance of the pre-selecting of their daughters' personal contacts which was still made use of by families in those days .[137]

Thus one may ask whether occupation brides could be seen as pioneers who broke the power of traditional moral standards—characterized by postponing and abstaining—in exchange for a consumer mentality not only when dealing with material goods, but also with respect to sexuality, enjoyment, hedonism, and so forth. [138] Moreover, one may ask if perhaps these women were part of an even bigger trend.

The sexual norms which aimed primarily at marriage and founding a family were already becoming blurred in the 1950s and the early 1960s by the first erotic wave in media and pop culture. Crucial impulses—which, of course, were vehemently held back in a cultural-conservative manner—came from rock 'n' roll and its eroticizing of the body. Also, movie idols who challenged traditional images of women and men—like Marilyn Monroe, Jane Russell, Sophia Loren, Brigitte Bardot, on the female side, or James Dean and Marlon Brando on the male side—encouraged this process. [139]

Veronika Ratzenböck has offered an interesting explanation for the effectiveness of a type of movie star who would become, "under the telling name 'bombshell,' the iconized ideal of the female up to the sixties." [140] The most powerful attribute which this cinematically constructed type of woman brought with her was her impressive physical form: the female body as a doll, sexualized, idolized, depersonalized, a tempting good ready to be consumed. Ratzenböck argues that these attributes in particular have made the "breast beauties" the ideal socially stabilizing model of order and steadfastness within the crisis-ridden postwar and reconstruction societies. Not surprisingly, the economic consequences of war and the effects of the war with regards to re-lationships had to be balanced. Apparently, this balance was achieved in the following way: Consumption was promoted, not least through the use of erotic and sexualized advertising.. But such a kind of "harmless" stimulation from the outside was also intended to encourage sexuality within the secure harbor of marriage and family.

So, is it true that the "bombshells"–as Veronika Ratzenböck states–were for the postwar generation a kind of stimulating model which reconciled conflicting demands and experiences—the necessity of marriage and reproduction, the experience of alienation caused by the long absence of men, the resulting autonomy of women, not to mention the many facets of war-induced male impotence? [141] According to Veronika Ratzenböck, the "bombshell" worked as an "icon of erotic desires for men" which did not endanger the family because of its unachievability. For the postwar women who had "returned to the stove in the mechanized kitchen of the period of the *Wirtschaftswunder*" in the meantime, too, [142] the "bombshell" as a role model revealed ways and means to commit their husbands again more to themselves, namely by inflaming their "desire to be sexually appealing". [143]

The occupation brides and their sexuality, as well as their more general hedonistic approach to life, did, however, irritate. Such forms of relationships and sexuality remained outside the social and—even more important—the national norms (which at least partly might also have to do with their dark underside).

In the media discourses of the 1950s, the escape stories of the occupation brides were integrated into a well-ordered framework by ending the stories in a way consonant with the traditional gender order of the reconstruction period.[144] This tactic only worked for a quite short period, however, for in the 1960s, the "sexual revolution" started to spread.

An example of such a "well-tempered" media discourse of the 1950s is a story published in the magazine *Die Frau*, and it may uncover the implicated mechanisms. It is the story of Hannerl from Hernals, a working class district in Vienna. Hannerl has met an U.S. American soldier, and she goes dancing and to the cinema with him. She enjoys, wears lipstick, and is proud of her completely different new life as a woman. The two marry, and she accompanies him to the United States. Later on, the first pictures from the other side of the Atlantic arrive in Vienna: Hannerl, who wears working clothes and a headscarf, is building a house together with her husband. The subtext of the story is clear: work (instead of hedonism) on either side of the Atlantic.[145] The young girl with her formerly transgressive desires, who had at least partly left the gender role which had been assigned to her, was, therefore, put back into her "normal" place.

Postscript: The End Is Not the End and the Story Still Goes on ...

Sexual encounters do very frequently have social consequences, also in a very immediate sense. Thousands of "occupation children" give evidence already through their pure existence that we cannot think about the "sexual encounters across (former) enemy borderlines" in the period after the end of the war without also speaking about their to this day lasting reverberations.

Labelled as "no-man's children"[146] in the postwar media discourse and, therefore, somewhat stigmatized as belonging to nobody and living in some kind of "no-man's-land", these children got blamed for the "shame" of being fathered by a man not belonging to their own nation. Needless to say, neither the (Austrian) nationality of the mother was considered, nor was the fact that it generally was the mothers who took care of the children and brought them up without their fathers. Within the logic of the time, only someone who was born to a mother "above all moral suspicions" (which also meant that she was married and, of course, married to a man with the "right" nationality) could become a "full" citizen.

These children, therefore, also got branded because of their "wrong" national belonging. For instance, the son of a Soviet soldier who had been stationed in Lower Austria recalled, "As a 'Russian child,' I was the most detested human being. The parents of my friends chased me out of their homes."[147] Another example is the daughter of a woman who had fallen in love with a Moroccan soldier, and who got pregnant within this relationship; this daughter found out about her father in the course of a quarrel with a neighbor girl. She remembered that this girl called her "*Marokkanerle*" which is the local form of the diminutive of Moroccan used in a disparaging way, "or, or, [...] 'hedgehog eater,' she said to me, 'hedgehog eater' (*Igelfresser*)."[148] Thus, the stigma lay not only in possessing the "wrong" nationality. It lay also in possessing the "wrong" culture, implied here by the insulting imputation that Moroccans could eat an animal as adorable as a hedgehog.

The so-called *Mischlingskinder*, the daughters and sons of African-American occupation soldiers (to a lesser extent also of Moroccan occupation soldiers) and Austrian women, were exposed to a very particular situation. These children were in many respects "too black" for the "white" Austrian postwar society into which they were born. Their appearance—classified as "alien"—and their "colored blood"—the term expressing another category of perception from that time— triggered modes of behavior within these children's social environment based on racist thinking ranging from an exotic fascination with the "sweet little Negro babies" to pity, awkward self-consciousness, prejudice, and stereotypical biases, all the way to unabashed discrimination.[149] The majority's view of them and the power of definition this exerted, forced these children to live their lives constantly "in between," passing through various scenarios of external and internal strangeness. "Somehow, it never stops," is how a man in this situation put it to one of the authors in a biographical interview, "In every new situation, we're right back at the beginning. You're black, and yet you're not a foreigner. A Negro with an Austrian dialect, that irritates people, even to this day."[150]

While the concerned mothers quite commonly tried to get rid of their mainly painful experiences by suppressing the past, to the point of not telling anything to their own kids, the children themselves were and still are in general intensely preoccupied with imagining their absent fathers and reflecting on their own identities.[151] Their search—whether physical, cognitive, or both—very often leads them far beyond the borders of Austria or even Europe. In their thoughts, Africa, Asia, or America play an eminent role in mentally locating themselves. The above mentioned daughter of a Moroccan soldier, for instance, characterized her identity in the following way, "Now I would stick by it. I would say, yes, I am only half European; the other half is Africa."[152] In a related way, the granddaughter of a member of the Red Army from Kirgisia, who left behind a son in the Soviet occupation zone in Austria, speaks about her roots in the Far East, "Well, in our family all are blond and blue-eyed apart from my father and me who look quite 'a bit' Asian. My grandmother loves me very much. She always calls me forcefully 'my little black hussy.' I know that I have inherited a lot of my grandfather and that my grandparents were tied together through a tender and ardent love."[153]

Around the occasion of the fiftieth anniversary of the end of the war ten years ago, the search for the unknown fathers at last slowly started to become a more public topic in the sense that it was not the elites and authorities of the Second Republic of Austria any more who "dealt with the problem," as had mostly been the case in the postwar period. At that time, the concerned children of occupation soldiers themselves started to speak up about their experiences. Almost half a century after the publication of the two letters to the editor which opened this article, further letters to the editor were written in the context of the "sexual encounters across (former) enemy borderlines." In 1995, the daughter of a British occupation soldier wrote the following letter to the national Austrian newspaper *Der Standard,* in order to remind the absent fathers—and, therefore, also the lovers of their mothers—of their failures:

Fifty years have passed since the end of the war—big parties, heart-rending speeches—old men, at that time young soldiers, visit the former theatres of war. [...] Then you tell your wives of your experiences in those days abroad. [...] What you are not telling are your encounters with young women and girls. [...]

Well, there you came in spring 1945, well fed, proper, self-confident, in victorious pose. You had chocolate, coffee, cigarettes, probably silk stockings as well. [...] You were courted and that pleased you. Surely you have not been the insensitive occupants, and you definitely had fallen in love with our certainly not ugly mothers. But the consequences of your encounters, the "burdens" of the occupation period, they had to be shouldered by these women alone. Do you tell your British, American, or French wives, or your "official" children, of the daughters and sons whom you had fathered here and whom you mostly also still experienced in their first or second years? As you did see me, father Paul Wade Brown. [...] Did it ever cross your mind that we "unofficials," stigmatized as "occupation children," had to suffer, that we often hid it shamefully until today? [...] Do not try to talk your way out of it because of the carelessness of my mother. Most of these "careless" women brought us up with great trouble and under very bad conditions. You left us behind as a "shame," but the shame is yours because you have absolutely failed as fathers. We are not only inevitable flotsam and jetsam of a war, but your children who do have the desire to be able to give their father a face and a story. [...] Before you finish your life, give our fathers a face, a character, a history and enable us to stand by our origin, that means by you.[154]

With this, we tie our argumentation back to the text passages at the beginning of our paper. Here again, there is ambivalence, another dark underside of the sexual relationships that occur in times of war and its aftermath—and, of course, here are the long-term reverberations with which the society still has not come to terms because they have remained unspoken. Until now, the aftereffects of the sexual encounters have in fact neither been part of public debates nor of national memory.

But let us open the circle again. What about the other side of the story? What about the children fathered by the soldiers of the *Wehrmacht* in the occupied countries of Europe during the war? Should we agree with an interviewee from Vorarlberg who would not like to know, as she put it, "How many [...] Austrians 'sprang around' in enemy country."[155] Apparently, this was meant almost only rhetorically as she immediately afterwards told the story of her fallen brother-in-law who had fallen in love with an Estonian woman with whom he fathered a baby. This story became known to his relatives only because this woman moved—which was undoubtedly exceptional—with her little girl to Austria after the end of the war in order to get assistance for the girl. According to the interviewee, some family members would have preferred to expunge the whole issue out of the family's memory because it clouded the moral reputation of this soldier as well as complicated claims upon his inheritance..[156]

So, what about the local fathers of such "occupation children" abroad? Should we not ask the same questions as Ebba D. Drolshagen did in her paper on the phenomenon of homecomers from the war keeping silent about their sexual relationships with women in the occupied countries?: "Did most of the soldiers leave behind them with their uniform also the memories of their girlfriends? [...] Did the former soldiers search for something (or for somebody) when they went back to the places of their stationing years later? With which hopes and fears did they look into the faces of the locals of the same age?"[157]

Last but not least-- in order to close the circle again-- what about the foreign fathers and former members of the Allied forces who have (as the writer of the letter to the editor above and daughter of a British soldier put it) "left us behind as a 'shame'"?[158]. What about them? Quite a few of them seem actually to be—at least according to our experiences as historians known for years to be working in this field—in search of their past, too. We have been contacted many times by former occupation soldiers, and usually they asked questions about finding a sweetheart from that time or a (presumed) own child. "Experiences of sexuality and love belonged to the experiences of the war—and, therefore, to the emotional education of this generation of men—as much as the experiences of brutality and cruelty,"[159] remarks Ebba D. Drolshagen in her paper. This may be true as well for at least one part of this generation of women. In a way, women *and* men across national borders in Europe might have had at their disposal comparable layers of experiences, including a spectrum of opportunities for sexual encounters that was much broader than usual in this period of postwar transition. However, the effects of such encounters had, without any doubts, gender-specific implications. Women were exposed to the social control of the public to a much greater extent, whereas most men could keep silent about their particular experiences abroad.

Nonetheless, keeping such relationships under wraps does not mean that they did not exist; quite the reverse is true. The threads woven by these relationships stretched and still stretch across Europe and far beyond.

Notes

1. H. J. W., Letter to the Editor, *Pinzgauer und Pongauer Zeitung*, 8 March 1947.

2. See as well Renate Huber, "'*I säg all, ma heat vrgessa höra schaffa* [—],' Alltagsleben von Frauen in Vorarlberg während der französischen Besatzungszeit 1945-1953 anhand lebensgeschichtlicher Interviews," M.A. thesis, University of Salzburg, 1996, 48-49.

3. See Ingrid Bauer, "'Besatzungsbräute': Diskurse und Praxen einer Ausgrenzung in der österreichischen Nachkriegsgeschichte 1945-1955," in *Nach dem Krieg: Frauenleben und Geschlechterkonstruktionen in Europa nach dem Zweiten Weltkrieg*, ed. Irene Bandhauer-Schöffmann and Claire Duchen (Herbolzheim: Centaurus, 2000), 261-76.

4. In the eastern countries, such encounters involved much more violence. Usually the voluntary character of sexual relationships was completely lacking; see Birgit Beck, "Sexuelle Gewalt und Krieg. Geschlecht, Rasse und der nationalsozialistische Vernichtungsfeldzug gegen die Sowjetunion, 1941-1945," in *Geschlecht hat Methode: Ansätze und Perspektiven in der Frauen- und Geschlechtergeschichte*, ed. Veronika Aegerter et al. (Zürich: Chronos, 1999), 223-34.

5. See Ebba D. Drolshagen, "Das Schweigen. Das Schicksal der Frauen in besetzten Ländern, die Wehrmachtssoldaten liebten," *metis* 8.15 (1999): 28-47; Ebba D. Drolshagen, *Nicht ungeschoren davonkommen: Das Schicksal der Frauen in den besetzten Ländern, die Wehrmachtssoldaten liebten* (Hamburg: Hoffmann und Campe, 1998).

6. Edith St., Letter to the Editor, *Pinzgauer und Pongauer Zeitung*, 22 March 1947, under the title "Response to 'Shame.'" This source was translated by the authors.

7. Ibid.

8. For a more detailed discussion, see Renate Huber, *Identität in Bewegung: Zwischen Zugehörigkeit und Differenz, Vorarlberg 1945-1965* (Innsbruck: StudienVerlag, 2004), 33-39 and 42-47.

9. See, e.g., Martina Gugglberger, "Den Feind lieben: Geschorene Frauen in Frankreich 1944-1945," in *Liebe und Widerstand: Ambivalenzen historischer Geschlechterbeziehungen*, ed. Ingrid Bauer, Christa Hämmerle, and Gabriella Hauch (Vienna: Böhlau, 2005), 362-75.

10. See *Nira* Yuval-Davis, Gender & Nation (London: SAGE Publications, 1997), 23, 45, and 61; see as well Ingrid Bauer, "'Die Amis, die Ausländer und wir': Zur Erfahrung und Konstruktion von 'Eigenem' und 'Fremdem' nach dem Zweiten Weltkrieg," in *Walz—Migration—Besatzung: historische Szenarien des Eigenen und des Fremden*, ed. Ingrid Bauer, Sylvia Hahn, and Josef Ehmer (Klagenfurt: Drava, 2002), 240; Ingrid Bauer, "Die 'Ami-Braut'—Platzhalterin für das Abgespaltene? Zur (De-)Konstruktion eines Stereotyps der österreichischen Nachkriegsgeschichte, 1945-1955," *L'Homme: Zeitschrift für feministische Geschichtswissenschaft* 7.1 (1996): 111-14.

11. See Ingrid Bauer, "Mächtige Fremde: Zur Erfahrung und Produktion von Eigenem und Fremdem im Nachkriegs- und Besatzungsjahrzehnt," in *Informationen zur Politischen Bildung* 22/2004, *Frei—Souverän—Neutral—Europäisch 1945 1955 1995 2005*, ed. Forum Politische Bildung (Innsbruck: StudienVerlag, 2004), 28-29.

12. See Huber, *Identität in Bewegung*, 95.

13. Important studies for Germany include Maria Höhn, *GIs and Fräuleins: The German-American Encounter in 1950s West Germany* (Chapel Hill, NC: Univ. of North Carolina P, 2002); see as well Annette Brauerhoch, Fräuleins und GIs. Geschichte und Filmgeschichte (Frankfurt am Main, Basel: Stroemfeld, 2005); for the social approach towards sexuality in the twentieth century as a whole, see the chapters on "fragile relationships" and on the "despairing search for normality" in Dagmar Herzog, *Die Politisierung der Lust: Sexualität in der deutschen Geschichte des 20. Jahrhunderts* (Munich: Siedler, 2005), 83-171.

14. See Monika Pelz, "Heiratsmigrantinnen 1945-1955: 'Österreich bedauert, einige seiner schönsten Frauen als Kriegsbräute an Angehörige fremder Militärmächte verloren zu haben […],'" in *Auswanderung aus Österreich: Von der Mitte des 19. Jahrhunderts bis zur Gegenwart*, ed. Traude Horvath and Gerda Neyer (Vienna: Böhlau, 1996), 395.

15. Barbara Stelzl-Marx, "Freier und Befreier: Zum Beziehungsgeflecht zwischen sowjetischen Besatzungssoldaten und österreichischen Frauen," in *Die Rote Armee in Österreich. Sowjetische Besatzung, 1945-1955: Beiträge*, ed. Stefan Karner and Barbara Stelzl-Marx (Graz: Oldenbourg, 2005), 432, translated by the authors.

16. See Regina Brunnhofer, "Liebesgeschichten und Heiratssachen: Das vielfältige Beziehungsgeflecht zwischen Britischen Besatzungssoldaten und Frauen in der Steiermark zwischen, 1945-1955," M.A. thesis, University of Salzburg, 2002, 19.

17. See Karin M. Schmidlechner, *Frauenleben in Männerwelten, Kriegsende, und Nachkriegszeit in der Steiermark* (Vienna: Döcker, 1997), 81-82.

18. See Pelz, "Heiratsmigrantinnen 1945-1955, 391; Ingrid Bauer; "'USA-Bräute': Österreichisch-Amerikanische Eheschließungen auf dem Salzburger Standesamt," in *Befreit und Besetzt: Stadt Salzburg, 1945-1955*, ed. Erich Marx (Salzburg: Pustet, 1996), 147-48.

19. See Pelz, "Heiratsmigrantinnen 1945-1955," 389.

20. See Ingrid Bauer, *Welcome Ami Go Home: Die amerikanische Besatzung in Salzburg 1945-1955. Erinnerungslandschaften aus einem Oral-History-Projekt* (Salzburg: Pustet, 1998), 159; Huber, "Alltagsleben," 29.

21. See Pelz, "Heiratsmigrantinnen 1945-1955," 390-91; Bauer, *Welcome Ami Go Home*, 57-63 and 143-92; Huber, "Alltagsleben," 20-21 and 31-33; see as well Renate Huber, "'Als Mann hätte er mich interessiert, als Mann […]': Beziehungen von Vorarlberger Frauen zu französischen Besatzungssoldaten auf der Basis lebensgeschichtlicher Interviews," in *Montfort* 49.2 (1997): 177-96; Renate Huber, "Beziehungen von Frauen in Vorarlberg zu französischen Besatzungssoldaten," in *50 Jahre gemeinsame Arbeit: Actes du colloque du 25 octobre 1996 à l'Institut français*, ed. Institut français (Innsbruck: Private publisher, 1997), 99-108.

22. Ingrid Bauer, "'Ami-Bräute,'—und die österreichische Nachkriegsseele," in *Frauenleben 1945—Kriegsende in Wien*, ed. Historisches Museum der Stadt Wien (Vienna: Eigenverlag, 1995), 75, translated by the authors.

23. See Pelz, "Heiratsmigrantinnen 1945-1955," 401.

24. Interview with a female contemporary witness, quoted in Bauer, "'Ami-Bräute,'" 78, translated by the authors.

25. These numbers are quoted by Franz Severin Berger and Christiane Holler, *Trümmerfrauen: Alltag zwischen Hamstern und Hoffen* (Vienna: Ueberreuther, 1994), 174, for the fall of the year 1945.

26. See Bauer, "'Ami-Bräute,'" 76.

27. Berger and Holler, *Trümmerfrauen*, 174, translated by the authors.

28. Anneliese Uhlig, *Rosenkavaliers Kind: Eine Frau mit drei Karrieren* (Munich: Herbig, 1977), quoted in Bauer, "'Ami-Bräute,'" 76, translated by the authors.

29. Interview with a female contemporary witness from Tyrol in the French occupation zone, quoted in Bauer, "'Ami-Bräute,'" 75, translated by the authors.

30. Interview with a female contemporary witness from Vorarlberg in the French occupation zone, born in 1921, quoted in Huber, "Alltagsleben," 118, translated by the authors.

31. Ibid., 118.

32. Interview with a female contemporary witness from Graz in the British occupation zone, born in 1922, quoted in Brunnhofer, "Liebesgeschichten und Heiratssachen," 27-28, translated by the authors.

33. See Bauer, *Welcome Ami, Go Home*, 226-27 and 259-81.

34. Interview with a female contemporary witness from the *Mühlviertel* in Upper Austria in the Soviet occupation zone, born in 1924, quoted in Andreas Praher, "'Wir waren die Verlierer und das waren die Sieger, da hilft einem alles nichts': Kriegsende und sowjetische Besatzung in lebensgeschichtlichen Erzählungen von Frauen und Männern aus dem Mühlviertel," M.A. thesis, University of Salzburg, 2005, 112, translated by the authors.

35. Interview with a female contemporary witness from Tyrol/French occupation zone, quoted in Bauer, "'Ami-Bräute,'" 75, translated by the authors.

36. The community of the folk (National Socialist terminology).

37. For the ambivalent implications of National Socialism and the Second World War on the living conditions of women in Austria, including the aspects of National Socialist policies that were positively received, see Ingrid Bauer, "Eine frauen- und geschlechter-

geschichtliche Perspektivierung des Nationalsozialismus," in *NS-Herrschaft in Österreich: Ein Handbuch*, ed. Emmerich Tálos, et al. (Vienna: öbv & htp, 2000), 409-43. Each policy enacted by the National Socialist government in favor of women, mothers, or families also regulated the exclusion of women who stood outside the "*Volksgemeinschaft*" with regard to racial and social criteria.

38. See Bauer, "'Ami-Bräute,'" 76.

39. For more detail, see Bauer, "'Die Amis, die Ausländer und wir,'" 197-202; Renate Huber, "Ein französischer Herr im Haus, ungebetene Gäste und ein Liebäugeln mit den Schweizer Nachbarn. Wahrnehmung und Deutungsmuster des Fremden und des Eigenen in Vorarlberg," in *Walz—Migration—Besatzung: historische Szenarien des Eigenen und des Fremden*, ed. Ingrid Bauer, Sylvia Hahn, and Josef Ehmer (Klagenfurt: Drava, 2002), 152-53, Huber, "*Identität in Bewegung*," 39-42.

40. George L. Mosse, *Nationalism and Sexuality: Respectability and Abnormal Sexuality in Modern Europe* (New York: Howard Fertig, 1985).

41. See also the analysis of Massimo Perinelli, *Liebe '47 – Gesellschaft '49: Geschlechterverhältnisse in der deutschen Nachkriegszeit, Eine Analyse des Films Liebe '47* (Hamburg: LIT, 1999).

42. See Bauer, "'Die Amis, die Ausländer und wir,'" 231-34; Christoph Kühberger, "Gescheiterte Männer? Über den Bruch der idealtypischen nationalsozialistischen Männlichkeit unter der amerikanischen Besatzung," in *Scheitern und Biographie: Die andere Seite moderner Lebensgeschichten*, ed. Stefan Zahlmann and Sylka Scholz (Gießen: Psychosozial, 2005), 191-206; Ernst Hanisch, *Männlichkeiten: Eine andere Geschichte des 20. Jahrhunderts* (Vienna: Böhlau, 2005), 99-105, the chapter entitled "Der Untergang des Kriegermythos"; Thomas Kühne, "'[…] aus diesem Krieg werden nicht nur harte Männer heimkehren': Kriegskameradschaft und Männlichkeit im 20. Jahrhundert," in *Männergeschichte—Geschlechtergeschichte: Männlichkeit im Wandel der Moderne*, ed. Thomas Kühne (Frankfurt am Main: Campus, 1996), 174-92.

43. Kühberger, "Gescheiterte Männer?," 191, translated by the authors.

44. Kühne, "'[…] aus diesem Krieg werden nicht,'" 174, translated by the authors.

45. For further details of mixing up the two concepts in practice, see Huber, "Identität in Bewegung," 80-83.

46. Interview with two female contemporary witnesses from Vorarlberg in the French occupation zone, born in 1921 and 1925, respectively, quoted in Huber, "Alltagsleben," 40, translated by the authors.

47. See, for example, "Amazon Corps," *Vorarlberger Tagblatt*, 8 January 1941, 1.

48. Interview with a female contemporary witness from Graz in the British occupation zone, born in 1932, quoted in Brunnhofer, "Liebesgeschichten und Heiratssachen," 24, translated by the authors.

49. See Brunnhofer, "Liebesgeschichten und Heiratssachen," 25.

50. Quoted in Huber, "Ein französischer Herr im Haus," 157; Huber, "Alltagsleben," 40-45; Huber, "'Als Mann hätte er mich interessiert,'" 178-82, translated by the authors.

51. See Huber, "Ein französischer Herr im Haus," 156-57; Huber, "Alltagsleben," 40.

52. See Bauer, *Welcome Ami, Go Home*, 167-68; see as well Ingrid Bauer, "'Leiblicher Vater: Amerikaner (Neger),' Besatzungskinder österreichisch-afroamerikanischer Herkunft," in "*Wir sind die Wunder, um die bittere Frucht der Zeit zu kosten*": *Afrika, Diaspora, Literatur und Migration*, ed. Helmut A. Niederle, Ulrike Davis-Sulikowski, and Thomas Filiz (Vienna: Wiener Universitätsverlag, 2000), 50-57.

53. See Ingrid Bauer, "'Schwarzer Peter'—A Historical Perspective: Peter Henisch's Novel *Schwarzer Peter* and the Postwar Austrian Occupation," in *Modern.History.Linz: Online-Texte zur Neueren Geschichte und Zeitgeschichte* 2002/007 <http://zeitgeschichte.uni-linz.ac.at/modern.history.linz/007.pdf>; Bauer, "'Leiblicher Vater: Amerikaner (Neger),'" 54; see as well Annette Brauerhoch, "'Mohrenkopf': Schwarzes Kind und weiße Nachkriegsgesellschaft," *Frauen und Film* 60 (1997): 120.

54. Bauer, *Welcome Ami Go Home*, 125; Bauer, "'Die Amis, die Ausländer und wir,'" 246.

55. Interview with a male contemporary witness from Salzburg in the U.S. occupation zone, born in 1926, quoted in Bauer, *Welcome Ami Go Home*, 226-27, translated by the authors.

56. Interview with a female contemporary witness from Salzburg in the U.S. occupation zone, born in 1927, quoted in Bauer, "'Die Amis, die Ausländer und wir,'" 219, translated by the authors.

57. Interview with a female contemporary witness from Salzburg in the U.S. occupation zone, born in 1931; she married a member of the occupation army in 1954 and is now living in the United States, quoted in Bauer, *Welcome Ami Go Home*, 227, translated by the authors.

58. Interview with a female contemporary witness from Graz in the British occupation zone, born in 1941, quoted in Brunnhofer, "Liebesgeschichten und Heiratssachen," 16, translated by the authors.

59. See Praher, "Kriegsende und sowjetische Besatzung im Mühlviertel," 110.

60. See, for example, the local study on Lower Austria by Hanns Haas, *Rosenburg am Kamp: Industriedorf und Sommerfrische* (work in progress).

61. See Praher, "Kriegsende und sowjetische Besatzung im Mühlviertel," 92; Stelzl-Marx, "Freier und Befreier," 437.

62. Marianne Baumgartner, "Zwischen Mythos und Realität: Die Nachkriegsvergewaltigungen im sowjetisch besetzten Mostviertel," *Unsere Heimat: Zeitschrift für Landeskunde von Niederösterreich* 64.2 (1993): 102, translated by the authors; Schmidlechner, "Frauenleben in Männerwelten," 58-59.

63. See Stelzl-Marx, "Freier und Befreier," 437.

64. Erika Thurner also refers to this fact: Erika Thurner, *Nationale Identität und Geschlecht in Österreich nach 1945* (Innsbruck: StudienVerlag, 2000), 64.

65. See Bauer, "'Besatzungsbräute,'" 262-63.

66. Josef Barth, "'Iwan war meine erste Liebe,'" in *Profil extra* (1945-1955. Vom Kriegsende zum Staatsvertrag), supplement of the edition of 13 May 2005, 82-84; all further information quoted from this article is translated by the authors.

67. See, for example, Praher,"Kriegsende und sowjetische Besatzung im Mühlviertel,"110.

68. *Vorarlberger Nachrichten*, May 19, 1952, 4.

69. See Brunnhofer, "Liebesgeschichten und Heiratssachen," 16.

70. See Huber, "Ein französischer Herr im Haus," 163.

71. See Stelzl-Marx, "Freier und Befreier," 431.

72. Interview with a male contemporary witness from Salzburg in the U.S. occupation zone, born in 1929, quoted in Bauer, "'Ami-Bräute,'" 81, translated by the authors.

73. Schmidt-Harzbach, Ingrid, "Das Vergewaltigungssyndrom. Massenvergewaltigungen im April und Mai 1945 in Berlin," in *Wiederaufbau weiblich: Dokumentation der Tagung "Frauen in der österreichischen und deutschen Nachkriegszeit' Frauen in der Nachkriegszeit,"* ed. Irene Bandhauer-Schöffmann and Ela Hornung (Vienna: Geyer-Edition, 1992), 186, translated by the authors.

74. Interview with a female contemporary witness from Vorarlberg in the French occupation zone, born in 1934, quoted in Huber, "Alltagsleben," 29, translated by the authors.

75. Interview with a male contemporary witness from the Soviet occupation zone, born in 1926, quoted in Praher, "Kriegsende und sowjetische Besatzung im Mühlviertel," 126, translated by the authors; for the French zone see as well Huber, "Alltagleben," 66-67.

76. See René Rémond, "Mémoire des guerres," in *Lieux de mémoire et identités nationales: La France et les Pays-Bas,* ed. Pim den Boer and Willem Frijhoff (Amsterdam: University Press, 1993), 265-66; see as well Barbara Porpaczy, "'Die schönsten Jahre unseres Lebens': Zur Idealisierung des Bildes von Tirol und Vorarlberg durch ehemalige französische Besatzungsmitglieder," in *Tirol zwischen Diktatur und Demokratie (1930-1950), Beiträge für Rolf Steininger zum 60. Geburtstag,* ed. Klaus Eisterer (Innsbruck: StudienVerlag, 2002), 159-74.

77. See Bauer, "'Ami-Bräute,'" 81.

78. Stephen E. Ambrose, *Band of Brothers: E Company, 506th Regiment, 101st Airborne from Normandy to Hitler's Eagle's Nest* (New York: Simon & Schuster, 1992), 287, also quoted in *Salzburger Nachrichten,* 21 October 2005, Lokalbeilage, 8.

79. See Bauer, "'Ami-Bräute,'" 80; see as well, Benjamin Richards, "B. Z: Brides," *The Spectator,* 22 June 1951, 810, quoted in Brunnhofer, "Liebesgeschichten und Heiratssachen," 21.

80. *Newsweek,* 24 December 1945, see as well Bauer, "'Ami-Bräute,'" 78.

81. See Pelz, "Heiratsmigrantinnen 1945-1955," 394-96.

82. Quoted in Pelz, "Heiratsmigrantinnen 1945-1955," 394-95, translated by the authors.

83. Quoted in ibid., 395, translated by the authors.

84. See Bauer, "Besatzungsbräute," 263.

85. *Chronik von Saalfelden,* vol. 1, ed. Marktgemeinde Saalfelden (Saalfelden 1992), 381, translated by the authors; see as well Bauer, "'Ami-Bräute,'" 77.

86. Bauer, "'Ami-Bräute,'" 77, translated by the authors.

87. This case was presented in Stelzl-Marx, "Freier und Befreier," 427.

88. *Zitiert nach* in ibid., 426-27, translated by the authors.

89. *Arbeiterzeitung,* 3 November 1955, 5.

90. *Kurier,* 19 June 2005, 4.

91. See Johannes Putz, "Zwischen Liebe und Business. Österreicherinnen und Amerikanische GIs in der Besatzungszeit," M.A. Thesis, University of Salzburg, 1995, 67-71; Bauer, *Welcome Ami Go Home,* 237-57; Brunnhofer, "Liebesgeschichten und Heiratssachen," 44-64; Schmidlechner, "Frauenleben in Männerwelten," 81; Stelzl-Marx, "Freier und Befreier," 438; Huber, "Alltagsleben," 54.

92. See Bauer, *Welcome Ami Go Home,* 146-48.

93. See notes of one author on a phone call on 13 October 1998 from a female contemporary witness from Vorarlberg in the French occupation zone, born in 1925.

94. See Bauer, "'USA-Bräute'—Österreichisch-Amerikanische Eheschließungen," 150.

95. See ibid., 148.

96. See Pelz, "Heiratsmigrantinnen 1945-1955," 394.

97. See Huber, "Alltagsleben," 50-53.

98. See Pelz, "Heiratsmigrantinnen 1945-1955," 408.

99. See Huber, "Alltagsleben," 51.

100. See Ingrid Tschugg, *Frauenalltag und Wiederaufbau: St. Johann in Tirol nach 1945* (Innsbruck: StudienVerlag, 2005).

101. See Putz, "Zwischen Liebe und Business," 92.

102. See Bauer, "'USA-Bräute'—Österreichisch-Amerikanische Eheschließungen," 148.

103. *Wiener Kurier*, 18 November 1950, 7, quoted in Putz, "Zwischen Liebe und Business," 91, translated by the authors.

104. See Marianne Baumgartner, "Vergewaltigungen zwischen Mythos und Realität: Wien und Niederösterreich im Jahr 1945," in *Frauenleben 1945—Kriegsende in Wien*, ed. Historisches Museum der Stadt Wien (Vienna: Private publisher, 1995), 64. She refers to entries in Viennese hospital books.

105. See Schmidlechner, *Frauenleben in Männerwelten*, 45.

106. Baumgartner, "Zwischen Mythos und Realität," 79, translated by the authors.

107. Ibid.

108. See ibid., 99.

109. See ibid., 99-100.

110. Praher, "Kriegsende und sowjetische Besatzung im Mühlviertel," 73, translated by the authors; see also Irene Bandhauer-Schöffmann and Ela Hornung, "Von Mythen und Trümmern: Oral History-Interviews mit Frauen zum Alltag im Nachkriegs-Wien," in *Wiederaufbau weiblich: Dokumentation der Tagung "Frauen in der österreichischen und deutschen Nachkriegszeit,"* ed. Irene Bandhauer-Schöffmann and Ela Hornung (Vienna: Geyer-Edition, 1992), 43-45; Baumgartner, "Zwischen Mythos und Realität," 95-102; Schmidlechner, "Frauenleben in Männerwelten," 47.

111. See Huber, "Alltagsleben," 59-60; Huber, "Als Mann hätte er mich interessiert," 189-90.

112. Bauer, "Die 'Ami-Braut,'" 110, translated by the authors.

113. Max Frisch, *Tagebücher 1946-1949* (Baden-Baden, 1974), 236.

114. See Bauer, "'Ami-Bräute,'" 79.

115. *Demokratisches Volksblatt*, 3 April 1952, 3, translated by the authors; see as well Bauer, "'Ami-Bräute,'" 79.

116. Siegfried Mattl, "Frauen in Österreich nach 1945," in *Unterdrückung und Emanzipation: Festschrift für Erika Weinzierl*, ed. Rudolf G. Ardelt et al. (Vienna: Geyer-Edition, 1985), 124, translated by the authors.

117. According to the manager of the department of skin and venereal diseases at the Salzburg hospital, quoted in *Salzburger Nachrichten*, 12 December 1946; see as well Putz, "Zwischen Liebe und Business," 75.

118. For the British zone, see Schmidlechner, *Frauenleben in Männerwelten*, 77-78.

119. See Stelzl-Marx, "Freier und Befreier," 432-33.

120. Interview with a female contemporary witness from Vorarlberg in the French occupation zone, born in 1926, quoted in Huber, "Alltagsleben," 62-63.

121. See Mattl, "Frauen in Österreich nach 1945," 112.

122. For a more detailed analysis of the social-psychological underpinnings of this aggressive critique, see Ingrid Bauer, "'The GI Bride': On the (De)Construction of an Austrian Post-war Stereotype," in When the War Was Over. Women, War and Peace in Europe, 1940-1956, ed. Claire Duchen and Irene Bandhauer-Schöffmann (London: Leicester Univ. P, 2000), 222-32; Ingrid Bauer, "'Austria's Prestige Dragged into the Dirt'? The 'GI-Brides' and Postwar Austrian Society (1945-1955)," Contemporary Austrian Studies. Vol. 6, Women in Austria. ed. Günter Bischof, Anton Pelinka, and Erika Thurner (New Brunswick, NJ: Transaction, 1998), 41-55.

123. Interview with a male contemporary witness from Salzburg in the U.S. occupation zone, quoted in Bauer, "'Austria's Prestige Dragged into the Dirt'?," 47, translated by the authors.

124. Quoted in Klaus Eisterer, "Fraternisierung 1945," in Dornbirner Schriften: Beiträge zur Stadtkunde 14 (May 1993): 29-30, translated by the authors.

125. Quoted in Bauer, "'Austria's Prestige Dragged into the Dirt'?," 48, translated by the authors; for the British occupation zone, see Brunnhofer, "Liebesgeschichten und Heiratssachen," 40.

126. Neue Zeitung, 4 April 1952, 3, quoted in Brunnhofer, "Liebesgeschichten und Heiratssachen," 40, translated by the authors.

127. See Ernst Hanisch, Der lange Schatten des Staates. Österreichische Gesellschaftsgeschichte im 20. Jahrhundert (Vienna: Ueberreuter, 1994), 427-28.

128. Interview with a female contemporary witness of Vorarlberg in the French occupation zone, born in 1933, quoted in Huber, "Alltagsleben," 63, translated by the authors.

129. See Brunnhofer, "Liebesgeschichten und Heiratssachen," 34-38; Schmidlechner, "Frauenleben in Männerwelten," 83; Bauer, "'Die Amis, die Ausländer und wir,'" 239-40; Michael John, "Das 'Haarabschneiderkommando' von Linz: Männlicher Chauvinismus oder nationalsozialistische Wiederbetätigung? Ein Fallbeispiel aus den Jahren 1945-1948," in Historisches Jahrbuch der Stadt Linz 1995, 335-59.

130. The Oak, 17 November 1945, 8; quoted in Brunnhofer, "Liebesgeschichten und Heiratssachen," 35.

131. One could even speak of a "relationship quartet" when also taking in the numerous initiatives from the part of the female population of the Allied countries.

132. See Bauer, "Die Amis, die Ausländer und wir," 236-41 Bauer, "'Austria's Prestige Dragged into the Dirt'?," 41-55; Ernst Hanisch, Männlichkeiten: Eine andere Geschichte des 20. Jahrhunderts (Vienna: Böhlau, 205), 224; Huber, Identität in Bewegung, 61-69, 90-91.

133. Volksbrief der Katholischen Schriftenmission, 6 June 1947, quoted in Bauer, "'The GI Bride,'" 229.

134. Christine Eifler, "Nachkrieg und weibliche Verletzbarkeit: Zur Rolle von Kriegen für die Konstruktion von Geschlecht," in Soziale Konstruktionen—Militär und Geschlechterverhältnis, ed. Christine Eifler and Ruth Seifert (Münster: Westfälisches Dampfboot, 1999), 155, translated by the authors.

135. See Eifler, "Nachkrieg und weibliche Verletzbarkeit," 157.

136. See Drolshagen, *Nicht ungeschoren davon gekommen*, 234.

137. Ibid., 136, translated by the authors.

138. See Ingrid Bauer, "Americanizing / Westernizing Austrian Women: Three Scenarios from the 1950s to the 1970s," in *Contemporary Austrian Studies*. Vol. 12, *The Americanization/Westernization of Austria*, ed. Günter Bischof and Anton Pelinka (New Brunswick, NJ: Transaction, 2004), 172.

139. See Franz X. Eder, "Die sexuelle Revolution—Befreiung und/oder Repression," in *Liebe und Widerstand: Ambivalenzen historischer Geschlechterbeziehungen*, ed. Ingrid Bauer, Christa Hämmerle, and Gabriella Hauch (Vienna: Böhlau, 2005), 397-414.

140. Veronika Ratzenböck, "Der Körper als Attrappe," in *Zeitgeschichte* 14 (1986/1987) 11/12: 464, translated by the authors.

141. See as well Mattl, "Frauen in Österreich nach 1945," 102-06.

142. Ratzenböck, "Der Körper als Attrappe," 465, translated by the authors.

143. Ibid., 467, translated by the authors.

144. See Huber, *Identität in Bewegung*, 111-25.

145. Franziska Tausig, "Ein Mädel aus Wien," in *Die Frau* 5.16 (1949): 3.

146. *Vorarlberger Nachrichten*, 12 February 1948, 2, translated by the authors; see as well Huber, "Alltagsleben," 53-58; Huber, "Identität in Bewegung," 91-97.

147. Quoted in Stelzl-Marx, "Freier und Befreier," 441, translated by the authors.

148. Interview with a female contemporary witness from Vorarlberg in the French occupation zone, born in 1946, quoted in Huber, "Identität in Bewegung," 187, translated by the authors.

149. See Bauer, "Schwarzer Peter," <zeitgeschichte.uni-linz.ac.at/modern.history.linz/007.pdf> (accessed 18 Feb. 2006).

150. Quoted in ibid.

151. See Huber, *Identität in Bewegung*, 184-98; Bauer, *Welcome Ami, Go Home*, 237-57; see as well Stelzl-Marx, "Freier und Befreier," 438-47; Brunnhofer, "Liebesgeschichten und Heiratssachen," 44-82.

152. Interview with a female contemporary witness from Vorarlberg in the French occupation zone, born in 1946, quoted in Huber, *Identität in Bewegung*, 191, translated by the authors.

153. Letter, 6 May 2004, quoted in Stelzl-Marx, "Freier und Befreier," 444, translated by the authors.

154. Brigitte Rupp, "Gebt uns ein Gesicht und eine Geschichte," *Der Standard*, 26 April 1995, 27, translated by the authors.

155. Interview with a female contemporary witness from Vorarlberg in the French occupation zone, born in 1926, quoted in Huber, "Alltagsleben," 68-69, translated by the authors.

156. See Huber, "Alltagsleben," 68-69.

157. Drolshagen, "Das Schweigen," 40, translated by the authors.

158. Rupp, "Gebt uns ein Gesicht," 27, translated by the authors.

159. Drolshagen, "Das Schweigen," 41, translated by the authors.

'The Nationalists' 'Healthy Sensuality' was followed by America's Influence': Sexuality and Media from National Socialism to the Sexual Revolution

Franz X. Eder

The decades between World War II and the so-called "Sexual Revolution" have remained rather neglected as far as research on the period's sexual history is concerned.[1] Until the early twenty-first century, an overly simplified, standard narration of postwar history dominated scholarly consensus. From this perspective, the National Socialists' control of and hostility toward sexuality were responsible for the conservative family values and restrictive sexual morals dominating also postwar Germany and Austria, at least until these were swept away by the so-called sex wave of the mid-1960s and a newly politicized sexuality. In recent years, however, this point of view has been met with growing criticism.[2] One strand of criticism challenged the assumptions undergirding the leftwing "liberation discourse" (*Befreiungsdiskurs*) of the 1960s-70s, which had assumed an enduring legacy of National Socialist (NS) sexual repression into the postwar era of reconstruction and economic miracles. In addition, critics pointed to the increasingly obvious fact that from the 1940s to the 1960s actual sexual practice had deviated quite far from the normative morals championed by the Catholic Church and by conservative circles, which demanded that sexuality only be expressed in the context of a marital love relationship. In fact, a closer look revealed that the postwar years in particular were distinguished by an erosion of conservative ideals of sexuality.

This article expands on the ascendant critical revision regarding the impact National Socialism had on sexuality by examining the issue through the dimension of the popular media. My central thesis is that from the 1940s to the early 1960s, public discourse and media coverage both fostered a "positive sexualization" (in the Foucaultian sense), causing a pro-sexual stimulus in Austria as well as in Germany. This dynamic resulted in vast parts of the population adopting a basically positive attitude towards sexuality, even *prior* to the Sexual Revolution —and this in spite of all sanctions against prostitution and homosexuality during the Nazi era and in spite of the measures taken against premarital or extramarital sex during the 1950s, which today are regarded as being sex-hostile and restrictive.

This investigation is based on a definition of media as comprising verbal and written media as well as visual media; that means newspapers and magazines, both in their reportage and in advertising, but also advice books, radio, literature, films, and also statistics and surveys.[3] Media does not represent some "simple" means of communication (following the input/output pattern), but rather needs to be understood as a "facilitating and identifying force supporting cultural manifestations and practices."[4] Accordingly, this article focuses on textual and discursive practices and on related social practices, as well as on visual media representations of sexuality and their social and cultural contexts.

"Positive" Sexualization during the National Socialist Era, 1933/38-1945

The NS regime was far from being as hostile to sexual issues as historians of sexuality tended to present it in the aftermath of the Sexual Revolution.[5] On the contrary, sexuality played a significant role for the regime, especially in its politics of *pronatalism*. Furthermore, as long as eroticism and sexual stimulation and satisfaction enhanced heterosexual desires in so-called "Aryan" men and women, they were more than welcome, even in the form of premarital and extramarital sexual intercourse as, for instance, the National Socialist support measures for unmarried women or the governmental organization of prostitution (during the war) suggest.[6] Cultivating and satisfying heterosexual desire was supposed to foster political peace, to encourage the stabilization of the Aryan family, and to aid in the implementation of NS socio-political ideologies, including those related to gender differences. In comparison, the Weimar Republic's sex reform movement was regarded as tawdry and degenerate. According to the NS regime, sex was supposed to be natural and healthy, an expression of new life standards as they were represented in the "Strength through Joy" program. This also offered new consumption and entertainment opportunities, or at least images thereof.[7] Moreover, one must not underestimate the significance of sexual politics in the fight against clerical values and against the clergy's influence. Christian sexual morals were criticized as aiming solely at reproduction while ignoring physical pleasure, and the prohibition of premarital sexual intercourse was regarded as simply being out of date. As opposed to the clerical sermon and its kingdom-come promises of redemption, NS culture aimed at paving the path for positive bodily experiences and sexual fulfillment. Christian transcendence was replaced by active participation in the holiness and divinity of nature. Meanwhile, however, the alleged antipodes of healthy Aryanism were sexualized in a demeaning way and consistently pathologized. Jews and black people were said to be of an exceptionally lecherous nature and victims of their own sexual desires. Prostitutes supposedly had an inbred affinity for their trade due to a genetic moral deficiency, and homosexuals, due to their pathological and perverted desires, were presented as a constant threat to the sexually unstable youth.[8]

Measures taken selectively either to support or to prevent expressions of sexuality included the "Mother's Cross" as well as forced sterilizations (conducted in hundreds of thousands of cases), the founding of *Lebensborn* homes for unmarried mothers, and the terrorization of men with an attraction to their own gender.[9] A broad repertoire of media applications served to diffuse NS ideas and to manipulate public perception and included, for instance, oral and written surveys of the genetic soundness of prospective spouses or information leaflets revealing that sterilization did not necessarily lead to a loss of sexual lust.[10] Soldiers of the German *Wehrmacht* were receiving elaborate written manuals concerning safe sex, and condoms were distributed in order to avoid contagious venereal diseases.[11] "Classical" advice books on sexuality were printed in tens of thousands of volumes and sold at affordable prices. Books like Hugo Hertwig's *Das Liebesleben des Menschen* (*The Love Life of Man*) (1940) reported the following on the significance of sexuality in heterosexual relationships:

> One must no longer remain silent on sexual matters that affect our people's future. Also, superficial sex education won't do. We have to comprehend love and one's sex life in all its depth. [...] On top of the necessity to educate both groom and bride thoroughly on love and the importance of their sex life with all its ups and downs prior to their wedding, they must remain open and straightforward on sexual matters throughout their marriage and refrain from delusions and concealments.

As to practice and technique, the reader receives the following information:

> Both partners must strive to attune the temporal occurrence of their respective orgasms. Many men will experience initial difficulties in doing so, being subject to a faster arising sexual high tension and

faster discharge owing to past experiences and frequent sexual contacts than the woman who has never had sexual intercourse before. [...] On the other hand there are women—and one might present many a famous name here—who never experience any sexual arousal whatsoever unless they are stimulated by soft caresses of their skin or certain parts of their genitals (clitoris).[12]

In their positive representation of sexuality and frank language, many of these advice books on sexuality produced during the NS era equalled the classics of the years between the wars, for instance, the bestsellers by Theodor van de Velde and Max Hodan.[13] But the important change since the 1920s was the closing of the gap between sexual education and the reigning political regime's ideology.

This is the reason why NS authors reached so many segments of the population: their writings were made available even in the remotest countryside dwellings, partly still supplied by hawkers. A seventeen-year-old woman from a very remote Lower Austrian village was able to purchase her copy of such an advice book:

There was this woman hawker walking around, and she had this book to sell, and I was on my own in the house. She kept talking to me and told me, "I have this book and it's written by a doctor and got all sicknesses of children and grown-ups inside and also pregnancy and birth and all the rest of it." I told her, "I want to see it," and she had one with her and showed it to me, and I just went through the pages quickly, and I thought to myself that I needed to have it. It had all these color pictures of giving birth and the different stages and the conception from the first month on, and the way things develop and keep growing. And I thought, "I'll get this book"; I had the money for it, and I bought it. Then I hid it. But I did literally study it, I really did! And from that very first day on I was, of course, fully sexually educated, I had gotten it all![14]

The textual strategies of these media fed on traditions dating to past decades, at times even past centuries. They contained fictitious doctor/patient dialogues, or formulas and rows of commands.[15] A new step toward "positive" sexualization, however, was the visual images included in some of these publications. In congruence with the NS exercise of "bio-power," the visual representation initially followed performative and incorporating strategies. In his book *Sieg der Körperfreude* (*Victory to Carnal Joy*) (1940), for instance, Wilm Burghardt delineated a counter-strategy to clerical spirituality: "Victory to carnal joy! The exclamation [...] is obvious. It relates to the secularist life. Joyfully anticipating the afterlife has been preached for thousands of years. The exclamation [...] means challenging a life principle." In contrast to Christian tradition, carnal joy could transform the entire physical and spiritual relationship with the environment: This attitude determines the spirit and has been determined by body language. Through personal hygiene such as washing, taking a bath, or brushing the body, and by physical exercises such as sports, outdoor games, and gymnastics, the body is being taught a certain language, sometimes having a playful disposition to begin with. However, carnal joy is more than that, it is impulse, laughter, upturn, and commitment to strength, health, and beauty. Therefore, the term "carnal joy" is closely connected to the naked body."[16]

Wilm Burghardt, *Sieg der Körperfreude*
(Dresden: Geist und Schöheit, 1940), 16.

Hugo Hertwig, *Das Liebesleben des Menschen* (Berlin: Verlag für Kulturpolitik, 1940), 369.

The NS regime's images and language regarding the body and their coding of nakedness have been subject to diverse interpretations, such as allegories of birth and violence, expressions of sexual repression, disguised body kitsch and anti-erotic poses, or even a continuation of the image repertoire of the nudist movement of the years between the wars.[17]

A further aspect, however, needs to be emphasized here: the (photographic) visual images of the naked, Aryan-compatible, orchestrated body were of great importance, but so was the fact that these visuals had now become standard fare and were no longer sources of moral indignation. The easy availability of images was clearly part of a political strategy, and representations of nakedness were an ideological requirement of it. Occasionally, an erotic-sexual context was used to eroticize what had originally been a purely aesthetic pose. As a result, simulacra and fantasies cropped up with the sole purpose of preparing for and heightening one's anticipation for the sexual experience with one's partner. Presumably, they also furthered autoerotic activity.

Erotic and pornographic photographs were sold in large quantities from the very moment the medium had been invented.[18] Particularly during the interwar era, these images appeared in related magazines and club newspapers. During the National Socialist era, however, they popped up in publications that transmitted governmental ideologies, in the process eliminating all reasons for shopkeepers to keep them under the counter. The integration was also supported by the fact that being accused of pornography ceased being an issue; even "dirty" and "degenerate" images could still be used as deterrents and be implemented for propaganda reasons. Among the condemned images was Josephine Baker's allegedly animal-like body language, or Hedy Lamarr's orgiastic facial expression in *Ecstasy* (Austria/Czechoslovakia, 1933, dir. Gustav Machatý). Reproducing and distributing American pin-ups was regarded as a shady financial exploitation of eroticism, and even as uncivilized.[19] After 1945, however, these very same images would increasingly be the ones to appear in magazines, sex advice books, and reform publications.

Shamefacedness in Crisis, 1945 to the early 1950s

The postwar years in Austria and Germany were characterized by a fundamental crisis of heterosexual, matrimony-focused sex life.[20] The subjacent social and cultural parameters are well-known. As far as men were concerned, war experiences (including possible sexual experiences at brothels or with fellow soldiers), the conflict-laden and, at times, delayed return home, and the competition with the victorious military occupiers and their sexual success with local women often led to somewhat serious psychological problems (for instance, impotence), to great difficulties in adapting to family and business routines, and to nearly irresolvable conflicts centered around patriarchal privileges in the face of the independent *Trümmerfrauen* (women clearing away the building debris from the war's bombings). Women were affected by the upheavals even more dramatically. By the end of the war, hundreds of thousands had fallen victim to rape; young women in particular had brief sexual involvements with soldiers of the occupying armies; and un-wanted pregnancies and abortions were the order of the day because effective contraceptives were hardly available. Owing to the unstable economic circumstances during the first postwar years, young couples refrained from getting engaged, let alone getting married and raising a family.[21]

This conjunction of circumstances resulted in high rates of illegitimacy, abortion, and divorce as well as in a great number of persons with venereal diseases. In Vienna, the number of divorces nearly tripled from 2,300 a year in 1945 to 6,700 a year by 1948, and then declined significantly; in 1953, there were only 4,400 divorces.[22] Illegitimate birth rates show an analogous development (see Table 1).

Table 1: Illegitimacy Rates in Vienna, 1939-1965[23]

Period	Illegitimate Birth Rates (in percentage)
1939-1940	12.8
1941-1945	13.9
1946-1950	15.0
1951-1955	12.9
1956-1960	10.7
1961-1965	9.5

Andreas Weigl, *Demographischer Wandel und Modernisierung in Wien* (Vienna: Pichler, 2000), 316.

If the spread of venereal diseases had been increasing during the war, it reached new peaks in 1945 with 70,100 newly registered cases of gonorrhoea and in 1946 with 12,900 new cases of syphilis.[24]

Some contemporaries interpreted these figures as an expression of a disastrous handling of one's own body and sexual feelings. Even

physicians such as Heinz Delsberg could not help addressing this
problem in their writings, referring mainly to young women:

> The overall postwar misery, the lack of housing, the young peoples'
> wishes to finally "have some fun in life," and, last but not least, the
> presence of foreign troops in Austria lured thousands of young girls
> and women into morally dubious and economically unpromising
> relationships, with the females ending up finding themselves in even
> worse a situation after a short period of pleasure. Furthermore, an
> irritating indifference of young women to their own bodies is
> evident, a frivolous presenting themselves to the next best male. The
> disruption of families due to the war, the fear of destruction, and the
> misery, they all contributed to the demoralization of men and women
> resulting from the uncertainty of the future and from attempts to
> enjoy the moment, regardless of the consequences.[25]

Random and thoughtless sexual encounters, detached from love
and marriage, were considered the epitome of emotional postwar
confusion.

Addressing this day-to-day experience of many citizens, advice
book authors were forced to take up the red-hot questions and to
approach explosive issues as serenely as possible. On the question of
masturbation, for instance, Arthur Schütz wrote:

> Parents should in time realize the futility of fighting against a natural
> drive and simply ignore their children's masturbation. This is the
> only way to refrain from transferring masturbation into the realm of
> "for-bidden fruit" and to reduce it to a reasonable frequency instead.
> Like eating, drinking and smoking, masturbation is a question of
> quantity. Anything *per se* innocuous can, at least temporarily, turn
> harmful when exaggerated.[26]

Other delicate questions were dealt with in a similarly pragmatic
way, for instance, abortions. Being lawfully prohibited, they were
nevertheless practiced everywhere owing to the countless rapes and
unwanted pregnancies. Different types of media also covered the discussion, publishing features on premarital sex, contraceptive practices
(mainly the temperature method and condoms), the absence of men, and
venereal diseases.

At its best, advice literature revealed a struggle for positive norms
located beyond the NS cultural and racist metaphysics, while at the
same time trying to remain free of conservative Christian sexual
morals, which seemed quixotic in the face of current living conditions.
Their authors had selected means of conveyance that would grow to be
an important source of "sexual scripts" in the following decades.

Among them were graphic representations of sexuality as van de Velde had distributed in the years between the wars. In his book *Die vollkommene Ehe* (*The Perfect Marriage*)—still being sold in countless editions after 1945 and one of the first products to be distributed by Beate Uhse— readers were presented with symbolic illustrations of coitus and orgasm, for instance. After 1945, these images were repeatedly modified.

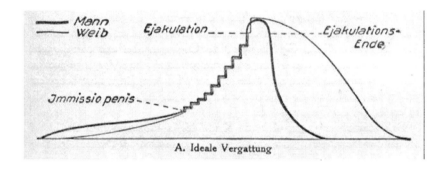

Theodor H. van de Velde, *Die vollkommene Ehe: Eine Studie über ihre Physiologie und Technik* (Leipzig: Konegen, 1926), 169.

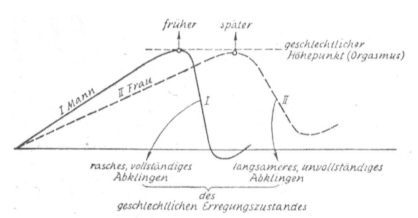

Fig. 1. Graphische Darstellung des Erregungsverlaufes (Erregungskurven) bei Mann und Frau.

Heinz Delsberg et al., *Ärzte raten der Frau. Antworten auf Fragen des Geschlechtslebens* (Vienna: Globus, 1949), 17.

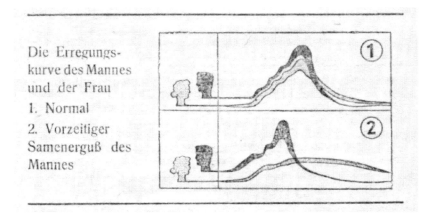

Mephisto: Illustriertes Magazin für Probleme der Erotik, des Liebes- und Sexuallebens 1.3 (1950): 6.

These illustrations invited readers to compare their own experiences to them and to use them as a benchmark for their own sexual activity. Coitus graphics offered readers ample room for interpretation. The imperative of simultaneous orgasm seemed just as obvious as the differing rates of arousal and sensitivity of men and women. The readers might have wondered what all those angular or linear graphs really represented, why they were drawn in waves or other up-and-down strokes, or why one of those lines for women seemed to never descend. Silently, a symbolism representing coitus and orgasm developed and found its way into scripts, fantasies, and regulations. The same applied to anatomic sketches and graphics, demonstrating, for instance, the positions of male and female genitals during various coitus techniques, while resorting to an age-old repertoire of images.[27]

By the end of the 1940s, two additional types of media exerted a strong influence on the field: statistics and surveys. Particularly worth mentioning are the first large-scale surveys in 1949 by the German Institute of Demography and the survey among female readers of *Constanze*, a glossy magazine preceding the still popular *Brigitte*. I will refer to the significance of these types of media later; for now, a summary of the most important survey results will suffice.

Table 2: Sexual Attitudes and Practices in Germany, 1949[28]

	Percentage	
	Men	Women
Did you ever have premarital (hetero) sexual relations?		
with various partners	63	18
with one partner	13	19
with the prospective spouse only	13	33
no premarital relations	10	28
Did you ever have extramarital sexual relations?		
Yes	23	10
No	68	87
Are sexual relations vital to your personal happiness?		
Vital	69	47
No vital	24	46
Undecided	7	7
Are you in favor of or against contraception?		
In favor of	71	62
Against	12	20
Undecided	17	18
Your opinion on § 218 (prohibition of abortion)?		
Abolish	19	14
Ease	33	43
Maintain	38	33
Sharpen	9	8
No opinion	1	2
What do you think about male homosexuality?		
Sickness	39	
Vice	48	
Habit	15	
Natural	4	
Undecided	3	
Do you think that masturbation is habitual with men?		
Yes	42	
No	21	
Undecided	37	

	Percentage	
	Men	Women
Do you think that masturbation is habitual with women?		
Yes		24
No		20
Undecided		49
Do you have any experiences with prostitutes?		
None	43	
One	14	
Many	43	

Ludwig v. Friedeburg, *Die Umfrage in der Intimsphäre* (Stuttgart: Enke, 1953), 84 ff.

While this survey may be of questionable quality, it still reflects a tendency to abandon marriage-focused love and sexual morals. Among the sampled group, premarital sexual intercourse was just as habitual as the use of various contraceptives,[29] and "intimate relations" were regarded as a vital element of (married) life. Severe restriction of abortion had lost support. Numerous men admitted to having had experiences with prostitutes and to engaging in frequent masturbation. In comparison, women reported fewer pre- or extramarital sexual experiences or masturbation. Generally, however, most peoples' sex lives remained focused on romance and (prospective) marriage, women tending to confine their premarital activities to their future husbands. Furthermore, it was evident that the Nazi regime had proved efficient as far as homosexuality was concerned: homosexual contacts remained unacceptable, an attitude that became obvious during the extensive persecutions and criminal proceedings in Germany and Austria during the 1950s.[30]

One question asked respondents to evaluate how erotic and highly stimulating certain situations were. The ranking was headed by "magazines with photographs and pictures" (46 percent men, 11 percent women), followed by "dancing" (24 percent men, 27 percent women) and "literature" (15 percent men, 16 percent women).[31] The sexualization of the public, especially the easy access to erotic images, was hotly discussed in those years. As far as the law was concerned, old regulations concerning "indecent behavior" were still valid in Austria until 1950, incriminating all visual representations and indecent activities constituting a public nuisance. The penalty for a conviction of indecent behavior in print material was six to twelve months. Like anti-abortion laws, these regulations were, however, seldom enforced, and newspaper stands offered plenty of glossies and magazines of dubious character.

Wiener Melange 4.2 (1949): 30 f.

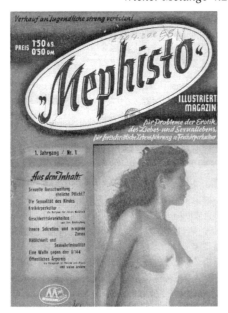

Mephisto: Illustriertes Magazin für Probleme der Erotik, des Liebes- und Sexuallebens 1.1 (1950): U1.

Wiener Illustrierte (1950): 15.

These illustrations and images could not only be found in similar magazines like *Mephisto: Illustriertes Magazin für Probleme der Erotik, des Liebes- und Sexuallebens*,[32] but also in average glossies like *Wiener Melange* or *Wiener Illustrierte*. In these periodicals, illustrations were placed amongst crossword puzzles, serialized novels, cartoons, juicy stories, and travel narratives. As opposed to the publications during the NS era, however, they were reduced to female subjects, whose representation alternated between natural poses, pin-ups, bikini sex bombs, and seductive vamps.[33] Here, too, the context frequently determined the erotic or sexual interpretation and, of course, its social

and cultural context. Eroticism and sex epitomized a better life (if only in the future), an easily available opportunity to experience pleasure and a distant promise of the "American way of life," including the consumerism associated with it. The sexualization of consumption had not yet become a common phenomenon; as a result, sex was only slowly turned into a consumer good.

Kunst ins Volk (1949): U4.

✱ *Die Premiere des Jahres*

LUXOR

die Schönheitsseife der Filmstars
– erstmalig in Deutschland

„Ich benutze immer Luxor" sagt

Hildegard Knef

LUXOR
TOILETTESEIFE

NUR **65** PFG

Constanze 13 (1951): 36.

The sexual context of the soap advertisement included herein was obvious to viewers at the time because the actress in it, Hildegard Knef, starred in the first big movie scandal of the postwar era. In *Die Sünderin* (*The Sinner*, Germany, 1951, dir. Willi Forst), Knef played a prostitute sacrificing herself for a lethally ill man. For a few seconds on-screen, she was visible naked. The Church called for a boycott of the movie, demonstrators clamored for censorship, and glossies competed in reporting on the "premiere of the year."[34] Apart from the nude scene, indignation focused on the allegedly ruthless narration of sexuality's commercial aspects, the main character, Marina's, greed for lust and erotic experiences, and the fact that this woman all the same proved to be a deeply moral and sentimental lover, communicated through an inner monologue voice-over.

Due to nude scenes in movies, erotic magazines at newspaper stands, revealing educational literature, classics of erotic literature at local book stores, and contraceptives via mail order services, the era between 1945 and 1950 resembled a miniature version of a short multimedia "sex wave." All the same, the media's sexualization of its content triggered ever more vocal demands for conservative reform, which was gradually realized during the early 1950s.

"Marilyn Monroe Doctrine" and the New/Old Family Values, Early 1950s to the Mid-1960s

Among the driving powers of this development were the Catholic and, to a lesser extent, the Protestant Churches, whose influence on personal lives, politics, and public discourse had continuously increased during the late 1940s and had a strong impact on the "dirt and trash" discussions taking place around 1950. Establishing new morals related to sexuality was considered highly significant for the project of re-Christianization; the clergy's representatives used the opportunity to turn against NS sexual ideologies, particularly against the secularization of marriage and against the government's direct intervention in an individual's private sexual and reproductive life through such activities as eugenic sterilization and forced abortions. In exactly the same way, the "Strength through Joy" ideology, which had celebrated the body and lust, had to be attacked to pave the way for a mental (re-)confessionalization. The postwar manifestations of marriage and sexuality were criticized for showing low support of matrimony and Christian child education, for the easy-going attitude towards premarital and extramarital sexual relations, for the tolerance of abortion, contraception, and masturbation, for the alleged wide-spread hedonism, for the lack of deep and consistent feelings of love and long-term relationships, and for the flourishing prostitution trade including its concomitant venereal diseases. In the words of the Catholic ethicist Franz Xaver Arnold:

> The aberrances that pervert and undermine the purpose of human sexuality, as well as their frightening spread, can be traced back to the fight against the basic truths of marriage, which is waged with the arsenal of mass media, fought jointly by the press, literature, movies, and radio. Mass media ridicule the virtues and natural marriage, all the while accepting and down-playing the impact of sexual degeneration, adultery, and divorce, or even praising them as achievements of the modern spirit, based on sham "science." [35]

The fact that conservative Christian attitudes gained increasing influence during the early 1950s not only resulted from the clergy's agitation, but also from general economic and social developments, such as the economic consolidation after the currency reform, the negotiations on wages and prices, successful modernization with the help of the Marshall Plan and the European Recovery Program, the establishment of social consensus politics, increasing efforts to push women off the employment market, and so forth.[36] In a climate of economic recovery, traditional family values and role models seemingly guaranteed social stability, as did the enforcement of values such as perseverance, tradition, diligence, and (for the time being) sacrifice. The unit of "family" was regarded as a prerequisite to the successful implementation of Ford's spiral of productivity and consumption. The imperative "Work to be able to consume, and consume (with your entire family) in order to secure jobs" was the social system's basis from the 1950s onwards and proved to be its stabilizer until the late 1970s and early 1980s, when the production crisis hit Austria. The productivity-consumption spiral was

Contemporary Austrian Studies

implemented successfully and swiftly thanks to Western, mainly U.S., economic support.[37] In order to achieve this feat, it was of vital importance to popularize the Western lifestyle, including its focus on consumption, and to make it an integral part of the public's vision of their future and their personal life plans. Regardless of whether one calls it Westernization, "Coca-Colonization,"[38] or the "Marilyn Monroe Doctrine,"[39] in the long run it proved to have a more decisive impact than any economic aid.

At around 1950, the Church focused mainly on the Christian up-bringing of the first postwar generation: those youngsters who were born during the war and now grew pubescent. The Church felt that religious education should provide this generation with sexual morals that went beyond NS ideology and postwar confusion. Actually, the Church's preferred sex norms differed very little from those preached in the first decades of the twentieth century. Christian wedlock as the sole and natural realm of sexual activity and the imperative to procreate as its sole legitimate purpose remained untouched. Premarital and extramarital sex were claimed to result in the very same physical, emotional, and spiritual problems that had characterized the NS era and the postwar years.

The sexual gender gap was part and parcel of this new/old family reform. Albert Niedermeyer, a pastoral physician, stated:

The male's sexual drive awakes spontaneously, boisterously, aggressively. With women, the sex drive proper, the *libido sexualis*, is not connected as closely to the beginning of puberty; their libido usually is initially latent, unconscious, and dozing, needing to be awakened by a male. Here, too, the contrast between activity and passivity, between aggression and expectation, is revealed. Once awakened, however, the female libido equals that of the male, at least during ovulation. The female libido's awakening usually occurs du-ring the first intimate sexual relation, thus being a crucial experience for the overall experiences of women and usually determining their entire lives. A woman usually remains tied all her life to the first man summoning her sexuality to consciousness. Herein lies the reason for many a disturbance of later life, resulting from premarital relations. Apart from getting accustomed to inadequate sexual stimulation and *abusus sexualis*, there is hardly a more frequent cause of future sensational disturbances suffered by married women than premarital psychological ties.[40]

Thus women were expected to resist sexual temptations until marriage, at least according to the maxims suggested to adolescents during the 1950s and early 1960s.[41] In a book on sexual education for

children and adolescents from 1953, a fictitious letter of a mother to her
fifteen year-old daughter phrased it in these words:

> You see, nature has wisely arranged the true venereal desire of a girl
> to awake later than her actual maturity. [...] A normally inclined
> woman has no need for sexual satisfaction at the age of fifteen. She
> merely yields to her partner's desire without actually being sexually
> aroused herself during intercourse. All the worse for her if unwanted
> consequences like pregnancy occur, which present a most awkward
> embarrassment that urgently requires elimination.[42]

Even with the lack of detailed oral histories, one can presume that
the sexual morals of the 1950s represented a generally accepted scope
of norms and values, including essential differences between the actual
experiences of men and women. Men still relied on double standards:

> We (male adolescents) had a burning interest in girls. They made us
> suffer, yet we never considered for a moment to take them seriously
> as individuals or to regard them, as one calls it today, as "partners."
> Their sexuality, too, seemed unimportant to us, even their lust wasn't
> accorded any significance by us since it seemed to be much inferior
> to our own. "Copulation is sensual for women as well, if not in the
> same way as for men." This was written in our Catholic booklet, and
> we believed it. I suppose the girls did, too. It made resistance easier
> for them, assuming they didn't miss much anyway. Perhaps they
> actually didn't miss much. I always had the impression that women
> of that decade didn't expect much of sexuality in the first place. They
> considered sexuality as a male thing one had to understand, but
> resist.

To overcome maiden resistance was, therefore, a success young
men were striving to achieve and to show off with. Their intentions
were, at times, verbalized rather crudely: "At the Catholic boarding
school, we used to call sexual intercourse 'to knock down' a girl. 'Did
you knock her down?' we'd ask, and the answer would usually be, 'No,
just felt her up.'"[43]

Many younger women experienced a threatening gap between
Christian family values and sexual morals and the contrasting cultural
alternatives for them to identify with. The media confronted them with
an image of womanhood crafted from both U.S. and local origins that
was hardly reconcilable with the ideal of the four Cs—children, church,
cooking, consumption—with the clergy's demand for premarital and
extramarital abstinence, and with marital sex being reduced to serving
the imperative of procreation. From the middle of the 1950s on,
competing images originated mainly in the "youth culture" and related

debates; rock 'n' roll musicians like "Elvis the Pelvis" capitalized on the potential that the "hot" topic of sex had on boosting sales figures. In Austria and Germany, sexual connotations emanating from Elvis's twitching pelvis were sneered at, for they seemingly represented a downfall of civilization. Consequently, people swiftly resorted to denunciations against the allegedly degenerate and lascivious "negro" music, denunciations which bore a striking resemblance to NS propaganda. Female rock 'n' roll fans' "hysterical" reactions and wild dancing styles, too, were hardly compatible with an image of womanhood centered on marriage and family. Neither did the male identification image, the "hooligan"—with its rebellious, provocative, and consumption-oriented attitudes (without actually having the necessary financial means at their disposal) and most of all impudent interest in girls—fit into the reconstruction mentality of the 1950s. The fact that the media and public opinion reviled this type of adolescent as violent thug actually added to its attraction for young men.[44] James Dean as the *Rebel without a Cause* (United States, 1955, dir. Nicholas Ray) provided the flashpoint for this furious and stubborn heroic archetype.

Until the 1960s, these hedonistic rock 'n' roller and hooligan identities were countered with a far more harmless juvenile icon, the so-called "teenager." Textbook stereotypes like "Conny and Peter" (Conny Froboess and Peter Kraus) were dreaming of a married, middle class life, of economic security, and of a world of colorful consumer products. Albeit being quite outspoken prior to marriage—words like "sexy" and "petting" were part of their active vocabulary, and they indulged in passionate French kissing and even reaching into each other's lingerie— sexual intercourse was postponed until they were married or at least involved in a stable relationship. The latter form of sexual contact seemed to be the only possible way to happiness for many couples, since creating a family was dependent on one's professional and, therefore, financial situation.

The family-focused image of femaleness was countered by the media-hyped exploitation of the female body, for instance, the eroticization of beachwear and tights or the staging of movie stars and "models," for instance, at beauty contests. These images again showed the unmistakable influence of America, as revealed in, say, the form of saucy pin-up poses. The eroticized/sexualized icons of the "Marilyn Monroe Doctrine" had found their way into printed advertisements, posters, and glossy magazines.

Wiener Magazin 7 (1955):U4 and Wiener
Magazin 8 (1955): U1.

Wiener Magazin 4 (1955): U4.

The movie and music magazine *Bravo*, being the most frequently read teenage magazine in Austria as early as 1960 with two-thirds of its readers being female,[45] displayed Marilyn Monroe in a saucy pose in 1957 next to an excited report on the alleged wave of nakedness in German movies.

Bravo 35 (1957): 30

Bravo 35 (1957): 38 f.

Due to the "dirt and trash" standard (Austria 1950, Germany 1953), however, illustration liberality was heavily restricted. With this standard, conservative parties and the clergy had created a seemingly highly flexible tool with which to censor public images and language. Unexpectedly, however, this obsession with repression and regulation also resulted in promoting sexuality as a prominent topic of public discussion, and "sex" became the number one topic during the allegedly uptight 1950s and early 1960s.

Many contemporaries considered an official limitation of sexualization in the media as being vital. Their comments also contained historical references. For instance, an article by Friedrich Sieburg published in the glossy *Constanze* in 1951 notes:

> The National Socialists' "healthy sensuality" was followed by America's influence. Americans' expression of sexual privation really is not our business. Not long ago, one would have suggested that they deal with their desires on their own. Today, they are in our midst with all their glamour girls, their award-winning buttocks, their young men, who claim to claiming to be experts and to use manometers to measure the excitement factor of competing female breasts. Today, they are being copied and even trumped. They have helped us generally to enforce the sportive approach to love which had already started to take shape under Hitler. [...] The atmosphere surrounding us grows more and more free of the refined currents of

female attraction and erotic courtship. Make the brassieres even smaller, design the slips to be even tighter, fill your horizon with the protruding spikes of the female torso, put nakedness on every butter wrapping, be sure no magazine cover goes without voluptuous thighs—none of this is going to help you; the world will only grow even more devoid of love. Erotic excitement [will] slacken and give way to sexual privation seeking hasty satisfaction.[46]

It is not surprising that the editorial staff of *Constanze* commented on this article having been written by a male, and that female readers must not necessarily share the author's opinion.

According to Austrian legislators, World War II and the postwar era had jolted conventions and morals, a situation that posed a great threat to the young generation:

The unhealthy military life in the rear and at the front, the overly increased will to survive and the awareness of life in the face of constantly threatening death, the deprivation of the other gender's company [...] and the resulting forced abstinence of satisfying the natural desires, the understandable eagerness to finally be able to enjoy the pleasures of life after all these years of misery and distress have created something close to an addiction to act out, to seek unlimited enjoyment, especially in the realm of sexuality.

Therefore, the law was called upon to avert the publication of works that "served no other purpose than to stimulate erotic sensations, [...] having a similar effect as drugs by evoking increased feelings of lust which were very dangerous owing to the fact that they aroused desires in adolescents that had until then been confined to their subconscious."[47]

Austrian pornography law, in short "dirt and trash law," in full named "federal law of 31 March 1950, for the prevention of licentious publications and the protection of the youth against the imperilment of morals," opened up special opportunities to enforce these standards. On the one hand, the law prosecuted the intention to sell licentious materials or to place them at the public's disposal. On the other hand, it prosecuted all those selling, offering, conveying, issuing, or otherwise publishing or making accessible "any writing, illustration, or other presentation qualifying to imperil the moral and sanitary development of juveniles by stimulating lecherousness or misguiding the venereal desire, or any such movie or sound carrier to persons under the age of 16."[48] As a result of this legislation, the circle of incriminated items expanded to include all those which could arouse "offensive behavior" or might sexually stimulate or misguide youth. At the same time, the law's intent was also to ensure that primarily artistic, instructive, or scientific items remained safe from persecution, especially when they remained difficult for youngsters to access.

As a result, more than the clergy's eyes were fixed on the commercialization of sex and eroticism, so, too, were the government's. Suspect media also included writings about sexual education and advice literature, fields which were booming because of both the images' ambivalence in terms of their representation of gender stereotypes and the moral ambivalence they created. Their authors moved cautiously along the paths of science and serious instruction. The increased demand for sex advice books in the 1950s was also related to the media's responses to the Kinsey reports. In *Sexual Behavior in the Human Female* (1954 Germany, 1953 United States) and *Sexual Behavior in the Human Male* (1955 Germany, 1948 United States), the full range of practiced human sex life was published for the first time. It revealed that numerous Americans—both male and female—masturbated, that about a third committed adultery, and that many people had homosexual experiences at some point in their lives, that in fact, there was a wide gap between moral ideals and actual sexual practices. The initial allegation that these survey results were solely applicable to American men and women, and that Austrians and Germans behaved differently, was soon dropped.

Apart from newspapers and magazines, related advice books on life and sexuality also supported the Kinsey reports' popularization[49] mentioning the famous "Kinsey Scale," optically qualifying the seeming polarity of heterosexuality and homosexuality, of healthy and ill, of normal and abnormal.

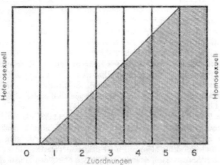

Abb. 63. Zuordnungsskala der heterosexuell-homosexuellen Anteile

Definitionen der Zuordnungen sind wie folgt: 0 = ausschließlich heterosexuell. 1 = vorwiegend heterosexuell, aber mit gelegentlicher homosexueller Betätigung. 2 = vorwiegend heterosexuell, aber mit deutlicher homosexueller Betätigung. 3 = heterosexuell wie homosexuell. 4 = vorwiegend homosexuell, aber mit deutlicher heterosexueller Betätigung. 5 = vorwiegend homosexuell, aber mit gelegentlicher heterosexueller Betätigung. 6 = ausschließlich homosexuell.

Alfred C. Kinsey,
Das sexuelle Verhalten der Frau
(Frankfurt am Main: Fischer, 1954), 362.

After the Kinsey reports, charts, graphs, percentages, and tables played a highly significant role in the media's presentation of sexuality. Initially, the media served to compare Kinsey's results with available Austrian and German survey data. The life advice book *1x1 des glücklichen Lebens* (*The Basics of a Happy Life*) (1956) phrased related differentiations as follows: "Among American young girls, only 22 percent reached orgasm by premarital petting or masturbation, while reliable surveys for Styria and Vienna report this figure to be higher (42 percent)." After comparing orgasm frequency during marriage—with Austrian women revealing lower figures—author Stefan Neiger concludes: "According to Kinsey, female premarital orgasmic experiences are also every important for a later marriage! That means that Austrian women enter matrimony with better preconditions, but find themselves subsequently neglected."[50]

Another example that reveals the reliance on statistical information can be viewed in the following illustration. The chart shows the frequency of marital and extramarital sexual intercourse in different age groups in the United States and Austria. The U.S. data were collected by Kinsey; the Austrian ones are based on "the author's observations in Austria."[51]

Kinsey and his successors molded the classification of sexuality into a central imaging technique, the purpose of which was to enable readers to allocate their own behavior and perceptions. At a glance, one could determine whether one's own feelings and behaviors were still within the tolerable realms of deviation or had developed beyond them into thoughts and/or activities possibly requiring therapy or even being criminal. Juveniles proved particularly addicted to the answers provided to inquiries about "when, how often, and how long?"[52] This was also confirmed by *Bravo*'s advice columns.

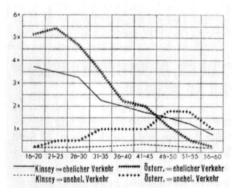

Kinsey = ehelicher Verkehr　Österr. = ehelicher Verkehr
Kinsey = unehel. Verkehr　Österr. = unehel. Verkehr

Die Häufigkeit des ehelichen und außerehelichen Geschlechtsverkehrs. Die waagrechten Linien zeigen die Häufigkeit pro Woche an, die senkrechten Linien die verschiedenen Altersstufen. Die Kurven, aus denen die Häufigkeit ersichtlich ist, wurden auf Grund nachstehender Erhebungen eingezeichnet: Kinsey-Bericht (USA): ehelicher Verkehr (glatte Linie), außerehelicher Verkehr (punktierte Linie); Beobachtungen des Verfassers in Österreich: ehelicher Verkehr (gekreuzte Linie), außerehelicher Verkehr (dickpunktierte Linie)

Georg Fischhof and W. A. Oerley, eds., *1x1 des glücklichen Lebens: Ein praktischer Wegweiser zum Erfolg im Alltag, Liebe und Erziehung* (Frankfurt am Main: Forum, 1956), 280.

The authors' textual repertoire exceeded the formerly known variety of textual types, practices, and styles. Interactive forms with which readers could identify were particularly popular. Publications contained inquiries and correspondences, psychological case studies, autobiographic confessions, rules and commands, manuals for self-therapy, exercises to improve physical performance, and so on. As opposed to pastoral writings, the mentioning of prohibitions, repressions, and moral appeals were exceptions. As long as the paradigms involving love were not violated, a positive sexuality, expressed by sexual perceptiveness, pleasurable sensation, and stimulation, was tne order of the day. Foreplay, stimulation of the clitoris, and varying coitus positions were suggested to meet the imperative of simultaneous orgasm.[53] Even matrimonial barriers were transgressed, not necessarily by welcoming premarital intercourse, but at least by refraining from condemning it.

Seeking sexual pleasure or sexual experiences without love, however, was frowned upon. This is the reason why the movie *Das Schweigen* (*The Silence*) (Sweden, 1963, dir. Ingmar Bergman) caused such a stir. Although the media and the Church scoffed at the (rather symbolic) sex scenes, they basically represented failing emotional ties being replaced by pure sexual experiences. Alleged craving for purely sexual hedonism (by women) was also mentioned in the context of the contraceptive pill. The first oral contraceptive, Anovlar, was introduced by Schering AG in 1961 and was sufficiently popularized by advertisements and media coverage that by the middle of the 1960s it became a widely accepted contraceptive, especially among younger women.[54]

In the second half of the 1960s, all moral barriers broke down, and the sex wave flooded the German-speaking region. The undermining of pornography laws by Denmark's extensive liberalization of the porno market (in 1967, Denmark abolished censorship of literature, and in 1969 of depictions) proved to have a significant impact in other European countries. With the sex wave's products, the media and discursive strategies and techniques were expanded and refined. Now even soft-porn magazines, the *School Girl Report* and *Housewife Report* easily claimed scientific credit by invoking survey data and pretending to offer serious life and sex counseling. What later presented itself as an enlightened attitude and an act of resistance against uptight parental morals and parents' middle class love and matrimonial ideals had already been characterized by Herbert Marcuse as "repressive de-sublimation": the dark side of the alleged sexual liberation proved to be "controlled production, marketing, and satisfaction of desires within the context of the production and trade of goods."[55]

Notes

1. For literature on this topic, see also Franz X. Eder, ed., *Bibliography of the History of Western Sexuality* <http://www.univie.ac.at/Wirtschaftsgeschichte/Sexbibl> (2 Feb. 2006).

2. Angela Delillie and Andrea Grohn, *Blick zurück aufs Glück: Frauenleben und Familienpolitik in den 50er Jahren* (Berlin: Elefantenpress, 1985), 116 ff.; Franz X. Eder, *Kultur der Begierde: Eine Geschichte der Sexualität* (Munich: C.H. Beck, 2002), 187 ff.; Franz X. Eder, "Die 'Sexuelle Revolution'—Befreiung und/oder Repression?", *Liebe und Widerstand: Ambivalenzen historischer Geschlechterbeziehungen*, ed. Karin Bauer et al. (Vienna: Böhlau, 2005), 397-416; Dagmar Herzog, *Sex after Fascism: Memory and Morality in Twentieth-Century Germany* (Princeton, NJ: Princeton UP, 2005) (German: *Die Politisierung der Lust: Sexualität in der deutschen Geschichte des 20. Jahrhunderts* (Munich: Siedler, 2005)); Elizabeth Heineman, "Sexuality and Nazism: The Doubly Unspeakable?", *Journal of the History of Sexuality* (Special Issue: Sexuality and German Fascism) 11.1/2 (Jan./April 2002): 22-66.

3. On this matter, see *Historische Medienwissenschaft* (Special Issue: Österreichische Zeitschrift für Geschichtswissenschaften) 14 (2003): 3.

4. Christa Karpenstein-Eßbach, *Einführung in die Kulturwissenschaft der Medien* (Paderborn: Utb, 2004), 10.

5. For more evidence on assumptions about the sexually repressive politics of the Nazi regime and for a revision of these assumptions, see Herzog, *Sex after Fascism*, 15 ff.

6. Gabriele Czarnowski, *Das kontrollierte Paar: Ehe- und Sexualpolitik im Nationalsozialismus* (Weinheim: Deutscher Studienverlag, 1991); Christa Paul, *Zwangsprostitution: Staatlich errichtete Bordelle im Nationalsozialismus* (Berlin: Edition Hentrich, 1994); Julia Roos, "Backlash against Prostitutes' Rights: Origins and Dynamics of Nazi Prostitution Policies," *Journal of the History of Sexuality* (Special Issue: Sexuality and German Fascism) 11.1/2 (Jan./April 2002): 67 ff.

7. Shelley Baranowski, *Strength through Joy: Consumerism and Mass Tourism in the Third Reich* (Cambridge: Cambridge UP, 2004), 5 ff.

8. Eder, *Kultur der Begierde*, 188 ff.

9. Stefan Maiwald, and Gerd Mischler, *Sexualität unter dem Hakenkreuz: Manipulation und Vernichtung der Intimsphäre im NS-Staat* (Hamburg: Ullstein, 1999); Irmgard Weyrather, *Muttertag und Mutterkreuz: Der Kult um die "deutsche Mutter" im Nationalsozialismus* (Frankfurt am Main: Fischer, 1993); Jürgen Simon, *Kriminalbiologie und Zwangssterilisation: Eugenischer Rassismus, 1920-1945* (Münster: Waxmann, 2001); Dorothee Schmitz-Köster, *Deutsche Mutter, bist du bereit ... Alltag im Lebensborn* (Berlin: Aufbau, 2002); Helga Amesberger et al., eds., *Sexualisierte Gewalt: Weibliche Erfahrungen in NS-Konzentrationslagern* (Vienna: Mandelbaum, 2004); Birgit Beck, *Wehrmacht und sexuelle Gewalt: Sexualverbrechen vor deutschen Militärgerichten, 1939-1945* (Paderborn: Schöningh, 2004); *Journal of the History of Sexuality* (Special Issue: Sexuality and German Fascism) 11.1/2 (Jan./April 2002): Burkhard Jellonnek, and Rüdiger Lautmann, eds., *Nationalsozialistischer Terror gegen Homosexuelle: Verdrängt und ungesühnt* (Paderborn: Schöningh, 2002); *Denunziert, verfolgt, ermordet: Homo-sexuelle Männer und Frauen in der NS-Zeit* (Berlin: Männerschwarmskript, 2002) (Invertito. Jahrbuch für die Geschichte der Homosexualitäten 4 [2002]); Stefan Micheler, *Selbstbilder und Fremdbilder der "Anderen": Männer begehrende Männer in der Weimarer Republik und der NS-Zeit* (Konstanz: UVK, 2005); Susanne zur Nieden, ed., *Homosexualität und Staatsräson: Männlichkeit, Homophobie und Politik in Deutschland, 1900-1945* (Frankfurt am Main: Campus, 2005).

10. Gisela Bock, *Zwangssterilisation im Nationalsozialismus: Studien zur Rassen- und Frauenpolitik* (Opladen: Westdeutscher Verlag 1986), 490.

11. Helke Sander and Barbara Johr, eds., *BeFreier und Befreite: Krieg, Vergewaltigungen, Kinder* (Frankfurt am Main: Fischer, 1995), 76.

12. Hugo Hertwig, *Das Liebesleben des Menschen* (Berlin: Schaffer, 1940), 352 ff.

13. Most popular were Theodor H. van de Velde, *Die vollkommene Ehe: Eine Studie über ihre Physiologie und Technik* (Leipzig: Konegen, 1926); Max Hodann, *Bub und Mädel: Gespräche unter Kameraden über die Geschlechterfrage* (Leipzig: Oldenburg, 1924).

14. *Ich weiß über die Liebe gar nicht viel: Waldviertler Frauen erzählen über Heirat, Liebe, Sexualität und Aufklärung*, ed. Verein für erzählte Lebensgeschichte (Vitis: Verein für erzählte Lebensgeschichte, 1990), 8.

15. See also the examples in Eder, *Kultur der Begierde*; for an analysis of such strategies and their tradition, see Franz X. Eder, "Discourse and Sexual Desire: German-Language Discourse on Masturbation in the Late Eighteenth Century," *Journal of the History of Sexuality* 13.4 (2004): 428-46.

16. Wilm Burghardt, *Sieg der Körperfreude* (Dresden: Geist und Schönheit 1940), 7, 20.

17. Hans Peter Bleuel, *Das saubere Reich: Theorie und Praxis des sittlichen Lebens im Dritten Reich* (Bern: Scherz, 1972); Klaus Theweleit, *Männerphantasien*, 2 vols. (Frankfurt am Main: Roter Stern, 1977-1978); Udo Pini, *Leibeskult und Liebeskitsch: Erotik im Dritten Reich* (Munich: Klinkhardt & Biermann, 1992); Mel Gordon, "German Life Reform and Weimar Vice," in *The History of Men's Magazines*, vol. 1, From 1900 to Post-WW II, ed. Dian Hanson (Köln: Taschen, 2004), 93-109; Arnd Krüger et al., "Nudism in Nazi Germany. Indecent Behaviour or Physical Culture for the Well-Being of the Nation," *The International Journal of the History of Sport* 19.4 (2002): 33-55.

18. Erwin J. Haeberle, "Der 'verbotene' Akt. Unzüchtige Fotos von 1850 bis 1950," *Das Aktfoto: Ansichten vom Körper im fotografischen Zeitalter. Ästhetik, Geschichte, Ideo-logie*, ed. Michael Köhler and Gisela Barche (Munich: Bucher, 1985), 240-52.

19. *The History of Men's Magazines*, vol. 1, From 1900 to Post-WW II, ed. Dian Hanson (Köln: Taschen, 2004).

20. Herzog, *Sex after Facism*, 64 ff.

21. See, for example, Delille and Grohn, *Blick zurück*; Gerhard Jagschitz and Klaus-Dieter Mulley, eds., *Die "wilden" fünfziger Jahre: Gesellschaft, Formen und Gefühle eines Jahrzehnts in Österreich* (St. Pölten: Niederösterreichisches Pressehaus, 1985); Roman Horak et al., eds., *Randzone: Zur Theorie und Archäologie von Massenkultur in Wien, 1950-1970* (Vienna: Turia and Kant, 2004).

22. *Zeitreihen zu Bevölkerung, Gesundheitsweisen und Umwelt in Wien, 1945-2001* 2 (Statistische Mitteilungen der Stadt Wien) (2002): 30.

23. For Germany, see Sybille Buske, *Fräulein Mutter und ihr Bastard: Eine Geschichte der Unehelichkeit in Deutschland, 1900-1970* (Göttingen: Wallstein, 2004), 19 ff.

24. Franz Puntigam and Anna Hiermann, *Die Einrichtungen Österreichs zur Bekämpfung der Geschlechtskrankheiten: Auf Grund amtlicher Unterlagen nach dem Stande von 1. Juli 1948* (Vienna: Österreichische Staatsdruckerei, 1949), 5.

25. Heinz Delsberg et al., *Ärzte raten der Frau: Antworten auf Fragen des Geschlechts-lebens* (Vienna: Globus, 1949), 9 f.

26. Arthur Schütz (pseud. Tristan Busch), *Darüber spricht man nicht* (Vienna: Kauf, 1951), 50.

27. See for the interpretation esp., Thomas W. Laqueur, *Auf den Leib geschrieben: Die Inszenierung der Geschlechter von der Antike bis Freud* (Frankfurt am Main: Campus, 1992).

28. There are no comparable surveys of Austria for this period.

29. When surveyed, 19 percent of the people asked used technical compounds (*Präparate*), 13 percent mentioned caution (*Vorsicht*), and 60 percent both of these methods.

30. Christian Michelides, "Die Republik ist schuldig: Homosexualität und Strafrecht in Österreich, Teil 2. Die Verurteilungen seit 1950," *Lambda Nachrichten. Zeitschrift der Homosexuellen Initiative Wien* 1 (1996): 38 ff.; Dieter Schiefelbein, "Wiederbeginn der juristischen Verfolgung homosexueller Männer in der Bundesrepublik Deutschland: Die Homosexuellenprozesse in Frankfurt am Main 1950/51," *Zeitschrift für Sexualforschung* 5.1 (1995): 59 ff.

31. Friedeburg, *Umfrage*, 88.

32. *Mephisto: Illustrated Magazine for Problems regarding Eroticism, Love and Sex Life for Progressive Lifestyles and Nudism.*

33. Delillie and Grohn, *Blick zurück*, 126 ff.

34. Burghardt, *Werk, Skandal, Exempel*, 18 ff.

35. Franz Xaver Arnold, *Sexualität und Menschenwürde* (Donauwörth: Auer, 1959), 33.

36. Franz X. Eder, "Privater Konsum und Haushaltseinkommen im 20. Jahrhundert," in *Wien im 20. Jahrhundert: Wirtschaft, Bevölkerung, Konsum* (Innsbruck: Studienverlag, 2003), 224 ff.

37. *The Marshall Plan in Austria*, Contemporary Austrian Studies, vol. 8, ed. Günter Bischof et al. (New Brunswick, NJ: Transaction, 2000).

38. Reinhold Wagnleitner, *Coca-Colonization and the Cold War: The Cultural Mission of the United States in Austria after the Second World War* (Chapel Hill, NC: Univ. of North Carolina P, 1994).

39. Günter Bischof, Introduction, in *Austria in the Nineteen Fifties*, Contemporary Austrian Studies, vol. 3, ed. Günter Bischof, and Anton Pelinka (New Brunswick, NJ: Transaction, 1995), 2.

40. Albert Niedermeyer, *Handbuch der speziellen Pastoralmedizin*, vol. 1, Das menschliche Sexualleben (Vienna: Herder, 1949), 118 f.

41. Alexandra Weiss, "... gilt es diesen alles beherrschenden Naturtrieb zu bändigen: Sexualität und Moral der 50er und 60er Jahre," in *Tirol: Gegen den Strom*, ed. Lisa Gensluckner et al. (Innsbruck: Studienverlag, 2001), 53 ff.

42. Anneliese Hitzenberger, *Wie sag' ich's meinem Kinde?* (Vienna: Jungbrunnen, 1953), 56 f.

43. Peter Huemer, "Angst vor der Freiheit," in *Die "wilden" fünfziger Jahre: Gesellschaft, Formen und Gefühle eines Jahrzehnts in Österreich*, ed. Gerhard Jagschitz and Klaus-Dieter Mulley (Vienna: Niederösterreichisches Pressehaus, 1985), 214 ff.

44. Wolfgang Fichna, "Rock 'n' Roll und Beat in Wien: Populäre Musikstile zwischen Untergrund und Oberfläche," in *Randzone: Zur Theorie und Archäologie von Massenkultur in Wien 1950-1970*, ed. Roman Horak et al. (Vienna: Turia und Kant, 2004), 169.

45. Leopold Rosenmayr et al., *Kulturelle Interessen von Jugendlichen: Eine soziologische Untersuchung an jungen Arbeitern und höheren Schülern* (Vienna: Hollinek, 1966), 107.

46. Friedrich Sieburg, "Vom Unfug der Entblößung," *Constanze* 10 (1951): 7.

47. EBRV 105 BlgNR VI, GP, 15 March 1950; quoted in Helmut Graupner, "Unzucht und Anstößigkeit: Rechtliche Rahmenbedingungen der Pornographie." Vortrag anlässlich der Fachtagung "Prostitution und Pornographie" des Österreichischen Institut für Familienforschung (ÖIF), 10-11 October 2001, Vienna <http://members.aon.at/graupner/documents/Vortrag-Porno-2001-1.pdf> (1 Feb. 2006).

48. Franz Erhart, *Das Schmutz- und Schundgesetz: Gesetz über die Bekämpfung unzüchtiger Veröffentlichungen und den Schutz der Jugend gegen sittliche Gefährdung vom 31. März 1950* (Graz: Styria, 1955), 37.

49. There were also books which summarized the Kinsey reports for a broader readership, for example, Paul Hugo Biederich and Leo Dembicki, *Die Sexualität des Mannes: Darstellung und Kritik des "Kinsey-Report"* (Regensburg: Decker, 1951); Carl van

Bolen, *Kinsey und die Frau: Kinsey und seine Kritiker* (St. Gallen: Bücher des Lebens Teufen, 1954).

50. Georg Fischhof and W. A. Oerley, eds., *1x1 des glücklichen Lebens: Ein praktischer Wegweiser zum Erfolg im Alltag, Liebe und Erziehung* (Frankfurt am Main: Forum, 1956), 273.

51. Ibid., 280.

52. Thommi Herrwerth, *Partys, Pop und Petting: Die Sixties im Spiegel der BRAVO* (Marburg: Jonas, 1997), 61 ff.

53. Robert Bergmann and Elisabeth Bergmann, *Wie bist du Mensch: Ein Buch über normales und krankes Seelenleben, Sexualität, Liebe, Ehe und Menschenkenntnis*, 11th ed. (Salzburg: Andreas, 1958), 177 ff.

54. Ralf Dose, "Die Implantation der Antibabypille in den 60er und frühen 70er Jahren," *Zeitschrift für Sexualforschung* 3.1 (1990): 25-39.

55. Ulrike Körbitz, "Zur Aktualität sexualpolitischer Aufklärung im post-sexuellen Zeitalter," in *Der "Fall" Wilhelm Reich: Beiträge zum Verhältnis von Psychoanalyse und Politik*, ed. Karl Fallend and Bernd Nitzschke (Frankfurt am Main: Suhrkamp, 1997), 259; see Herbert Marcuse, *Triebstruktur und Gesellschaft: Ein philosophischer Beitrag zu Sigmund Freud* (Frankfurt am Main: Suhrkamp, 1965); Reimut Reiche, *Sexualität und Klassenkampf: Zur Abwehr repressiver Entsublimierung* (Frankfurt am Main: Neue Kritik, 1968).

Queering Austria for the New Europe

Matti Bunzl[*]

This essay explores the place of "Europe" in the context of Austria's lesbian/gay movement and its continuing struggle to achieve full social and legal equality for the country's queers. In short, it is my argument that Europe—as cultural trope, social reality, and legal entity —has come to occupy a central position of political and discursive mobilization. More than any other relevant motive, the vision of queering Austria for the New Europe has thus come to dominate both the emancipatory discourse of the country's lesbian/gay-rights organizations as well as the publicized construction of homosexuality in Austria's mass media.

To investigate the place of Europe in Austria's lesbian/gay discourses in their variously overlapping dimensions, this essay addresses three empirical domains. First, I account for the use and deployment of Europe by the country's lesbian/gay-rights organizations. As I show, Europe not only occupied the central position of a comparative imaginary from the very inception of Austria's lesbian/gay movement in the late 1970s, but it served as the crucial rallying point for the successful mass mobilization of the country's queers in the mid-1990s. Second, I turn to the function of Europe as a supranational legal domain. I argue that it was pan-European organizations, both within and beyond the European Community (EC)/European Union (EU), that generated the most significant pressure on Austria's political field, a pressure that, in turn, has engendered an ongoing project of legal reform. Third, I turn to the mass-mediated discourse of homosexuality. As I demonstrate, that

* An earlier version of this essay was presented as a paper at the 2002 conference of the Council for European Studies (CES). I would like to thank Don Kulick and Sonya Michel for their comments on that occasion. I would also like to thank Günter Bischof and Dagmar Herzog for their appraisals as well as their invitation to contribute the essay to this volume. Parts of the essay draw on my book *Symptoms of Modernity: Jews and Queers in Late-Twentieth-Century Europe*. The specific overlaps are indicated in the endnotes.

discourse has undergone a massive transformation over the last decade. While publicized opinion used to sustain the homophobic insulation of Austria's national sphere, the status of homosexuality has emerged as a central question in debates on Austria's *Europareife* (maturity for Europe). In that context, the country's mass media have come to articulate a virtual consensus that regards the persistent discrimination of homosexuals as a key obstacle to Austria's genuine membership in the New Europe.

Based on my investigation of these three domains, I advance my main conclusion which holds that the abjection and containment of homosexuals was tied to a project of nation-building. It is in superceding this exclusionary project that the New Europe can function as a pluralistic space, its imagination above and beyond a national project of sexual purity allowing for the affirmative integration of queers into the body politic. In turn, I argue that this analysis has important ramifications for progressive politics, whose goals might be more readily realized in the neo-liberal spaces of late capitalism than the standard analysis of the political and academic left would suggest.

Before I can turn to the investigation of my three empirical domains, however, I need to provide the basic historical parameters of lesbian/gay existence in post-World War II Austria. In legal terms, the situation of queers in Austria's Second Republic has been unusually harsh. While the Nazis' violent persecution ended in 1945, the postwar state continued to criminalize Austria's homosexuals, interdicting all same-sex sexual activities and threatening violations with prison sentences of up to five years. As a consequence, thousands of lesbians and gay men were incarcerated in the postwar era—a situation that only ended in 1971 when Austria's Socialist Party (SPÖ) spearheaded a legal reform that decriminalized most consensual same-sex sexual activity.[1]

The timing and nature of this legal measure coincided with a number of other countries (Great Britain and Germany, for example) that also liberalized their legislation of homosexuality in that period. Where the Austrian case differed, however, was in the creation of new discriminatory legislation. In place of the total interdiction of all homosexual acts, the country's parliament introduced a new set of laws designed to ensure the protection of Austria's national sphere. On the one hand, this resulted in two statutes respectively outlawing the creation of lesbian/gay organizations (§221) and the dissemination of any material that could be construed as an advertisement for homosexuality (§220). On the other hand, the legal reform resulted in the creation of §209, a statute outlawing consensual sexual relations between adult men and their fourteen to eighteen year-old counterparts, a measure designed to protect Austria's national body from seduction to male homosexuality (no equivalent interdictions existed for relations between males and females and females and females of the same age brackets).

In combination with Austria's social conservatism centrally embodied by the cultural stronghold of the Catholic Church, the country's legal situation inhibited the public emergence of lesbians and gay men that characterized such countries as Germany, France, and Great Britain in the years after the Stonewall Rebellion of 1969. Austria's homosexuals, in other words, did not come out of the closet in the course of the 1970s; consequently, it was the struggle against the dual oppression of legal and social subordination that came to stand at the heart of the country's lesbian/gay movement when it came into existence at the end of that decade.

Europe and the Movement

From its initial inception, Austria's lesbian/gay movement took recourse to an affirmative vision of Europe in its efforts to improve the situation of the country's lesbians and gay men. Its first political act, in fact, rested on an argument that came to dominate the movement's political discourse. HOSI—as Austria's pioneering lesbian/gay rights organization was called in an acronym for *Homosexuelle Initiative*—had barely come into existence in 1979 when it addressed a formal petition to Austria's Socialist chancellor, Bruno Kreisky. In it, the group demanded the abolition of Austria's anti-lesbian/gay laws based in part on the argument that the country's regressive legislation put it out of step with developments in Europe's other democracies. In language that betrayed a residue of ethnocentric nostalgia, HOSI thus warned Kreisky of Austria's singularly archaic position when compared with the "other cultured states (*Kulturstaaten*) of the Western world."[2]

The conception of Austria's homophobic legislation as an impediment to the country's standing as a contemporary European civilization remained a central trope in the discourse of the lesbian/gay movement. Indeed, throughout the 1980s and early 1990s, it underwrote the countless legal and political initiatives spearheaded by HOSI. Ranging from petitions and demonstrations to legal challenges and lobbying efforts, these initiatives sought to demonstrate Austria's deficiency when measured against a putatively European standard, a standard that was variously seen as embodied by such progressive countries as Scandinavia and the Netherlands or such standard bearers of Europeanness as Germany and France.[3]

For nearly two decades, the lesbian/gay movement's deployment of this "European discourse" had little political effect. Ignored or belittled by Austria's mass media and placated by the country's political elite, the queer movement could show next to no legal gains by the early 1990s. Even more importantly—and related to its political ineffectualness—the lesbian/gay movement had failed to break through homosexuality's inherent privatization. While a small group of activists promoted and performed the ideal of politicized public disclosure, the vast majority of Austria's homosexuals remained firmly entrenched in the closet.[4]

This situation changed in the mid-1990s, and once again, it was a deliberate act of "Europeanization" that underwrote the transformation. More than anything else, this development centered on the initiation in 1996 of the *Regenbogen Parade* (Rainbow Parade), Vienna's version of a gay pride parade. HOSI had marked the anniversaries of the Stonewall Rebellion throughout the 1980s and early 1990s. But in a political mode that took recourse to such national models as May Day demonstrations, the organization had resisted the creation of the kinds of irreverent parades that had come to characterize Western European gay pride celebrations. The resulting events—earnest marches accompanied by posters and political slogans—failed to draw more than a few dozen participants.[5]

The creators of the Rainbow Parade sought to overturn this very situation when they announced their initiative. Rather than an overtly political demonstration against Austria's injurious legislation, it would be a self-consciously cosmopolitan event that took its immediate inspiration from similar celebrations in the rest of Europe. It was in that sense that the modest Pride Guide, a pamphlet issued to advertise and to accompany the Rainbow Parade, went to great lengths in the effort to establish the Viennese event as part and parcel of an international network. That network had originated in the United States, and the extensive list of other cities staging gay pride parades in 1996 made mention of many of them. But it was the European cities —from Amsterdam to Zurich—that were printed in bold letters, thereby serving as the immediate model for the new venture.[6]

This European strategy helped engender a triumphant event as the first Rainbow Parade exceeded the hopes of even the greatest optimists. With nearly 30,000 participants, the parade was a completely unprecedented display of lesbian/gay visibility and prowess; it set the stage for ever-more aggressive attempts at resisting Austria's provincialism through recourse to an overtly European logic. Indeed, over the next few years, the Rainbow Parade organizers actively sought to rearticulate Vienna's status as capital of an ostensibly homogeneous nation-state along the lines of an explicitly European-coded cosmopolitanism.

Witness, for example, the official poster for the third Rainbow Parade, held in 1998. In a catchy slogan, the poster proclaimed "*Europa ist anders. Wien auch. Wir sowieso*" ("Europe is different. Vienna too.

We are anyway."). Reflecting the organizers' original intention of bringing an international quality of lesbian/gay existence to Vienna, the slogan enacted a performative parallelism between Europe, Vienna, and its queer population. All these entities were figured to be of the same order due to their queer capacity for difference and diversity. Reading the slogan forward, Europe was thus constructed as an intrinsic site of a diversity that encompassed Vienna and its lesbian/gay population. Read backward, the chain of signification made an even more daring proposition, suggesting that it was Vienna's queer populace that bestowed the degree of difference on the city that could, in turn, render it a constitutive part of Europe. The parade organizers thus intimated that Vienna needed the Rainbow Parade in order to become genuinely European.

This strategy of Europeanization became even more apparent when the parade organizers put in a bid to host the 2001 EuroPride celebration. A month-long festival held annually in a different city which comes to function temporarily as "Europe's lesbian/gay capital," EuroPride was the very embodiment of a cultural vision that saw the construction of a cosmopolitan space of sexual diversity as the most potent resistance against the social homogeneity of the exclusionary nation-state. As early as 1999, the Rainbow Parade backers thus advertised EuroPride with the slogan "*Ganz Europa in Wien*" ("All of Europe in Vienna"), a motto that could similarly be read in the manner of an anagram.[7] In that sense, EuroPride was not only seen as a vehicle for bringing Europe's queers to Vienna, but also as a means of bringing Vienna into Europe.

Indeed, when the festival was held in June of 2001, it engendered this very sensation. With thousands of queers from all over the continent in town for the festivities, Vienna's EuroPride brought a veritable transformation of the city's urban space. As scores of male and female same-sex couples happily walked through Vienna's streets and as the city's venerable street-cars were adorned with Rainbow Flags, the affirmative vision of a European space of sexual diversity became a (at least) temporary reality. As the organizers of EuroPride put it in introduction of the lavish Pride Guide, which had become fully bilingual in German and English:

> Europe represents the removal of borders. Borders European rulers
> have erected over the centuries to restrict people's freedom and indi-
> viduality, deriving power from doing so [sic]. Borders were not only
> drawn to demarcate states—social borders were erected as well,
> imposing restrictions on basic rights, individual freedom and chances
> of a self-determined life protected by the law. Europe, however,
> represents the notion of emancipation from such restrictions. The

European Idea represents the freedom to live one's own self-determined life. Europe means emancipation.[8]

Europe and the Law

That Austria's lesbian/gay movement should figure Europe in such florid and slightly pathos-laden language was not surprising. Indeed, it was Europe and specifically pan-European institutions that generated the political pressure underwriting nearly all of the legal advances made in the effort of lesbian/gay equality. As early as 1981, the parliamentary assembly of the European Council had issued a recommendation designed to curb homosexuals' legal subordination; and in 1984, the European Community itself began to champion an anti-homophobic agenda when the European Parliament voted for a resolution designed to fight discrimination against lesbians and gay men in the workplace.[9] Numerous other initiatives followed as the organization transformed itself into the European Union; in 1994, these efforts resulted in an affirmative vote on a wide-reaching declaration that demanded full equality for lesbians and gay men in all areas of criminal and civil law. With this vote, the European Parliament acted on a report compiled by the EU Committee for Basic Freedoms and Inner Affairs; and while the resolution was not binding for individual member states, it clearly signaled the Union's pluralizing trajectory toward lesbian/gay equality. It was in that sense that the declaration not only envisioned anti-discrimination legislation and the possibility of registered partnerships, but specifically criticized those countries that had different ages of consent for heterosexuals and homosexuals and inhibited the social visibility of lesbians and gay men.[10]

When Austria joined the European Union in 1995, it did so at the very moment the organization intensified its efforts on behalf of lesbians and gay men. In that context, the country's overtly homophobic legislation not only appeared as an obstruction of the European-wide quest for lesbian/gay equality, but also came to be seen as a blemish on a state seeking to integrate itself into the New Europe. This conjuncture produced an unprecedented degree of pressure on Austria's legislature, and within a few months of the country's entry into the European Union, the first serious efforts at repealing Austria's anti-lesbian/gay laws were underway. After much deliberation in various committees, the proposed abolition of §§ 209, 220, and 221 came to a parliamentary vote in the fall of 1996. In the process, the latter two statutes were eliminated, while the vote on the former produced a tie that kept Austria's unequal age of consent law on the books.[11]

Austria's conservative parties—the Christian Social People's Party (ÖVP) and the nationalist Freedom Party (FPÖ)—may have sought to protect Austria's collective body with their votes for a retention of §209. But in an integrating Europe, the legal autonomy of individual states was rapidly waning. In this context, international pressure to abolish §209 only mounted, especially given that the European Union was dedicated to championing the very open and pluralistic society Austria's conservative parties opposed on religious and nationalist grounds. More than any other document, it was the Amsterdam Treaty that signaled the Union's commitment to fight the legal subordination of lesbians and gay men. Negotiated in 1996/1997 and ratified in 1999, the treaty expanded the founding charter of the European Union, paying particular attention to the question of human rights. Article Thirteen of the document thus professed a commitment to oppose discrimination on the basis of gender, race, ethnicity, religion, disability, age, and sexual orientation. The inclusion of the latter was an unprecedented recognition of lesbians and gay men as a group whose basic rights needed special protection, and while the treaty of Amsterdam enunciated fundamental principles rather than binding laws, its acceptance by all fifteen member states—Austria among them—was widely seen as a milestone on the path toward a European future of lesbian/gay equality.[12] The treaty of Amsterdam, however, was not the only European entity that generated pressure on Austria's homophobic legislation. In the context of the European Union's growing commitment to the protection of lesbian/gay rights, Austria emerged as a veritable target of the European Parliament. Between 1997 and 2000, the country was "urgently called upon" to "abolish the laws against homosexuals" on five separate occasions.[13]

Given this constellation, it became exceedingly likely that Austria would abandon its discriminatory age of consent law. Indeed, in the summer of 2002, §209 was abolished in the wake of a ruling by Austria's constitutional court (*Verfassungsgerichtshof*) that held, following the European Union's argumentation, that the statute violated the country's principle of equality (*Gleichheitssatz*).[14]

But European pressure is certain to have even more far-reaching legal ramifications. For as the struggle against Austria's injurious penal code came to an end, the center of debate shifted to the domain of civil law. By the early 2000s, it was thus the quest for registered partnerships for same-sex couples that came to occupy the lesbian/gay movement and its supporters. Once more, the transnational domain of the European Union provided the immediate impulse for this model of legal recognition. In general terms, the treaty of Amsterdam warranted the institutionalization of "gay marriage" as the only viable means to combat the discrimination of lesbians and gay men in regard to inheritance law, tax law, and immigration law, among others. Such legal regulations were, in fact, becoming exceedingly common in other EU countries. The demand for registered partnerships had been advanced by Austria's lesbian/gay movement since the 1980s, but it was only in this European context that the issue gained wider political currency. A 1998 initiative on the occasion of Austria's EU presidency exemplified this dynamic. Under the motto "E(u)quality now," it comprised a series of events designed to highlight the disjunctions between European principles of non-discrimination and Austria's legal realities. To "render Austria fit for Europe," the campaign suggested, the country needed to overcome its position as "tail end in human rights for lesbians and gay men." The "securing of [same-sex] partnerships" would do much to alleviate the situation; whereas similar arguments had been made in the past, their re-articulation in a European framework resulted in an unprecedented level of political support.[15]

Indeed, by 1999, the introduction of registered partnerships was not only championed by Austria's Green Party, but also by the SPÖ which officially adopted the cause as part of its program for legal reform.[16] Neither Greens nor Social Democrats have been in Austria's government since the initial formation of the coalition between the ÖVP and the FPÖ in early 2000, but with the possibility of different majorities in the future, the legal recognition of same-sex couples has become a certain prospect. Even without a change in government, the extension of civil rights to lesbians and gay men is not inconceivable given Europe's steadily mounting pressure.

Europe and the Media

The pressure exerted by the New Europe on behalf of lesbian/gay equality was resisted by Austria's conservative parties which continued to pursue a policy designed to safeguard the nation's heteronormative boundaries. But if transformations in the political field were thus slow to come, the Europeanization of the "lesbian/gay question" engendered a genuine revolution of mass-mediated discourse.

Until the early 1990s, Austria's mass media was actively complicit in the systematic subordination of the country's homosexuals. Prior to the early 1980s, coverage of the issue was essentially restricted to sensationalized accounts of lesbians and gay men as criminals. With the emergence of the lesbian/gay movement, the coverage did diversify. But while the occasional report on the movement's activities brought the topic of homosexuality closer to the journalistic mainstream, the mass-mediated coverage enforced the hegemonic strictures against lesbian/gay visibility. In practice, this meant that the efforts of the lesbian/gay movement were usually held up for censure and public ridicule.[17]

As late as 1995, Austria's mass-media enacted this discursive pattern in their coverage of the so-called "outing affair." In the summer, gay activist Kurt Krickler had identified four Catholic bishops as clandestine homosexuals to protest the ongoing discrimination of Austria's lesbians and gay men and to call attention to the Church's role in that state of affairs. This agenda was completely silenced by the media, however, as coverage exclusively focused on the activist and the ostensible pathology that drove him to his supposedly desperate measures. Failing to show any tangible concern for the quality of life among Austria's lesbians and gay men, the mass media thus ultimately safeguarded a national sphere constituted through the systematic subordination of the country's homosexuals.[18]

It was in the context of Europe's growing pressure on Austria that the mass-mediated construction of homosexuality began to change drastically in the second half of 1990s. The left-liberal weekly *Profil* was a case in point. As late as the summer of 1995, it had still distinguished itself with the publication of a blatantly homophobic cover story on the outing affair.[19] A few months later, and in the wake of some protests, however, it began to embrace a very different agenda; the resulting three-part series on "Homosexuality in Austria" broke new ground in the representation of the country's queers. A publishing project of unprecedented breadth and depth, the series not only took a strong stance against ongoing discrimination, but pioneered an affirmative mode of representation that constructed lesbians and gay men as worldly arbiters of lifestyle and taste.[20]

Profil's celebration of queer culture as a marker of cosmopolitanism stood at the beginning of a larger trajectory that replaced a set of criminalizing and pathologizing tropes with the assemblage of affirmative representations that came to characterize constructions of homosexuality in the course of the late 1990s. Indeed, by the turn of the millennium, the old figures of homosexual abjection had all but disappeared from Austria's mass media; as more and more coverage was devoted to lesbian/gay issues, publicized homophobia seemed increasingly inappropriate. Instead, the normative position came to be defined in terms of explicit support for lesbian/gay concerns, a position that characterized the unprecedented amount of media coverage generated by EuroPride in June of 2001.

From such left-leaning publications as the daily *Standard* and the weekly *Falter*, whose extensive reporting of the "rainbow over the city" extolled Vienna's ascent to the "capital of the gay Europe" to the more conservative *Kurier*, which celebrated Vienna's queers' "self-confidence and lust for life" to *Die Presse*, the principal newspaper of Austria's right, where critical articles on the country's lackluster record on lesbian/gay rights were paired with lavish praise for EuroPride's film festival, Austria's mass media had adopted the emerging rhetoric of queer affirmation.[21]

This rhetoric was fueled, in turn, by a trope that figured Austria's lesbian/gay-rights situation as an explicit gauge for the country's standing in the New Europe. In the developmental schema transported in this new discursive context, Austria's *Europareife* seemed in severe doubt, a position expressed in paradigmatic fashion in a cover story on gay marriage, published by *Profil* in August of 2001.[22] Written on the occasion of the legalization of registered partnerships in Germany, the piece functioned as an indictment of Austria's social conservatism. Pointing to the fact that forms of gay marriage were not only available in Germany, but have been in place for a "long time in many other countries in Western Europe," the article constructed Austria as an effective backwater whose ascent to the standard of the New Europe presupposed a radical change in the country's policy toward lesbians and gay men.[23] This point was brought home by the article's centerpiece: a large map of Europe with superimposed boxes detailing the forms of registered partnerships available or about to be available to queers in various countries. Presented under the heading of "A Europe of Partnerships," the absence of Austria effectively erased the country from this map of European civilization—a civilization centrally defined by the pluralizing commitment to lesbian/gay rights.[24] It is a trope that has been reaffirmed by the countless articles charting the various legal breakthroughs in Europe, from Spain's 2005 authorization of same-sex marriages to the creation of civil unions in the United Kingdom later in the same year.

Queering Transnationalism: A Provocative Conclusion

In a recently published book on the trajectory of Jews and queers in post-World War II Vienna, I offer an overarching interpretation of Europe's function in the struggle for lesbian/gay rights.[25] As I argue in respect to both Jews and queers, the modern configuration of the groups, particularly in the German-speaking world, was a product of the exclusionary project of nation-building. That project created the "German" through recourse to the fiction of an ethnically pure space whose normative reproduction needed to be ensured through acts of social engineering. It was that ideology that rendered Jews and queers the principal symptoms of modernity: the abject by-products of a normalizing process that presupposed the groups' existence at its constitutive margins.

In this conceptual framework, the Holocaust emerges as the ultimate project of nation-building, a catastrophically radicalized attempt to rid the body politic of those elements that threaten its normative reproduction. But the postwar period, too, needs to be understood in the context of modernity's constitutive exclusions. As I show in considerable detail in the book, and as I hint at in the present essay, the decades after World War II were marked by the ongoing subordination of Jews and queers, both of which continued to function as the constitutive outsides of a body politic imagined along the lines of an exclusionary nationalism.

This structural configuration was not challenged until the late 1980s when the end of the Cold War and the incipient transformation of the European Union from a collection of nation-states to a more federally organized entity began to undermine the integrity of the nationalist project. In the ethnographic realities of Austria, this development was transported in and coded through "Europe." In contrast to an ethnically and sexually homogeneous Austria, Europe thus stood for a pluralizing logic that imagined the body politic not in opposition to the Jewish and queer symptoms of modernity, but through their very inclusion.

In this light, it is hardly surprising that Jews and queers supported Austria's membership in the European Union with enormous enthusiasm. In fact, I do not know of a single Austrian Jew who voted against Austria's entry into the European Union. The fervor of the queer support was similarly palpable and can be gleaned quite accurately from the sentiments expressed in the EuroPride Guide.

In this context, it is worthwhile to pause and think about the larger political constellations operative in Austria as well as in other EU countries. When Austrians went to the polls in 1994 to vote on the country's potential membership in the European Union, the political parties were divided in their recommendations. While the SPÖ and the ÖVP recommended the ratification of the membership agreement they had negotiated as partners in the then-ruling coalition, the then oppositional FPÖ urged voters to cast a "no" as a means of preserving the integrity of the Austrian nation-state. Coming from an avowedly nationalist party with an overtly xenophobic platform, this recommendation was not surprising.

What was more surprising was the recommendation by the socially progressive, left-wing Green Party. Its leadership also recommended a negative vote—in this case, based on a familiar theme of anti-capitalist resistance against the neoliberal forces of globalization. In its place, the

Green Party advocated a kind of leftist nationalism, a retrenchment of sorts in an Austrian tradition of national welfare.

In light of the present analysis of the function of Europe and the European Union in Austria's lesbian/gay context, the Green Party's stance is somewhat ironic. After all, it was the Greens who were Austria's first party not only to champion lesbian/gay rights, but also to run openly queer candidates for office. More generally, it is the Green Party that has the strongest record on questions of human and minority rights.

This constellation is not unique to Austria, of course. Throughout Europe, as well as in the United States, the most progressive parties and organizations—the respective Green Parties as well as the many anti-globalization movements—combine a genuine commitment to social pluralism with an anti-capitalist stance that identifies entities like the European Union as their primary target. I am not a booster for the neo-liberal utopias envisioned by the champions of globalization. But I am struck by the fact that the institutions designed to effect their realization seem far more effective at engendering the kinds of legal and cultural transformations associated with an agenda of social progress than the political and academic left seems to realize.

If Jews and queers were constructed as the abject symptoms of the modern nation-state, it would seem that this process was linked in no small part to the purification of national economies. The prevention of their exploitation by "foreign capital" does account, at least partially, for the persistence and violence associated with the exclusion of Jews and queers from the national realm. In the logic of national economies, Jews, after all, were figured as inherently alien, while homosexuals could be seen as having a rather tenuous relationship to the nation's reproduction.

This is all to highlight the fundamental transformation brought on by a transnational economy. Simply put, such concepts as "Jewish capital" would seem to lose their salience, while the support for lesbian/gay rights would become an affirmative issue of human resource management. These are the very dynamics that seem to be playing out in the United States where more and more corporations, especially among Fortune 500 companies, extend benefits to partners of lesbian/gay employees. In the process, corporate America has emerged as the most potent ally of a lesbian/gay rights movement beleaguered by a religiously driven and overtly nationalist backlash.

Admittedly, these are very preliminary thoughts. But they hint at the possibility that the weakening of the nation-state in the context of globalization might be good, not only for the Jews, but for the queers as well. If that were the case, we might want to rethink the position of a self-consciously progressive politics to better push for social progress in this new century.

Notes

1. For the basic contours of Austrian lesbian/gay history, see Matti Bunzl, *Symptoms of Modernity: Jews and Queers in Late-Twentieth-Century Vienna* (Berkeley, CA: Univ. of California P, 2004); Michael Handl et al., eds., *Homosexualität in Österreich* (Vienna: Junius, 1989); Wolfgang Förster et al., eds, *Der Andere Blick: Lesbischwules Leben in Österreich* (Vienna: Eigenverlag, 2001).

2. Homosexuelle Initiative Wien, "Unser Brief an Bundeskanzler und Justizminister," *Warme Blätter* 1/1 (July 1979): 4-6, here 5.

3. HOSI, ... Und sie bewegt sich doch. ...: 15 Jahre Homosexuelle Initiative (Vienna: Eigenverlag, 1994); see also Handl et al., *Homosexualität in Österreich*.

4. Bunzl, *Symptoms of Modernity*, 73-81.

5. Ibid., 129-33.

6. Connect-Sonderausgabe (June 1996), 10.

7. CSD Wien, *Pride Guide 99* (June 1999), 2.

8. CSD Wien, *EuroPride Guide* (June 2001), 5.

9. *Lambda Nachrichten* 3-4 (1981): 3, 6; *Lambda Nachrichten* 2 (1984): 30. Cf. Bunzl, *Symptoms of Modernity*, 102.

10. *Lambda Nachrichten* 2 (1994): 51-53. Cf. Bunzl, *Symptoms of Modernity*, 192.

11. *Lambda Nachrichten* 1 (1997): 8-14. Cf. Bunzl, *Symptoms of Modernity*, 192-93.

12. *Lambda Nachrichten* 3 (1997): 42-44; *Lambda Nachrichten* 2 (1999): 49-51. Cf. Bunzl, *Symptoms of Modernity*, 194.

13. *Lambda Nachrichten* 3 (1997): 12; *Lambda Nachrichten* 2 (1998): 13-14; *Lambda Nachrichten* 1 (1999): 8-9; *Lambda Nachrichten* 2 (2000): 20-22. Cf. Bunzl, *Symptoms of Modernity*, 194.

14. *Der Standard*, 26 June 2002.

15. *Lambda Nachrichten* 4 (1998): 42-43, 46-47. Cf. Bunzl, *Symptoms of Modernity*, 195.

16. *Lambda Nachrichten* 2 (1999): 7. Cf. Bunzl, *Symptoms of Modernity*, 195.

17. Bunzl, *Symptoms of Modernity*, 81-85.

18. Ibid; Bunzl, "Outing as Performance/Outing as Resistance: A Queer Reading of Austrian (Homo)Sexualities," *Cultural Anthropology* 12.1 (February 1997): 129-51.

19. Robert Buchacher and Christian Seiler, "Gestehe, dass du schwul bist," *Profil* 31 July 1995, 26-29.

20. *Profil*, 11 Sept. 1995; *Profil*, 18 Sept. 1995; *Profil*, 25 Sept. 1995; *News* 5 Feb. 1996; *News*, 11 May 2000. Cf. Bunzl, *Symptoms of Modernity*, 203-04.

21. *Der Standard*, 5 June 2001; *Der Falter* 22 (2001); *Wiener Zeitung*, 29-30 June 2001; *Kurier*, 1 July 2001; *Die Presse*, 1 June 2001; *Die Presse*, 9 June 2001. Cf. Bunzl, *Symptoms of Modernity*, 205.

22. Nina Horowitz and Dagmar Schwelle, "Bis die Zeit reif ist," *Profil*, 6 Aug. 2001, 30-37.

23. Ibid., 30.

24. Ibid., 32.

25. Bunzl, *Symptoms of Modernity*.

A Scandal in the Seminary

Pieter M. Judson

"There goes his bride!" someone cried, followed by a chorus of "the devil and his bride!" reiterated most vociferously by the youngest, as if it were a matter of course. [...] Nothing less than an open, strict disciplinary treatment of the case could now save the convent and its integrity."[1]

In the summer of 2004 when a considerable quantity of pornography—including child pornography—was found on the main computer of a conservative seminary in St. Pölten, a sex scandal rocked the Catholic Church in Austria. As more details about life in the St. Pölten seminary were reported, the emerging scandal narratives in the Austrian press had less and less to do with the specific issue of child pornography. Instead, the discovery of pornography in the seminary produced a broad public discussion of some familiar and ongoing questions about religion, homosexuality, and family in Austrian society. This broader scandal combined diverse concerns about three different topics that, when brought together, incited considerable public outrage. The most obvious set of concerns had to do with allegedly deviant sexual behaviors in the Church, especially in its educational institutions. This panic developed from the discovery that someone in the seminary had downloaded child pornography on the main computer. Given the nature of power relations in educational institutions and the discovery of pornography that depicted minors, however, the original panic about sexual deviance developed into fears about potential sexual abuse by teachers of their students (in this case, all adults). When the bishop of St. Pölten, the outspoken (and conservative) Kurt Krenn, downplayed the seriousness of the matter, a third element was added to the scandal. The radically conservative, ideological character of this particular seminary—and indeed of the diocese of St. Pölten—had consistently raised questions among Austrian Catholics about the apparent arrogance of power that the Church hierarchy displayed toward the faithful.[2] The origins of this last issue can be traced as far back as Austria's distinctive *Kulturkampf* in the 1860s and 1870s, when a few ultramontane bishops chose adamantly and very publicly to oppose the popular reforms enacted by Austria's new liberal government. This panic has been revived in new forms every few years, but it has recently taken on greater significance because of alleged attempts by fundamentalist organizations in Austria to turn the clock back on religious practice. Lay groups are quick to blame both the fundamentalist organizations and some traditional Church doctrine—such as celibacy requirements for the priesthood—for scandals in the Church that produce public mistrust.

Above all, however, the scandal built on specifically homophobic tropes involving alleged gay threats to Austrian society, tropes which had not diminished in their fundamental power, despite the recent liberalization of Austrian society and the growing acceptance toward queer culture in the public mainstream. As we will see, even some of the more socially liberal media outlets in Austria that regularly support homosexual initiatives for legal and social equality in Austrian society could not help falling back on traditional storylines that linked homosexual behavior to pedophilia and the endangerment of Austrian society.[3] This was ironic indeed, given the spate of pedophilia scandals involving priests that have cropped up in the last fifteen years and the steadfast condemnation by the Church of homosexual practices.

On 31 October 2003, a fifty-three year-old seminarian from St. Pölten, Ewald S., was found dead in the Alten Donau (a backwater of the Danube near Vienna). The police listed the official cause of death as drowning, but did not completely rule out foul play. This first episode in the scandal narrative actually had nothing to do with the story, until the following July when newspapers retroactively added it to their coverage, sometimes making it a central element of their articles. The story really begins on 10 November 2003, when technical experts working on a computer available for common use at the St. Pölten seminary discovered that pornographic material had been downloaded and reported this discovery to seminary director Ulrich Küchl. On 27 November, twenty-nine boarding students at the seminary petitioned Küchl to investigate this clear misuse of the Internet. The next day, Küchl himself informed the State Attorney's Office of suspicions that child pornography had been downloaded on this computer. His superior, Bishop Kurt Krenn of St. Pölten, informed the Lower Austrian police as well. The police then confiscated the computer.

Almost four months later, on 19 March 2004, the investigation yielded thousands of pornographic images, including some that involved minors. On the basis of this discovery, the police conducted a search of the seminary on 24 June, confiscating private laptops in an effort to discover who had downloaded the child pornography.[4] On 19 July, the state prosecutor indicted a Polish seminarian, Piotr Z., for possession of child pornography. On 13 August, Piotr Z. was convicted of possession of 1,700 pornographic photos, most of which involved minors. He was given a six-month suspended sentence (the maximum being two years). Meanwhile, under pressure, the Vatican had instituted its own investigation on 20 July, and on 12 August, the papal visitor, Bishop Klaus Küng of Vorarlberg, closed the seminary, remarking that a completely new beginning would be necessary. On 10 September, the Vatican required Krenn to resign his post, due to health reasons. Küng eventually replaced Krenn as bishop of St. Pölten.

Let us return to early July 2004, however, when a far more lurid, if legally inconsequential, set of revelations about the seminary stole media attention almost completely away from the original child pornography investigation, offering the public a new lens for interpreting events in St. Pölten. A week after the police had visited the seminary and confiscated the laptop computers, an ex-seminarian accused director Ulrich Küchl of homosexual behavior. Two days later, Küchl resigned, in order, he said, "to calm a difficult situation." In his resignation letter to Bishop Krenn, Küchl wrote, "The slanders being circulated against my person in the media by an ex-seminarian have created such a negative influence on public opinion, that my staying here would only cause a greater burden on the seminary and the diocese of St. Pölten."[5] On 11 July, the news magazine *Profil* published photos showing the seminary's's assistant director Wolfgang Rothe kissing a seminarian, purportedly at a Christmas gathering. (This photo induced much subsequent speculation about the nature of the kiss in question, and whether it was, in fact, what Americans would call a "French kiss"). Subsequently, several other photographs were circulated, some obtained and published by the media, that purported to show Küchl, Rothe, and several of their seminary charges engaging in what appeared to be homosexual activities. Some of the photos were delivered anonymously to Bishop Krenn, who questioned openly their authenticity (had they been altered by means of computer technology?) and then later characterized the whole thing alternately as *Bubendummheiten* (youthful pranks) or as a witch-hunt against his person.

In order to understand the character of the scandal, as opposed to the stories that produced it, I examine three overlapping popular narratives that framed public discussion and media coverage. They are old and familiar stories. One involves the relationship of the Church hierarchy to the society it purports to serve, and the other two involve panics around accusations of homosexual behavior and pedophilia. The "discovery" of homosexual behavior at the seminary seemed to reinforce the moral position of those within the Church who had long demanded reform of the hierarchy. (Here, "discovery" seems to be the wrong term, since so many people seem, rather, to have turned a blind eye to the homosexual behavior of some churchmen before *Profil* published its photographs.) The photos only confirmed what so many others claimed to have already known instinctively. But the discovery also served a conservative institutional agenda within the Church that sought to turn public attention away from alleged systemic abuses within the Church. By framing the story in terms of the dangers to society of homosexuality and pedophilia, Church leaders clearly hoped to deflect accusations of laxness and irresponsibility within this conservative seminary. Homosexual behavior became the unquestioned explanation both for the presence of pornography and for any abuse of power on the part of Küchl or Rothe in the seminary. In the end, the scandal helped to reinforce several homophobic norms in Austrian public culture, even among people who described themselves as more liberal and tolerant of homosexuality in Austrian society. As is so often the case with this issue and in the face of evidence to the contrary, pedophilia was figured publicly as a problem particular to homosexuals. The real problem for most observers was that the St. Pölten seminary endangered society by consecrating homosexual priests who would gain unfettered access to Austria's children. This re-focusing of attention on homosexual behavior ensured that critical issues such as the sexual abuse of minors by priests (or child pornography) would be buried under the avalanche of "homopanic."

The *Kulturkampf* Updated

For many Catholic Austrians, the events in the St. Pölten seminary offered the welcome opportunity to debate questions internal to the Catholic Church, questions that recalled struggles among Austrian Catholics dating from the 1860s and 1870s.[6] Reformers, fundamentalists, and conservatives battle periodically in the public media for influence over the national Church in Austria. The position of the minority fundamentalists was generally enhanced under John Paul II, given the close personal ties many of them had to Rome. While a more traditionalist, conservative faction controls the conference of Austrian bishops, the conservatives are unable to curb the more controversial statements and practices of the fundamentalist group. This would not normally be a problem, except that many fundamentalists have in the past decades taken provocative blame-the-victim positions, especially on issues like sexual abuse of children by the clergy. Seeing their chance, progressive reformers took this opportunity to blame social problems like priest abuse of minors on the Church's unyielding and outdated policies regarding celibacy and the potential role of women in the priesthood. In recent years when scandal has hit the Austrian Church, the conservatives have scrambled to adopt an attitude of greater responsiveness to public misgivings in order to diffuse the moral power behind the demands of the more liberal reformers. Publicly, conservatives began to pursue a more responsive and sympathetic style, while continuing to adhere strictly to traditional doctrine. Fundamentalists, meanwhile, accuse the conservatives of moral relativism.

Newspapers, television reports, public commentators, and letters to the editor all placed the St. Pölten scandal firmly in the context of two broader recent controversies internal to the Austrian Catholic Church. One issue was the "fundamentalist line" embodied by the outspoken bishop of St. Pölten, Kurt Krenn. The other issue was the Groer affair of a decade before. In 1995, a former seminary pupil had accused Groer, a teacher and confessor to the pupil, of sexual abuse. Later, four others had come forward with similar accusations. The police had been hampered by the statute of limitations from pursuing the case, and Groer had remained silent about the accusations until his death. At the time, Krenn had characterized the affair as stupid boyish pranks, the same language he used to describe the events at the St. Pölten seminary in 2004.[7] In the wake of the Groer scandal, close to 400,000 Catholics left the Church.[8]

This time, Bishop Krenn interpreted the uproar around the St. Pölten seminary in 2004 as a personal attack on his authority, especially his fundamentalist practices. Krenn's harsh intransigence and denials in the face of mounting revelations about the seminary reminded many people of the Church's unresponsiveness to accusations of the sexual abuse of children in the Groer scandal. The evocations of Groer produced by Krenn's attitude allowed critics and reformers to characterize the St. Pölten scandal as merely the tip of an iceberg and certainly not a unique case. Conservatives, too, tried hard at first to frame the St. Pölten scandal as an isolated set of incidents, but Krenn's megalomania made this tack impossible. If Krenn had learned nothing about managing public relations from the Groer affair, however, the mainstream conservatives had learned their lesson well. Thus when the St. Pölten stories became public, the conservative bishops could not risk appearing insensitive to Austrian Catholics' legitimate concerns. They swiftly changed their dismissive line to a studied pose as the champions of Church reform. Still, the conservative reforms that were meant to address the St. Pölten situation were internal and largely bureaucratic in nature. They did not touch on controversial issues such as celibacy or women in the priesthood that many reform-minded Austrian Catholics raised in public forums.

The St. Pölten story itself involved far more complex internal Church politics than I have as yet touched on. As we have seen, Krenn himself had a reputation as an extreme fundamentalist who rarely hesitated to speak his mind. Krenn was hardly a consensus builder; he was a combative type who liked to transform issues of doctrinal differences into personal crusades. Krenn's followers were well aware of this dimension of the scandal. A July letter to the conservative and normally sympathetic *Kronenzeitung* asked whether the Church only had room nowadays for so-called progressives, or whether there might also be room for a few conservatives.[9] Playing on public outrage against Krenn's intransigence, this writer portrayed Krenn as the protector of authentic Catholicism. Clearly Krenn's ability to polarize Austrian Catholics was nothing new. In fact, news of Krenn's appointment as bishop of St. Pölten in 1991 had been greeted by a silent protest march of over a thousand believers in the streets of the city on the day preceding his installation.[10] The lay group Forum had criticized Krenn on the occasion of his tenth anniversary as bishop, complaining that he had provoked over ninety different controversies in the past decade alone. Calling him a "militant champion of the anti-conciliar restoration," the group accused Krenn of an authoritarian leadership style.

In the case of the St. Pölten seminary, Krenn had fired its allegedly liberal director, Franz Schrittwieser, in 2001 and had replaced him with the extremely conservative Prior of Eisgarn, Ulrich Küchl.[11] Küchl in turn had instituted several "reforms" that, according to a reporter for *Die Welt*, had almost "encouraged students in St. Pölten to leave the Catholic path of virtue." Taking a tone of "I told you so," *Die Welt* described how an increasingly isolated St. Pölten seminary had quickly degenerated into an institution that collected fundamentalist Catholics who were mentally unfit for the priesthood and who would not have gained admission to any other seminary. Along with the new "political" direction of the seminary, Krenn had evidently encouraged Küchl to lower the entrance qualifications for candidates as well, in order to increase their numbers and to end their required year of probation as priests. The news reports framed these developments in St. Pölten as a systematic effort by Krenn to further the goals of radical sects like *Opus Dei* by producing greater numbers of fundamentalist priests. *Die Welt* reported in shocked tones that Krenn had tried to reintroduce the reading of the mass in Latin "with the priest facing away from the faithful" in some churches. He had also consecrated priests in secret who would otherwise not have been approved by the diocese, in order to pursue his radical agenda.[12] The news magazine *Profil* reported similar stories about this new fundamentalist crop of priests, stories that recalled an implied connection between the priest and some vaguely threatening sexual danger of the kind traditionally found in nineteenth-century anti-clerical propaganda such as the Oscar Panizza story quoted at the outset. A priest in a suburb of St. Pölten who was a member of one fundamentalist group, for example, had allegedly forbidden the parishioners to take the host in their hands during Communion, claiming that only a priest's hands might touch the host. When a host fell into a woman's blouse during Communion, this priest forced her into the sacristy so that he could fish it out himself. On another occasion, the same priest told a mother whose sixteen year-old son lay dying from a motorcycle accident that if the boy had already had sexual relations he would certainly burn in hell.[13]

"Frau Pröpstin in der Sakristei…": Pedophilia or "Homo-Panic"?

The stories that emerged about Küchl and Rothe's alleged participation in homosexual orgies with their seminarian charges lent a useful urgency to Catholic reformers' ongoing critique of Krenn's arch-conservative agenda. The fundamentalist agenda was not only distasteful to the sensibilities of modern Catholics, but the discovery of homosexual activities within the seminary allowed the reformers to argue that this same agenda had produced hidden and sexually deviant activities within the Church.

The St. Pölten diocese had frequently gone out of its way to damn specifically homosexual behavior as unnatural and perverse. But, as *Profil* explained, daily practice in the hothouse atmosphere behind the seminary walls was far different, "[Homosexual] passion and jealousy ruled the day, embedded in a complex interpersonal dynamic between favorites and outsiders."[14] Küchl had allegedly brought those who counted as his favorites with him to his Eisgarn residence on the weekends. Küchl and one of his former favorites had even allegedly "exchanged" their new favorites on one occasion. Moreover, Küchl had also brooked no opposition to his behavior within the seminary. Those who had allegedly objected to these goings-on were harassed and threatened. Küchl, referred to as "Frau Pröpstin" by his young favorites, had allegedly carried out perverse ceremonies blessing male couples, which the press characterized in shocked tones as "homosexual marriages."[15] "K," a favorite of Küchl's who was twenty years old, was allegedly appointed to be organist at Eisgarn by Küchl. The latter, reported *News* knowingly, had given the former "private lessons." Once, reported a witness, two high school students visiting the seminary in St. Pölten had overheard K. call out to the sacristy where Küchl was putting on his vestments for mass, "Frau Pröpstin, what lovely outfit are we wearing this evening?"[16] "Loving thy neighbor below the belt" was the way *News* characterized the general practices in the seminary.

Other commentators linked this theme of "homo-sex in the seminary" directly to the Groer pedophilia/abuse scandal and the endangerment of Austria's children. Once again, the Church became figured as a site for the abuse of minors, despite the fact that the seminarians were all over Austria's age of consent. In this particular case, the pedophilia link was made through the discovery of child pornography at the seminary and was not linked to any substantive accusation of abuse. Yet the press and commentators contextualized the child pornography story in terms of the homosexual behavior of Küchl and Rothe. There was no evidence to suggest that either man had an interest in child pornography. The discovery of child pornography on the seminary computer and the media's sexualization of the teacher/student relationship (even if the students were not statutory minors) encouraged many observers to see the homosexual behavior of Küchl, Rothe, and their circle as predatory and as a danger to Austria's children. Eliding pedophilia with homosexual behavior, many observers conveniently ignored the fact that the only descriptions of the child pornography available in the Austrian press (as far as I could determine) referred to images of young girls abused by older men. Many journalists fed the pedophilia theme by hinting at the possibility that the teachers and priests had misused their power and sexually abused many of the young seminarians.[17] *Corriere della Sera*'s headline for this story captured the tangle of popular associations and reproduced them with the simple words, "Pedophilia Scandal in Seminary: Shock in Austria." The accompanying article referred melodramatically to a "theater of perversion" and a "Habsburg Sodom in St. Pölten."[18]

These fevered attempts to link homosexuality to sexual abuse of children culminated in one of the more bizarre elements of the scandal: the sudden and retroactive press interest in the drowning death of former seminarian Ewald S. back in October of 2003. On 27 July 2004, the press questioned the prosecutor about whether, perhaps, Ewald S. had committed suicide because of his involvement in a homosexual affair in St. Pölten. The truth, however, was more interesting indeed. It turned out that far from having participated in the homosexual orgies in St. Pölten, Ewald S. had actually been involved with a woman, Gabriele H. Ewald's diary revealed that he believed that Küchl and Rothe were spying on him.[19] In a breathtaking feat of media acrobatics, the magazine *News* now portrayed Ewald S. as the unlikely hero of the story, the only *real man* in the St. Pölten seminary—his unimpeachable heterosexual credentials supported by the testimony of his "Gabi." She claimed that her Ewald had frequently complained to her about the goings on in the seminary, calling it "psycho terror." Had he ever mentioned child pornography or "homo-sex [sic]" in the seminary wondered *News*? Not directly, but Gabi did recall that Ewald had once told her that things were sometimes bad in the seminary. How did Ewald describe his colleagues in the seminary? Oh, he liked most of them a lot, but he said that three of them were evil people. "Once we walked hand-in-hand to the train station and ten minutes later [Küchl] knew all about it." Gabriele H. commented in closing, "It's good that the affair in St. Pölten exploded. Now everything is coming to light, and Ewald's death will not have been in vain."[20]

Ewald Did Not Die in Vain ...

The interviews of Gabriele H. alone offer the historian a superb snapshot of the ways in which the Austrian media and public interpreted the events surrounding the scandal. They so beautifully captured the self-contradictory nature of the stories woven together by the media to produce a reassuring whole that the public could believe. They also captured the very limited scope of the imaginations of the journalists involved. First, the interviews reframed the St. Pölten scandal for the public as a story about the persecution of a good and "normal" man by evil, perverted predators. Heterosexual Ewald S. had refused to put up with the goings-on in the seminary and was subsequently driven to his death. Like Austria's abused children (although fifty-three years old), he was the victim of those homosexual pedophiles who held power over him in the seminary and who had wielded that power for ill. At the same time, Ewald S. was also something of a poster boy for those who earnestly argued that it was specifically the celibacy requirement that created deviance in the Church and attracted homosexuals to the priesthood. This good man of the community who innocently loved a good woman was not fit to be a priest, but the evil homos and their arrogant ally Bishop Krenn continued to exercise enormous power within the Church. Something must be done to reverse this terrible power dynamic.

Letters to local newspapers throughout Austria that summer confirmed this linkage between the celibacy requirement and all manner of deviant behaviors in the public mind. When asked whether celibacy requirement should be ended, readers of the *Vorarlberger Nachrichten* responded: "[Yes] to protect our children." "It's about time!" "It's ridiculous to speak of 'boyish games' when we are dealing with forty year-olds!" "A priest with a family would have a greater sense of responsibility and empathy." "Everyone should have a healthy sex life. Get rid of celibacy and we'll have satisfied priests—after all, they, too, are only men." "Celibacy is against nature." "No, it's media, TV, and theater that created a sex wave and have made all humanity rotten to the core." "A married priest with a good woman who can support him with help and advice, that would be a good model."

The public discussions and debates among Austrians about the scandal at the seminary demonstrate that despite the visibility and legitimacy Austria's queer community has achieved in the past decade, homophobic constructions of the crisis remained an important default mode of interpretation.[21] After all, the sexual deviance reported in the media focused on accusations of homosexual behavior among seminarians and not on the images of young girls molested by adult men, or on the facts of Ewald S's affair. After all, legally or morally, should homosexual behavior among allegedly celibate seminarians have been considered a deeper form of moral corruption than the heterosexual activity of Ewald S?

In this crisis, queer voices could be heard occasionally challenging precisely this default understanding of the scandal in Austrian society, although none of the voices that questioned the fundamentally homophobic approach of the media made a lasting mark on this discussion. They were unable to offer an acceptable alternative framework for understanding the course of events, and their assertions were simply ignored by other commentators. But at least their opinions were not derided by the mainstream media as they had been during the "outing" scandal of the mid-1990s, when the media made clear that homosexual behavior could be tolerated in Austria, but only as long as it remained closeted away from public view. Those queer voices who did question the shape of the public discussion offered Krenn some (undoubtedly unwanted) support. The left-of-center *Der Standard* carried at least two guest editorials lambasting the hypocrisy of the liberal media. Lawyer Helmut Graupner of *LAMBDA Wien* wrote that the real scandal in Austria was the double standard encouraged by Church leaders who preached one thing and did another. According to Graupner, the liberal media made no mention of this particular form of Church hypocrisy and its countless victims in its reporting. Instead, the media characterized homosexual intimacy as degenerate and perverse and branded homosexual unions as somehow cynically disdainful of Church teachings, while labeling homosexual partnerships freely entered into by adults as "open perversion." Graupner also pointed out that the discovery of child pornography in the seminary had still not produced any admission of responsibility or resignations by responsible individuals in power. "Only adult men attend seminary. When a liberal media, which otherwise vehemently supports the end of discrimination against homosexuality, now demands the resignation of the bishop because seminarians are living out their homosexuality, that constitutes an unbearable form of hypocrisy."[22]

Probably Austria's only celebrity to comment critically in the same vein was actor Alfons Haider (no relation to Jörg). Austria's only openly gay theater, musical, and cabaret star (who is also popular with Austrians outside of Vienna), Haider expressed anger that child pornography had been mixed up with homosexuality in the public debate. Interviewed while rehearsing for the summer season at Stockerau, Haider angrily commented that "the entire discussion is a big lie! [...] The Church has a problem with sexuality, not with homosexuality. For Krenn to resign because of homosexual attachments in the seminary is the scandal." What is considered normal nowadays in Austria anyway wondered Haider? "Normal," he opined, "is when a man does it with his secretary on Thursday and with his girlfriend on Friday, goes to a gay bar on Saturday and to Church with his wife on Sunday. And at the *Stammtisch* complains loudly about queers."[23]

In his analysis of the so-called "outing scandal" of 1995 when gay activist Kurt Krickler threatened to expose four Austrian bishops as homosexuals, Matti Bunzl deftly shows how the Austrian press consistently argued for the privacy rights of those threatened with outing as a means of maintaining the cloak of invisibility that surrounded a demoralized Austrian queer community. A decade later, Austria's queer communities have achieved significant and lasting visibility in the public sphere. As Bunzl's analysis demonstrates, their annual Rainbow Parade on Vienna's prestigious *Ringstrasse* constitutes both symbolic and real appropriations of public space by communities whose existence a decade ago was only tolerated as long as they remained invisible to the public.[24] The parade is only one example of a range of vibrant queer institutions that promote the community in public. Not surprisingly, the public and media responses to the goings-on at the seminary in St. Pölten also demonstrate that the queer community's rising visibility has not diminished the ongoing explanatory power of certain tropes about homosexuality for many Austrians. Indeed, one might argue that it is precisely with regard to Church issues that these tropes show their staying power: what began as a story about heterosexual child pornography in a seminary swiftly became overshadowed by accusations about homosexual perversion and pedophilia.

Notes

1. Oscar Panizza, "A Scandal at the Convent," in *Herculine Barbin: Being the Recently Discovered Memoirs of a Nineteenth-Century French Hermaphrodite*, intro. Michel Foucault, trans. Richard McDougall (New York: Pantheon Books, 1980), 177-78.

2. Although elements of this scandal would be familiar to Americans, the particular conflicts within and about the Catholic Church in Austria, conflicts that go back at least to the Austrian *Kulturkampf* of the 1860s and 1870s, shaped many of the specific ways the scandal resonated in Austrian society.

3. For a superb analysis of these traditions and tropes in the Austrian media, see Matti Bunzl's groundbreaking study, *Symptoms of Modernity: Jews and Queers in Late Twentieth-Century Vienna* (Berkeley, CA: Univ. of California P, 2004).

4. For a chronology, see *Austria Presse Agentur (APA)*, 10 September 2004, WNL0069 5 II 0388. For the police search of the seminary and seizure of the laptops, see *APA*, 29 June 2004, APA0771 5 II 0082.

5. *APA*, 5 July 2004, WNL0053 4 CI 0262.

6. In many ways, the internal Church conflicts of the last three decades echo internal conflicts from the time of Austria's own *Kulturkampf*, which pitted Catholics who were also political liberals (and sometimes so-called "*Alt-Katholiken*") against Austria's few but loud ultramontane bishops, and the latter against the more traditionally conservative or Josephenist bishops. It is not difficult to imagine Bishop Krenn or Cardinal Groer in the role of nineteenth-century activist Bishop Franz-Joseph Rudigier of Linz, with conservative Cardinal Schönborn playing the role of Vienna's Cardinal Rauscher in the 1870s. For an excellent recent analysis of those earlier struggles, see Max Vögler, "Religion, Liberalism, and the Social Question in the Habsburg Hinterland: The Catholic Church in Upper Austria, 1850-1914," Ph.D. diss., Columbia University, 2005, draft currently available at <http://www.voegler.name/defense_voegler_050623.pdf> (17 Feb. 2006).

7. *Kurier*, 5 October 2004, p. 9; *Profil*, 19 July 2004, p. 18.

8. *APA*, 12 July 2004, WNL0040 5 II 0870.

9. "Das grosse Krenn-Stechen," *Kronenzeitung*, 19 July 2004, p. 8.

10. *APA*, 12 July 2004, WNL0022 5 II 0320.

11. *Profil*, 19 July 2004, p. 18.

12. *Die Welt*, 22 July 2004, p. 6.

13. *Profil*, 19 July 2004, p. 18.

14. *Profil*, 20 December 2004, p. 46.

15. Most of these references are to stories recounted in the magazine *News*. See, for example, the article "Kirche Orgien, Saufgelage, Exzesse im Krenn-Reich: Ein Priesterschüler packt aus," *News*, 5 August 2004, p. 30, or "Das geheime Tagebuch des Alumnen," in the same issue, p. 35. Readers looking for lurid speculation and homophobic detail need go no further than *News*, a truly magnificent source for dirt.

16. *News*, 5 August 2004.

17. While I do think that a misuse of power clearly took place in the seminary, it did not specifically involve sexual abuse.

18. *APA Pressestimmen: Schlagzeile in Italien*, 14 July 2004, WNL0043 5 II 0251.

19. "Das geheime Tagebuch des Alumnen," *News*, 5 August 2004, p. 35

20. "Die Seminar-Leitung hat Ewald in den Tod getrieben," *News*, 29 July 2004, p. 15.

21. On this transformation, see Bunzl, *Symptoms of Modernity*.

22. "Homophobe Treibjagd," *Der Standard*, 13 July 2004, p. 27. See also Martin Traxler's insightful editorial, "Die Buben Ideologie," *Der Standard*, 21 July 2004, p. 23.

23. "Das ist eine große Verlogenheit," *Die Presse*, 15 July 2004, p. 7.

24. Bunzl, *Symptoms of Modernity*, 81-85, 117-51.

Romancing the Foreigner? "Fictitious Marriages" and the Crisis between Immigration and Human Rights

Julia Woesthoff

In early January 2006, the Austrian newspaper *Die Presse* announced, "In Austria, around two thousand marriages are not based on love [*bestehen nicht der Liebe wegen*]. They were formed to make it possible for a person without Austrian citizenship to stay" in Austria.16. Juli 2006[1] One of the only ways foreign-native interpersonal relationships has been publicly discussed in Austria in recent years is in the context of so-called "fictitious marriages" (*Scheinehen)* between Austrians and third-country nationals—immigrants from outside the European Economic Region (*Europäischer Wirtschaftsraum*, EWR for short). Public officials as well as the media understand these marriages as partnerships of convenience, having been established for the sole purpose of providing the foreign spouse with a relatively easy way to circumvent Austria's restrictive immigration and naturalization regulations and to gain Austrian citizenship.[2] In fact, the Austrian government has considered this phenomenon serious enough to tighten the law in this regard in the latest version of the *Fremdenpolizeigetz* (Foreigner Police Law, one of three laws pertaining to foreigners in Austria that was reformed last year and which took effect on 1 January 2006).

This paper seeks to locate the current debate about "fictitious marriages" in Austria in a broader context, considering both the evolution of binational marriages in the country more generally while also discussing the trajectory of official Austrian debates on immigration and integration and the place of *Scheinehen* within this discourse. This historical overview is followed by a closer look at the various ways in which the different constituencies in this debate—the government, the media, as well as advocacy groups for people in binational and bicultural partnerships—have interpreted the persistence and even rise of binational marriages. As will become clear, these debates are not just about divergent opinions regarding why Austrians enter into these marriages; they also inadvertently expose how official and popular understandings of marriage ("true" or "fictitious"), love, and desire are very much informed by the racial and/or ethnic context in which they are discussed.

The phenomenon of the "New Fictitious Marriage Boom," as one paper titled it, emerged in the mid-1990s. To understand why such marriages drew the public and political interest they did, it is helpful to provide a broad outline of the way in which the Austrian government has handled immigration since the early 1990s. Not surprisingly, perhaps, the appearance of the "fictitious" marriage coincided with a number of other developments related to migration issues in Austria, particularly the country's concerted effort not just to limit immigration, but also to decrease the number of foreigners already in the country.[3] As in other European nations that had experienced post-World War II guest-worker migration, Austria's approach to it had long been guided by economic considerations. It was only in the 1990s that a new—and somewhat negative—public and political consciousness developed about the growing number of immigrants in Austria's midst. This was partly due to the ever longer residency of many who had come as guest-workers from the 1960s onwards. Another factor, however, was the sharp rise in immigration that took place after the fall of communism in the late 1980s and the wars in former Yugoslavia in the early 1990s. Within four years (from 1989-1993), the number of legal immigrants to Austria rose by 80 percent, raising the percentage of foreigners in Austria by 3.5 percentage points to 8.6 percent.[4] The Austrian government, not surprisingly, took note and initiated the reform and introduction of a number of laws—the Asylum Law of 1992 and the Foreigner Law of 1993, as well as the new Residency Law (*Aufenthaltsgesetz*) of 1993. For the first time, the emphasis of migration-regulatory priorities shifted toward the issue of entry and arrival of foreigners (rather than being focused on those immigrants already in Austria).[5]

In 1990, the government had already passed an amendment to the Law on the Occupation of Aliens (*Ausländerbeschäftigungsgesetz*) that, while providing legal improvements for those foreign laborers already in Austria, also, and very crucially, introduced an immigration quota system geared toward reducing the number of immigrants coming into the country. The system was refined when the new Residency Law took effect in 1993, setting up two different quota systems—one specifically for family unification. The effect was a decrease in immigration figures back to their levels in the mid-1980s.[6] As scholars have noted, in content this law very much had the character of an immigration law, but because of concern about public opinion—most likely because Austria would have had to admit openly that it was a *de facto* immigration country—it was not called that.[7]

According to Dilek Çinar, it was not until the mid-1990s—a time when "fictitious" marriages were brought to the public's attention as well—that a thorough public and political debate took place about the (lack of) *integration* of migrants in Austria.[8] The Residency Law's restrictive policies, especially the quota system—which even regulated and limited family reunification among immigrants and created a massive backlog—had caused a lot of uncertainties among immigrants, effectively hindering any true integration process. In response, in 1995 the government proposed a so-called "integration package" (which ultimately included, among others, the 1997 Foreigner Law as well as a revised Law on the Occupation of Aliens), which eventually took effect in 1998. The goal of anchoring already-present immigrants' residential status more firmly was realized, rather than improved employment rights or social rights.[9] Relatives of immigrants at that time still had to wait eight years to be allowed to take up employment.[10]

Applying for Austrian citizenship, particularly for people from third countries, is a rather arduous process. Despite numerous reforms in the last decades, the law is still based on citizenship through descent (*ius sanguinis*) and a rejection of dual citizenship. A ten-year residency requirement has been in place since the law's inception in 1812. Adequate language skills, sufficient income, and a willingness to integrate, for example, are also required. While in the past it has been possible for certain groups of immigrants (like EWR members, asylum seekers, and foreigners married to Austrians) to shorten the waiting period, since the reformed citizenship law took effect in January 2006, the earliest opportunity for naturalization now occurs after six years of residency. Prior to this reform, waiting periods varied depending on the status of the immigrant and could in certain cases be requested after only three years. Indeed, Austria's minister of justice, Karin Gastinger, had complained that 60 percent of all naturalizations occur before the general ten-year waiting period is up, thus providing further incentives for migration to Austria.[11] Given Austria's goal to keep immigration numbers low, yet another factor to consider is Austria's entry into the European Union in 1995. People from its member states as well as Lichtenstein, Norway, and Iceland are now exempt from much of Austria's restrictive regulatory policies related to immigration. Since Austria's entry into the European Union, citizens from all EU nations can more easily find employment in Austria.

Despite, or rather because of, Austria's attempts to keep immigration low and despite the country's continuing difficulties in integrating its migrant population, binational marriages in the country have increased significantly over the last decade. While 13.9 percent of married couples in Austria were binational in 1998, by 2002 the figure had risen dramatically to almost one in four, or 23.8 percent.[12] One indication of the growing presence and increasing visibility of as well as public interest in binational/interethnic marriages and partnerships in Austria was the founding of the organization *Fraueninitiative Bikulturelle Ehen und Lebensgemeinschaften* (FIBEL) in 1994. The impetus for its founding came in 1992, the year the international bestseller *Not without My Daughter* by Betty Mahmoody chronicled the American author's traumatic experiences with her Iranian husband, effectively making the difficulties she experienced in her binational/interethnic marriage front page news all over the world. Moreover and as already discussed, in the early 1990s, the Austrian government had tightened immigration restrictions, which also greatly affected the foreign partners of Austrian women, most of whom came from third countries. In response to both the popular reaction to Mahmoody's work as well as the amendments to existing migration regulations, that same year the Social Democratic Party of Austria (SPÖ) invited women in bicultural partnerships to a seminar where they could exchange their experiences.[13]

It was in this broader context that the term "fictitious marriage" first appeared as a politically and legally viable concept and thus became an integral part of the public and political discourse on immigration in Austria. While the term had already been scrutinized in 1984 in an article published in *Öffentliche Sicherheit*, the organ of the Austrian Ministry of the Interior, it had been dismissed as irrelevant and even (legally) non-existent. As the Austrian Administrative Court declared, "Neither the Civil Law Code nor the Austrian Marriage Law know the term 'fictitious marriage.'"[14] Ten years later, however, the term appeared again in the pages of the same publication. In the meantime, it had attained legal recognition in the context of Austria's marriage law, declaring a marriage null and void, for example, if it only existed to gain Austrian citizenship. While it became easier for a third country national married to an Austrian to gain a residency permit as a consequence of the migration reforms in the late 1990s, the concept of the "fictitious marriage" also became codified in law.[15] Thus the concept attained growing significance in the minds of officials and the public, creating and/or reinforcing an ideological framework in which binational unions (especially with a partner from third countries) were already viewed as suspicious. It is not surprising then, that *Kurier* reported a "boom" in fictitious marriages in 1995, that a series of so-called *Scheinehe-Befragungen*—inquiries about marriages that were suspected of having been formed exclusively to facilitate immigration of the foreign partner—were being conducted in Vienna in 1996, or that fictitious marriages were inscribed in the law in 1997 (which took effect in 1998). The fact that binational marriages were (and are) on the rise only fed the flames, and the phenomenon has gained in importance since.

In 2005, the Austrian government introduced a new "foreigner law package," containing a new Asylum Law and Foreigner Police Law, as well as the new Residency Law, all of which came into effect on 1 January 2006.[16] One of the explicit reasons for this overhaul of immigration and integration policies has been to introduce a number of more effective measures against what the government warns is "the problem of fictitious marriages [*Aufenthaltsehen*] that should not be underestimated."[17] In fact, one of the explicit goals has been to provide deterrents for *Austrians* to agree to participate in fictitious marriages. According to the new Foreigner Police Law, Austrians entered into what are found to be fictitious marriages now have to fear punishment as well. If the Austrian partner accepts money or gifts in exchange for marriage, for instance, he or she faces the threat of prison for up to one year. If no money or gifts change hands, the Austrian partner has to pay a fine. If, however, the Austrian partner feels remorse about having entered into this kind of marriage and turns him- or herself in before the authorities might investigate, no penalties arise for the Austrian. The foreign partner has to fear expulsion and, as the case may be, revocation of citizenship.

To understand the full scope of the debate and the official and public excitement about fictitious marriages, one has to look more closely at the statistics. As the organization FIBEL reported in their "Country Report Austria 2002," in 2000, 16.3 percent of marriages contracted in Austrian registry offices were binational in nature.[18] That number rose to 23.8 percent in 2002.[19] According to the magazine *Profil*, also citing official Austrian statistics, a combined total of 37,195 couples entered into marriage in 2003. Of them, 5,161 were marriages between Austrians and foreigners, making up around 13.8 percent of all new marriages in Austria that year.[20] Another more recent report in the Austrian magazine *News* states that in 2004, 8,496 marriages of a total of 38,528 marriages that were contracted in Austria happened between Austrian and non-EU members; in other words, 22 percent of all marriages entered into in Austria have occurred between Austrians and non-EU members. Given the fact, as it has been repeatedly announced by various news outlets—often citing Willfried Kovarnik, head of the foreigner police in Vienna—that an estimated 2,000 binational marriages each year in Austria are suspected to be "fictitious," anywhere between one fifth and one quarter of these marriages are under suspicion.[21]

In the Austrian press, where the issue of "fictitious" marriage has received growing attention, the stories about it have been told in very particular—and lopsided—ways. Most generally, reports usually focus on Austrian women who have married foreign men (rather than vice versa), even though the gender differential is not that high: 60 percent of all binational marriages are between an Austrian woman and a foreign man; 40 percent are between an Austrian man and a foreign woman.[22] Within the stories about the suspicious unions, the foreign male partners never receive much attention beyond their nationality (most of them are Turkish or Yugoslav), and interest in their lives or mention of their religion in particular—a topic that in other contexts has drawn ample attention, especially in connection with Turks in Europe—is largely absent.[23] A little more attention is paid to the middlemen who broker the "deal," although, again, the reader learns little other than their nationalities—which are rather diverse—and the savvy with which they do business.

Given the general attitude that these relationships cannot be considered "real" begs the question and leaves newspapers with the task of explaining what would prompt Austrian women to agree to such a marriage. Variously described as "in financial straits," "jobless, single, and desperate," as single mothers "with children and a burden of debts,"[24] or, more explicitly, as prostitutes, alcoholics, or drug addicts,[25] the women's despair is presented as the key factor motivating them to agree to marry third-country nationals. According to various reports, a fictitious marriage costs between 5,000 and 15,000 Euros, but the women are often short-changed by the middle men.[26] In an article about another bust of suspected fictitious marriage brokers, *Der Standard* reflected the general tenor present in other news articles and explicitly designated these women as "the victims."[27] Thus, despite their far superior legal standing *vis-à-vis* their foreign husbands, it is the Austrian women—rather than their foreign husbands—that are pitied and in need of compassion. A 2005 article in *Profil* about the (then) impending changes in foreigner law, particularly as they targeted fraudulent binational couples, illustrates most clearly the dominant framework for the fictitious marriage narrative even as it also acknowledges the problems inherent in it.

Profil provided for its readers what the head of the Vienna foreigner police confirmed was the "classic case" of a fictitious marriage. The young woman, who had agreed to not one but two marriages with foreigners for the purpose of providing them with legal papers, was addicted to heroin. She had quit her apprenticeship as a painter and had little hope of finding gainful employment again because of a visual impairment she had sustained when she was the victim of a hit-and-run. As the article put it, "she helped [these men]—also to help herself"— financially.[28] When her second husband demanded that she sign an ever-increasing number of legal documents, she had the marriage annulled despite being massively threatened by the marriage broker's body-guards. The article also provided further examples of the suspicious nature of binational marriages by citing the Justice Minister Karin Miklautsch's fear that the number of fictitious marriages could be "considerable" (*beträchtlich*), given that "in Vienna alone 60 percent of all marriages are between people where at least one of the partners is not Austrian." (Interestingly, marriages between foreigners in Austria were counted in this statistic as well, thus seriously inflating the figures of potentially unsavory unions.) The article's subsequent assertion that there is "no marriage mafia" at work in Austria or that the investigations by foreigner police are informed by ethnic and gender bias ("Hardly anybody asks about the reasons why a fifty year-old Austrian would marry a nineteen year-old woman from Thailand") relativized its opening story, but was still secondary to the grand narrative of the destitute woman that *Profil* set in scene so effectively. Certainly, some Austrian women in these relationships were also victims; however, by making this the dominant narrative, all women married to third-country nationals (and their relationships) becme suspect in this way.

Moreover, inherent in the news coverage is an apparent inability to imagine that desire and love for these men is a real possibility. When papers made pronouncements in their headlines like "Great Love Only an Illusion," or "6,000 Marriage Partners Lie When They Say 'Yes,'" or, as the report from *Die Presse* at the opening of this article stated, that "2,000 marriages are not based on love" (that is, only those that are binational and suspected of being fictitious), binational marriages were overtly being condemned as illegitimate partnerships of convenience, as commercial enterprises to circumvent laws.[29] That there might be marriages between Austrians that are also not based on love, and/or that financial considerations could be motives for intra-Austrian marriages as well, is simply elided.

Some of the articles that were published on fictitious marriages also drew—at times numerous—responses from readers.[30] Only one reader dared to comment jokingly that the greatest number of fictitious marriages surely exists *among* Austrians, and thereby implicitly challenged the very definition of the term. Mostly, those who criticized the rigid new foreigner law were concerned about the dangers it was going to pose for couples in "true" binational marriages, in other words, marriages based on love. Others worried about the law's implications when it came to proving the existence of real love. For example, one reader empathized that if her marriage were ever under suspicion, she "wouldn't even know the name of the toothpaste [her] loved one uses."[31] While opinions were overall split regarding the changes in the new law, there was near unanimity that a real marriage was first and foremost to be based on proper emotions. Neither side, in other words, condoned marriage for any reason other than love.[32]

Providing an insightful counter-narrative to the more typical media and popular assumptions, the Vienna street paper *Augustin* instead called these unions "protective marriages" (*Schutzehen*), acknowledging not only the legal precariousness of non-marital binational relationships, but also frankly revealing the hubris that migrants in Austria "are supposed to be the only ones not allowed to use a marriage license as a means to an end," and in this way exposing the questionable assumptions about marriage popularly applied as a yardstick to gauge the validity of binational marriages.[33] This double standard (making it both harder for binational couples to cohabit while also legitimizing their legal unions only if based on "real" love) becomes especially apparent when comparing it to figures on cohabitation and divorce in Austria more generally. In a 2003 press release, Statistik Austria declared that "Cohabition is Booming!" marking a rise in non-married couples from 7 percent in 1991 to 10 percent ten years later.[34] Equally informative is the fact that in 2003 almost one in two marriages in Austria (43 of 100) ended in divorce. While this marks an improvement of 4.4 percent over the previous year, it does not speak well for the strength of the institution.[35]

Binational partnerships, then, need to be understood in a multifaceted (inter)national political, legal, social, cultural, and ethnic context. According to FIBEL's 2003 annual report, foreign marriage partners of Austrian women come, first and foremost, from Turkey, followed by the various countries of former Yugoslavia (ranks second, fourth, and fifth) and Germany in third place.[36] This means that the vast majority of these binational partnerships have to contend with Austria's strict regulations in regards to third-country nationals. FIBEL itself has voiced criticism of the phenomenon, arguing that "binational couples marry much too fast."[37] However, this objection is not focused on the couple's decision to marry quickly, but on the *circumstances* that leave them with extremely limited choices and that force them to do so. The narrative about binational couples thus takes on a much different valence when considered from this angle—in particular the role of Austrian women within it undergoes a shift. Similar to *Augustin*'s reading of binational marriages as potentially "protective" marriages, FIBEL understands the Austrian women in these relationships as "rescuers." According to the organization, women's actions are oftentimes selfless and exhibit a willingness to marry quickly to ensure their partner's domicile in Austria and to take on the financial burdens that might arise due to the fact that their foreign partner's chances on the job market are less than ideal.[38]

So, while marriage alleviates some of the legal strains, it also engenders others, like an official investigation to which the couple might be subjected once married. Defended at times by the authorities as a protective measure for the "Austrian partner against marriage fraud," these probes further circumscribe what are deemed proper parameters of a marriage.[39] According to the website *Tu Felix Austria Nube* (a tongue-in-cheek reference to the marriage policy of the Habsburg monarchy) with its slogan "Marriage is Not a Crime," certain legal circumstances like the imminent denial for request of asylum or the immigrant's illegal status can be considered evidence for a fictitious marriage. However, much more subjective reasons based on cultural stereotypes can trigger an investigation as well, such as a considerable age gap between partners, if the partners speak different languages, or if they do not reside together. Last but not least, an investigation is initiated if the couple is reported to the authorities.[40]

Moreover, since the inception of the new "foreigner package" in January 2006, all marriages between Austrians and third-country nationals now have to be reported to the foreigner police. In addition, before the law reform it was possible for the foreign partner who had come into the country as an illegal or an asylum seeker to apply for a residency permit in Austria—which was usually granted—if he or she agreed to withdraw his or her application for asylum first. Now, hundreds of binational couples face the threat of "illegalization" through no fault of their own. Under the new law, all applications for residency have to be filed in the foreign partner's country of origin (which is insensitive and potentially very dangerous for those who fled their country fearing harm).[41] In other words, foreign partners who had applied for a residency permit in Austria in 2005 after they had gotten married (and therefore had legal standing), but whose application had not been processed before the new law took effect 1 January 2006, were now in the country illegally and had to fear being put into remand pending deportation. This fear indeed became reality for some in the wake of the new law. Rather than admit that a problem existed because the new law did not provide for an interim solution, the spokesperson for the Ministry of the Interior instead reiterated the legitimacy of taking those into custody who broke the law under the new ruling because no exceptions could be made "for 'old cases' [of fictitious marriages] from the previous year."[42] In a highly critical commentary that explicitly accused the Austrian government of racism, Doris Knecht in *Die Presse* not only explained the destructive nature of the new law by citing a case in which a Chinese wife in an "apparently intact [binational] marriage" was deported back to her native country as a result of the new foreigner law; she also noted that the husband—on top of this—was billed for the cost. Knecht further pointed to the highly problematic official stance of suspecting every binational marriage as potentially fictitious and the concomitant difficulty of "proving" one's love, especially after deportation of the foreign partner. Even as official policy is harshly condemned, insistence on love to validate a marriage informs Knecht's criticism as well.[43]

Ultimately, most of the concern about binational couples is focused on partnerships between Austrian women and foreign men—this is true in the case of the authorities and the media, as well as the advocates of international partnerships. Unions between Austrian men and their foreign partners, on the other hand, have not received nearly the same level of public and legal scrutiny. Certainly, gendered assumptions about interethnic relationships play a role here, so that age differences or the history of the relationship, for example, are left unquestioned. Another reason, however, has to do with the national and ethnic background of most of the female foreign partners in binational marriages, which has changed considerably since the late 1990s. While the home countries for both foreign husbands and wives were largely the same in earlier years (Germany, Turkey, and Yugoslavia), there has been a recent shift in national origin among the foreign female marriage partners. Since the late 1990s, they have come mainly from Romania, followed by Serbia and Montenegro, then Germany, Slovakia, and Poland. Turkish women now only rank in sixth place in binational marriages in Austria. Three among the top five nationalities (like Germany, Slovakia, and Poland) now enjoy EU privileges, which partly helps to explain the lower level of publicity these couples receive. Another reason given by FIBEL is that this shift indicates a "growing-together" of Europe and is the result of an increasingly expanding European job market. However, further study is needed to explore this shift in more depth.[44]

Overall then, the phenomenon of the fictitious marriage can offer us a more intimate look at Austrian national self-understanding. At the current juncture, it reveals assumptions about the nature of marriage and the place of love within it, and a striking unwillingness to admit the many layers informing love and matrimony no matter who the partners are. After all, a multiplicity of factors is currently exposing the complexity of marriage as an institution, such as the drive to legalize same-sex unions, the growing tendency for heterosexual couples to cohabitate rather than to marry, and the phenomenon of a growing number of binational marriages.[45] Even those fighting for the rights of binational couples base their arguments on a concept of marriage weighted with aspirations of love and companionship and mutual care and the "human right of marriage and family."[46] Marriage as an institution that also bestows legal privileges is, thus, located completely outside of this powerful set of associations that inform all facets of the debate. Given, then, that notions of love and desire occupy a central role in people's understanding of marriage, it is crucial to note that the media and the popular response point to the limits of reporters' and the public's capacity to imagine the possibility of genuine desire and affection in the context of interethnic relationships. Whether fantasies and anxieties of financially desperate or pathetic Austrian women and racist notions of undesirable foreign men are driving policy or whether such stories are being circulated in a deliberate attempt to justify policy is a question that must remain open.

Notes

1. Klaus Stöger, "Neues Gesetz: Kampf gegen Scheinehen verstärkt," *Die Presse*, 7 January 2006.

2. The EWR is made up of countries of the European Union as well as Lichtenstein, Norway, and Iceland.

3. "Neuer Scheinehe-Boom," *Kurier*, 30 August 1995.

4. See Rainer Münz, Peter Zuser, and Josef Kytir, "Grenzüberschreitende Wanderungen und ausländische Wohnbevölkerung: Struktur und Entwicklung," in *Österreichischer Migrations- und Integrationsbericht* (Klagenfurt: Drava Verlag, 2003), 25-30. For a very helpful overview on immigration in Austria, see also International Organization for Migration, ed., *The Impact of Immigration on Austria's Society: A Survey of Recent Austrian Migration Research* (Vienna, 2004), available for download at <http://www. emn.at/News-index-idc-30-topic-3.phtml>.

5. See August Gächter und Recherche-Gruppe, "Von Inlandarbeiter-Schutzgesetz bis Eurodac-Abkommen," in *Gastarbajteri—40 Jahre Arbeitsmigration*, ed. Hakan Gürsels, Cronelia Kogoi, Sylvia Mattl (Vienna: Mandelbaum Verlag, 2004), 41; also see See Münz et al., "Grenzüberschreitende Wanderungen," 26.

6. See Münz et al., "Grenzüberschreitende Wanderungen," 27. While the number of immigrants has at times risen since then, it never reached the level of the early 1990s. In fact, in the 2005 *Niederlassungsverordnung* determining the quotas, numbers were lowered once again to 7,500 (compared to 8,050 the previous year); 5,460 of those go toward family unification. One reason given for the lower numbers is the successful reduction of the backlog in family unification requests from previous years. See the announcement on the ÖVP's website at <http://www.oevp.at/sicherheit/artikel. aspx?where=11206>.

7. See Irene M. Tazi-Preve, Josef Kytir, Gustav Lebhart, and Rainer Münz, *Bevölkerung in Österreich* (Vienna: Österreichische Akademie der Wissenschaften, 1999), 76.

8. Dilek Çinar, "'Geglückte Integration' und Staatsbürgerschaft in Österreich," *L'Homme* 10, 1-2 (1999): 53.

9. See Karin König, "Das österreichische Migrationsregime von 1945 bis heute," *Vor der Information* 7/8 (1998), 153; cited in Çinar, "'Geglückte Integration,'" 54-55.

10. The waiting period was reduced to four years in 2002, and with the reform of the Residency Law in 2005, family members from third countries joining their relatives in Austria are now immediately given restricted access to the job market and full access after twelve months.

11. "Staatsbürgerschaft wird strenger," *Vienna Online*, 6 December 1995 <http://www.vienna.at/engine.aspx/page/vienna-article-detail-page/dc/tp:vol:oesterreich/cn/vol-news-egunz-20060222-070324/nav/prev> (accessed 8 March 2006).

12. See "Anhang E: Statistik zu binationalen Eheschließungen in Österreich im Jahr 2002," FIBEL, "Jahresbericht 2003 plus Statistiken," I, <http://www.verein-fibel.at/download.htm>.

13. See "Wer Wir Sind—10 Jahre Fibel," at <http://www.verein-fibel.at/10jahre.htm#> (accessed 8 March 2006).

14. "Scheinehe existiert nicht," *Öffentliche Sicherheit* 3 (1984): 17; cited in Renée Winter, "Migration kontrollieren?" in *Gastarbajteri—40 Jahre Arbeitsmigration*, ed. Hakan Gürsels, Cronelia Kogoi, Sylvia Mattl (Vienna: Mandelbaum Verlag, 2004), 55.

15. Winter, "Migration kontrollieren?" 55-56. Apparently, as the law is cited here, it still held particular gender connotations, declaring a marriage null and void if it served only to help the *wife* obtain the husband's name or to gain the citizenship of her *husband's* country.

16. For an overview of an explanation of the legal changes in these laws, see Thomas Marth, Hans-Peter Doskozil, and René Bruckner, "Fremdenrechtspaket 2005," *Öffentliche Sicherheit* 9-10 (2005): 99-105.

17. Ibid, 103.

18. Verein Fibel, "Austrian Country Report 2002," <http://www.verein-fibel.at/download.htm>.

19. Ibid.; "Anhang E: Statistik zu binationalen Eheschließungen in Österreich im Jahr 2002," I.

20. Josef Barth, "Jetzt trau dich doch!" *Profil*, 10 March 2005, 33. Considering that this estimate is presumably based on figures that include marriages between Austrian and EWR members, in other words, unions that are much less likely to arouse the suspicion of the foreigner police, the rate of those suspected of fraud among Austrians and third-country nationals is even higher.

21. For a reference to the number of estimated fictitious marriages each year, see, for example, "Skandal um Scheinehen," *Salzburger Nachrichten*, 1 July 2003; Klaus Stöger, "Scheinehen: Unkomplizierte From der Schleppererei," *Die Presse*, 19 October 2004; "Jagd auf falsche Bräute," *News*, 15 December 2005; "Härtere Gangart gegen Scheinehen," *Kurier*, 5 January 2006.

22. See "Härtere Gangart gegen Scheinehen," *Kurier*, 5 January 2006.

23. In the Federal Republic, relationships between German men and foreign (guest-worker) women have been similarly treated as a non-issue in the German press. See Julia Woesthoff, "Industrial and Loyal: Ideal Workers, Ideal Wives, 1960-1966," in "The Ambiguities of Anti-Racism: Representations of Foreign Laborers and the West German Media, 1955-1990," Ph.D. diss, Michigan State University, 2004, 73-86.

24. "Skandal um Scheinehen," *Salzburger Nachrichten*, 1 July 2003; "Jagd auf falsche Bräute," *News*, 15 December 2005.

25. See, for example, Klaus Stöger and Heinz Müller, "Justiz: Scheinadoptionen werden erschwert," *Die Presse*, 22 April 2004; Oliver Jaindl, "Einwanderungsstrom durch die Hintertür," *Kurier*, 4 October 2004; "Eine Scheinehe kostete 7000 Euro—Sex kostet allerdings extra," *Kurier*, 12 March 2005.

26. See, for example, "Härtere Gangart gegen Scheinehen," *Kurier*, 5 January 2006; Klaus Töger, "Scheinehen: Unkomplizierte Form der Schlepperei," *Die Presse*, 19 October 2004; "Skandal um Scheinehen," *Salzburger Nachrichten*, 1 July 2003.

27. "Neun Scheinehen-Vermittler in Wien ausgeforscht und angezeigt," *Der Standard*, 21 February 2006.

28. Barth, "Jetzt trau dich doch!" 32.

29. Gertraud Walch, "Große Liebe nur zum Schein," *Kurier*, 21 January 2006—note the double entendre in the headline; 6000 Ehepartner lügen beim 'Ja,'" *Kurier*, 30 August 1995; Klaus Stöger, "Neues Gesetz: Kampf gegen Scheinehen verstärkt," *Die Presse*, 7 January 2006.

30. See, for example, online letters to the editor about the issue of *Scheinehen* in *Die Presse* <http://www.diepresse.com/Artikel.aspx?channel=p&ressort=i&id=539054&archiv=false>, as well reader responses to "Ehe-Betrugsfälle in Linz aufgeflogen," *Der Standard*, 12 May 2003 and "Neun Scheinehen-Vermittler in Wien ausgeforscht und angezeigt," *Der Standard*, 21 February 2006 (both at <http://www. standard.at>).

31. Susi Stattnam, "Lesebrief in Response to 'Ehe-Betrugsfälle in Linz aufgeflogen,'" 12 May 2003, <http://www.standard.at> (accessed 25 February 2006).

32. Gerd Sängerin, "Leserbrief: Schein und Sein," 14 February 2006, <http://www. diepresse.com/Artikel.aspx?channel=p&ressort=i&id= 539054&archiv=false> (accessed 4 March 2006).

33. Katharina Osoma, "Liebe und die Fremdenpolizei," *Augustin*, 10 no. 168 (2005); Tina Leisch, "Der letzte Sommer der freien Liebe," *Augustin* 7, no. 163 (2005).

34. "Lebensgemeinschaften boomen!" *Statistik Austria*, 3 August 2003; <http://www. statistik.at/cgi-bin/pressetext.pl?INDEX=2003127_txt>.

35. "Scheidungsrate weiter rückläufig. 43 von 100 Ehen enden vor dem Richter," 3 June 2004, <http://www.statistik.at/cgi-bin/pressetext.pl?INDEX=2004001541>.

36. FIBEL, "Anhang E: Statistik zu binationalen Eheschließungen in Österreich im Jahr 2002," III.

37. Ibid.; "Anhang B: Statistik zu binationalen Eheschließungen in Österreich im Jahr 2001," in *Jahresbericht 2002*, B IV.

38. Ibid.; "Austrian Country Report 2002."

39. Ibid.; "Bericht zur Situation bikultureller Paare 2000," 21, <http://www.verein-fibel.at/download.htm>.

40. The home page is at <http://www.8ung.at/traudich/index.htm>. Information about the investigation of "fictitious" marriages can be found at <http://www.8ung.at/traudich/heiraten.htm#5a>.

41. Irene Brickner, "Hunderte Ehepaare in Angst vor 'Illegalisierung,'" *Der Standard*, 4 February 2006.

42. Ibid.; "Binationale Paare: Erste Schubhaftfälle," *Der Standard*, 2 March 2006.

43. Doris Knecht, "Quergeschrieben: Beweisen Sie uns doch mal Ihre Liebe," *Die Presse*, 30 March 2006.

44. FIBEL, "Jahresbericht 2003," III.

45. See, for example, George Chauncey, *Why Marriage: The History Shaping Today's Debate over Gay Equality* (New York: Basic Books, 2004); Göran Therborn, *Between Sex and Power: Family in the World, 1900-2000* (New York: Routledge, 2004); Stephanie Coontz, *Marriage, a History: From Obedience to Intimacy, or How Love Conquered Marriage* (New York: Viking, 2005).

46. Austrian Thailand Portal, "Fremdengesetz Neu: Niederlassungs- und Aufenthaltsgesetz NAG 2005," <http://thailand.8ung.at/fremdengesetz.html> (accessed 12 March 2006).

II. FORUM

Memory Boom:
The "Year of Reflection" 2005

After the Game is Before the Game:[1]
A Review of the 2005 Commemorations

Katharina Wegan

Sixty years since liberation, fifty years since the signing of the State Treaty, ten years of EU membership. One has to expect that the so-called anniversary year of 2005 will bring a surge of historical distortions and jingoism, of victim myths and assorted constructions of national identity to Austria. As the seventieth anniversary of the events of February 1934 has shown, there was no comprehensive debate of Austro-fascism and its continuity in the present. Instead, the discourses of politics, media, and society shifted to the right. This is a symptom of two periods of office of the ÖVP/FPÖ administration, which since 2000 has been engineering a thorough integration of neo-liberal and nationalist orientations. For the anniversary year of 2005, a further hegemonic stabilization of these policies must be expected.[2]

The activists of the platform "Austria 2005: A Protection Kit against a Year of Homeland Celebrations" (better known as "Austria minus 2005"[3]) alerted to a reinforced jingoistic patriotism in the run-up to the so-called "*Gedankenjahr*" (Helene Maimann).[4] They wanted to be prepared in time to answer any construction of a "homeland of great sons" as mentioned in the Austrian National anthem, exploiting conservative icons (from Leopold Figl and Julius Raab to Alois Mock and Wolfgang Schüssel).[5] But less "suspicious" persons like journalist Barbara Coudenhove-Kalergi deplored a patriotism demanding a univocal sense of belonging as a kind of oath of disclosure. Following philosopher Rudolf Burger who considered producing an "ethos" as the only legitimate reason for anniversaries, it seemed to her that a kind of "Austria-ethos" was being established by an increasing use of Austria's national colors combined with traditional costumes and Austrian folk music in daily politics. Mountains, music, skiing, the Empress Sisi, the skiing star Hermann Maier, Wolfgang Amadeus Mozart, Leopold Figl, tourism, and organic food are clichés propagated as typically Austrian by the Austrian public broadcasting station ORF, the daily newspaper *Neue Kronenzeitung*, and the People's Party. Despite the criticism voiced by intellectual elites, these national images would be petrified in that *"Gedankenjahr 2005,"* she presumed.[6]

The Opening

Then the tsunami disaster in Asia's coastal regions shook the entire world. It seemed a poor augury for the anniversary year; celebrating when others were dying or barely surviving in extreme penury did not appear honest. Therefore, the government finally decided to integrate the funeral commemorations for the tsunami victims with the official 2005 opening ceremony taking place in the historical chamber of the Austrian Parliament on 14 January 2005. "Is it impudent to remember Austria, and in particular Vienna, in ruins sixty years ago in view of the pictures of the disaster area?" Wolfgang Schüssel asked and immediately answered in the negative:

[... A]ll political earthquakes on this continent also reached us; sometimes we even were in the epicenter: two world wars, a painful reconstruction, the Hungarian fight for liberty in 1956 [...], the construction of the Berlin Wall, the impact of the suppression of the Prague Spring, of the imposition of martial law in Poland, of the turmoil in Bucharest, the consequences of the crisis and war in the Balkans—all that had to be overcome and was eventually overcome.[7]

The tsunami had obviously facilitated once again what many of his predecessors had done: Wolfgang Schüssel drew an analogy between the natural disaster and National Socialism and World War II.

Surprisingly, such analogies provoked no outcry; the only exception being that of author Robert Menasse who criticized not only the government for linking both commemoration ceremonies, but also the opposition for stepping into the government's trap. "The message was: even in the aftermath of the biggest disaster one can arise from the ruins by the mean of solidarity and helpfulness, or was the message, rather, that fascism was a natural disaster after all, which befell, like a spring tide, completely unprepared people, who really could not have wanted that at all, took countless victims and devastated everything?" he asked, alluding to Austria's "victim myth."[8]

Flashback

The founding myth of the Austrian Second Republic is anchored in the "zero hour" (1945) and "hour one" (1955).[9] The Second Republic was first established on 27 April 1945 when a group of politicians around Karl Renner (1870-1950) and Leopold Kunschak (1871-1953) declared both Austria's independence and at the same time Austria's "annexation" by the Third Reich on 13 March 1938 as "null and void." This break of 1945 is preceded by one related date and followed by another one: the "Moscow Declaration concerning Austria"[10] by the foreign ministers of the USSR, the United States, and the United Kingdom on 30 October 1943, and the "State Treaty concerning the reestablishment of an independent and democratic Austria" on 15 May 1955. The days of "liberation" (27 April 1945) and "freedom" (15 May 1955) constitute benchmarks in the Austrian calendar of commemorative events. These dates symbolize the rebirth of both democracy and the Austrian state itself. Since 1955 (at least), Austrian (interpreting) powers have exploited the memory of this "double foundation" of the Second Republic. One of the first aims was to create Austrian self-confidence by assuring Austria's position as an independent and neutral state and by convincing those Austrians who lacked trust in it (and in particular in neutrality, which was criticized by its opponents as too high a price for freedom) that it was sound policy.

A sense of togetherness, however, never exists as a given emotion, but is constructed by means of strategies of imagination; symbols and political "liturgies"[11] make "the imaginary unseen bonds visible and, thus, politically effective."[12] Within the scope of historical-political "stagings," central events are re-enacted by returning to meaningful historical sites and activating their "sacral" aura. In such "repetitions" of historical events, new meanings are generated again and again—matching the new context every time—and at the same time practicing and actualizing present encodings by virtue of this iteration.[13] So commemoration ceremonies mostly serve to construct and strengthen the sense of togetherness and to legitimize current politics.

Austria's liberation and State Treaty anniversaries have consistently presented a welcome opportunity to legitimize the internal and external politics of the time. Once the Austrian State Treaty had been signed, the reasons for "liberation," "occupation," and "freedom" were willingly omitted. The emphasis has been put on the event that reestablished Austria's sovereignty and its consequences. The "hour one" of the Second Republic eclipsed even the "zero hour" of 1945 and the previous seven to ten years to such an extent that it formed the basis of Austrian national identity. The narrative followed the "typical" rhetoric of political speeches of the postwar period. The privations of the civilian population and the commitment of the "Austrian people" in the years of reconstruction after 1945 formed a paraphrase of the victim thesis. In general, however, the reconstruction and the industriousness of the Austrians after 1955, as well as Austrian neutrality and its mediation between East and West, dominated. At the same time, politicians' efforts after 1945 to get a State Treaty were assimilated with the myth of the "struggle for freedom" from 1938-1945 and interpreted as a contribution to Austria's liberation which the Allies had called for in the Moscow Declaration. With the help of such "inventions of tradition" (Eric Hobsbawm), the present, in which the population fully supported the desire of the politicians for state sovereignty, was positively represented and projected onto the National Socialist past. This narration led down the path of forgetfulness (especially concerning the involvement of Austrians in National Socialism) to a self-assigned victim status that allowed the self-portrait of an industrious and determined nation, which of its own accord had built up a new, peaceful country and now had taken its place in the community of nations recognized by the world powers.[14]

In the months following 15 May, this legitimate narrative of the past was concentrated in a symbolic picture: Leopold Figl (1902-1965) on the balcony of the Belvedere Palace, surrounded by his colleagues and representatives of the Austrian Federal Government, presenting the just signed State Treaty to the waving and celebrating masses below. It was the most reproduced photograph of this historic moment.

Today, we are confronted with it not only in places of remembrance like the "Consecrated Room for the Victims of the Austrian Struggle for Freedom," which since 1965 has been located in the left wing of the outer *Burgtor* on Vienna's *Heldenplatz*. We also find it, for example, on the cover of popular documentaries and academic publications such as the fourth volume of the *Austria II* series edited by Hugo Portisch and Sepp Riff and the second volume of the textbook *Austria in the Twentieth Century* by Rolf Steininger and Michael Gehler.[15] It apparently came to symbolize the Second Republic itself. It is clearly attached to an identifiable moment of (re-)cognition.[16] In the memories of many people—as Willi Resetarits admitted in an interview in 2003—the sound and pictures of the *Wochenschau* were mixed: Leopold Figl's "Austria is free!", shouted from off-screen, is still ringing in the ears of those looking at the balcony picture:

Today it seems to me that I did hear Leopold Figl's "Austria is free!"
then. But in reality, he didn't say it on the balcony but in the room
behind it. On the balcony, he only presented the signed State Treaty.
But we have heard this eternal phrase so often that all of us, who were
in Belvedere Park or even in the vicinity, think we really heard it. And
today even I have this impression. I, who was standing on a tall building where I could barely see the balcony of the Belvedere.[17]

The picture of the balcony scene is thus stamped on the visual
memory of Austrians. It has taken on various meanings since 1955.
First, the narrative of the "Austrian struggle for freedom," substantiated
by pointing to those few people who had resisted the NS regime, was
exploited in an opportunistic way by the political elites in their representations of Austria to the occupation powers. This narrative has also
included the self-assertion of the Austrian "*Ständestaat*" against the pan-
German "Third Reich" and likewise the "anit-fascist resistance" of the
communist and socialist parties against "Austro-fascism." However, in
this narrative the "Austrian struggle for freedom" continued after
1945—this time against the occupation powers. In this way, the
politicians who achieved the signing of the State Treaty became
"Austrian freedom fighters," even though they never had to risk their
lives in this struggle.

The second narrative deals with Austria's role as a mediator between East and West in the Cold War, referring back to the old Habsburg
ideas of "Austria's cultural mission" and of Austria as the "intellectual
center of Europe." Already in the *Wochenschau* Special Edition from
October 1955 (no. 44/55), the commentary linked this mediating role
with Austria's neutrality. Later, this narrative would be reproduced in a
strikingly similar manner on the occasions of the anniversaries of the
State Treaty in 1965 (in the middle of the escalation of the Vietnam
War), in 1980 (during the Afghan Crisis), and in 1985 (in the context of
the Ministers of the Council of Europe that coincidentally met to discuss
questions of human rights). As a result, this narrative became part of the
nation's collective consciousness.

After 1985, however, the balcony scene was losing its attractiveness. As a consequence of the debate on Kurt Waldheim's service in
the *Wehrmacht*, historian Robert Knight and others showed the State
Treaty as being a product of the victim thesis.[18] The signatory powers
also did not see any reason to send a signal for their "willingness for
peace" and "understanding among peoples" based on the State Treaty
after the fall of the Iron Curtain and the collapse of the Soviet Union
(1989-1990). The State Treaty appeared to lose its significance under
these conditions. The balcony picture no longer functioned as a sign for

"freedom," "patriotism," or "peace mediation" in this new era of revised orientation and positioning. The print media used it to illustrate the virulent annual debates surrounding 15 May about the validity of the State Treaty and neutrality, which have been associated with discussions about Austria's accession to the EC/EU since the 1990s. In this new context, this photographed historical moment apparently lost its legitimizing function and its significance for both present and future.

It was Wolfgang Schüssel who first re-appropriated the old codings of "freedom" and "patriotism" in his "State of the Union" address on 15 May 2000, which was overshadowed by the so-called "sanctions" of the EU member states against the People's Party/Freedom Party Coalition.[19] This resurrection of old codes by the People's Party, however, had something anachronistic about it. Numerous commentators in Austrian (and German) newspapers humorously noted that on the forty-fifth anniversary of the State Treaty, Benita Ferrero-Waldner and Wolfgang Schüssel rhetorically climbed onto the "pedestal of Figl and Raab."[20] The former foreign minister and the federal chancellor called for a fight against the "inner occupation powers" of "comfortability, lack of courage, aversion to decision, greed, and the struggle to retain entrenched privileges, as well as against the so-called 'sanctions' of the EU partner nations."[21] In this way, they placed themselves and the People's Party in the (invented) tradition of "patriotism" and the "Austrian struggle for freedom" of the so-called fathers of the State Treaty. The opposition replied to this with the equally invented tradition of "antifascist resistance" and also by interpreting "EU sanctions" against Austria as the international protest which one had wished for in 1938. Thus, the "Austrian struggle for freedom" and the "antifascist resistance" faced one another as two different encodings of Austrian patriotism.

This reactivation of old narratives considered more or less obsolete since the "Waldheim debate" indicated a revival of the victim theory. Wolfgang Schüssel spoke, thus, in an interview with the *Jerusalem Post* of Austria as "the first victim of the Nazi regime," even though he acknowledged that Austrians have "a moral responsibility" for their past.[22] In addition, politicians of the Freedom Party did not hide their rather revisionist ideas of the Nazi past. But whatever they said, the federal chancellor remained silent and did not even distance himself from these statements. The perspectives on the past were obviously shifting.

In 2005

In 2005, the balcony scene once again became almost omnipresent, and it soon turned out that the anniversary of the State Treaty would stand in the center of interest. A team of historians (Stefan Karner, Manfried Rauchensteiner, Wilhelm Brauneder, and Karl Scholz) affiliated with the People's Party, the Freedom Party, and the Social Democrats were given the task of organizing an official State Treaty exhibition at the *Künstlerhaus* in Vienna. However, even after it had been cancelled (for budgetary reasons according to Secretary of Education Elisabeth Gehrer), the focus did not change. State Secretary for Cultural Affairs Franz Morak, and his *Planungsbüro 2005* (directed by *Presse* journalist Hans Haider), charged with the coordination of the anniversary (*Gedankenjahr 2005*), named as main points of the commemorations the establishment of the Austrian Second Republic and the end of World War II (sixty years ago), the signing of the State Treaty (fifty years ago), and Austria's entry into the European Union (ten years ago)—besides the anniversaries of the Federation of Austrian Trade Unions, the Austrian Armed Forces, the re-opening of the State Opera and the *Burgtheater*, and the public broadcaster ORF:

> The year 2005 stands not only for multiple memories; it also is on the threshold of the future: Austria is crossing it after the enlargement of the European Union in 2004 and is looking forward to its EU presidency in 2006. This is the reason why we remember not only the end of World War II sixty years ago and the signing of the State Treaty fifty years ago, but also the need to redefine our role in enlarged Europe. Thus 2005 is a year of taking stock between Austrian past and future, remembrance and expectancy, on the threshold of a new Austrian self-image.[23]

Teresa Indjein and Andrea Sutter, charged with editing the official 2005 reader, outlined the government's ideas concerning the *Gedankenjahr 20005*: the year of commemorations should strengthen a "new" self-consciousness and should guide Austrians into the future, in particular towards Austria's EU presidency in 2006. The look back was supposed to include thankfulness to the reconstruction generation and pride in their achievements. It should thus provide a self-image composed of creativity in dealing with problems, of the commitment to peace (from Nobel Peace Prize laureate Bertha von Suttner, 1843-1914, to Austria's neutrality and engagement in the European Union), of successes in culture as well as in economy, of the beautiful landscape and its protection, and last but not least of a sense of humor.[24] The 2005 reader painted a "success story" lasting sixty years and describing the Austrian qualities that would enable citizens to continue it. It also mentioned a (joint) moral responsibility for the "horrors of the twentieth century."[25]

This "success story" actually is a new variant on the "victim" and the "reconstruction myth." It now includes the acceptance of a (joint) responsibility for—supposedly Nazi—crimes. However, sixty years after the Allies' victory over the "Third Reich," this admission seems to be fuelled by opportunism rather than signifying a voluntary commitment to Nazi victims. On the one hand, the general European perspective on the Nazi past and, thus, Austria's position as a member of the European Union require a "politically correct" engagement with the past. On the other hand, sixty years after the victory over the "Third Reich" only a few contemporary witnesses are still alive. Thus paying compensation now seems advantageous in budgetary terms and for strategic reasons alike.[26]

Some political speeches given at official commemorations indicated this slight change in the hegemonic narration of the past. However, Austrian Nazi past and moral responsibility were only brought up on anniversaries of the liberation of the Auschwitz and Mauthausen concentration camps. At the United Nations' commemoration ceremony on 27 January 2005, State Secretary Franz Morak, for instance, gave a rather clear statement of "Never Again" and committed Austria to compensation and to fighting against anti-Semitism, racism, and xenophobia. But in retrospect, this "Never Again" and also the commitment to fighting against racism and xenophobia appeared rather hypocritical, or at least opportunistic. First, one year later and after the United Nations had designated 27 January as the International Holocaust Remembrance Day,[27] no official ceremony for the liberation of Auschwitz took place in Austria, even though it currently holds the EU presidency. Austria celebrated Mozart's 250th birthday instead and chose this date for the conference "Sound of Europe," discussing "fundamental questions as to the future of Europe, European values, identity and culture."[28] Actually, 27 January is a reminder of the most radical antithesis to the values of democracy and human rights upon which the European Union is based. Thus the link between Mozart's birthday and the conference discussing European values, identity, and culture seems rather astonishing.[29]

Second, by half-time of the *Gedankenjahr 2005,* the Austrian market research institute IMAS published the survey "World War II perceived by Former Enemies." According to this study, 49 percent of Austrians would prefer to stop discussing Nazi crimes during World War II.[30] The study's finding provoked Michael Fleischhacker, for instance, to demand a focus on the future instead and de-criminalization of those who wished for an end of discussions about the past.[31] His editorial can be considered a symptom of the skepticism shown towards history that was also expressed by Rudolf Burger, philosopher and confident of Wolfgang Schüssel.[32] From this point of view, dealing with the past is considered useful as long as it provides bearings for the future, but it must not constrain society, "There are memories providing options for the future [...] neither because they suggest imitating the past nor because they function as a warning sign, but because they make clear what else could be done."[33] Here philosopher Konrad Paul Liessmann was obviously pleading for the famous "*Schlussstrich*," literally translated as "final stroke," meaning coming to terms with the past. "So much future is not fortuitous," stated Barbara Tóth in the daily newspaper *Der Standard* referring to the *Zukunftsfonds* (Fund for the Future), which should link "the efforts of coming to terms with the Nazi past with the future."[34]

The debate on the *Schlussstrich* has to be considered in the context of other debates about the past: incidents like a neo-Nazi demonstration on Vienna's *Heldenplatz* on 13 April 2002, and clashes with counter-demonstrators, a commemoration ceremony organized by neo-Nazi and nationalist fraternity members sympathizing with the Freedom Party on *Heldenplatz* in Vienna on the occasion of the anniversary of the end of World War II on 8 May 2002. Ewald Stadler's (FPÖ) statement in 2003 that Austria had been liberated in 1955 (instead of in 1945 by the Allies) preceded this *Gedankenjahr 2005*, but the People's Party usually adopted a defensive or at least indifferent stance, and Chancellor Schüssel kept silent in such cases. Therefore, the emphasis on the future has been understood as indicative of a desire for the *Schlussstrich*.

Third, in springtime 2005 the motion to rehabilitate deserters from the *Wehrmacht* proposed by the Green Party in 2002 was debated anew in parliament.[35] This debate reached a new peak when Siegfried Kampl, deputy of the Federal Council (BZÖ), declared deserters from the *Wehrmacht* to be killers of their own comrades. He said he was was committed to facing the past, but "[...] then we have to face really all parts of the history," meaning also the "persecution of Nazis" in the postwar period.[36] Only a few days later, John Gudenus, also deputy of the Federal Council (FPÖ), in an interview suggested an examination of whether there really were gas chambers in the Third Reich. Later he backpedaled, saying that "there were gas chambers, although not in the Third Reich, but in Poland."[37] These statements provoked a general outcry and overshadowed the sixtieth anniversary of the Austrian Second Republic.

In his address on the occasion of the commemoration festivities, Federal President Heinz Fischer stated that historical debates were necessary and that politicians had to know about the past in order to be able to make decisions for the future.[38] Even the federal chancellor, who used to keep silent in such cases, by then distanced himself from revisionist ideas.

"How can we make this 'Never Again,' which had been the resolution of the founders of the republic, an unwritten fundamental law of this republic and of this new Europe?" he asked and answered:

> The victims of this horror have to be named: 100,000 Austrians died in concentration camps or in captivity, most of them Jewish. Many had to die for their political and religious beliefs, thousands of Sinti and Roma, and sick and disabled were murdered; 50,000 civilians were killed; 100,000 political prisoners lost years of their lives; 250,000 soldiers were killed, 250,000 came back from war badly injured and mutilated, and 500,000 prisoners of war had to wait for their return home in the following years because this war had been started [...]. And it appears a ghastly parallel that the number of victims—about 400,000 Austrians—reflects the number of perpetrators—nearly half a million of Nazis and their sympathizers. Thus, it seems clear to me and hopefully to all of us, that those who deny the atrocities of the regime and the existence of concentration camps and gas chambers, have no place in our institutions [...] especially in this country, which had resisted Hitler and National Socialism longer than any other country, but in which many, too many, have become guilty [...]. On this day of recollection, we owe respect to the founding ideals of the new Austria, and we have to remember them. There were new parties, new programs which avoided the mistakes of the past.[39]

Wolfgang Schüssel did not distinguish the victims, but listed them as one group among others, regardless of the reasons for their suffering or their engagement. It also seemed to his critics rather curious that his voice was breaking with emotion:

> What unbalanced Schüssel? The FPÖ-politician Gudenus has already doubted the existence of the gas chambers [...]. In front of Schüssel in the Redoutensaal there sat Jörg Haider who had praised the *Waffen-SS* [...]. In the back sat the deputy of the Federal Council, Siegfried Kampl, former member of the FPÖ, now of the BZÖ, who considered himself as a victim of a brutal persecution of Nazis after 1945 and loudly affirmed it when leaving the hall. The FPÖ/BZÖ put those people into "our institutions." The Federal Chancellor knew it. But right on this day of celebration [...] his voice was breaking with emotion."[40]

Because Schüssel usually kept silent and because it had not been the first lapsus of the FPÖ/BZÖ, his critics considered Wolfgang Schüssel a hypocrite. John Gudenus' and Siegfried Kampl's statements bore little consequence for them, for Siegfried Kampl in particular. He cannot assume the (rotating) presidency of the Federal Council anymore, whereas John Gudenus only now is going on trial for his revisionist statements. But he remained deputy of the Federal Council until the elections for the Viennese parliament in October 2005, and Siegfried Kampl still is a deputy of the Federal Council.[41]

Actually, this lack of immediate consequences seemed unacceptable to many critics. They stated that the administration had failed because it did not discourage such statements.[42] Linguist Ruth Wodak, for instance, pointed out keeping silent even for strategic reasons could be counterproductive, "One cannot come to terms with the past by keeping silent; *Schlusstriche* have to be justified and argued comprehensibly and rationally. In this case, this means that such statements by high functionaries have to be condemned publicly and that they have to distance themselves from them once and for all. There is an end to it!"[43]

Compared to the reactions to John Gudenus' and Siegfried Kampl's statements, the quick arrest of the British Holocaust denier David Irving on 20 November 2005 and his sentence to serve three years in jail three months later appeared as though Austria was changing its policy in regard to this matter. However, a discussion about the "usefulness" of the *NS-Verbotsgesetz* from 1945, prohibiting (neo-)Nazi activities in Austria, has flared up. Opponents of this law considered revisionism and Holocaust denial as "opinion offense." Sociologist Christian Fleck, for instance, argued that putting Holocaust deniers like David Irving on trial instead of perpetrators of Nazi crimes still enjoying freedom like Aribert Heim or Milovoj Asher is not worthy of a liberal democracy.[44] Moreover, those who thought this law necessary apparently assumed that people today would blindly follow a "crude thesis of such a fool like Irving."[45] Actually, the opponents of this law proscribing Nazi activities have not considered that the Holocaust denial is similar to the tale of ritual murder (*Ritualmordlegende*) and, thus, is a type of hate speech (*Hassparole*) as writer and historian Doron Rabinovici stated.[46] Besides, neither have they borne in mind Clause 9 of the State Treaty which commits Austria to proscribing any Nazi activity, nor international law. The condemnation of Nazism indeed constitutes a part of the (judicial) foundation of the Austrian Second Republic as well as of the United Nations.[47] Therefore, the *NS-Verbotsgesetz* can be seen as a ju-dicial symbol of the "Never Again" to which Wolfgang Schüssel referred on the Republic's anniversary.

On 15 May, these shadows of Austria's Nazi past had seemingly dwindled. The politicians neither mentioned John Gudenus nor Siegfried Kampl on the occasion of the official ceremony at the Upper Belvedere. Only Austria's reconstruction and economic boom after 1945—especially after 1955—and the Allies'—particularly the United States'—contribution stood in the center of their speeches:

You [the signatory countries] not only gave us freedom with the State Treaty, but you also had faith in Austria. And we, we did not bury this credit, as the Bible says, but we repaid the credit of 15 May 1955 in multiple ways to the world. The Marshall Plan of the Americans helped us very much to make Austria a prospering country. This country, which, in 1945 and the following years, was experiencing hunger, penury, privation and devastation [...] today exports and imports annually goods worth 25 billion Euros alone from the four signatory countries. It was worthwhile. And today you can see the political faith you invested in us embodied in Vienna's UNO city, in the OSCE headquarters, and in the future Human Rights Agency of the European Union. We returned the freedom you gave us in the form of the international aid program *Nachbar in Not*. We took in hundreds of thousands of refugees. We used the new autonomy also to pay compensation, though sometimes very late. For one and a half decades, we have used the chance Austria was granted fifty years ago to lobby for our neighbors and for their integration into Europe. The neutrality chosen by us was never meant to keep us aloof; we participated in UN and EU peacekeeping missions in the Balkans.[48]

The government wished to turn the fiftieth anniversary of the State Treaty into "a red-letter day," with celebrations of Austria becoming "part of a new Austrian self-confidence," and to stop criticizing negative aspects that day.[49] Thus a folklore fair with music of the last five decades and talks with contemporary witnesses took place in the park of Belvedere Palace, climaxing in a reenactment of the famous balcony scene. It was intended to symbolize the "success story" told by Wolfgang Schüssel and would be applauded by about 10,000 Austrians and tourists. It implied similarities between 1955 and 2005: new difficulties and crises have to be confronted, but the government will rise to meet these new challenges.[50] However, the festivities met with little approval. On the one hand, many newspaper articles complained that the mood for celebrating, the pathos, or nostalgia were lacking.[51] On the other hand, critics like historian Gerhard Jagschitz called them "opium" and "nasty fuss" and criticized that the government had missed the opportunity to "discuss very important questions of Austrian self-consciousness."[52]

Actually, no politician touched on the subject of bilingual topographical signs in Carinthia; only some activists reminded them of the
debt Austria owed its ethnic minority groups (*Volksgruppen*). This was
also politely ignored by the representatives of the signatory countries
who were present.[53] The debate about the failing implementation of
Article 7 of the State Treaty has reached a new peak, though. The erec-
tion of more bilingual topographical signs on 12 May 2005 should have
been a "birthday present"[54] to Austrian Slovenes. However, not all the
signs have been erected yet, and there is no agreement about how many
there should be.[55] Therefore, the debate continues; nowadays, Jörg
Haider is obviously using this subject for his campaign in the run-up to
the elections for the National Council in the fall of 2006.[56]

However, this debate reached a new dimension when Austrian
public broadcaster ORF blocked the airing of a documentary on the
matter. The film *Artikel 7—Unser Recht / Èlen 7—Naša Pravica!"*
(*Article 7—Our Right*) by Thomas Korschil and Eva Simmler (A/SLO
2005) focuses on the development of the *Ortstafelsturm* in 1972, when
Carinthian nationalists uprooted freshly erected bilingual topographical
signs. ORF and RTV Slovenija, the Slovenian public broadcaster,
contributed archive material and also made joint decisions with regard
to the film's content.[57] The film was meant to be aired on 4 December
2005. By then, ORF and Franz Grabner, directing the editorial department for documentaries, canceled it, claiming worries about violating
ORF's commitment to full objectivity.[58] Thomas Korschil and Eva
Simmler suspect political pressure caused this decision, for the film had
moved through ORF's standard screening procedures and had been
accredited without any objection.[59]

Actually, the debate on minority policy and its implementation is
inextricably linked with the question of national self-confidence. There
have been long continuities between denying minority rights and
allowing discrimination and non-integration of Slovenians in Austrian/
Carinthian society since the Austrian First Republic and the Nazi
regime, as Thomas Korschil pointed out in a recent interview. Eva
Simmler criticized the fact that the partisan fight and the Slovenian
minority's history are still unrepresented in school curricula. Scru-
tinizing the roots of this conflict is not only the film's purpose, but also
a means for discussing Austria's past and, thus, national identity.[60]

In the run-up to the jubilee year, Wolfgang Schüssel explained that,
fifty years after the signing of the State Treaty, its articles which were
not yet obsolete, like Article 7, became "our second nature" so that "we
made it a rule."[61] The widespread resistance to bilingual topographical
signs proved that he was not right, just as he was not right either when
in his address of 15 May 2005 he spoke of restitution and compensation

as if they were successfully closed chapters of the past. A heated debate flared up after a final decision reached by arbitration on the restitution of five paintings by Gustav Klimt (1862-1918) (among others the portraits *Adele Bloch-Bauer I* and *II*) to Maria Altmann, heir to Ferdinand Bloch-Bauer, on 15 January 2006. After six years of legal debate, Peter Rummel, expert in civil law and head of the appointed arbitrators, declared that the paintings had to be returned to the heirs.[62] This decision provoked a national outcry. Everybody was relieved that finally there was a decision, but questions arose as to whether the Austrian republic should try to buy the paintings or not. Gustav Klimt ostensibly has been turned into a national icon, and there was anxiety about "losing" his works. Arthur Rosenauer, head of the Department of Art History of the University of Vienna and member of the Austrian Fine Arts Commission for Restitutions, even spoke of a cultural downturn, "The paintings are part of the patrimony of our Republic [...]. These paintings are irreplaceable. The 'golden' *Adele Bloch-Bauer I*, along with *The Kiss*, is the most important opus of the *Österreichische Galerie* [Austrian Gallery] at the Belvedere."[63]

But, in fact, the question which touched Austria's self-consciousness was not whether or not the Klimt paintings would remain in Austria. Even though thousands of people waited in line to see them one last time after the government had decided not to buy them, Austrians mostly agreed both with the decision to return them to Maria Altmann and with the government's decision not to buy them back from Mrs. Altmann.[64] The emotional issue has been the way of dealing with the past which is linked with Austria's self-image. Therefore, Ilsebill Barta, art historian and former member of the Fine Art Commission of Restitutions, pleaded for buying back the portraits of Adele Bloch-Bauer, but as a meaningful highlight of a museum of the republic, where they could represent some of the many facets of Austrian history.[65]

Actually, the Altmann/Bloch-Bauer case can be considered as symbolic of Austrian restitution policy. After the arbitration decision, a political debate on the judicial interpretation of the Altmann/Bloch-Bauer case and the restitution law from 1998 flared up. The government's critics wondered why the Fine Arts Commission for Restitutions had not come to the same decision in 1999 as the arbitrators had in 2005; it seemed that they had interpreted the same documents differently.[66] The jurists of the Commission for Restitutions focused on Adele Bloch-Bauer's last will of 1923—she had asked her husband to give her portraits by Gustav Klimt to the *Österreichische Galerie* at the Belvedere after his death—and on the fact that these paintings were not part of the restitution action in the 1940. The arbitrators followed Maria Altmann's intentions and reasoning instead.

Since Ferdinand Bloch-Bauer had been persecuted and his posses-
sions expropriated by the Nazis, the Austrian Republic did not acquire
the paintings because of Adele Bloch-Bauer's will, but because of a
restitution agreement achieved with Gustav Rinesch, Ferdinand Bloch-
Bauer's heir's attorney, in 1948. In addition, the arbitrators criticized the
restitution law of 1998 because it limited the claims on spoiled property
which had already been the object of a restitution action, and they
pointed out that some objects probably were not claimed because of
"anticipatory obedience" (aus vorauseilendem Gehorsam).[67] In this way,
they considered this case not from a pure judicial point of view, but also
from an historical perspective.[68]

However, Education Ministry Elisabeth Gehrer only responded
rather tersely to the arbitration agreement, "Even though these five
paintings by Gustav Klimt represent prominent examples of Austrian
fine arts of the early twentieth century, the Republic will abide by the
arbitration agreement."[69] Her critics found missing any words of regret
for the unfair restitution policy of Austrian Second Republic since 1945
and have been wary about the administration's good will. Even though
Wolfgang Schüssel spoke in obviously proud terms about the resitution
policy (since 1998), not only on the occasion of the fiftieth anniversary
of the State Treaty, they have not been expecting a change of the restitution law in terms of the arbitration agreement.[70]

Holes in History

As long as the government had not decided for or against
purchasing the Klimt paintings, the Österreichische Galerie at the
Belvedere announced that "the restitution of these chief works by
Gustav Klimt represents an immense damage to Austria as a cultural
nation. Therefore, the Österreichische Galerie Belvedere greatly supports the acquistion of those paintings."[71] The label describing the Adele
Bloch-Bauer I portrait, however, contained neither an apology nor a hint
about the criminal restitution policy of the Austrian Second Republic
after 1945.[72]

These proceedings are, indeed, symptomatic of the way the past has
been handled during the Gedankenjahr 2005. Both portraits of Adele
Bloch-Bauer were shown in the State Treaty exhibition Das Neue
Österreich (The New Austria), for instance. However, the exhibit's
curators did not consider the restitution policy of Austrian Second
Republic worth mentioning. Only the text beneath the painting Adele
Bloch-Bauer I told its history, but from the administration's perspective.[73] The same has been true in regard to minority rights. Article 7 and
non-enforcement were never mentioned. Both topics represented blanks

in both of the semi-official State Treaty exhibitions, *Das Neue Öster-reich* and *Österreich ist frei (Austria is Free)*.

Official and semi-official statements and narratives during this jubilee year 2005 either omitted the dubious way Austrians have been dealing with their past after 1945 or integrated part of it into the Austrian "success story." However, a few exhibitions and comme-moration activities tried to fill those blanks; examples are the remar-kable exhibitions "*Heiss umfehdet, wild umstritten. ....*" *Geschichts-mythen in Rot-Weiß-Rot* ("*Hotly Contested ....*" *Historical Myth in Red-White-Red*) in the museum of the city of Villach in Carinthia and *Jetzt ist er bös, der Tennenbaum: Die Zweite Republik und ihre Juden* (*Now Tennenbaum is Upset: The Second Republic and its Jews*) in the Jewish Museum Vienna.

Werner Koroschitz and Lisa Rettl, both historians, understood their work as a clear statement against patriotic commemoration ceremonies and a revival of the "victim myth" in the context of the *Gedankenjahr*.[74] In "*Heiss umfehdet, wild umstritten ....*" they wanted to show the prevailing interpretation of the past since 1945 and to confront it with historical documents telling histories of minorities, especially of the partisans and Slovenes in Carinthia. Farewell letters of victims that died and their portraits in front of the museum drew passers'-by attention to the exposition and served as an emotional introduction to the subject. In the museum itself, a timeline of historical facts and documents showed continuities between the times before and after 1945 and contrasted them to various "myths" arising after 1945. In this way, Werner Koro-schitz and Lisa Rettl filled in the blanks of Austria's past and success-fully avoided turning the year 1945 into a "zero hour."

Curator Felicitas Heimann-Jelinek chose a different focus: the Second Republic's relationship to its Jewish citizenry. The title *Jetzt ist er bös, der Tennenbaum*[75] (taking a quotation from Helmut Qualtinger's and Carl Merz's *Der Herr Karl*, a satirical one-man play that reveals the perpetual opportunism of the Austrian *petit bourgeoisie* indicated the ironic character of the exhibition). Games juxtaposed with historical documents showed how easily former Nazis could continue their careers after 1945; how compromising parts of their past have been elided, even in encyclopedias that are supposedly "objective"; how difficult and frustrating it has been for Jews to get their property restored; and how strong and obvious anti-Semitism has been even after 1945.

Felicitas Heimann-Jelinek originally did not envision making a "critical contribution" to the jubilee year. Moreover, the idea for this exhibition arose after the People's Party/Freedom Party coalition had been formed in February 2000. Other incidents like the Austrian Science Fund's (FWF) refusal of a research project regarding the Nazi past by the Department of Musicology of the University of Vienna in 2000 and its argument that not enough time had passed to make critical research possible, caused Heimann-Jelinek to demand vehemently a critical exhibition.[76] The exhibition eventually took place during the anniversary year and presented, more or less unwillingly as far as the administration was concerned, a critical statement about the Second Republic's "success story" as it was told in 2005.

Both exhibitions explicitly tried to uncover "the hidden mirrors of the past"[77] emerging every now and then from the Austrian unconsciousness as demonstrated by the debates on bilingual topographical signs and the restitution of the five paintings by Gustav Klimt. For instance, the "Waldheim debate" has been resumed in a sophisticated way, whereas still current controversies over the Nazi past had been more or less willingly omitted both in *Das Neue Österreich* and *Österreich ist frei.*[78] Instead, both exhibitions told a "success story" and turned Austrians into heroes and heroines building a prosperous country out of ruins. The year 1945 represents a turning point. Before then, Austrian politicians and civilians had made mistakes and committed crimes, but they had learned from history and the Austrian Second Republic is the proof of that. However, this idea of the Second Republic as an antithesis to the Nazi regime and to the authoritarian and near fascist *Ständestaat* of the Austrian First Republic seems to imply that after 1945 everything had changed for the good, that the dream of a "New Austria" had eventually become true in 1955 with the signing of the State Treaty.

In this way, the State Treaty stood in the center of both exhibitions. The show at the Schallaburg Castle quoted this moment by choosing Leopold Figl's final sentence of his address, "Austria is free," as its title. Accordingly, the storyline culminated in the signing of the State Treaty. In the last room, the visitor was embraced by an almost holy atmosphere. The surroundings were modeled on the signing scene of 15 May 1955: a rococo table was arranged between a black silhouette adumbrating the balcony scene with Leopold Figl surrounded by his colleagues and representatives of the Austrian Federal Government on the balcony of the Upper Belvedere, and for about three weeks (from 15 April to 9 May), a showcase displayed the original treaty.

The original State Treaty clearly was the crowd-puller of *Österreich ist frei* and *Das Neue Österreich* alike. On the first weekend after its opening, *Österreich is frei* (15 April 2005) registered about 5,000 visitors who wished to see the original State Treaty. On the two preceding days, the treaty had been shown at the Belvedere Palace. There, too, people waited in line in order to catch a glimpse of it. Here, one could observe the power of the original document, but also how strongly and emotionally anchored the State Treaty still seems to be in Austrian memory. "For us Austrians, it is an absolutely important document," explained Gerbert Frodl, director of the *Österreichische Galerie*, on the occasion of the opening of *The New Austria*.[79]

Actually, *Das Neue Österreich* dealt with the *genius loci* of the Upper Belvedere. A neon sign over the balcony visible for miles depicted the territorial contours of Austria and, thus, indirectly emphasized the balcony scene. Behind the balcony, in the Marble Hall, the original document of the treaty was displayed in a kind of "shrine" (10/15 May to 27 May). The Marble Hall, the center of the *bel étage* of Prince Eugene's summer residence, represented also the heart of the exhibition: there were only a few exhibits so that the visitor's attention was directed to the State Treaty and to the freshly renovated frescoes by Martino Altomonte (1659-1745). Here, the storyline contained a break. After a chronological tour through Austrian history from the collapse of the Austro-Hungarian empire to the signing of the State Treaty, the Second Republic's history was told in thematical order: "Neutrality and the United Nations," "The Cold War and the Iron Curtain," "Identity," "Cliché and Reality," "Crisis and Prosperity," and "Austria in Europe." Visual representations of the Austrian flag throughout the exhibition signaled the State Treaty's importance for the Second Republic's rise.[80] The second part compared the (successful) Second Republic with the (abortive) First Republic, which was tormented by a lacking consensus about the character of democracy, about Austria's position in Europe, and about Austrian self-identity.[81] Fascism and National Socialism were its consequences—the flag accompanying this topic was not red-white-red anymore, but grey like the uniforms of the *Wehrmacht*. Little by little, it was rising again. At first, overshadowed by the flags of Allied occupation powers, but in the first decade after Austria's liberation in 1945, with the signing of the State Treaty, it started waving freely again.

Das Neue Österreich turned over a new leaf insofar as it integrated the "dark chapters" and social and political conflicts of Austrian history. One of the organizers' concerns was indeed to put the signing of the State Treaty in a broader context.[82] In this way, no prelude outside the exhibition had been necessary (such a prelude occurred at Schallaburg Castle where the victims of Nazi crimes were commemorated on the steps leading to the exhibition and the experience of war was symbolized by a swastika at its entrance). However, judgment was avoided: the hats of the paramilitary organizations in the First Republic, for instance, were arranged side by side; a brochure about the Civil War of 1934 by Julius Deutsch (1884-1968) could be seen next to a poster of Engelbert Dollfuß (1892-1934).[83] All sides appeared equally legitimate or illegitimate, no matter what they did. Thus current controversies regarding Austria's past were avoided.[84] An uninformed and unaware visitor could easily think that Austrians had come to terms with their past and would not think that the past is still affecting the present.

This impression was amplified by the choice of exhibits in the section "Occupation" (*Besatzungszeit*). The Allied occupation powers, the destruction caused by the war, the extreme penury, and the lot of ethnic Germans (*Volksdeutsche*) dominated this section. Only five items (out of more than seventy-three) like *Publication Nr. 1 of Registering National Socialists in Vienna* (*Kundmachung Nr. 1 über die Registrierung von Nationalsozialisten in Wien*) from 18 June 1945, or a photograph of the first war crimes trial at the Austrian People Courts in Vienna on 17 August 1945, indicated how the Austrian Second Republic had been dealing with its past.[85]

Even though *Österreich ist frei* told more extensively about deNazification than *Das Neue Österreich*, it likewise focused on destruction caused by the war, penury, and Austrian reconstruction efforts. The fate of minorities, like Jews or Slovenes, or controversies dealing with the past, like the "Waldheim debate" in 1986, were not brought up. In both exhibitions, Austrian history was presented as rather smooth. It seemed that curators had acted in accordance with the intention of the committee of *Das Neue Österreich* that no "self-adulation" but no "self-flagellation" either would appear in the exhibits, "commemorating in a joyful and thankful way, including the dark sides like Mauthausen," as Günther Düriegl, director of the exhibition team, explained,[86] referring to Viktor Frankl (1905-1997) who had pleaded, "Forgiving yes, forgetting no."[87]

However, neither have Frankl's reasons for this attitude ever been scrutinized, nor has the question whether he had been willingly misinterpreted by those wishing to forget and firmly to embrace the victim myth. Instead, *Das Neue Österreich* hailed him along with Rosa Jochmann (1901-1994) and Franz König (1905-2004) as "unimpeachable Austrians of our time."[88] Doubtless, there has been a certain reciprocity between the building of the "victim myth" and Viktor Frankl's concept of reconciliation.[89] Therefore, it had been rather reminiscent of the "victim myth" when Hannes Androsch, inaugurating the exhibition *Das Neue Österreich* at the Upper Belvedere together with Herbert Krejci and Peter Weiser, called the research on "brown [Nazi] stains" in the *Bund Sozialistischer Akademiker* (BSA)[90] a "stain cleaning action."[91] The big State Treaty exhibition should, thus, emphasize that the Austrian Second Republic has been a "success story," in particular when compared to the workhouse of the First Republic.[92]

At this point, the exhibition committee went along with the government. Franz Morak wished in the run-up to the anniversary year "that we know more about us, including the awareness that we live in a country worth living in. And that this self-confidence will help us to cope with future challenges. [Since anniversaries are a kind of] trampoline to the future [...] it is important to understand what it means to live in peace for sixty years."[93]

Strategies of Success

These State Treaty exhibitions and their history were actually para-digmatic for the government's remembrance policy that year. Initially, a team of historians affiliated with the People's Party, the Freedom Party, and the Social Democrats (Stefan Karner, Manfried Rauschen-steiner, Wilhelm Brauneder, and Karl Scholz) should have organized the official State Treaty exhibition at Vienna's *Künstlerhaus*. But from the very beginning, there were problems. The opposition and contemporary historians in particular disagreed with the government's choice of the exhibition team and expressed concerns about the intended way of representing Austrian history. For instance, leftwing politicians worried that the exhibition would focus on conservative politicians and that the contributions of social democrats would be omitted.[94] On the other hand, contemporary historians criticized the cumulative character of the exhibitions which would display a series of iconic events and lack structural as well as moral dimensions. Furthermore, they would have wished for a conference bringing together all departments of contem-porary history of Austrian universities from the very beginning. But when Manfried Rauchensteiner invited them at the last moment to discuss the exhibition concept, it seemed to them that the point was to integrate potential critics without fundamentally changing the concept.[95]

However, after the death of Peter Mahringer, general director of the Education Ministry who had been heavily involved in this affair, the government only reluctantly followed up this exhibition project and finally canceled it for budgetary reasons in September 2003.[96] It envisaged instead an overall plan including all commemoration projects, exhibitions, and events. State Secretary for Cultural Affairs Franz Morak and his *Planungsbüro 2005* (directed by *Presse* journalist Hans Haider) were charged with coordinating all anniversary activities. "We want to involve the whole country in this anniversary year which is so important to the history of the Second Republic. We want to draw a bow over the anniversary that spans all federal states, schools, museums, and cultural institutions,"[97] Franz Morak explained and further made clear that "[t]here will not be any imposed governmental interpretation of history. We are just raising issues, thereby allowing for discussions."[98] By calling on the "civil society" to take the initiative,[99] the government retreated to a coordinating position and ostensibly left the field open to other players. This strategy seemed like a maneuver intended to silence its critics.

Very soon after the government had backed out of the official project, Stefan Karner was appointed to organize a State Treaty exhibition for the province of Lower Austria honoring Leopold Figl and Julius Raab (1891-1964) as "fathers" of the State Treaty. Since his affiliation with the People's Party and his friendship to Chancellor Wolfgang Schüssel is well known, the opposition and critics of the administration objected to his nomination and once again worried that the Social Democrats' share in the achievement of the State Treaty would be diminished.[100] At the same time, Hannes Androsch, Herbert Krejci, and Peter Weiser initiated plans for the exhibition *Das Neue Österreich* at the Upper Belvedere. According to them, the signing of the State Treaty could not be commemorated anywhere else than at the place where it had been signed. They finally convinced the government and the city of Vienna to support this exhibition in a public-private partnership.[101]

Obviously, there was a whiff of the rivalry between *Das Neue Österreich* and *Österreich ist frei*. Therefore, the committee of *Das Neue Österreich* repeatedly stressed that their exhibition would not hide anybody's share in Austrian history nor recreate the signing scene (like *Österreich ist frei* did at the Schallaburg), but would contextualize the State Treaty in the political context of the twentieth century.[102] However, during the *Gedankenjahr 2005* this potential rivalry failed to materialize. "All these controversies which had been prophecied seem ridiculous today [...]."[103]

Actually, both exhibitions told a variant of the Austrian "success story." They focused on the postwar period of 1945-1955, on penury and destruction by the war, and on reconstruction under difficult conditions. The achievement of the State Treaty was presented as a climax and turning point, drawing a *Schlussstrich* under the tragic period of the Third Reich and making Austria's political and economical rise possible.[104] Furthermore, both exhibitions presented a history matching the experiences of the majority of Austrians and showed items evoking emotional (hi)stories, like personal souvenirs in *Österreich ist frei*, Russian Foreign Minister Molotow's broken and glued champagne glass in *Das Neue Österreich*, or the original document of the State Treaty in both exhibitions. Maybe this mainstream history was a reason for the exhibitions' success in terms of attendance (about 220,500 at the Schallaburg and about 310,000 at the Belvedere) as well as in (most) reviews.[105]

The mostly positive reviews in the media are indicative of a new consensus on Austrian history. The new "master narrative"[106] has integrated all controversies by easing them through. Whatever one's political or ideological stance and involvement were in the past, nobody would be judged. For instance, it has seemed satisfying that Andreas Khol, president of the National Council and "voice"[107] of the People's Party, admitted Engelbert Dollfuss had abrogated democracy in 1934, although he still defended his party's worship of Dollfuss as an anti-Nazi resistance fighter and as one of the Austria's first patriots.[108] More-over, this new "master narrative" focuses on the "success story" of the Austrian Second Republic. The year 1945 continues to be Austria's "zero hour,"[109] even though it has not always been intended as such.[110] For it omits the Austrian Second Republic's dealing with the past and how the past is still interfering with the present. The emphasis on the hard years of reconstruction from 1945 to 1955, on the State Treaty, and on the Second Republic's successful and prospering development after 1955 further amplifies this interpretation of history.

This "success story" is intended to instill patriotism among young people in particular. Hannes Androsch pointed out the purpose of *Das Neue Österreich*, "We want to convey patriotism to our descendants: you can be proud of what your parents and grandparents have built! You stand on a solid foundation. But now, it's your turn!"[111] It corresponded with Wolfgang Schüssel's speech held on the occasion of the opening of *Österreich ist frei*. In that speech, he once again stressed the success-ful rise of the Austrian Second Republic. Leopold Figl and Julius Raab, the "fathers of the State Treaty" served as examples: they were looking backwards only to learn from history how to cope with the future. The point of the commemorations was, according to the chancellor, to strengthen the values guiding Austrian society and to proceed in buil-ding the nation, for "Austria has set a great example. The state that nobody wanted in between the wars has turned into a country which all stand by [...] The country which did not have enough perspectives has turned into a successful country, a lighthouse serving as a beacon."[112]

A consensus has obviously been reached here, not over contro-versial chapters of the past, but over the Second Republic's "success story." Once again, this is exemplified by the well-known balcony scene: today it should cause Austrians to recall how they have used their freedom since 1955 for social and economical success. It is inextricably linked with the narrative of 1945 as the "zero hour" and with the updated victim theory. This narration should further patriotism and serve as a guide in the future. But in the context of the European Union, it clearly is intended to support Austria's position, at least during its EU presi-dency.

Conservative politician Andreas Khol deliberatedly admitted to agreeing with philosopher Rudolf Burger who defined the creation of an "ethos" as the anniversary year's purpose.[113] This "ethos" points to the future and stresses Austria's wish to engage in solving the problems of a globalized world. The past is of no consequence as long as it does not provide bad examples for the future. History has been pushed aside, reduced to a legitimizing function. Therefore, it has not been important to reach a consensus about the sore spots of the past.[114] The red-white-red flags, which led visitors through *Das Neue Österreich* exhibition, will soon serve as a unifier of Austrian patriotism and self-confidence[115]—at least in the run-up to the elections to the Austrian Parliament. Perhaps they will also guide visitors in a "House of History" (*Haus der Geschichte*), which Hannes Androsch is advocating and which Wolfgang Schüssel has recently requested,[116] in order to make the invisible bond visible. The *Gedankenjahr 2005* has passed, but already the next round has begun with Austria's EU presidency.[117]

Notes

1. Martin Wassermair, "Nach dem Spiel ist vor dem Spiel: ÖVP und Bundeskanzler gehen nach dem Jubeljahr in die EU-Verlängerung," *Kulturrisse* 0405 (December 2005): 40-43.

2. *Austria 2005: A Protection Kit against a Year of Homeland Celebrations.* <http://oesterreich-2005.at/english/> (accessed 10 February 2006).

3. Cf. St. Gr., "Die Minus-Republik," *profil*, no. 49, 29 November 2004.

4. Literally translated "year of thoughts" or "thoughtful year." Indeed, it is a play on words, wishing people would think about the past (*sich Gedanken machen*) by commemorating (*Gedenken*).

5. Cf., for example, Martin Wassermair, "Heimatdienst in Dolby Surround: Das Jubiläumsjahr 2005 als Hegemonial-Spektakel der ÖVP," *Kulturrisse* 0404 (December 2004): 8-9; Tina Leisch, "Überdösis ÖÖÖ," ibid.: 10-11; Oliver Marchart and Nora Sternfeld, "60 Jahre Schüssel: Die Regierung feiert sich selbst, und die Opposition feiert die Regierung," ibid.: 12-13.

6. Cf. Barbara Coudenhove-Kalergi, "Österreich 2005: Da die Heimat!," *Die Presse*, 29 January 2005. Cf. also Peter Huemer, "Wut: Schulter? Schluss!," *Die Presse Spectrum / Zeichen der Zeit*, 5 March 2005.

7. Speech of Federal Chancellor Wolfgang Schüssel on the occasion of the anniversary year opening celebration, "Rede von Bundeskanzler Dr. Wolfgang Schüssel," *Jubiläumsjahr 2005*, 14 January 2005 <http://www.oesterreich2005.at/DesktopDefault.aspx?TabID=4537> (accessed 7 February 2006). Cf. also the speech of Vice-Chancellor Hubert Gorbach on the occasion of the jubilee year opening celebration, "Rede von Vizekanzler Hubert Gorbach," *Jubiläumsjahr 2005*, 14 January 2005, <http://www.oesterreich2005.at/DesktopDefault.aspx?TabID=4536> (accessed 6 February 2006).

8. Robert Menasse, "Österreich: Wende und Ende," *Die Presse Spectrum/Zeichen der Zeit*, 26 February 2005.

9. This is the title of the radio show on *Radio Österreich 1* on the occasion of the fifteenth anniversary of the signing of the Austrian State Treaty. Cf. Gedächtnisprotokoll zwecks Festlegung des Rahmens, in dem das Programm der verschiedenen aus Anlass des 25. Jahrestages der Befreiung Österreichs und der 15. Wiederkehr der Staatsvertrags-

unterzeichnung geplanten offiziellen Maßnahmen gestaltet werden soll, Zl. 11.636-Pr.1a/70, ÖStA, AdR, BKA, 54/1, GZl. 100.220-III/70.

10. It is important to point out that the Moscow Declaration about Austria was just a partial result of the conference of foreign ministers in Moscow, in which the postwar order had been predominantly discussed. Cf. Gerald Stourzh, *Um Einheit und Freiheit: Staatsvertrag, Neutralität und das Ende der Ost-West-Besetzung Österreichs, 1945-1955*. Studien zu Politik und Verwaltung 62 (Vienna: Böhlau, 1998), 11-28.

11. Cf. Claude Rivière, *Les Liturgies Politiques* (Paris: Presses universitaires des France, 1988).

12. Peter Berghoff, *Der Tod des politischen Kollektivs: Politischen Religion und das Sterben und Töten für Volk, Nation und Rasse* (Berlin: Akademie Verlag, 1997), 16.

13. Cf. Sybille Krämer, "Sprache—Stimme—Schrift: Sieben Gedanken über Performativität als Medialität," in *Performanz: Zwischen Sprachphilosophie und Kulturwissenschaften*, ed. Uwe Wirth (Frankfurt am Main: Suhrkamp, 2002), 323-46.

14. Cf. i.g. Hans Petschar and Georg Schmid, *Erinnerung & Vision: Die Legitimation Österreichs in Bildern, Eine semiohistorische Analyse der Austria Wochenschau 1949-1960* (Graz: Akademische Druck-u. Verlagsanstalt, 1990), 18.

15. Cf. Hugo Portisch, Sepp Riff, *Österreich II: Die Geschichte Österreichs vom Zweiten Weltkrieg bis zum Staatsvertrag*, Vol. 4, *Der lange Weg zur Freiheit* (Munich: Sachbuch, 1993); Rolf Steininger and Michael Gehler, eds., *Österreich im 20. Jahrhundert: ein Studienbuch in zwei Bänden*, Vol. 2, *Vom Zweiten Weltkrieg bis zur Gegenwart* (Vienna: Böhlau, 1997).

16. Cf. Petschar and Schmid, *Erinnerung & Vision*, 47.

17. "Ein Bewohner mehrerer Heimaten. Gespräche über Österreich 5: Willi Resetarits," *Kleine Zeitung*, 17 August 2003.

18. Cf. Robert Knight, "Dieses schlaffe Land," *profil*, 22 June 1987, 16-17.

19. Cf. Katharina Wegan, "'Heilige Zeiten': Der österreichische Staatsvertrag und seine Jubiläen," *Zeitgeschichte* 28/5 (2001): 279-91.

20. "Ferrero-Waldner und Schüssel klettern auf das Podest von Figl und Raab," *Oberösterreichische Nachrichten*, 16 May 2000.

21. "Schüssel im Kampf gegen 'innere Besatzungsmächte': Eine Rede zur Lage der Nation," *Neue Zürcher Zeitung*, 16 May 2000.

22. Jeff Barak, "Austrian Chancellor to '*Post*': We were Nazis' First Victim," *Jerusalem Post*, 9 November 2000.

23. Teresa Indjein and Andrea Sutter, Introduction, *Österreich 2005: Das Lesebuch zum Jubiläumsjahr mit Programmübersicht*, ed. Bundeskanzleramt Österreich (St. Pölten: Residenz, 2004), 5-6, here 5. Cf. also *Jubiläumsjahr 2005* <http://www.oesterreich 2005.at/> (accessed 9 February 2006).

24. Cf. Bundeskanzleramt Österreich, ed., *Österreich 2005*.

25. Cf. ibid., 9.

26. Cf. Franz Schandl, "Kommentar der anderen: Staatsmythos im Umbau," *Der Standard*, 2 February 2005.

27. Cf. "General Assembly Designates International Holocaust Remembrance Day." *UN News Centre Home*. 1 November 2005 <http://www.un.org/apps/news/story.asp?News ID=16431&Cr=holocaust&Cr1=#> (accessed 12 February 2006); *Remembrance and*

Beyond. United Nations. 2006 <http://www.un.org/holocaustremembrance/> (accessed 12 February 2006).

28. Additional information on the conference on 27-28 January 2006 in Salzburg is at "'The Sound of Europe' as the Starting Point for a Wide-ranging Debate on the Future of Europe." Press Release. *Presidency of the Council Home Page*. 19 January 2006 <http://www.eu2006.at/en/News/Press_Releases/January/1901soundofeurope.html?null> (accessed 12 February 2006).

29. Cf. Heidemarie Uhl, "27. Jänner: Tag des Gedenkens an Holocaust," *ORF on Science*, 27 January 2006 <http://science.orf.at/science/uhl/143183> (accessed 12 February 2006).

30. Cf. "Der Zweite Weltkrieg aus der Sicht der ehemaligen Gegner," *IMAS* 9 (May 2005): 5a.

31. Michael Fleischhacker, "Leitartikel: Wir können nur die Zukunft bewältigen," *Die Presse*, 7 May 2005.

32. Cf. among others Roman Sandgruber, "Wir basteln uns ein Fest," *Die Presse Spectrum/Zeichen der Zeit*, 31 December 2004.

33. Konrad Paul Liessmann, "Auf der Insel der Seligen: Österreich und seine Formen der Erinnerung," in *Österreich 2005*, ed. Bundeskanzleramt Österreich, 62-65, here 62.

34. Barbara Tóth, "Der Schlussstrich," *Der Standard*, 21 December 2004.

35. Cf. Bericht des Justizausschusses über den Antrag 21/A der Abgeordneten Mag. Terezjia Stoisits, Kolleginnen und Kollegen betreffend ein Bundesgesetz zur Rehabilitierung der Opfer der NS-Justiz, 1023 der Beilagen zu den Stenographischen Protokollen des Nationalrates XXII. GP <http://www.parlinkom.gv.at/pls/portal/docs/ page/PG/DE/ XXII/I/I_01023/FNAMEORIG_045217.HTML#> (accessed 13 February 2006).

36. Siegfried Kampl, in Dringlicher Anfrage zur NS-Militärjustiz insbesondere der Wehrmachtsdeserteure im von der Bundesregierung ausgerufenen "Gedenkjahr 2005" (2307/J-BR/2005) in Stenographisches Protokoll, 720. Sitzung des Bundesrates der Republik Österreich, 14 April 2005, 101-29, here 124-25.

37. Quoted in Gudenus, "Es gab Gaskammern, aber nicht im Dritten Reich. Sondern in Polen,"*Der Standard*, 8 June 2005.

38. Cf. Fischer, "Historische Debatten notwendig," *Die Presse*, 27 March 2005.

39. "Festrede von Bundeskanzler Wolfgang Schüssel anlässlich des Festaktes zur Wiedererrichtung der Republik am 27. April 1945," *Jubiläumsjahr 2005* <http://www.oesterreich2005.at/DesktopDefault.aspx?TabID=4506&Alias=jubilaeum2005&cob=1 1087> (accessed 13 February 2006).

40. RAU, "Stimmversagen," *Der Standard*, 28 April 2005.

41. Cf. "Wiederbetätigungs-Anklage gegen Ex-Bundesrat rechtskräftig," *Der Standard*, 29 January 2006; "'Lex Kampl': Mitterer als Bundesrats-Präsident nominiert," *Die Presse*, 29 June 2005; "Ing. Siegfried Kampl." *Österreichisches Parlament*. 2 November 2005 <http://www.parlinkom.gv.at/portal/page?_pageid=907,663602&_dad=portal&_ schema=PORTAL&P_PAD=B> (accessed 13 February 2006); "Mag. John Gudenus." *Österreichisches Parlament*. 17 November 2005 <http://www.parlinkom.gv.at/portal/ page?_pageid=907,175478&_dad=portal&_schema=PORTAL&P_PAD=B> (accessed 13 February 2006).

42. Cf. i.g. Hans Rauscher, "Gibt es doch ein Nazi-Gen?," *Der Standard*, 7 June 2005.

43. Ruth Wodak, "Kommentar der anderen: Strategie des Schweigens," *Der Standard*, 7 June 2005.

44. Cf. Christian Fleck, "Kommentar der anderen: Lasst den Irving doch reden," *Der Standard*, 23 November 2005.

45. Michael Fleischhacker, "Leitartikel: Und jetzt noch ein EU-Kritik-Verbotsgesetz," *Die Presse*, 26 November 2005.

46. Cf. Doron Rabinovici, "Gastkommentar: Märtyrer schauen anders aus," *Die Presse*, 25 February 2006.

47. Cf. Alfred J. Noll, "Die Abschaffer," *Die Presse Spectrum*, 17 December 2005.

48. "Rede von Bundeskanzler Wolfgang Schüssel anlässlich der Feierlichkeiten zum 50. Jubiläum der Staatsvertragsunterzeichnung im Schloss Belvedere," *Jubiläumsjahr 2005* <http://www.oesterreich2005.at/DesktopDefault.aspx?TabID=4506&Alias=jubilaeu m2005&cob=11305> (accessed 13 February 2006).

49. Quoted in Iris Mostegel, "Österreich erinnert sich seiner Freiheit," *Wiener Zeitung*, 14 May 2005.

50. Cf. Gerald Mandlbauer, "Leitartikel: Erfolgsgeschichte da capo," *Oberösterreichische Nachrichten*, 14 May 2005.

51. Cf. i.g. Uta Hauft, "Festakt fast ohne Feierlaune," *Tiroler Tageszeitung*, 17 May 2005; Erwin Zankl, "Offen gesagt: Ein Tag ohne Nostalgie," *Kleine Zeitung Graz*, 15 May 2005; "Sperrige Pflichtübung, reichlich unterkühlt," *Die Presse*, 17 May 2005.

52. Martin Link, "Die Feiern sind nichts als Opium," interview with Gerhard Jagschitz, *Kleine Zeitung*, 15 May 2005.

53. Cf. i.g. "Überschattete Feierstunde," *Salzburger Nachrichten*, 14 May 2005; Uta Hauft, "Festakt fast ohne Feierlaune: Wenige Fahnen, viele Reden," *Tiroler Tageszeitung*, 17 May 2005; Wolfgang Weisgram, "Barocker Rasen, republikanisches Fest," *Der Standard*, 17 May 2005.

54. Samo Kobenter, "Gedenktagsgeschenk," *Der Standard*, 15 March 2005.

55. Cf. "Zahl der Tafeln unklar," *Die Presse*, 12 May 2005.

56. Cf. among others the collections of articles in the online editions of *Die Presse* <http://www.diepresse.com/diashow/default.aspx?id=489872&channel=p&template=e> and *Der Standard* <http://derstandard.at/?url=/?ressort=kaernten> (accessed 13 February 2006).

57. Cf. "Austrian Broadcaster Blocks Airing of Documentary on Minority," *NavigatorFilm Online*, 14 December 2005 <http://www.artikel7.at/index.php?Art_ID= 67> (accessed 13 February 2006).

58. Answer by Franz Grabner to the letter of IG Kultur from 5 December 2005: "Antwort von Franz Grabner, ORF," *NavigatorFilm Online*, <http://www.artikel7.at/index.php? Art_ID=52> (accessed 13 February 2006).

59. Cf. Thomas Korschil and Eva Simmler, "Film zu Minderheitenkonflikt muss in den ORF!," *NavigatorFilm Online,* 26 January 2006 <http://www.artikel7.at/index.php? Art_ID=68> (accessed 13 February 2006).

60. Cf. Berthold Eder, "Wir sehen das Vorgehen des ORF als Wortbruch," *Der Standard*, 26 January 2006, <http://derStandard.at>.

61. "Staatsvertragsjubiläum: 'Ein Jahr der Identität,'" *Die Presse*, 23 January 2004.

62. On the chronology of this suit cf. "Rechtsstreit zog sich über sechs Jahre," *Der Standard*, 6 February 2006, <http://derStandard.at>.

63. Artur Rosenauer, Gastkommentar, "Ein kultureller Supergau," *Die Presse*, 17 January 2006.

64. Cf. "Abschied nehmen voller Bedauern," *Der Standard*, 6 February 2006.

65. Cf. Ilsebill Barta, "Gastkommentar: Juristen und historisches Recht," *Die Presse*, 9 February 2006.

66. Cf. i.g. Anne-Catherine Simon and Barbara Petsch, "Klimt, Rückkauf nur zu Weltmarktpreisen," *Die Presse*, 18 January 2006; Alfred J. Noll, "Kommentar der anderen: Institutionalisierte Unverantwortlichkeit," *Der Standard*, 18 January 2006.

67. Cf. "Der Schiedsspruch und sein Hintergrund," *Der Standard*, 17 January 2006, <http://derStandard.at>.

68. Cf. Ilsebill Barta, "Gastkommentar: Juristen und historisches Unrecht," *Die Presse*, 9 February 2006.

69. Quoted in Thomas Trenkler, "Gönnerhafte Gehrer," *Der Standard*, 18 January 2006.

70. Cf. ibid.; Alfred J. Noll, "Kommentar der anderen: Institutionalisierte Unverantwortlichkeit," *Der Standard*, 18 January 2006; the Green Party demanded an amendment to the restitution law. Cf. "Restitution: Grüne fordern Novellierung des Gesetzes," *Die Presse*, 31 January 2006.

71. Quoted in Matthias Dusini, "Adele, ade!," *Der Falter*, No. 4, 25 January 2006.

72. Cf. ibid.

73. Cf. Monika Mayer, "Gustav Klimt: Bildnis Adele Bloch-Bauer I," in *Das Neue Österreich. Die Ausstellung zum Staatsvertragsjubiläum 1955/2005. Oberes Belvedere, 16. Mai bis 1. November 2005*, ed. Österreichische Galerie Belvedere (Vienna, 2005), 101.

74. Cf. Werner Koroschitz and Lisa Rettl, "Erläuterungen zur Ausstellung," in *"Heiß umfehdet, wild umstritten ... " Geschichtsmythen in Rot-Weiß-Rot: Katalog zur Sonderausstellung im Museum der Stadt Villach, 21. April – 30. Oktober 2005*, ed. Werner Koroschitz and Lisa Rettl (Villach: Drava, 2005), 11.

75. Cf. "Exhibitions 2006," *Jüdisches Museum Wien* <http://www.jmw.at/en/vorschau_ septemberii_2005en_ko.HTM#Tennenbaum> (accessed 13 February 2006).

76. Cf. Karl Albrecht-Weinberger, "Ein 'vatermörderisches Projekt'? Eine Ausstellung zum heuchlerischen Umgang von Österreichern mit der NS-Zeit," in *"Jetzt ist er bös, der Tennenbaum": Die Zweite Republik und ihre Juden, Eine Ausstellung des Jüdischen Museums Wien, 20. April – 4. Juli 2005*, ed. Felicitas Heimann-Jelinek et al. (Vienna: Jüdisches Muesum Wien, 2005), 7-8.

77. Matthias Horx, "Quergeschrieben: Schilder und Bilder," *Die Presse*, 21 January 2006.

78. Cf. Heidemarie Uhl, "Kommentar der anderen: Welches Haus wollen wir?," *Der Standard*, 7 January 2006.

79. Quoted in and cf. "50 Jahre Staatsvertrag: Dokument wieder im Schloss Belvedere," APA 03381005, 10 May 2005.

80. Cf. Hannes Androsch, Herbert Krejci, and Peter Weiser, "Kommentar der Anderen: Die Patrioten sind überall," *Der Standard*, 12 February 2005. This is the letter sent in January 2004 to numerous intellectuals, business leaders, and politicians to support and

to organize one big State Treaty exhibition after the government had cancelled its own exhibition project.

81. Pelinka, "Die Zwischenkriegszeit," 60.

82. Cf. Hannes Androsch, Herbert Krejci, and Peter Weiser, "Geleitwort der Proponenten," in *Das Neue Österreich*, 19.

83. Exhibits no. 2.33.1 to 2.33.3 (hats of *Heimwehr, Republikanischer Schutzbund*, and SA), no. 2.35 ("*Der Bürgerkrieg in Österreich. Eine Darstellung von Mitkämpfern und Augenzuegen*", 1934 by Julius Deutsch) and no. 2.36 ("*Österreich über alles! Unser Bundeskanzler Dr. Dollfuß ruft: Wer Österreich liebt und schützen will, hinein in die Vaterländische Front!*," 1933/34, poster). Cf. Anton Pelinka, Walter J. Fend, Brigitte Halbmayr, and Walter Manoschek, "Zwischenkriegszeit," in *Das Neue Österreich*, 50-77, here 65.

84. Cf. also Cf. Uhl, "Welches Haus wollen wir?"

85. Manfried Rauchensteiner, Andrea Brait, and Gregory Weeks, "Besatzungszeit," in *Das Neue Österreich*, 108-45, in particular, 123.

86. Quoted in Reinhold Reiter, "Warten auf die Originalurkunde aus Moskau," *Kleine Zeitung Graz*, 1 February 2005; cf. also i.g. "Stadt Wien gibt für Aktivitäten im Gedenkjahr vier Millionen Euro aus," *Wiener Zeitung*, 22 January 2005.

87. Cf. Margaretha Kopeinig, "Langer Schatten," *Kurier*, 27 April 2005.

88. Peter Weiser, Ursula Haspel, Emmie Montjoye, and Eva Zitterbart, "Klischee und Wirklichkeit," in *Das Neue Österreich*, 270-81, here 280.

89. Cf. Timothy Pytell, *Viktor Frankl: Das Ende eines Mythos?* (Innsbruck: Studien Verlag, 2005), 149-62.

90. Cf., Wolfgang Neugebauer and Peter Schwarz, eds., *Der Wille zum aufrechten Gang: Offenlegung der Rolle des BSA bei der gesellschaftlichen Reintegration ehemaliger Nationalsozialisten*, Bund sozialdemokratischer AkademikerInnen, Intellektueller und KünstlerInnen (BSA) (Vienna: Czernin, 2005).

91. Hans Werner Scheidl, "Eine Schau, die Jugendliche stolz machen soll," *Die Presse*, 4 May 2005.

92. Cf. ibid.

93. Quoted in Walter Hämmerle, "Ein Sprungbrett in die Zukunft," *Wiener Zeitung*, 25 Septemebr 2004.

94. Cf. i.g. "Staatsvertragsschau strittig," *Die Presse*, 2 April 2002; Andreas Schwarz, "Meinung: Knapp ober der Fläche," *Die Presse*, 2 April 2002; Erich Witzmann, "Der Streit um die Staatsvertrags-Schau: 'SPÖ sollte sich nicht abkoppeln,'" *Die Presse*, 5 April 2002.

95. Cf. email from Siegfried Mattl to Katharina Wegan on 20 February 2006.

96. Cf. Hans Werner Scheidel, "Österreich feiert sich selbst—und Schüssel ist immer dabei," *Die Presse*, 15 November 2004; "Staatsvertrag: 'Offensive für die Bildung ist wichtiger,'" *Die Presse*, 24 September 2003.

97. Quoted in "Staatsvertragsausstellung: Regierung kündigt 'Gesamtkonzept,'" in APA 0499 5 II 0144, 16 December 2003.

98. Christian Böhmer, "Jubiläumsjahr 2005: Blick durch die Österreich-Brille," *Kurier*, 31 July 2004.

99. Cf. Andreas Koller, "Das neue Österreich," *Salzburger Nachrichten*, 6 August 2004.

100. Cf. i.g. "Verbeugung vor der Wiederaufbaugeneration," *Salzburger Nachrichten*, 10 March 2005.

101. Cf. i.g. "Staatsvertrag: Wird das Jubiläum 2005 noch gerettet?," *Die Presse*, 28 October 2003; "Staatsvertragsausstellung: Häupl zur Kostenbeteiligung bereit," APA 04021612, 16 December 2003; "Komitee: Nun Aufruf für Ausstellung zum Staatvertrag," *Die Presse*, 22 December 2003; "Gerettete Staatsvertrags-Ausstellung," *Salzburger Nachrichten*, 5 January 2004.

102. Cf. i.g. Barbara Tóth, "Kolportiert: Jubeljahr 2005: Historiker geht ab," *Der Standard*, 3 September 2004; "Jubiläums-Schau soll Weg Österreichs zu 'zeitgemäßem Land' zeigen," APA 00271601, 16 January 2005; Brigitte Borchardt-Birbaumer, "Die Staatsvertragsausstellung: Rückblick ohne wenn und aber?," *Wiener Zeitung*, 31 January 2005; Otto Klambauer, "Nachgefragt: 'Keine Jubel-Ausstellung,'" *Kurier*, 22 April 2005; "Das neue Österreich," *preview. Kunst. Zukunftsweisend*, January 2005; "Österreichs Weg in Stationen," *Kurier*, 15 May 2005.

103. Kurt Scholz, "Erinnerung ohne Pathos," *Die Furche Feuilleton*, No. 21, 26 May 05.

104. Cf. "Komitee: Nun Aufruf für Ausstellung zum Staatvertrag," *Die Presse*, 22 December 2003.

105. Cf. i.g. Robert Preis, "Erlebnis Geschichte 'Österreich macht frei!'," *Kleine Zeitung Graz*, 14 April 2005; Andreas Feiertag, "Über Berg von Leichen in die Freiheit," *Der Standard*, 15 April 2005; Helmut Schliesselberger, "Zeitreise zum Staatsvertrag," *Salzburger Nachrichten*, 16 April 2005; Ingrid Teufl, "Der lange Weg zum Staatsvertrag," *Kurier*, 16 April 2005; Herbert Lackner, "Staatsvertrag und Nähmaschine," *profil*, 18 April 2005; "Österreichs Weg in Stationen," *Kurier*, 15 May 2005; Andreas Feiertag, "Rot-weiß-rote Spur durch hundertjährige Geschichte," *Der Standard*, 11 May 2005; Helmut Schiesselberger, "Lernen S' Geschichte," *Salzburger Nachrichten*, 12 May 2005; Uta Hauft, "Nicht behübscht, nicht zerknirscht," Kurier, 12 May 2005; Kurt Scholz, "Erinnerung ohne Pathos," *Die Furche Feuilleton*, No. 21, 26 May 2005.

106. Uhl, "Welches Haus wollen wir?"

107. Günter Traxler, "Im Heucheljahr," *Der Standard*, 21 January 2005.

108. Cf. Peter Huemer, "Der keine Ruck," *Die Presse*, 10 December 2005; Michael Fleischhacker, "Österreich: 'Wer ist schon makellos?'," *Die Presse Spectrum/Zeichen der Zeit*, 5 March 2005.

109. Cf. Michael Kerbler and Claus Philipp, "Gedankenjahr als 'Ausblendungsprozess,'" *Der Standard*, 10 March 2005.

110. Cf. Kopeinig, "Langer Schatten."

111. Hans Werner Scheidel, "Belvedere."

112. "Rede von Bundeskanzler Schüssel anlässlich der Eröffnung der Jubiläumsausstellung 'Österreich ist frei,'" *Jubiläumsjahr 2005*, 15 April 2005 <http://www.oesterreich2005.at/DesktopDefault.aspx?TabID=4506&Aliasjubilaeum2005&cob=11 086> (accessed 19 February 2006).

113. Cf. Fleischhacker, "Österreich."

114. Cf. Huemer, "Der keine Ruck."

115. Cf. Uhl, "Welches Haus wollen wir?"

116. Cf. "Schüssel gibt Auftrag für 'Haus der Geschichte,'" *Die Presse*, 24 February 06.

117. Cf. Wassermair, "Nach dem Spiel ist vor dem Spiel," 40-43.

Austrian Exhibition-ism:
The Year 2005 and Its Commemorations of the Recent Past in Exhibition Catalogues

Teresa Indjein and Bundeskanzleramt Österreich, ed., *Österreich 2005: Das Lesebuch zum Jubliäumsjahr mit Programmübersicht* (St. Pölten-Salzburg: Residenz Verlag, 2004)

Das Neue Österreich: Die Ausstellung zum Staatsvertragsjubiläum 1955/2005 (Vienna: Österreichische Galerie Belvedere, 2005)

Stefan Karner and Gottfried Stangler with Peter Fritz and Walter M. Iber, eds., *"Österreich ist frei!" Der Österreichische Staatsvertrag 1955: Beitragsband zur Ausstellung auf Schloss Schallaburg 2005* (Horn: Verlag Berger, 2005)

Hans Petschar, *Die junge Republik: Alltagsbilder aus Österreich 1945-1955* (Vienna: Ueberreuter, 2005)

Susanne Breuss and Vienna Museum, ed., *Die Sinalco Eoche: Essen, Trinken, Konsumieren nach 1945* (Vienna: Czernin Verlag, 2005)

Helmut Lackner and the Technisches Museum Vienna, ed., *Österreich Baut Auf/Rebuilding Austria* (Vienna: Technisches Museum, 2005)

Werner Koroschitz and Lisa Rettl, eds., *"Heiss umfehdet, wild umstritten..."*: *Geschichtsmythen in Rot-Weiss-Rot* (Klagenfurt/Celovec: Drava, 2005)

Günter Bischof

Introduction: A Surfeit of Memory?

The year 2005 produced a memory blitz in Austria of unprecedented proportions. The major commemorations celebrated were the fiftieth anniversary of the Austrian State Treaty and the end of the four-power occupation, the sixtieth anniversary of the end of World War II and the reestablishment of an independent republic, and the tenth anniversary of the Austrian accession to the European Union. A cornucopia of additional anniversaries were thrown into the hopper of the big year of commemorations: Bertha von Suttner's Peace Nobel Prize 100 years ago, the Allied liberation sixty years ago, the establishment of the Austrian Army, the reopening of the State Opera and the national theater (the *Burgtheater*), and the beginning of Austrian state television, as well as the conclusion of the Austrian neutrality law and membership in the United Nations fifty years ago, and the less "round" anniversary of the beginning of Austrian soldiers serving in UN missions forty-five years ago. In the age-old tradition of Josephinian state paternalism, the federal chancellery gave marching orders to make 2005 not only a memory year (*Gedenkjahr*), but also a year of thoughtful reflection (*Gedankenjahr*). The many historical exhibits were also designed to impart a deeper historical knowledge in a citizenry often innocent of the knowledge of basic facts.[1] The State Secretary for the Arts and Media, Franz Morak in the State Chancellery, set up a separate planning bureau to coordinate this festival of commemorations and exhibits and launched the website <www.oesterreich.2005.at>. Austrian museums in the capital, Vienna, went into a frenzied national competition of who could design the fanciest and most popular anniversary exhibit. The interest of the citizenry in the provincial capitals weakened the further one got away from Vienna. Clearly, the echoes from the past of the liberation, occupation, and "liberation from the liberators" were much stronger in Vienna and Eastern Austria, where the Soviets had been occupiers.

The year 2005 was a good one for historians; this one included. They were involved in designing the many exhibits; writing essays for catalogues, magazines, and newspapers; jet-setting about the world, participating in symposia and conferences; giving lectures and keynotes; and being present in the media. Without a doubt, they were in the forefront of producing and defining the national historical memory, sometimes even acting as water boys (and girls) and *Handlanger* to politicians who wanted to impress their versions of historical memory onto an unsuspecting public. The politicians defined the often partisan versions of the past in commemorations as acts of state such as the ceremonies in the National Parliament on 14 January and the signing of the State Treaty in the historic *Marmorsaal* of the Belvedere Palace on 15 May. Clearly, most of the political class and the Austrian population (including former Nazis) were more comfortable celebrating the "liberation from the occupiers"—independence and freedom gained in 1955—rather than the liberation from the Nazis in 1945.[2] Historians had to remind the ever-opportunistic politicos that 1945 was the more significant "liberation event" for the Austrian people than 1955. The year 2005 produced an even larger avalanche of publications, TV documentaries,[3] commemorations, and "events" than the fiftieth anniversary of the 1938 Anschluß had in 1988. Nevertheless, the recognition of 1988 as a "memory year" may well be the more important turning point in Austrian postwar historical memory culture.[4]

I was in Vienna in March, May, and June of 2005 and in Innsbruck in July/August of the year for openings and conferences and so made a point of seeing all the major exhibitions, some twice. I presumably was counted multiple times among the 1.25 million visitors (in a population of 8 million) that crowded into these shows.[5] At the Schallaburg in Lower Austria on a Sunday morning, I stood in line for half an hour and got pushed by steady throngs of visitors through the exhibit to see the original copy of the Austrian State Treaty, which had been shipped from its permanent home in Moscow. In all the other exhibits I visited in Vienna on weekdays, the crowds were solid and steady, such as at the major Belvedere show, where tens of thousands visited in the course of the summer (and where the original State Treaty was on display, too, for a couple of weeks); they were moderate to light in all the other shows. At some shows, such as the postwar photo exhibit by the National Library in the magnificent *Prunksaal*, I was a lonely and forlorn visitor. A small exhibit in Innsbruck's *Zeughaus* on the occupation years in the Tyrol was so anemic that it seems to have been a perfunctory exercise of participating in the national carnival of commemorations rather than a labor of love such as the innovative shows on economic reconstruction and the Marshall Plan at the Technical Museum, everyday life and food culture at the *Wien Museum*, and the pictorial iconography of the postwar decade in the photo exhibit at the National Library. It appears that many Austrians tired quickly of the Austrian commemorative circus, especially in the provinces where the spectacles in Vienna seemed to have been observed with some puzzlement.

Then there were the theatrical "25 PEACES," designed to evoke World War II and the difficult beginnings of the Second Republic in a "jocular" fashion (Schüssel), connecting a broader public with the past which otherwise might ignore it.[6] Americans like to *reenact* significant events of their past such as battles of the Revolutionary War and the Civil War in order to make a personal connection with the heroism of those historical turning points, to keep history "alive," and to promote a participatory patriotism. These "25 PEACES" designed by event managers hoped to reconnect Austrians with some of the most difficult events of the wartime and postwar eras and to encourage them to count their blessings for a peaceful history since then.[7] A World War II night of bombing was staged in the inner city of Vienna with sirens and the chilly sounds of B-24 bombers dropping their payloads. The huge equestrian statues on the *Heldenplatz* were walled in as they had been during the war when they needed protection against bombs. Gardens were planted on the *Heldenplatz* as they had been in 1945/46 as a reminder of the years of postwar starvation. In a similar vein, cows were once again grazing in the Belvedere Gardens. Instead of chilly reminders of *temps perdu*, the "PEACES" produced a fierce debate over millions of Euros being wasted by these peddlers of Viennese theatricality, bathos, and historical nostalgia. Passing through the *Heldenplatz*, I witnessed willy-nilly tomatoes and green beans being grown and archdukes and princes high on their houses made invisible by fake brick walls. In the Belvedere Gardens, I spotted the somewhat disoriented cows that must have seen better times on their Alpine pastures. Even though I was in Vienna in March, I could not get myself to listen to the terrors of bombs falling over the *Gauhausptstadt*. Reading G.W. Seebald and Jörg Friedrich will do for me to relive the bombing nights.[8]

Exhibition-ism: A Carnival of Exhibit Catalogues

The impressions one gathers from the pictures, documents, and artifacts at an exhibit are fleeting and transitory. A catalogue documenting and contextualizing an exhibit, on the other hand, casts the intentions of the designers into a more permanent mold and leaves a record for more intense study. One can read the texts pregnant with meaning and linger over the pictures and designs in such documentations. Konrad Paul Liessmann is correct in arguing that the usually highly-selective historical exhibitions "serve the interests and perspectives of the present by presenting and giving meaning to the past, especially in the context of producing group specific strategies of identification."[9] Austrians seem to love to put on historical exhibitions. The nine Austrian federal states usually have "state exhibits" (*Landesausstellungen*) almost every summer, competing with one another for viewers. Particularly the *Land* Lower Austria spares no expense to put on mega-shows such as the Austrian millennium show in 1996 or previous exhibits on the "Age of Emperor Francis Joseph." These shows are good for maintaining a vast assortment of castles and cultural sites in the "heart of Austria," they are good for local tourism and provide a rich return on initial investments over time, and they build local identity, as Liessmann suggests, and define patriotism as a sense of pride in one's regional and national past. In 2005, the concatenation of dozens of *Zeitgeschichte* exhibits dealing with Austria's post-World War II recent and immediate pasts was unusual and multiplied such opportunities. They presented multiple venues in which to give meaning to the past, to engage in the (frequently partisan) politics of history, to re-forge local and national identities, and to re-inject citizens with a sense of specific local and/or national pride and patriotism.

The exhibits referred to here were on display either in some of Vienna's principal state museums or in regional museums. It is crucial to remember the function of museums in the creation of national and/or regional identities in such a memory year.[10] Experts remind us that "museums are powerful sites of cultural transmission and public education [...] the state museum is an important site not only for the exhibition of objects, but also for the exhibition of national beliefs; it is a place where the 'imagined community' of the nation becomes visible."[11] Objects become part of "our" history when they are displayed in a museum. Museums are special places for the "construction of a public sense of the past."[12] Museums also provide "one of the principal means by which people can gain access to the past and a special historic legitimacy is conferred upon events and objects when they are included in museums."[13] More importantly, when objects become part of museum exhibits, they "cease to be just part of history and instead have the potential to become a part of our shared, national, *heritage*" (emphasis in the original).[14] The distinction is that "history" represents the past, while "heritage" takes aspects of the past and inscribes them "as especially significant in the collective history of a group of people, be it class, region or nation"; heritage is closely linked "with our need for a sense of the past, a sense of continuity, belonging and identity."[15] These museum exhibits and the catalogues that document them are both "sites of memory" designed to build and to firm up Austrian identity in the 2005 *Gedenkjahr*.

I selected one national reader and six catalogues from the most important exhibits to test these propositions and to give the reader a sense of whether the *Gedankenjahr* indeed produced a more complex rethinking and reinvention of the recent past and Austrian historical memory culture. All these catalogues are lavishly illustrated; *Das neue Österreich* even includes gorgeous color pictures of the exhibit's paintings. To carry them across the Atlantic produced a minor effort (the U.S. Transportation Security Administration even left a conspicuous "Notice of Baggage Inspection" in *Österreich ist frei*, informing me that the anonymous snooping inspectors did not consider it terrorists' literature—the homeland is secure). Put on a neat pile onto my scales, together these catalogues at 24 pounds seem weighty.

The reader *Österreich 2005* is an official publication by the "Grand Central Station" of memory year coordination, the Federal Press Agency in the Federal Chancellery. Published in the fall of 2004, it provided a complete survey of all the exhibits, symposia, and events launched in the memory year 2005 for enthusiasts of history and the Austrian memory cult. But it is more than a guide. It is also a primer of brainy texts, dreamy poems, and evocative photographs celebrating postwar Austria and its intellectual, artistic, economic, and social achievement. In half a dozen chapters, some of the country's best and brightest present shrewd, thoughtful, and quirky essays, interspersed with more pedestrian texts by the chancellor and some of his favorite (ex)ministers (and/or their speechwriters).[16] The axes of reflection are a mile wide and an inch deep: "Memory & Renewal," "Crisis & Creativity," "Peace & Integration," "Work & Inspiration," "Harmony & Irony," "*Heimat* & Europe." There is the quirky novelist "Franzobel" who thrives on both the ironic and less sublime in the Austrian character, its mistrust of the Enlightenment and reason and its indulgence in a culture of feelings. Franzobel loves to point out the contradictory traits of Austrians, "Try to imagine a country, where no one is serious, which is not to say that people don't wish to be taken seriously." He gleefully pooh-poohs their determined underachievement at home and overachievement abroad, "All higher aspirations are pointless here. You can't get anywhere in Austria. On the one hand, the dictum holds true that one can't be special, on the other hand, one lives up to the rule: to shut up is sufficient praise. This results in Austrians who want to get somewhere must either die or go abroad, where they almost always succeed" (pp. 258f).

Then there is the smart essayist Karl-Markus Gauss, son of Balkan German DP's, and his discovery of Austria. He reflects critically on the false patriotism of postwar Austria, where former Nazis turned teachers retained their German nationalism but dutifully pressed their government dictated love of country (*staatsoffizielle Heimatliebe*) on their charges in the classroom: It is true, "Austria" was an excuse, a magical code for those who had betrayed it prodigiously before but put it up on a pedestal after 1945. It was a powerful tool to free them of the constrictions [of the past] and expiate their guilt. The pervasive Austrianization (*Verösterreicherung*) of every day life nestled in a state that was presenting Austria as an innocent victim of the Third Reich so successfully that not only foreign politicians swallowed it hook, line, and sinker but also those natives that had eagerly participated in it. It was this savvy state opportunism that later made it exceedingly difficult for me and many others to design a critical image of Austria [...] (pp. 299f).

This *Lesebuch* presents a smorgasbord of impressions, which makes for an unusually reflective primer. There is Franz Bauer's wise plea for the acceptance of the existing multicultural society in Austria rather than fighting it endlessly in Carinthia with the eternal row over dual-language German/Slovene place name signs, "The two different writs on the *Ortstafeln* signify the existence of two languages, two cultures. They signal multiplicity. Only simple-minded people can't live with this" (p. 151). In addition, the insights of the gifted essayist and philosopher Konrad Paul Liessmann trace a continuity between Pope Paul VI's 1971 dictum of Austria being an "island of the blessed" and the ancient feudal myth of *"felix Austria"*: "Others may arm themselves to the teeth with nuclear weapons, but you happy Austria continue your role as an island and bridge between the hostile blocs" (pp. 63f). An excerpt from Ingeborg Bachmann's war diary betrays an unusual sensibility. A young British occupation soldier turns out to be a Viennese Jew who managed to save his life on a *Kindertransport* to England before the war. She dates him in order to engage him in discussions of Arthur Schnitzler and Hugo von Hofmannsthal. Her Carinthian neighbors look askance at her for "going out with a Jew" (p. 47). Ernst Jandl is represented with a whimsical four-word poem and Peter Turrini with a longer one about guardian angels. Of course, to demonstrate tolerant magnanimity, such an official reader cannot do without Thomas Bernhard, Austria's favorite *Nestbeschmutzer*. Yet the book's charm lies in the outstanding selection of photography: gorgeous Austrian landscapes, Jedermann-type people, and curious motives are interspersed with the texts. Images of the proud traditional cheese-makers and *"Biobauer"* in the Alpine region appear next to one of the Americanized youth who sports "Kylie, Britney, Christina, Pamela, Pink" on his t-shirt.

The reader also has to suffer through the trite texts of the chancellor and some of his ministers. Wolfgang Schüssel cannot help but deliver his usual denunciations of the Kreisky era, "Austria was more than reconstructed. Austrians created a comfortable prosperity for themselves, but not without the blemish of growing state deficits. Joining the EU ten years ago Austria was forced to consolidate" (p. 55), presumably all single-handedly under Schüssel's aegis. The book starts with a brilliant text by Friedrich Heer, one of Austria's greatest postwar intellectuals. In the year 1955, he calls on the political parties and cliques to cease with the poisoning of the political arena through their perennial backbiting (p. 22). The juxtaposition of the street-fighting Schüssel and the high-minded Heer produces an inherent tension. Minister of Education, Science, and Culture Elisabeth Gehrer waxes less eloquently about change in the globalizing educational arena and arrives at the knock-out insight, "Education and science both have to create the conditions for mastering the challenges of our time and strengthening people's confidence in new accomplishments" (p. 181). But then, this is an official reader coming out of the federal ministry, and the reader has to live with these jarring variances in the quality of the texts.[17] Imagine the White House one day issuing an anniversary-year reader with texts by President Bush and Secretary of Defense Donald Rumsfeld juxtaposed with the writings of, say, Joyce Carol Oates, Toni Morrison, Gore Vidal, and e.e. cummings, along with the photography of Ansel Adams and Robert Maplethorpe. Get the idea? Yet they, too, in Whitmanesque fashion would encompass all that is America as this reader tries to represent Austria. The best one can say of this reader, then, is that it presents Austria's multiple identities in a highbrow fashion.

A record half million people saw the exhibits in the Belvedere Palace and at the Schallaburg in rural Lower Austria. Presumably, they were commercial successes. The politics of history in the contentious genesis of the Belvedere show *Das Neue Österreich* is a classic case study of the partisan politics of history in Austria and surely will find a patient Ph.D. student (like Heidemarie Uhl in her 1988 book) to analyze the details of the Viennese community of envy (*Neidgenossenschaft*)—a baroque tale of sinister intrigue and petty backbiting *Wadlbeisserei*, as well as grandstanding one-upmanship.[18] In the end, a vast bipartisan ÖVP/SPÖ team of "black" and "red" historians produced an appealing exhibit in the tradition of consensual history financed with both public and private monies. The counterpoint in the provinces was that conservative "black" Lower Austria hired the enterprising Stefan Karner and his team of young historians at the *Boltzmann Institut für Kriegs-folgenforschung* in Graz to design the Schallaburg exhibit. Chancellor Schüssel, the current resident in the *Hofburg*, in the age-old tradition of Emperor Maximilian I, has anointed Karner as his favorite *Haus- und Hof* historian.[19]

The creative conceptualization of the Belvedere exhibit by a team of architects and designers was quite brilliant exhibition-ism. The choice of Prince Eugene's baroque Belvedere Palace as one of *the* national sites of memory where the Austrian State Treaty was signed on 15 May 1955 with huge acclaim by the Viennese population was a natural. Its *genius loci* provided a dignified context for the parallel three-tracked exhibit throughout the marbled rooms of the upper floor of the palace. The designers devoted one track on the outer walls to traditional historical artifacts, original sources, and objects. On the opposite inner walls, an "art track"—*Kunstspur*—displayed respective works of art by Austria's leading painters and sculptors associated with the times and themes of the historical objects. The central track in between—the patriotic red-white-red *Fahnenspur* of the Austrian flag—tied the show together with a flag running (mostly) on the ceilings of the rooms and with audiovisual exhibits. The three tracks offered different perspectives and associations on a given historical period and, thus, offered multiple readings of history (*Das Neue Österreich*, pp. 345), the art track being the most tenuous yet perceptive. Thus in the World War II room, private photos of an Austrian soldier on the Eastern front and an original guillotine used by the Nazis in the Vienna regional court to execute 1,200 "criminals" were juxtaposed with paintings by Oskar Kokoschka and Gustav Klimt's famous "aryanized" portrait *Adele Bloch Bauer I*, now returned to its rightful owner in the United States. In this room, the Austrian flag came down to the floor—quasi-trampled by the Nazis and their Austrian admirers in 1938—and vanished during the war only to rise again out of the ashes of the war to proudly fly high again in the postwar rooms.

Obviously, the catalogue cannot do justice to the rich feast of visual imagery in the three exhibit tracks. But it provides a complete documentation of all the exhibit's historical artifacts with brief descriptions, along with complete color reproductions of the art displayed. The running commentary by Tobias Natter and his team of art historians on the paintings provides a brief survey of twentieth century Austrian art history and may well be the most evocative and original contribution in this exhibit catalogue, along with Natter's essay on 1955 and Austrian postwar art (pp. 181ff). The most substantive chapters with new information even for the specialist are Verena Traeger's artful "Biography of One Day" in Vienna—15 May 1955—the day of the signing of the State Treaty (pp. 150ff) and her keen analysis of the arcane commissioning of the official painting of this event (pp.167ff). Her microhistory of 15 May is a masterpiece devoted to the arcana and significance of diplomatic protocol, which is fitting in a show on a key international treaty. It begins with the cleaning of the rooms (documented from the original invoices); the ordering of flowers ("pale red hortensia"), carpets, and ink pens for the signing ceremony; the number of journalists admitted and unobtrusively placed in preparation for the 11 a.m. arrival of the delegations for the signing ceremony. After the foreign ministers put their signatures on the complex treaty (only completed the day before), they went out on the balcony to show it to tens of thousands of cheering people assembled in the gardens of the park. After a quick bite to eat, they had a 1:15 p.m. reception and "*dejeuner*" in the *Hofburg* offices of President Körner. The entire Austrian government and the French and British Foreign Ministers gathered at St. Stephen's Cathedral at 5 p.m. for a festive *Te Deum*. Understandably, Foreign Minister Vyacheslav Molotov was a no-show, but where was the staunch Presbyterian Secretary of State John F. Dulles? At 7 p.m. the Austrian government and elites, along with the foreign delegations and 1,300 invited guests in formal attire and fancy evening gowns (who among Vienna's rich, glamorous, and mighty was *not* invited?) gathered at the Imperial Habsburg Summer Palace Schönbrunn for a lavish state dinner. A dinner of *Caneton a la Nivernaise* was served with lots of *Dürnstein Riesling Spätlese* and *Burgenländer Blaufränkischer* (but what in the world is "Sauce Bagration"?). What a day for the Vienna caterers! The party went without a glitch (*ohne Zwischenfall*) until one in the morning; only Dulles, who left town that night, left Schönbrunn at 10 p.m., but not without a rousing rendition of the "Star Spangled Banner" on behalf of the American secretary of state. Molotov obviously enjoyed the lavish celebrations and left the capitalist city two days later.

Compared with Traeger's excessive details, the rest of the catalogue's chapters are quite tame and recount the well-known. They briefly outline the course of Austrian history from World War I to the present in a largely consensual fashion. The chapters from the First to the Second Republic, and from the Cold War to Austrian accession to the European Union, along with the drama of the ups and downs of Austrian identity formation (from "*Ent-*" to "*Verösterreicherung*") are common fare. Austria's remarkable postwar economic trajectory from poverty to prosperity and the inventiveness of Austrian *Erfinder* is nicely represented, too. It is annoying that the South Tyrol problem is not included in the general foreign policy chapters on the Cold War; it receives a separate chapter (pp. 325). This is a piece of stubborn Austrian territorial revisionism—in one of Europe's best-resolved ethnic minority conflicts[20]—that will not go away. Think of it—the Federal Republic of Germany producing such a catalogue with the "lost provinces" of Eastern Prussia and Silesia added in as part of the national master narrative! These essays together, then, produce a consensual master narrative of Austrian history that most historians can embrace and with which most of the public can identify.[21]

Only the World War II chapter represents a jarring and bolder statement, as Austrian perpetrator history is now fully included in the master narrative, as are the sordid tales of persecution and exile. No longer are Austrians portrayed as Adolf Hitler's hapless victims, as they were only twenty years ago; now they figure as chief culprits in launching the Holocaust. Predictably, there were voices from the right who felt the focus on Austrian Nazis was excessive. But the official version of Austrian postwar history is prepared now to include what the German Holocaust survivor Ralph Giordano calls the burden of "second guilt": no longer denying their first burden of guilt, their support of Hitler, as they had done for the first two postwar generations.[22] In the postwar trajectory of Austrian historical memory, this marks a significant breakthrough.

The attractive culmination of Austrian exhibitionism comes in the final room (and pages of the catalogue) devoted to *"Über Österreich"* (this can be read as "About Austria" or "Super Austria"). Katarina Schmidl's ironic sculpture of a shapely female rear end, made from red-white-red drinking straws and aptly entitled "a nice piece of Austria" (*Ein schönes Stück Österreich*), hopefully did not unhinge too many American visitors. It was juxtaposed with quotations from famous Austrians: "One dies in Vienna, but one never ages there" (Charles de Montesquieu); "Austria is a labyrinth that everybody is familiar with" (Helmut Qualtinger); "Everybody likes his country. Me too. I only don't like the state" (Thomas Bernhard); "Once at home I am a stranger" (Theodor Kramer) (pp. 341ff). Go figure.

Plate 1: Katharina Schmidl (b. 1973), *Ein schönes Stück Österreich* **(2002)**

Source: Image 13.1 in *Das Neue Österreich*, p. 343; reprinted with the permission of the artist.

The exhibit in the Schallaburg and its catalogue, *Österreich ist frei*, lacks such playful irony and represents straightforward traditional history. The layout of the medieval castle offered few opportunities for imaginative museum design and was quite plain compared to the spectacular "retraceable past" (*"begehbare Geschichte,"* p. 345) in the Belvedere. *Vis-à-vis* the expansive layout of the Belvedere halls, the galleries were narrow, almost producing pangs of claustrophobia. One did not quite feel free. *Österreich ist frei* provides no documentation of the artifacts, but brief essays by specialists on the postwar occupation decade. They amount to an encyclopedia of sorts for these years. Allied postwar planning during the war is covered, as is the liberation of Austria by Allied armies and the difficult beginnings of the Second Republic.[23] All four occupation powers and their Austrian policies are represented as are domestic politics, including controversial issues such as de-Nazification and restitution. Given the interests of Karner and his Graz team of historians in World War II prisoners of war and their return after the war, the essays on Soviet POW treatment are particularly informative (Austrian POWs in Western captivity are predictably missing). Social and economic history is extensively treated, including sensitive topics such as *Russenkinder* and the Communist strike of 1950. The chapter on culture is surprisingly strong with essays on literature, film, theater and the arts, and sports (obviously, in the field of arts there is no comparison with the Belvedere exhibit). The entire final third of the catalogue covers the history of the State Treaty negotiations and its final culmination in 1945.[24] Individual essays are dedicated to the chief architects of the State Treaty, the one on the American architects such as Dulles being particularly uninformative. Ernst Bruckmüller's two-page essay on Austrian national identity (p. 397) is trite compared with his treatment of the same topic in *Das neue Österreich* (pp. 241-54). Clearly, some in the tribe of historians ran out of steam writing their way through the demands of the *Gedankenjahr*. To sum up, in an archeology of postwar Austrian history, the Schallaburg show would represent the surface layer of traditional political, diplomatic, and economic history, while the Belevedere show also provides a deeper layer of Austrian subtle mentalities through its playful art track.

Even deeper layers of everyday life and an Austrian iconography, as well as an ethnography of sorts, are uncovered in the next two shows/catalogues under review. *Die junge Republik* and *Die Sinalco-epoche* offer a rich fare and provide the most substantive scholarly contributions among 2005 memory year exhibit catalogues. They both cover the postwar decade—the *Sinacloepoche* reaching into the 1960s—the trajectory from shocking poverty to rich plenty. Hans Petschar is the director of the photographic archives in the Austrian

National Library, located in the vast *Hofburg* palaces in the center of
Vienna.[25] For his visually stunning *Die junge* Republik exhibit,
exhaustively documented in the catalogue, Petschar selected the
photographs from an embarrassment of riches of some 10,000 negatives.
This constitutes the entire archives of the United States Information
Service (USIS) branch of the U.S. occupation government, employing
some forty Austrian photographers in the postwar decade. These
negatives were handed over by the U.S. Embassy to the National Library
in 1977. Petschar begins each of his nine chapters which brief intro-
ductions, providing the reader with both pointers on the motives and
iconic images and the photographers and their stylistic tools. Yoichi R.
Okamoto, who joined the U.S. Army as a photographer in 1942 and
came to Austria as High Commissioner Mark Clark's personal press
photographer, became the head of the USIS in 1948. He trained some
forty young Austrian photographers, thus giving a head start to some of
Austria's most talented photographers of the postwar period (p. 300).
Okamoto, who in the 1960s became President Lyndon Johnson's personal photographer, thus may be seen as the *spiritus rector* of sorts of this
intriguing exhibit. The lush catalogue with its often stark pictures
deservedly was a bestseller in the summer of 2005.

Petschar's visually rich photographic essay represents the entire
trajectory of Austrian life from the stark days at the end of the war to the
giddy excitement in Vienna on the day of the signing of the Austrian
State Treaty. Nothing brings the complex characteristics of Austrian
existence, rising like a phoenix out of the ashes of war, to life as do
these photos. Petschar uses the original captions of the American USIA
photographers, thus offering the viewer subtle insights into U.S. Cold
War propaganda as well. There are the bombed out streets of Vienna
(looking a bit like parts of New Orleans these days) and the *Trümmerfrauen* and Nazis cleaning up the rubble. Hungarian DP's marching
home from Mauthausen KZ and young forlorn Austrian soldiers with
despair written all over their faces returning from their POW camps look
out from the pages as well. There is the intriguing "Joseph Goldyn
Story" (pp. 40-3). The young American flyer lost both of his eyes in a
bombing raid against Vienna in November 1944. Seven year later, he
returns to Moosbierbaum and gives a winter coat to a seventeen year-old
local girl who also lost an eye during that air raid. It may have been
genuine, but more than fifty years later, it appears a bit like a staged
Cold War melodrama. The USIS photographers obviously eagerly
photographed the human side of such moving tales of postwar reconciliation between the victors and the vanquished. The sadness of the
desperate poverty and enormous want in 1945 is richly displayed in
images of a five year-old boy who collects cigarette butts, pathetic old

women digging for remnants of coal in the rubble, carrying bundles of firewood on their backs into Vienna from surrounding areas, along with the blossoming of brazen black market activity.[26]

The subtext of the "Americanization" of Austria is writ large in this exhibit catalogue.[27] The beginning of U.S. food aid to Austria by way of CARE packages is documented, as well as the rich volume of Marshall Plan aid and the recovery of economic life in both industrial and rural economic life. The USIS photographers obviously had orders to document the export of American popular culture to postwar Austria and its eager reception in the land: cinemas showing Hollywood movies, performances of *Porgy and Bess*, and a young "Lionell Hampton and his 16 Black Bombers" jazzing it up in Vienna's prestigious *Konzerthaus*, traveling "bookmobiles," a large Boy Scouts meeting in Bad Ischl, and placid American GIs dancing with eager Austrian women in Vienna's "Rainbow Club." In contrast, Soviet soldiers are portrayed among themselves playing chess in their free time in a house that they had "seized" from the Austrians—no Austrian "chocolate girls" for them! U.S. generosity displayed in numerous Marshall Plan projects vital for Austrian economic recovery are juxtaposed with Soviet economic exploitation of their Austrian zone: oil transports leaving Austria, embarrassed Austrian workers in factories taken over by the Soviets, price dumping USIA stores in the Soviet zone, and a picture of a Soviet pack of cigarettes, "looking like an American pack of [popular] Chesterfields" (p. 139). The high drama of long-winded propaganda speeches of the 1952 Communist Peace Congress in Vienna is fittingly captured with an Egyptian delegate napping during the endless speeches of Communist propagandists (p. 211). Modern times were juxtaposed with the harsh life of farmers in the Alpine region. While in the cities the motor scooters arrive and Austrian hairdressers done up like Hollywood starlets gather around bars drinking American cocktails and listening to jazz (p. 219 ff), life remains a grind in the high regions of the hard-working Alpine farmers where nature is merciless (pp. 260-63). Some of these scenes may be lowbrow, but they are engagingly presented.

The final chapter is entitled *"Lebenskünstler,"* named after the 1938 Frank Capra film first shown in Vienna in 1947. It offers a fascinating "ethnographic gaze" (p. 249) from the outside—a visual biographical cross section of Austrian archetypes documented in the USIS photo series "Meet Some Austrians": carefree kids eating candy in Vienna's amusement park *Prater*, chimney sweeps, a "coal shoveler" (in its dramatic visual iconography resembling 1930's Dorothea Lange-style gnarly Great Depression figures), the busy female mayor of Gloggnitz, women on the job (*"Frauen stellen ihren Mann"*), farmers, steel workers, teachers, office workers, window cleaners, and librarians.

These iconic Austrians represent everyday life in the early 1950s and suggest that the country was well on its way towards economic recovery and prosperity. The gaunt and desperate looks on the faces of 1945 survivors were gone. Now they are marked with determination and comfort signaling the advent of what Eric Hobsbawm calls the postwar "golden age." These iconic visual biographies of the common people suggest a very deep level in our archeology of the postwar era.

The arrival of the "Austrian economic miracle" with its "golden age" of consumerism and widespread prosperity is the topic of *Die Sinalcoepoche*, the exhibit by the City of Vienna Museum on everyday food, drink, and consumer culture after the war (*Sinalco* was the name of a popular Austrian soda pop with instantly recognizable gentle twist bottle-top design). The curators collected an astounding number of posters, cookbooks, food culture items, tableware, kitchen tools, and historical bottles, mostly from private collectors. These objects may well be the best examples for Lucy Noakes's assertion quoted above that selecting specific artifacts for museum display may lift them from the obscurity of "history" to the public realm of national "heritage." The trajectory of everyday material culture of consumption addressed in this show (and the catalogue documenting it) again runs from "scarcity to affluence," as Franz Eder's thorough essay on consumerism in Vienna from 1945 to 1980 notes (pp. 24ff). The years 1951/52 represented a "turning point" from black market activity and "squirreling away" survivalist rations (*hamstern*) to richly set tables and celebratory food culture, observes Wolfgang Kos in his subtle introduction. In the immediate postwar years, the desire for good food was a symbol of freedom. In a kind of "voluntary reeducation," observes Kos, by the 1950s the Austrians had eagerly adopted U.S. consumption models. "Americanization" became fashionable as a sign of rationalization and organization of everyday life.[28] Clearly, the quasi-"guardian angel" of *"Americanization"*—the adoption and/or rejection of everyday objects from the U.S. way of life—hovers over this exhibit. The housewife became the manager of domesticity. She had to learn new shopping and kitchen techniques on a daily basis. *Trümmerfrauen* transmogrified into *Hausfrauen*. A growing number of exotic import products came to Austria. Oranges from the south and pineapples from Hawaii signaled the arrival of the world at large, eradicating postwar poverty with its provincial ill-humor. A new consumer elite began traveling and bringing back new tastes; "the internationalization of consumption offerings destabilized traditional food customs" (p. 17).

The essays in *The Sinalcoepoche* offer the most unconventional scholarship to those who are looking beyond master narratives covering the well-tread celebratory anniversary history. They are specimen of social and cultural discourses at its best. Sándor Békési covers the postwar rise and fall of the *Greisler*—the tiny one-room neighborhood grocery store to which one could walk to buy the essentials of life. Whereas a housewife did most of her shopping at the bakery, the butcher's shop, and other small neighborhood stores, the arrival of self-service grocery stores by the 1970s changed basic shopping habits. By the 1990s, most Viennese drove to huge supermarkets, many of them on the periphery of town, just as they are in American cities. People began talking of the *Greisler* in nostalgic terms. In the old city, he had functioned as the next-door distributor of groceries and as a vital local communications hub. For many Viennese overwhelmed by the rapid modernization of postwar life with its escalating anonymity, the *Greisler* became a "site of memory" (p. 41).[29] The first supermarket opened in a Vienna suburb in 1970 and quickly became the *chiffre* of American modernity and "consumer democracy." Big self-service grocery stores signaled "the American way of life" (p. 50) and rapidly became the norm in daily Austrian consumerism as well. The culture of friendly clerks asking, "How may I help you?" rapidly vanished. Instead, shoppers were directed through narrow isles, lured by new products and cheap prices. The "supermarket paradise" ended a Viennese way of life. In a second essay, Küschelm provides a keen analysis of the advent of Austrian classic brand names such as *Thea* margarine, *Meinl* coffee, and *Haas* baking products.

Gabriele Sorgo's shrewd essay is on the archetypical *Hausfrau* who does it all. She manages the household and takes care of her man (*"Alles für ihn,"* proclaims a reprinted poster, p. 79). Sorgo shows how bourgeois hierarchies were played out in daily rituals around the dinner table. Preparing the family's food was not only a duty, but also an activity that gave women power in the family setting. In the 1970s, more and more women began taking jobs, but their husbands still wanted them to be *Hausfraus*. Austrian women had a hard time shedding their archetypical postwar roles associated with food and love (p. 85).

Susanne Breuss' two insightful chapters cover the revolutionary arrival of refrigeration in households and other technological advances that made life in the kitchen much easier. Next to cars, TVs, and washing machines, the refrigerator became *the* status symbol for Austrian households. Refrigerators filled with culinary delights signaled "prosperity reaching palpably close" (p. 96). Electrical technology eased life for the modern cooks, "sped up" work processes, and rationalized the kitchen. Mixers and *"presto"* pressure cookers were the "kitchen robots" that saved time and energy for the housewife. The "electrification" of postwar Austria signaled modernization of all aspects of economic life, the private household included (p. 114). Electrical kitchen gadgets were part and parcel of the Austrian economic miracle. The rationalized "American kitchen" became the fad in Austria as well, even though such kitchens had already been experimented with in the public housing projects of "Red Vienna" during the 1920s. During the initial postwar years, Austrian women contributed more than their share to the reconstruction of economic life. Reproduction and most of their other contributions were not remunerated by society. They needed relief and more freedom to improve their quality of life. The modern electrified kitchen gave it to them.

It may come as a surprise to many that fast food culture had existed in Austria long before McDonald's and Burger King. Nicole Dietrich's essay shows that fast food in Vienna was a homegrown tradition. The Viennese tradition of mobile sausage stands goes back to the nineteenth century, when sausage vendors walked the city with contraptions carried on their chests. After the war, an average of 320 *Würstlstände* spread across the city, giving the inebriated night owls a chance for a late supper on the way home from their favorite bar or the sober early birds a quick breakfast on their way to work. McDonald's came to Vienna in 1977 and was accepted slowly. It is mainly popular among young people. Similarly, the arrival of the *espresso* challenged the existence of the traditional coffee house. While the coffee house invited customers to linger, to talk, and to take their time reading the daily newspaper, *espressos* served their harassed customers in the fast moving urban arena. It is this dictate of time that speeds up postwar life, and these essays present fascinating case studies how Austrians adapted to the "fast life" and "fast food." On a personal note, many of the artifacts in this exhibit evoked a warm nostalgia, transporting this viewer back to the bygone era of his own youth when *Sinalco, Libella*, and *Austro-Cola*, along with *Petz* and *Manner Schnitten*, indeed defined one's well-being, which is to say that many consumer products were homegrown and that not everything "modern" came from America. In our archeology, the history of every-day life, where a growing number of Austrians participated in prosperity and its changing consumer patterns, is the most familiar layer of the past with which most people can identify. These trivial objects of daily life are part of average Austrian postwar identity and are presented in the most highbrow fashion.

The National Library photo exhibit presented the brilliant U.S. public relations effort in selling the Marshall Plan's generosity to Austrians to remind them on whose side Washington expected them to be in the Cold War. The Marshall Plan exhibit and its catalogue *Öster-reich Baut Auf/Rebuilding Austria*, covering the initial phase of postwar Austrian economic reconstruction in the Vienna Technical Museum, recounted the inner workings of the European Recovery Program

(ERP).[30] The Technical Museum staff seemed to have been the only exhibitor anticipating that an international audience might want to visit these shows, too, and provided bilingual German/English captions and catalogue texts. (During the Schallaburg exhibit, I personally translated some captions for American visitors.) This show told the story of postwar Austrian economic recovery and the crucial role the Marshall Plan played in it. The postwar economy was in shambles and suffered from serious bottlenecks in raw materials and critical infrastructure. The ERP provided the raw materials and machines, as well as the technical know-how needed to spark a quick recovery of the Austrian economy. It also produced the vital "counterpart funds" that gave the federal government the sorely needed investment funds for the oversized national economy and the many private industries to rebuild and to modernize. The state-sector steel factories, the nationalized hydro-electric industry, and the state railway system were principal recipients of such investment funds. In the private sector, the paper and textile industries, along with tourism and agriculture, were the beneficiaries. All of this was carefully documented in the exhibit. Unusual for the rest of Europe, food aid characterized the early years of the Marshall Plan in Austria. In a brilliant cameo of material history, original 100-pound flour sacks from mills in Minneapolis, St. Louis, and New Orleans, carrying U.S. grain to hungry Austrians, filled an entire wall. One almost could hear empty postwar stomachs growl. U.S. technical help designed to increase productivity and to introduce U.S. management know-how was another focus.

Naturally, the ERP sped up the "Americanization" of Austria by providing "food for the mind" as well. The American occupiers and keen Cold War propagandists filled suitcases with books and sent them to the most remote corners of Austria. The only remaining such *Bücherkoffer* was displayed filled with books and fiction on U.S. history and culture. A history in private photos of an unknown Austrian family through the postwar years concluded the exhibit and its catalogue. The well-known Austrian theologian Adolf Holl commented on these photos with a text about the generational unfolding of history and the intersection of individual and national lives. The Marshall Plan, in a way, still is alive and well in Austria. The U.S. government turned over all counterpart funds to the Austrian government in 1962. The *ERP-Fonds* was established to provide low-interest loans to and to fund innovation in Austrian businesses to this day (p. 136). Curators Helmut Lackner and Georg Rigele assembled a remarkable "themed display," fulfilling their role as "interpreters of the past" who give "credence and legitimization to one particular version of event" that does not usually show up in traditional museum displays.[31] Key Marshall Plan documents are appended to the catalogue as is a complete scholarly bibliography of the Marshall Plan in Austria. While most of the exhibit catalogue essays make concessions to popular audiences and feature minimal bibliographies—and most approach their references from an inbred perspective citing no foreign language sources—this extensive Marshall Plan bibliography not only includes all the contemporary literature of the Marshall Plan years (1948-1952), but also includes the vast and relevant foreign language literature to the present. This exhibit finally dispelled the well-liked myth among many Austrian politicos that the country's economic recovery was sparked by the brawny hard work of the Austrian people and did not require foreign help.

The final catalogue under review here addresses more troubled subterranean layers of Austrian historical mythology and postwar mentalities of historical memory. *"Heiss umfehdet, wild umstritten . . ."* is the catalogue of an exhibit in the City Museum of Villach. It is dedicated to postwar political myths, some of which are advocated—and perpetrated, one is tempted to say—with particular fervor in embattled Carinthia. It is fitting that such an exhibit should hold the mirror of historical truths and deceptions up to Carinthians. It is audacious and surprising that such a show should have been produced in "Haider country." The essays in the catalogue are easily the most thought-provoking of the entire *Gedenkjahr* literature. They are iconoclastic and hard-hitting. They challenge the reader by inviting him or her to penetrate into the deeper layers of postwar trauma and historical myth-making and to confront the ugly face of the Carinthian politics of history. Acting as the principal iconoclasts themselves, Lisa Rettl and Werner Koroschitz assembled a younger team of historians. Heidemarie Uhl's essay covers the well-known path of Austrian historical postwar memory and its social functions, so often treaded by her before. Katharina Wegan recounts the myth-making surrounding the Austrian State Treaty during its regular five-year commemorations staged by the federal government since 1965. The State Treaty was canonized as a sacred event in collective postwar Austrian memory culture. In state-directed identity formation by way of an hierarchization of sites of memory, the signing of the State Treaty was given top billing, and the Belvedere Palace became sacred ground for political "pilgrimages" (p. 47). The government chose not the *Heldenplatz*, site of Hitler's Anschluß speech, nor the building where the Control Council met on the *Schwarzenbergplatz*. Prince Eugene's Palace had the aura of Austria's heroic age.[32] Thomas Albrich summarizes the postwar myth of Austrian victimhood during the war. Peter Pirker touches on contentious issues dealing with *Wehrmacht* deserters and the failure of most Austrian politicians even today to give them credit for having been the true patriots. No pangs of "second guilt" ("*zweite Schuld*") surfaced in Carinthia.

Yet by dealing with the barbarities perpetrated by Carinthians during the war and the deceptive local and regional Carinthian memorial culture, Rettl and Koroschitz go the furthest in challenging official histories. In a relentless unmasking of defiant Carinthian public memory culture, Lisa Rettl shows how public memorials in Carinthia from 1947 until today have always insisted on the collective memory of Austrian victimhood. While the true victims of the war (Jews and Slovene resistance fighters, among others) have been excluded from the Carinthian "victims' collective," public memory culture has eagerly embraced *Wehrmacht* veterans and "victims of Allied de-Nazification." There has not been a single monument built for Slovenian anti-Nazi resistance fighters, who fought bravely with the Allies and Tito Communists, that has not been defaced multiple times. In fact, the rightwing nationalist Carinthian *Heimatdienst* has been acting like Ku Klux Klan-type enforcers of public memory culture, regularly defacing Slovenian monuments. Everybody knows who brazenly defaced the monuments, but no one has ever landed in jail. The *Heimatdienst* has doggedly intimidated Slovenian attempts to gain the ethnic equality promised in Article 7 of the State Treaty. Continued Carinthian refusal to live up to the international law of the treaty amounts to a persistent violation of the State Treaty; the governments in Vienna and the former occupation powers have been tolerating this breach, maybe the loudest silence ringing through this memory year. These young historians in a myth-shattering catalogue demonstrate what the actual job of the professional historian ought to be, namely to debunk historical myths, not to reinforce them as many texts in the catalogues under review here tend to do. No "eternal verities" or trite sermonizing here!

Conclusion

Are "memory years" useful, and are such a plethora of exhibits necessary? Is a surfeit of historical memory[33] healthy for a nation? It is always good if the people get a better sense of their own past, especially young people who increasingly learn their history not in classrooms, but from television, the movies, and video games. If such rare "memory years" as 2005 are only used for popularizing grand narratives of national history and for reinforcing official myths through the traditional politics of history, then a great opportunity is wasted. If, however, deeper layers of historical meaning are unearthed and evoked such as the social and economic, cultural, and mental trajectories of the postwar past, along with everyday life of people, then citizens are reconnected with the complexities of their personal identities and their own family histories. If, on top of this, people get a sense of how blatantly governments and official histories often misrepresent the past and how they build false monuments and deceptive collective memories, then they get an inkling of how febrile and fragile the construction of public historical memories is and how contentious the business of writing national master narratives can be. The stuff most citizens learn in school usually only represents the tip of the iceberg of a nation's historical trajectory. That it is the lowest common denominator most historians can agree on. Master narratives do not represent the real archeology and ethnography of the deeper subterranean pasts. To the credit of some of the 2005 memory year exhibits, deeper layers of history were probed. Strangely, the deepest layers were dug up in a local exhibit in the provinces far removed from Vienna's official *Gedankenjahr*. Quite amazingly and unexpectedly, then, the most daring and unconventional challenges to the *Gedankenjahr* emanated from the heart of Carinthia as a counterpoint to the traditionally smug Viennese intellectual community. In the Carithians' "heart of darkness," alternate routes into the recent Austrian past were tested. Some flashes of brilliance occurred in Vienna, too, yet official memory cultures were frequently reinforced too facilely. At its worst, the exhibitions embarked on a stale, theatrical historical-memory-as-nostalgia trip.

One of the most glaring lacunae was the intellectual history of the Second Republic. True, it is hard to portray visually great critical minds such as Friedrich Heer, Hans Weigel, and Elfriede Jelinek's, or moral consciences such as those of Franz König, Simon Wiesenthal, Ruth Klüger, and Hilde Spiel in an exhibit. One must turn to the sixtieth anniversary issue of the Austrian Catholic weekly *Die Furche* to enter the discourses of these and other fine Austrian minds.[34] Of course, many of the best minds were Jews who left Austria in the 1930s or were forced to leave the country in 1938 (if they were lucky). The Ludwig von Mises, Paul Lazarsfelds, and Erwin Kandlers made their weighty contributions in Anglo-American exile. Most Austrians do not want to be reminded of such self-inflicted trauma. Postwar Austrian intellectual history—the most highbrow kind of history—largely remains a history *manqué*. That may be the reason why it is so hard to write about or to display for a larger audience. While culture—the arts and literature—are represented in some of the exhibits and their catalogues reviewed above, ornery minds, such as Friedrich Heer and Tomas Bernhard's, only get a cursory hearing.

Notes

1. Speech by Chancellor Wolfgang Schüssel on the occasion of the presentation of the program for "Österreich 2005," 7 November 2005 [*recte* 2004], reprinted in Bundeskanzleramt/Bundespressedienst, ed., *Gedanken – Termine – Bücher: 1945 – 1955 – 1995 – 2005* (Vienna: 2006), p. 10. This is part of a handy three-volume documentation— namely this book of speeches, dates, and anniversary books quoted here, as well as two DVDs—reflecting the major events of the 2005 memory year. In the supposedly complete list of dates (*Termine*) of the memory year, conferences in New Orleans, Minneapolis, and Ottawa, as well as in Budapest and Vienna, that this author attended were not included— a snub of North American sites?

2. See Heidemarie Uhl, "Europäische Tendendenzen, regionale Verwerfungen: Österreichisches Gedächtnis und das Jubliläumsjahr 2005," in: *"Heiss umfehdet, wild umstritten. ..."*, p. 21.

3. Television journalist Hugo Portisch continued to be one of the principal myth-makers with his popular Austrian television documentaries. Chancellor Schüssel anointed him to be the "Cicerone leading through the past," establishing the "cultural guidelines" (*Leitkultur*) in the memory year, see his 7 November 2004 speech (n 1), p. 11.

4. For an outstanding analysis of the media's response to the 1988 memory year, see Heidemarie Uhl, *Zwischen Versöhnung und Verstörung: Eine Kontroverse um Österreichs historische Identität fünfzig Jahre nach dem "Anschluss"* (Vienna: Böhlau, 1992).

5. For the 1.25 million quoted in Chancellor's Schüssel's self-congratulatory final accounting of the *"Gedankenjahr 2005,"* see <http://www.oesterreich2005.at/site/cob__14011/4381/default.aspx> (accessed 3 May 2006).

6. "Wir wollten zum Schmunzeln anregen," ibid., and 7 November 2004 speech (n. 1), p. 11.

7. See the documentation in the DVD (n. 1) Bundeskanzleramt/Bundespressedienst, ed., *25 Peaces: Die Zukunft der Vergangenheit* (Vienna 2006).

8. G.W. Sebald, *On the Natural History of Destruction*, transl. Anthea Bell (New York: The Modern Library 2004); Jörg Friedrich, *Der Brand: Deutschland im Bombenkrieg 1940-1945* (Munich: Propyläen, 2002); see also now the massive critique of the Allied bombing war by the British philosopher A.C. Grayling, *Among the Dead Cities: The History and Moral Legacy of the WW II Bombing of Civilians in Germany and Japan* (New York: Walker & Co 2006).

9. Konrad Paul Liessmann, *Die Insel der Seligen: Österreichische Erinnerung* (Innsbruck: StudienVerlag, 2005), p. 37.

10. Chancellor Schüssel even avers that ever since the Baroque era "celebration is part of Austrian identity," see 7 November 2004 speech, (n. 1), p. 12.

11. Lucy Noakes, "Making Histories: Experiencing the Blitz in London's Museums in the 1990s," in *The World War II Reader*, ed. Gordon Martel (New York: Routledge, 2004), 422-34 (here 423, 425f).

12. Ibid.

13. Ibid.

14. Ibid.

15. Ibid.

16. The chancellor had a busy year of opening exhibits and delivering speeches. If one looks at the collection of Schüssel's memory year sermons, the principal ideas of the Austrian postwar trajectory from war and dictatorship via occupation to freedom and

sovereignty, from poverty to prosperity, from Cold War neutrality to European integration tended to become repetitive; see his speeches in *Gedanken* (n. 1), pp. 9-12, 17-20, 21-25, 41-45, 49-52, 59-63, 71-74, 77-81. In the case of his brilliant opening speech at the Marshall Plan exhibit in Vienna's Technical Museum on 16 March 2005 (not reprinted in *Gedanken*), his principal ideas were directly excerpted from—but not attributed to—this author's introductory essay to the exhibit catalogue.

17. A similarly uneven product with interesting perspectives from abroad, but too many politicians writing their usual edifying trivialities on "European identity" and "historical milestones" is the anniversary issues of "Österreich und die Welt: 50 Jahre Staatsvertrag," of *Europäische Rundschau* 33/1 (Winter 2005).

18. For a possible first draft of such a book, see Katharina Wegan's essay in this volume.

19. For an uncomplimentary portrait of Karner, see Herwig G. Höller and Thomas Wolkinger, "Ein Mann der Geschichte," *Falter* 13/2006, 2f.

20. See Rolf Steininger, *South Tyrol: A Minority Conflict of the Twentieth Century* (New Brunswick, NJ: Transaction, 2003).

21. There seems to be a growing movement in Austria to make the artifacts and the narrative of the Belvedere show the permanent core exhibits of an Austrian "*Haus der Geschichte,*" the idea of which has been contentiously debated for almost ten years amongst historians and politicians.

22. Ralph Giordano, "Die Internationale der Einäugigen," in *Aus Politik udn Zeitgeschichte*, 24 April 2006, 7.

23. Full disclosure requires that this author note his contribution to the first chapter with an essay on the Moscow Declaration for 1943, pp. 22-26.

24. The doyen of Austrian State Treaty historians, Gerald Stourzh, is only represented with a short essay on Foreign Minister Leopold Figl, one of the Austrian architects of the Treaty. He contributed a more substantive essay to *Frei – Souverän – Neutral – Europäisch: 1945 1955 1995 2005*, in *Informationen zur Politischen Bildung* 22 (2004), 7-20. His principal contribution to the State Treaty celebrations was his memorable keynote address to the Austrian Academy of Sciences in mid-May, reprinted in "Wie Kam es zu Staatsvertrag und Neutralität?," in idem, *1945 und 1955: Schlüsseljahr der Zweiten Republik* (Innsbruck: StudienVerlag, 2005), 65-82.

25. For a parallel volume dealing with both the history and the analysis of film on the occupation period, see Karin Moser, ed., *Besetzte Bilder: Film, Kultur und Propaganda in Österreich 1945-1955* (Vienna: verlag filmarchiv Austria, 2005).

26. The well-known American economist Charles P. Kindleberger visited Vienna in August 1946 as a State Department official dealing with Austrian economic affairs. On 16 August he wrote to his wife: "[…] Vienna is a sad city. Like Berlin, but even more so. Everybody is carrying a package, or a bundle or a rucksack. I saw a women this evening with a netzli [sic] which showed the contents of at least some of the packages—six or eight pounds of potatoes." Charles P. Kindleberger, *The German Economy, 1945-1947, Charles P. Kindleberger's Letters for the Field*, with an historical introduction by Günter Bischof (Westport, CT: Meckler, 1989), p. 79.

27. It thus provides the imagery for the scholarly analyses in Günter Bischof and Anton Pelinka, eds., *Contemporary Austrian Studies*, vol. 12, *The Americanization/Westernization of Austria* (New Brunswick, NJ: Transaction, 2004).

28. The larger trajectory of Americanization by way of consumerism is covered in the profound new book by Victoria de Grazia, *Irresistible Empire: America's Advance through 20th-Century Europe* (Cambridge, MA: Harvard UP, 2005). See also Charles S.

Maier, *Among Empires: America's Ascendancy and Its Predecessors* (Cambridge, MA: Harvard UP, 2006).

29. Interestingly, the *Greisler* was not included in the three-volume encyclopedic Austrian *lieux de memoires* by Emil Brix, Ernst Bruckmüller, and Hannes Stekl, eds., *Memorie Austriae I – III* (Vienna: Böhlau, 2004/2005).

30. Again, full disclosure demands that the reader know this author wrote the scholarly lead essay in the exhibit catalogue; see Günter Bischof, "Der Marshall-Plan in Österreich/The Marshall Plan and Austria," in *Österreich baut auf/Rebuilding Austria*, pp. 12-66.

31. Noakes, "Making Histories," p. 426.

32. See also Wegan's essay in this volume.

33. I take the notion from Charles S. Maier, "A Surfeit of Memory? Reflections on History, Melancholy and Denial," in *History & Memory* 5/2 (Winter 1993): 136-51.

34. *Die Furche*, 1 December 2005. The Viennese daily *Kurier*, launched by the Americans, celebrated its fiftieth birthday with a less high-minded special anniversary issue on 18 October 2004 by picking a signal headline from each year and having it analyzed by a prominent contemporary (for example, Ambassador Ludwig Steiner commenting on the special edition of 15 May 1955 *"Wir sind frei!"*).

Of Affluence and Amnesia

Felix Butschek, *Vom Staatsvertrag zur EU: Österreichische Wirtschaftsgeschichte von 1955 bis zur Gegenwart* (Vienna: Böhlau Verlag, 2004)

Oliver Rathkolb, *Die paradoxe Republik: Österreich 1945 bis 2005* (Vienna: Paul Zsolnay Verlag, 2005)

Emmerich Tálos, *Vom Siegeszug zum Rückzug: Sozialstaat Österreich 1945-2005* (Innsbruck, Vienna: StudienVerlag, 2005)

Peter Berger

Two of the three books under review here appeared in 2005. Since this was the year marking the fiftieth anniversary of Austria's regained sovereignty in the wake of World War II, both Oliver Rathkolb and Emmerich Tálos's volumes may be seen as intellectual contributions to a national commemorative effort. One can safely assume that Böhlau publishers also wished to exploit the *"annus mirabilis"* effect when they launched Felix Butschek's economic history of Austria (somewhat prematurely) in 2004. Readers familiar with this author's earlier work will, however, find out that large sections of *Vom Staatsvertrag zur EU* are a revised and updated extract from a long essay published in the mid-1990s. It was printed in 1996 under the auspices of Vienna's chamber of labor (*Kammer für Arbeiter und Angestellte Wien*), but due to the limited number of copies in circulation failed to attract the attention of a wider public.[1]

Half a century elapsed since the signing of Austria's State Treaty in 1955, but we still lack a comprehensive and critical historical narrative of this country's rise from the ashes of postwar destruction (in both the physical and the moral sense) to its present degree of prosperity and stability. *Die paradoxe Republik*, though written by a distinguished

contemporary historian, does not aspire to fill the gap. While some
readers may deplore this, others will welcome the author's decision to
focus on a limited number of issues which are considered important for
an understanding of the Austrian mentality, institutions, and achievements. In ten chapters, each one an essay in its own right, Rathkolb sets
out to challenge—as he puts it in his foreword—the "founding myths"
of the Second Republic and proposes to replace them by unprejudiced
analysis. One is tempted to ask whether anything else can be expected
from an honest disciple of Clio. Unfortunately, the question is off the
mark. All too often, Austrian historians have deliberately avoided analy-
tical clarity, sometimes for want of a deeper understanding of their
subject, but more often because, in a highly politicized environment,
outspokenness would have exposed them to charges of political
partisanship. Rathkolb never tried to conceal his close ties with Austria's
Social Democracy. He is known as the editor of two volumes of
memoirs of Bruno Kreisky,[2] head of four consecutive socialist governments in the 1970s and early 1980s. Rathkolb's admiration for Kreisky's
attempts at modernizing Austrian society is reflected in every paragraph
of *Die paradoxe Republik* devoted to this statesman of undeniable
stature. Where he turns a blind eye on Kreisky's shortcomings, as in his
treatment of the chancellor's actions during the infamous Wiesenthal-
Peter affair of 1975, Rathkolb can be reproached for transgressing the
line that separates legitimate empathy from unwarranted bias. But
throughout most of his book, he remains an impeccably dispassionate,
and exceptionally well informed, guide to post-1945 Austrian politics,
economics, and culture, as well as the welfare system and the media.

As its title suggests, *Die paradoxe Republik* is mainly concerned
with contradictions present in almost every aspect of daily Austrian life.
To begin with, the concept of an Austrian identity is fraught with ambivalence. During the interwar period, Austrians thought of themselves as
a branch of the German nation, compelled to live outside the boundaries
of Germany proper by the ignorance and vindictiveness of those who
had defeated and dismembered the Habsburg Empire in 1918-1919. Pan-
German sentiment was deeply entrenched in all sectors of Austrian
society, inclusive of the socialist and catholic camps, though it was a
catholic politician, Engelbert Dollfuss, who after Adolf Hitler's seizure
of power in Berlin resorted to slogans of local patriotism as a means to
counteract the growing appeal to Austrian youths of the Nazi's radical
Anschluß rhetoric. In March 1938, jubilant crowds welcomed the *Führer*
in Linz and Vienna. Following their country's incorporation into
Germany, Austrian adherents of the swastika hoped to be given a decisive share in the business of running the Third Reich. Rathkolb
maintains (against other historians like Evan Burr Bukey[3]) that their

disappointment was pivotal in leading to an anti-German emotional backlash during the final stages of World War II. Be that as it may, the Allied liberation/occupation of Austria in 1945 made it impossible for pan-Germanism to prevail as the official Austrian state doctrine. It came to be replaced with surprising speed and efficiency by an alternative dogma, consisting mainly in the full-scale denial of any common traits between Austrian and German culture and history. Thus, the communist minister of public education after the war, Ernst Fischer, reminded all schools under his jurisdiction to avoid using the term "German language" in their written curricula. "Language of instruction" was considered appropriate. In a similar vein, Austria's prominent role in German politics between 1815 and 1866 received scant attention in history classes, while Hitler, if mentioned at all, was usually introduced as a German, and not as the child of a Habsburg customs official born and raised in Upper Austria.

This reviewer, who went to Austrian schools in the late 1950s and 1960s, can testify to the relative ease with which a new national identity, tinted with anti-German feelings, was adopted by a generation born around 1950. Rathkolb is also right in asserting that, for all the emphasis laid by our teachers on Austria's glorious past as the centerpiece of a powerful dynastic empire, the very fact that this empire's well-being depended on the loyalty of its forty-odd million non-German speaking subjects was largely ignored. If Austrians of today are skeptical of Germany, their attitude toward former compatriots like the Czechs, Poles, and Romanians, among others, can be called hostile. Eastern European immigrants in particular are readily identified with criminal behavior, illicit work, and abuse of the welfare system—all of which happens, of course, but not to an extent the general public (influenced by the tabloid press) takes for granted. The paradox here lies in the Slavic roots of much of the population of Austria's Eastern provinces. One finds as many Czech or Polish names in Vienna's telephone directory as in those of Prague or Krakow.

If, after 1945, Austria could avoid a rerun of its sad prewar history, this was mainly due to efficient political power sharing arrangements and to the unexpected speed of economic recovery followed by almost two decades of stable growth. Austrian postwar democracy rested on two pillars. There was a seemingly perennial coalition of two mass parties, one socialist, the other catholic, who divided between themselves all available jobs in government and bureaucracy according to their respective electoral returns (*Proporz*). At the level of interest associations, the grand coalition regime was supplemented by "social partnership," a consultative arrangement obliging the workers' and employers' key organizations to exercise wage and price moderation, which

duly resulted in high rates of export-led growth. Leading functionaries
of these key organizations, who almost invariably were either Socialist
or Catholic party members, routinely occupied government posts and/or
carried legislative mandates. The ubiquitous presence of interlocking
elites made Austrian politics seem special, and somehow suspicious, in
a larger European context. Rathkolb shows how social partnership
survived the break-up of the original grand coalition in 1966 to remain
influential while first the catholic ÖVP (until 1970), and then the
socialist SPÖ (until 1983) governed alone. The year 1986 saw a return
to joint government of "Reds" and "Blacks" and to the habit of pro-
portional sharing of the spoils as well. Since Austria's joining the European Union in 1995 and the advent to power of a center-right coalition
of Catholics and the Freedom-Party (FPÖ/BZÖ) in 2000, the social
partners lost a great deal of their former clout. A future entirely without
them is hard to imagine, says Rathkolb. But the recent involvement of
Austria's Trade Union Federation (ÖGB) in a potentially destructive
bank scandal may prove him utterly wrong.

The "tribal" nature of Austria's post-1945 political system (where
backroom deals between all-powerful party bosses made debates in
parliament look almost like a sham) drew many critical comments over
time. Rathkolb's treatment of consensual politics, Austrian style, is
generally sympathetic because of their undeniable contribution to social
peace and prosperity. The author convincingly argues that a gradual
strengthening of democratic pluralism has taken place in Austria over
the past decades. But he finds no indication for a parallel growth of
enlightened attitudes among individual Austrian voters. It seems
paradoxical that while the Second Republic's state institutions developed to a reasonable degree of maturity the electorate should have
continued to include a sizable minority of "authoritarian personalities"
in the sense of Theodor W. Adorno and Max Horkheimer.[4] Rathkolb's
claim is backed, however, by the outcome of relatively recent opinion
polls. They show (too) many Austrians harboring feelings of hatred
against Jews and foreigners, preferring to have a strong man instead of
democratically elected politicians at the helm of the state, and advocating the death penalty for rapists and "terrorists." Somewhat surprisingly for a country with Austria's cultural credentials, objects of art and
dramatic plays are popular targets of law-and-order rhetoric. Outcries of
popular indignation, and calls for censorship, accompanied the performance in 1988 of Thomas Bernhard's play, *Heldenplatz*, at the Viennese
Burgtheater. In 2004, the display of a backward-bending male figure
with an erected penis, sculptured by the art-group *Gelatine* and named
Arc de Triomphe, brought the peaceful citizens of Salzburg to the edge
of revolt.

In what may well be the best chapter of his book, Rathkolb offers an elaborate account of the history and power of Austria's print media—including that self-styled mouthpiece of sound popular instinct, a tabloid paper called *Kronenzeitung*. The first Austrian newspaper after the war, *Neues Österreich*, was controlled by Soviet military authorities and jointly produced by the three legal political parties of that time, Socialists, Catholics, and Communists. Editor-in-chief was Ernst Fischer, the Communist. Later, each party was granted permission to print its own daily. As a result of a paper shortage, it took some time for independent journalists to find ways of reaching the public. In Vienna, Ernst Molden founded *Die Presse*, a nominally non-partisan paper, yet closely aligned with the conservative camp. Its counterpart in Salzburg was named *Salzburger Nachrichten* (SN). Several members of the SN writing staff were known as Nazi sympathizers, which, however, did not adversely affect their careers in democratic Austria. Two SN journalists became the founding fathers of a political movement called "Association of Independents." Its constituency was former Nazis and/or men and women who held former Jewish property and wished to avoid restitution.

The socialist and catholic parties fought acrimonious battles over the control of an emerging market for mass-circulation tabloids. Enterprising newspaper publishers were offered "red" and "black" financial support—and often switched from one sponsor to the other. Hans Dichand who, together with Kurt Falk, launched the *Kronenzeitung* in 1959 was lent a helping hand by Franz Olah, a charismatic socialist leader holding the functions of both interior minister and president of the Trade Union Federation. Olah diverted trade union funds to secure the *Kronenzeitung*'s successful launch. Later he was sentenced to one year of prison for not having disclosed the deal with Dichand to his fellow trade unionists. Selling approximately 1.1 million copies per day, the *Kronenzeitung* today occupies a dominant position in its Austrian home market while ranking seventh among Europe's most influential tabloid papers. Like its chief national competitor, *Kurier* (with a daily circulation of 310,000 copies), it is partly owned by the German media conglomerate WAZ. Whereas a high degree of economic concentration in the media sector is not uncommon for small European countries, it is bound to have dangerous consequences if media monopolists (or near-monopolists) pursue a political agenda. Dichand's agenda is xenophobic, narrow-minded populism, and Rathkolb correctly if sadly states that whoever aspires to a career in Austrian politics cannot escape seeking some sort of arrangement with his power over Austrian public opinion.

If the *Kronenzeitung* is an Austrian institution, such, too, is neutrality. Rathkolb gives a detailed account of its genesis and describes how it functioned as a lodestar of Vienna's foreign policy from the mid 1950s to the mid 1980s. Prior to the conclusion of the Austrian State Treaty, Chancellor Julius Raab's efforts to get rid of Allied tutelage by "neutralizing" his country in a Swiss fashion drew skeptical reactions from various quarters. U.S. Secretary of State John F. Dulles feared that West Germany might emulate the Austrian example and offer to become neutral in return for Soviet willingness to sanction German reunification. Dulles' Russian counterpart, Vyacheslav Molotov, initially refused to consider withdrawing the Red Army from Austrian soil and hence ignored Raab's overtures until he was forced by Premier Nikita Khrushchev to reverse his stance. In Vienna, leading socialist politicians warned that if Austria's government struck a deal with the Kremlin it would be considered a Soviet puppet by the West. As a matter of fact, Austria since the late 1940s was an unwavering, if undeclared, ally of the United States. Washington assisted in the build-up of a clandestine Austrian military force ready to quell potential communist violence and to reinforce NATO's Eastern flank in the eventuality of a Russian onslaught. That Austria possessed a small pro-Western army in all but name made U.S. President Dwight D. Eisenhower favorably disposed to granting it full independence in 1955 and also to accept its Russian-sponsored neutral status. Khrushchev's chief motive for supporting the State Treaty, says Rathkolb, was his desire to bring about a temporary reduction of East-West tensions. *Détente* was bound to facilitate modernization of the Soviet economy, a project to which Joseph Stalin's successor felt strongly committed.

After its formal adoption by Federal Parliament on 26 October 1955, neutrality quickly became a factor which buttressed Austrian self-confidence, as did the astonishing growth of the national economy and the emergence of an efficient welfare state regime. (Rathkolb deals with economic and social developments in two separate chapters of his book not reviewed here due to limitations of space.) In contrast to their Swiss fellow neutrals, Austrians saw no difficulty in their country's joining the United Nations (1955), while the option of full membership in the European Economic Community was dismissed by experts as a breach of international law. During the 1970s—a period Rathkolb calls the Golden Age of Austrian "active neutrality"—Chancellor Bruno Kreisky's personality left a strong imprint on Vienna's handling of foreign affairs. While preserving its traditional interest in the promotion of U.S.-Soviet *détente*, Austrian diplomacy under Kreisky extended its field of action to include bridge-building between industrialized and developing nations. As a leading statesman of the Socialist International, Kreisky also mediated in the conflict between the Israelis and Arabs. Whatever one's opinion is of his excursions into the Near Eastern minefield, it seems safe to assume that from a domestic Austrian perspective they always looked more spectacular than they actually were. Inasmuch as Rathkolb fails to see this, he is guilty of the kind of "Austro-solipsism" justly denounced in the first chapter of *Die paradoxe Republik*. Rathkolb's discussion of the present state of Austrian neutrality within the framework of the European Union seems to suffer from the same solipsistic slant. He is keen to demonstrate how Catholics, Socialists, and "Freedomites" prevaricate whenever the subject of Austria's possible future association with NATO is broached. But nowhere does he offer an explanation for the obvious paradox of a neutral country whose constitution obliges it to support Europe's Common Foreign and Security Policy (CFSP).

Everyone mindful of Marc Bloch's famous dictum that historians ought to be like cannibals who, when they smell human flesh, know that their prey is near must welcome Rathkolb's choice to include in his book ten biographical profiles of Austrian postwar heads of government, from the Socialist Karl Renner (1945) to the incumbent Conservative Wolfgang Schüssel. The author focuses on each of these men's period of tenure at the *Ballhausplatz* (no woman ever was Chancellor of Austria!) and tries to assess their long-term political impact. There are two more chapters of *Die paradoxe Republik* devoted to the personality factor, one dealing with art and artists in the aftermath of World War II, the other with Austria's unmastered Nazi past and those who, like presidential candidate Kurt Waldheim in 1986, instead of facing its horrors preferred to forget them altogether. The international scandal caused by Waldheim's refusal to disclose important details of his wartime record and his stubborn insistence on having fulfilled a patriotic duty during the Nazi era proved to be instrumental in undermining Austria's self-perception as an innocent victim of Hitler's schemes. Collective amnesia may now have been overcome, Rathkolb says. What remains to be seen is if Austrians will respond to the challenge of globalization by learning to understand their country's history as part of a larger picture including not only Europe, but the world as a whole.

The title of Felix Butschek's *Vom Staatsvertrag zur EU* contains the promise of a European perspective. The author is a retired long-time director of Vienna's renowned Economic Research Institute (WIFO), an advisory body counseling the government and the social partners. His approach to postwar Austrian economic history is that of an economist mainly concerned with problems of growth and stagnation in a long-term, comparative perspective. Hence, *Vom Staatsvertrag zur EU* offers an impressive array of statistical tables testifying first and foremost to

Austria's miraculous transformation from neglected European Cinderella in 1945 to wealthy princess of the old continent only a few decades later. If in terms of GDP growth the Alpine republic outperformed most of Western Europe (as it did from the late 1950s to the late 1970s), this was primarily due to a set of institutional arrangements promoting internal stability, Butschek tells us. In a similar vein, he argues that lower and/or discontinuous Austrian growth in the 1980s and 1990s resulted to a large extent from flaws in the domestic governance structure. Yet his emphasis on "institutionalist" explanations does not lead him to ignore the restricted size and openness of the Austrian economy which have always exposed it to external influences, whether beneficial (like the fall of the Iron Curtain in 1989) or malign (like the twin oil crises of 1974/75 and 1979/80).

Vom Staatsvertrag zur EU begins with a cursory description of Austria's plight in the immediate aftermath of World War II. Austrian civil and military casualties were high (the author does not bother to quantify them, but 350,000 is probably a good estimate). Approximately 750,000 POW's could not return home. Buildings and traffic facilities suffered extensive damage from aerial bombing. Butschek asserts that Austria, though it remained occupied by the four victorious Allied powers until 1955, could neither be held responsible for the outbreak of the war nor be considered a belligerent in the legal sense of that term. The Anschluß had reduced it to being a marginal German province. While there is nothing wrong in saying this, one should be aware that there was another side to the coin. Bereft of its national sovereignty, Austria may have been innocent of Hitler's crimes, but individual Austrians certainly participated in them. Shortly after the Germans' arrival in 1938, this country witnessed the largest forcible transfer of economic assets from one group of citizens to another since the times of the Counter-Reformation. "Aryanization" was carried out mainly by native Austrians (not Germans from the Reich!) eager to reap the benefits of their Jewish neighbors' reduction to pariah status. After Hitler's defeat, "unclaimed" Jewish property helped lay the foundations of Austria's economic miracle which thrived on short memory. Butschek prefers not to touch upon this sensitive topic. He contents himself with pointing at less controversial factors facilitating postwar recovery. In spite of Anglo-American air raids, large portions of German wartime productive capacities in Austria had remained intact. Skilled labor was abundant and, thanks to Marshall Aid flowing in from the United States, so was fresh capital. Business and labor engaged in joint efforts to curtail inflation and to reduce the risk of social unrest. If the trade unions and their economic brain-trust, the Austrian Chamber of Labor, occasionally reverted to mild anti-capitalist rhetoric, this was not meant to challenge fundamentally the notion of functioning markets as a precondition to growing national wealth. In 1952, Reinhard Kamitz, who during the Nazi era taught economics at Vienna's notorious *Hochschule für Welthandel*, was promoted to the post of finance minister. He remained in office until 1960. Somehow Kamitz acquired the reputation of being an unbending liberal (in the anti-interventionist sense), but Butschek correctly emphasizes his penchant for state activism. Federal income taxes were lowered, nationalized banks and insurance companies gained access to public subsidies, and export promotion was introduced as an instrument of growth policy. During Kamitz's tenure, but more actively supported by ÖVP Chancellor Julius Raab than by him, the "Parity Commission for Wages and Prices," a cornerstone of Austrian social partnership, began functioning in 1957. Two years earlier, Catholics and Socialists had agreed on the Magna Charta of Austrian "welfare capitalism," the General Social Insurance Law (ASVG 1955). In accordance with the electoral strength of Christian Democracy, Austria's welfare provisions resembled the German rather than the Swedish model, placing strong emphasis on salaried employment and family as the criteria for access to social rights. In his chapter devoted to social partnership and the emergent welfare state, Butschek stresses the ideologically motivated reluctance of ÖVP politicians to acknowledge the justification of a tightly woven social security net. Austria's conservatives, he says, merely gave in to socialist pressure without ever taking the initiative in welfare matters themselves. If that is true, things were rather different in the area of wage and price management. Here, employers' organizations dominated by the ÖVP actively militated for cooperation with the trade unions, rightly presuming that mutual confidence would pave the way for a reduction of transaction costs and, hence, for a competitive edge of Austrian products on their export markets.

The prosperous years of 1953-1962 were followed by a brief recession lasting until 1968. In that year, Austria's economy entered another sustained boom period extending beyond the first oil price crisis in 1973 and withering away in 1975-1978. Butschek identifies several domestic factors which contributed to the remarkable steadiness of Austrian growth during the 1970s. To begin with, there was a healthy infusion of scientific professionalism into politics, as senior politicians of both the leading parties were replaced with younger "technocrats" who learned to base their decisions on expert advice from think tanks like Butschek's own *Wirtschaftsforschungsinstitut*. Austrian industry, which comprised a large nationalized basic goods sector, had suffered from a fall in demand for steel in the early 1960s; this situation was partly reversed in the 1970s, although with hindsight one cannot say that efforts under-

taken by Chancellor Bruno Kreisky of the SPÖ to reorganize nationalized industry and to increase its productivity came anywhere near to
success. Kreisky and his finance minister, Hannes Androsch, were,
however, successful in practicing what later came to be called Austro-
Keynesianism. Chief elements of that singular economic policy mix
were the pegging of Austria's currency to the hard German Mark (to
prevent imported inflation), an emphasis on wage moderation in the
manufacturing and service sectors, and occasional deficit spending
which helped Austria to insulate itself from the impact of the global
recession in 1973-1974 (but failed to achieve a similar result during the
second oil crisis in 1979-1980). Somewhat surprisingly, Butschek down-
plays the salutary effect of Austro-Keynesianism on overall employment, while admitting that well into the 1980s Austria did have lower
unemployment rates than most other advanced European economies. But
this, he says, resulted from legalized premature retirement of jobholders
and large-scale dismissal of foreign workers rather than from the creation of new job opportunities.

While the peoples of non-communist Europe enjoyed a degree of
affluence unknown to earlier generations, the mid-1970s witnessed the
advance of popular movements opposing "unbridled consumerism,"
widespread ignorance of nature's vulnerability, and the seemingly un-
shakeable belief in scientific progress. Growth skepticism found an early
expression in Dennis Meadows' report for the Club of Rome of 1972,
which predicted total exhaustion of the world's natural resources within
a few decades. Butschek heaps scorn not only on Meadows and his
associates, but especially on Austria's "68ers" and "Greens," whom he
accuses of having sown the seeds of hostility towards everything potentially conducive to capitalist expansion: from the construction of high-
ways and nuclear power plants to genetically manipulated agriculture.
How much of the blame for Austria's uneven and sometimes sluggish
growth performance of the 1980s and 1990s should be put on the shoul-
ders of environmentalists is a moot question. But Butschek surely has a
point when he chastises Austrian lawmakers and the bureaucracy for
their sometimes irrational fear of innovation. A recent example is provided by the slowness of Austrian traffic planners to acknowledge the
need for new transit roads following from the increase of trade between
Western and Eastern Europe since the demise of Communism in 1989-
1990. Butschek deals with this problem in a chapter called "Misallo-
cation of Resources." It is one of the very few parts of his book where
an uncompromisingly technical writing style is enlivened by injections
of polemical fervor.

In the mid-1980s, the deficit of Austria's federal budget rose to
record levels of around 5 percent of GDP. Thus, when in 1987 a grand

coalition of the SPÖ and ÖVP headed by Franz Vranitzky (a socialist and former banker) took office, the government could have been expected to abandon Austro-Keynesianism and to follow a course of retrenchment. Indeed, Chancellor Vranitzky displayed a firm commitment to privatize state-owned industries which previously had been a major drain on public finances. But according to Butschek, the two SPÖ-ÖVP coalition governments of 1987-1994 lacked the political will to curb public expenditure while a favorable international business climate would have made such a venture socially acceptable. Instead, Butschek says, social costs (mainly in the form of state contributions to pension insurance carriers) were unduly expanded. As the federal elections of 1994 approached, Finance Minister Ferdinand Lacina (SPÖ) proposed to abolish several taxes on property and trade and to reduce the tax levied on income from financial investments. Parliament passed the new tax laws in 1993, despite predictions of an imminent reversal of the global business cycle. During the tenure of Vranitzky's last two cabinets (1994-1998), efforts at budget consolidation were counteracted by developments beyond any government's sphere of influence. As a freshly accepted member of the European Union, Austria was obliged to contribute 0.5 percent of its yearly GDP to the common European household. While prior to 1994 the problems of Austria's pension system had been attributable to excessive utilization of early retirement rights, now they increasingly stemmed from the rise in the ratio of old people to total population. Last but not least, Austria's social partners, on whose cooperation and advice previous cabinets had relied during their efforts at balancing public finances, suffered a loss of prestige. Under incessant attacks from Jörg Haider's populist FPÖ, but more so because of the difficulty in convincing their clientele of the merits of membership in an increasingly competitive environment, trade unions and chambers of labor now discontinued the practice of scaling down their social claims (as they had done in the 1960s and 1970s) in order to secure smooth functioning of the economy and the state. Consequently, says Butschek, the budget situation remained unsatisfactory until Vranitzky's successor, Federal Chancellor Viktor Klima (SPÖ), was ousted by a combination of Wolfgang Schüssel's Christian Democrats and the Freedom Party early in 2000.

Did the Socialist's removal from power bring about a paradigm shift in Austrian economic policy? While fourteen EU governments seemed more concerned about the political consequences of cabinet posts falling to the extreme right (and accordingly proceeded to impose diplomatic sanctions on Austria), there were some indications that the new finance minister in Vienna, Karl-Heinz Grasser, sympathized with neo-liberalism and supply-side economics. Austria's Association of

Industrialists, known for its penchant for Reaganomics and Thatcherism, was so impressed by Grasser that it sponsored his personal homepage, the copyrights of which were held by an "Association for the Promotion of the New Economy." Butschek in the last chapter of his book reports such details with obvious amusement. However, he denies that Schüssel's government at any time in its existence followed a consistently neo-classical agenda. Whenever it sold state property (which happened at increased speed), pursued the goal of budget equilibrium (not without success), or supported the creation of private pension funds as a supplement to the public social insurance system, governments of a different color would have done the same, and maybe with less regard for the rights of the worker, says Butschek, citing the example of Germany's reform of unemployment insurance under the auspices of a red-and-green cabinet led by the Socialist Gerhard Schröder.

Butschek's argument is squarely rejected by Emmerich Tálos in his short history of the postwar Austrian welfare state entitled *Vom Siegeszug zum Rückzug. Sozialstaat Österreich 1945-2005*. Tálos is a renowned political scientist at the University of Vienna and the author or editor of several standard textbooks on Austria's political system, National Socialism in Austria, and social partnership. In the first chapter of *Vom Siegeszug zum Rückzug*, he discusses the emergence and gradual strengthening of the Second Republic's social security system. Chapter Two is devoted to the retreat of social policy which began in the 1980s and took on a distinctly new quality after the ÖVP-FPÖ coalition's entering office in January 2000. The foundations of an Austrian welfare state, says Tálos, were laid by imperial governments of the Habsburg era in the 1880s and expanded after World War I. While both Austrofascism (1933-1938) and Hitler's dictatorship (1938-1945) restricted social rights, the Socialists' return into government offices paved the way for a steady improvement of welfare legislation from the late 1940s until the late 1970s. Factors which helped to finance costly social provisions were sustained economic growth, a steady rise of the wage level, and high birth rates. In contrast to earlier periods, social insurance was extended to include self-employed persons, which made the welfare state more attractive for Austria's conservatives. At its heyday around 1980, Austrian social policy protected every gainfully occupied citizen from falling prey to poverty as a consequence of illness, accident, unemployment, or old age. However, there were structural flaws in the system, as Tálos rightly points out. Protection was more efficient for men than for women, and practically nonexistent for people who never possessed a regular job and/or a family.

In the 1980s and 1990s, social rights in Austria were certainly not dismantled, says Tálos. While substantial progress occurred in several areas like worker codetermination or gender mainstreaming, others witnessed slow but steady erosion. Like their counterparts elsewhere in Europe, Austrian governments adapted their welfare strategies to an increasingly unfavorable politico-economic environment. Average GDP growth rates failed to reach the level of previous decades. Unemployment soared, while a growing percentage of wage earners worked irregularly or part-time. Demographic change implied lower birth rates and increased life expectancy, causing a drain on the pension system's reserves. After joining the European Union in 1995, Austria opted to introduce the Euro at the earliest possible date and, thus, was compelled to comply with the Maastricht criteria. This resulted in additional pressure to reduce budget deficits and to curb social spending. But Tálos insists that prior to the year 2000 occasional measures to retrench the welfare state (such as the pension reforms of 1984 and 1988) were hardly motivated by ideological considerations. Not before Wolfgang Schüssel replaced socialist Chancellor Viktor Klima did a neo-classical turn in social policy occur, says Tálos. The current Austrian government has repeatedly professed belief in a "lean state." Its aim is to strengthen what it calls the individual's sense of social responsibility and to shift the emphasis of the welfare state from providing security for everyone to assisting those who are in need. After more than four decades of socialist dominance in welfare policies, that would certainly amount to a revolution. However, revolutions are for the French rather than for the Austrians. On this, Rathkolb, Butschek, and Tálos will probably agree.

Notes

1. Felix Butschek, *Vom Konflikt zur Konsensorientierung. Die Kammer für Arbeiter und Angestellte und die Wirtschaftspolitik Österreichs, 1920-1995* (Vienna: Kammer für Arbeiter und Angestellte für Wien, 1996).

2. Bruno Kreisky, *Im Strom der Politik: Der Memoiren zweiter Teil* (Berlin: Siedler, 1988). Bruno Kreisky, *Der Mensch im Mittelpunkt: Der Memoiren dritter Teil* (Vienna: Kremayr & Scheriau, 1996).

3. Evan Burr Bukey, *Hitler's Austria: Popular Sentiment in the Nazi Era, 1938-1945* (Chapel Hill, NC: Univ. of North Carolina P, 2000).

4. Theodor W. Adorno et al., *The Authoritarian Personality: Studies in Prejudice* (New York: W.W. Norton, 1969).

III. BOOK REVIEW

Gabriele Anderl and Alexandra Caruso, eds.,
NS-Kunstraub in Österreich und die Folgen
(Innsbruck: StudienVerlag, 2005)

Jonathan Petropoulos

A writer of popular "art crime novels" recently sent me an e-mail in which he inquired whether I could "identify the one most significant action taken by the Nazis during their methodical looting of the citizens and institutions they held sway over as they conquered most of Europe from 1933 forward." After considering his question, I replied that it was the events that transpired in Vienna after the Anschluß in March 1938—and more specifically, the proclamation of the *Führervorbehalt* in which Hitler asserted his authority in the chaotic Austrian metropolis. The more I thought about it, the more I realized that Vienna was central to the history of the National Socialists' *Kunstraub*: the plebiscitary support and avarice that accompanied the early "wild Aryanizations"; the creation of rival plundering agencies; the complicity of art dealers and auctions houses; Adolf Eichmann's creation of the *Wiener Modell* that denuded departing Jews of their property; and ultimately, the inextricable link between the expropriations and the Holocaust. This impression was confirmed and, indeed, more fully developed, while reading the important volume edited by Gabriele Anderl and Alexandra Caruso. Growing out of a conference held in Salzburg in 2003, *NS-Kunstraub in Österreich und die Folgen* features twenty contributions of wide-ranging and cutting edge research that take the reader from the most recent scholarship on *Sonderauftrag Linz* (the "*Führermuseum*" planned for Linz, but also a collecting initiative designed to bolster other provincial museums in Austria) to the renewed restitution efforts that followed the 1998 Austrian *Bundesrückgabegesetz* (federal restitution law). Since the late 1990s, no other nation has done more than Austria to rectify past injustices concerning Holocaust victims' property, and this includes the 2001 agreement to pay into a

General Settlement Fund, as well as numerous instances (involving more than 2,000 objects), where property in state institutions was returned to victims and heirs. Recent events have only amplified the significance of the history of *Kunstraub* in Austria.

Among the most important articles in the volume are those that focus on specific institutions that either carried out or benefited from the expropriations. Sabine Loitfellner's piece on the Vugesta ("Verwaltungsstelle für jüdisches Umzugsgut der Geheimen Staatspolizei"), for example, brings together recent research on this notorious agency that "processed" Jewish victims' property. Most of the Vugesta's records were closed to researchers until the late 1990s (the opening of archives was a key element in the 1998 *Bundesrückgabegesetz*). Similarly, the essays by Claudia Sporer-Heis, Martin Kofler, and Gerhard Plasser, which treat the *Ferdinandeum* in Innsbruck, the *Museum der Stadt Lienz*, and the *Landesgalerie Salzburg* respectively, take advantage of recently granted archival access. In their introduction to the book, Anderl and Caruso argue persuasively that "*das Thema NS-Kunstraub in Österreich keineswegs als systematisch wissenschaftlich aufgearbeitet gelten*" (12), meaning there still is a lot of research to be done. The way to remedy this situation rests upon the close study of specific institutions. Even though the vast majority of Austria's pre-Anschluß Jewish population (approximately 200,000) lived in Vienna, their property quickly migrated beyond the former capital. The examination of museums and individuals in the provinces is central to the project of understanding *Kunstraub* in Austria.

The specificity of many of the articles in this book is also a strength—a way of realizing the goal of a systematic scholarly treatment. Michael Wladika's examination of the gothic panels of Dr. Victor Blum and Walter Schuster's study of the art dealer Wolfgang Gurlitt are two notable case studies. The latter shows how this important dealer for *Sonderauftrag Linz* avoided justice after 1945—as was most often the case for those complicit in the *Kunstraub* program of the regime. Gabriele Anderl examines the art market in Vienna during the Third Reich and offers a series of illuminating case studies. Alexandra Caruso's treatment of the state auction house, the Dorotheum, also offers path-breaking research (although many of their records were "lost" during the war). Reading these varied articles on an array of institutions and individuals, one comes away agreeing with the startling insight provided by Birgit Kirchmayr in her study of *Sonderauftrag Linz*, "Der *'NS-Kunstraub' in Österreich war im Wesentlichen 'hausgemacht'*" (36). In other words, the expropriations and attendant persecution did not emanate from authorities in Berlin or elsewhere, but were perpetrated in large part by Austrians themselves.

Monika Meyer adopts a biographical approach in her piece on the director of the *Österreichische Galerie*, Dr. Bruno Grimschitz. Because of privacy laws and the frequently successful rehabilitation of careers in the post-1945 art world, many key figures have avoided scrutiny. Monika Mayer, who since 1996 has been director of *Archiv und Künstler-dokumenation* at the *Österreichische Galerie*, is well-positioned to study the art historian who directed the institution from 1938 to 1945. She articulates many of the criticisms leveled at Grimschitz in the postwar period and notes how he himself avoided a critical treatment of his career, but she also approaches her subject with caution. Most notably, she treats his role in acquiring three of the Bloch-Bauer Klimt paintings in a cursory manner. While Mayer notes that Grimschitz engaged in deals with the trustee of Ferdinand Bloch-Bauer's property (Dr. Erich Führer)—citing the 1941 trade and the 1943 purchase—she limits herself to a terse summary and does not avail herself of the interpretive potential of this episode. She also does not examine his part in the "de-Jewification" of many of Klimt's portraits. In wartime catalogues, for example, the golden portrait of Adele Bloch-Bauer (a prominent Jewish Viennese patron) took on the more anonymous title *Dame in Gold*. Grimschitz also helped the Austrian state retain the pictures in the post-1945 era; despite having been released from his post as director, he provided shrewd and sometimes cynical counsel on ways to deflect restitution claims by the heirs. Because six of the paintings by Klimt in the collection of the *Österreichische Galerie* were the subject of a lawsuit filed by Adele Bloch-Bauer's niece (Maria Altmann) and the other heirs, and because Dr. Mayer helped draft one of the expert reports about the provenance of the pictures in question (in the interest of full disclosure, so did the author of this review, who was commissioned by the plaintiffs), it is perhaps understandable that she would exhibit some reticence concerning this topic. This consideration aside, Mayer's treatment of Grimschitz is balanced. She is clear about how he joined the Nazi party in May 1938 and helped evaluate Jewish collections that were liquidated (a point emphasized in Alexandra Caruso's treatment of Grimschitz in her article), and Mayer gives a good sense of the rapacious acquisition policies of the *Galerie*; on the other hand, she notes that Grimschitz also helped to safeguard the museum's collection.

The failure to include a fuller treatment of the Bloch-Bauer Klimts is the greatest shortcoming of this volume. The lawsuit, which was by-and-large resolved in January 2006 when an Austrian arbitration court (*Schiedsgericht*) ruled that five of the paintings should be returned to Maria Altmann and the other heirs, is the most important restitution case since the immediate post-1945 period (note that a decision concerning

241

the sixth and final Klimt painting was deferred to a later point). The paintings represent the most valuable cultural property returned in many decades (they would certainly bring more than the $90.7 million earned by the sale of the Rothschilds' property in London in 1999); the case, where the jurisdiction of a U.S. court was upheld by the U.S. Supreme Court in a June 2004 ruling, exhibits the extent to which the American legal system will provide recourse for Holocaust victims' claims, and the Austrian *Schiedsgericht* is an important model for alternative dispute resolution. Of course, important developments in the case *Altmann v. Austria* occurred subsequent to the publication of this volume. But the claim dated back to the late 1990s and deserved more careful treatment (if not by Monika Mayer, then by another author).

This (one) criticism of the anthology, however, is offset by the volume's quality. The contributors to this book represent many of the best provenance researchers and scholars in the world who are working on Nazi art looting. All of these individuals strive to clarify this often murky history and are playing important roles in rectifying past injustices. Many served on the relatively recent *Historikerkommission der Republik Österreich* that produced the careful and extensive reports on Austria during the Third Reich. In short, the individuals in this volume are on the front lines as they "fight the good fight."

Furthermore, one of the strengths of this book lies in the contributions about recent restitution efforts. Gerhard Plasser's article on the *Landesgalerie Salzburg*, for example, includes photographs of the backs of paintings in the gallery and provides instruction regarding how to read the signs and to interpret the extant clues. Evelyn Adunka's essay on stolen books brings the reader up to date on restitution efforts for this category of cultural property. In addition, the contributions of Michael Franz, Ingo Zechner, Maren Gröning, and Esther Tisa Francini—all important figures in on-going provenance research—help to make this the best single volume on the topic of recent restitution efforts. *NS-Kunstraub in Österreich und die Folgen*, which balances the specific and the general and features cutting-edge scholarship, constitutes a tremendously important contribution to the field.

Thomas Klestil, *Der Verantwortung verpflichtet: Ansprachen und Vorträge 1992-2004*, ed. Herbert Schambeck (Vienna: Verlag Österreich, 2005)

Anton Pelinka

Thomas Klestil was elected Austria's federal president in 1992 as the candidate of the Austrian People's Party (ÖVP). In 1998, a multiple party platform of conservatives, social democrats, FPÖ representatives, and independents backed him for his successful re-election bid. In the process, he alienated himself increasingly from his own party, the ÖVP. After the parliamentary elections of October 1999, Klestil as a principal mediator in the coalition negotiations openly favored the prolongation of the traditional SPÖ/ÖVP "grand coalition." The president tried to prevent Wolfgang Schüssel from assuming the leadership position as chancellor of a "black-blue" (ÖVP/FPÖ) coalition. Such partisanship made most of his former friends in the ÖVP turn against him. By the end of his second term, Klestil had numerous friends in the SPÖ, outside his party, but few in the camp that had nourished his political ambitions. Most in the ÖVP considered him a traitor.

This unusual trajectory of political estrangement could not have been predicted after his first years as president. In 1994, Klestil unleashed a constitutional and political conflict with Chancellor Franz Vranitzky, a social democrat who governed Austria via grand coalitions from 1986 to 1997. Klestil contrived a legal argument to argue that the president and not the chancellor should represent Austria in the European Council. Vranitzky retorted with equal consistency that the chancellor was predestined to represent the country in the European Union's most prominent institution. Vranitzky ended up winning that battle more for political than constitutional reasons—not the least of which was his ÖVP coalition partner did not support Klestil.

Of course, these political conflicts are common knowledge in Austria and are well documented. However, they are missing in their entirety in the recently published collection of speeches under review here, edited by the prominent former member of the *Bundesrat* (the second Austrian parliamentary chamber), Herbert Schambeck. This collection is designed to underscore Klestil's role as a well-respected national and international statesman. Without any background knowledge of Klestil's dramatic years as president, then, succeeding his former colleague in the Foreign Ministery, Kurt Waldheim, and acting as major obstacle to Wolfgang Schüssel's pragmatic political alliance with Jörg Haider's party, such a documentation of his public speeches is misleading. Klestil in his public utterances comes across as a man representing the undisputed wisdom of the Austrian political mainstream, as a man favoring international openness, as a principal figure standing for Austrian responsibility for the Holocaust, and as an integral figure defending the success story of Austria's Second Republic.

Indeed, Klestil the *homo politicus* did reflect and express all these trends. Following in the footsteps of Chancellor Vranitzky's speeches, he was the second official Austrian spokesman to find the right words for characterizing Austrians' complex identity as both "victims and perpetrators" during the dark Nazi years between 1938 and 1945. His 15 November 1994 speech in Israel's parliament, the Knesset, is indeed a key document in recent Austrian history (pp. 277-82). Klestil also happened to be among the first politicians to consider Austria's new role as a member of the European Union, namely asserting that it was mandatory no longer to consider "EU Europe" as foreign territory, but as the community to which Austria now belonged. He expressed this sentiment in his televised speech of 4 February 2000, immediately after accepting (and appointing) the Schüssel cabinet, which at the same time constitutes his most significant political defeat (pp.119f).

A documentation of Klestil's political life through speeches alone does not come close to fleshing out this complex man, above all his unfulfilled promise to become a "strong" president, his failed ambition to prevent the ÖVP/FPÖ coalition government (Klestil clearly foresaw Austria's painful isolation within the European Union). The Klestil presidency was overshadowed by these setbacks and honorable political defeats, none of which is reflected in this volume of speeches.

Undoubtedly, Klestil was a key figure in Austria's most recent history. Yet part of his political legacy will be defined by these defeats, though first and foremost by his defeat in blocking the first Schüssel coalition government. His valiant struggle against the center-right coalition may serve as an excellent argument for Klestil's ethical and moral fortitude and for his keen diplomatic skill at balancing domestic and European perspectives. But it will go down as the Armageddon of his political life nevertheless.

Klestil's life includes one of the more distinguished careers in diplomacy and politics of the Second Republic. As a career diplomat, he

Contemporary Austrian Studies

represented Austria as ambassador to the United Nations in New York, as well as to the United States in Washington. This distinguished service abroad catapulted him into the position of political director in the Foreign Ministry, the pinnacle of a career in the Austrian Foreign Service. For most of his professional life, then, he was a loyal (and able) civil servant, much more so than a politician. His successful campaign as a "dark horse" for the presidency in 1992 came as a surprise. Yet his open ambition to be a "strong president" defied all political tradition and constitutional practice. The unwritten rules of Austrian politics call for strong chancellors such as Vranitzky and Schüssel. Austria's constitutional practice (*Realverfassung*) clearly specifies the central figure of Austrian politics to be the chancellor, backed by a majority in parliament, the National Council. The President is mostly a representative figurehead—a bit of a monarch in state visits at home and abroad, a bit of a promotional speaker during the opening ceremonies of many summer festivals—with real powers only in the appointment of governments. All of Klestil's predecessors in the president's office have resigned themselves to this secondary political role. Klestil tried to reinvent the office and to challenge the borders defined by tradition and constitutional practice—in vain.

This lesson Klestil learned the hard way. The political complexity in Klestil's career in the *Hofburg* is not reflected in this documentation of some 100 official speeches. It does not diminish the content and the messages of those speeches. However, the historical contexts and the political background of the man who delivered them through all the ups and downs of his political ambitions and defeats are missing. The editor should have this pointed out. Observant readers need to know it, particularly those who are not familiar with the daily partisan infighting in Austrian politics. As an introduction to Thomas Klestil as political actor and idea man, this documentation of his official speeches as federal president is helpful. The biography and/or political history of the real Klestil still needs to be written.

Thomas Hanifle, "Im Zweifel auf Seiten der Schwachen": Claus Gatterer, Eine Biographie (Innsbruck: Studienverlag, 2005)

Rolf Steininger

South Tyrol is a region about half the size of Connecticut located in the heart of the Alps. It had been part of Austria for over 500 years and almost totally German-speaking before it was awarded to Italy as "spoils of war" after World War I. The fascist regime under Benito Mussolini embarked on a full-scale policy of Italianization and industrialization of this rural land, largely colonizing it from the *Mezzogiorno*, that is, immigration in large numbers from the south, introduction of Italian as the official language, closing down of all German public schools, and Italianization of German place and family names, including even the defacement of tombstones. In 1939, an agreement was reached between Hitler and Mussolini known as the *Option*: South Tyroleans could "opt" between retaining Italian nationality or migrating to the "Greater German Reich" as German citizens. About 86 percent, or 200,000, voted for the Reich; 75,000 actually left South Tyrol.

This was the world into which Claus Gatterer was born in Sexten in 1924. As a child and student, he experienced the fascist policy all the way up to the Option; he never forgot this first example of ethnic cleansing. To get some kind of higher education and to learn German, one had to go to a high school run by the Church which was protected under the so-called Lateran treaties between the Vatican and the fascist state. Gatterer went to this school until 1943. In the same year, Mussolini was overthrown, Italy switched sides, and northern Italy was occupied by German troops. To escape the draft into the German *Wehrmacht*, Gatterer fled to Padua; at the university there, he studied history and philosophy. Early in 1944, he went back to Sexten and from there to Parma, where he stayed until the end of the war.

Early in 1939, he had met Friedl Volgger, one of the most prominent "*Dableiber*" (as those who had not opted for Germany in 1939 were derisively called) who after the war became one of the most

influential persons of the newly founded South Tyrolean People's Party
(*Südtiroler Volkspartei*, SVP) and a kind of mentor to Gatterer. For three
years, Gatterer was press officer of the SVP. In 1948, he crossed the
border again and went to Innsbruck to take a job at the daily *Tiroler
Nachrichten*. He stayed there until 1957, then went to the *Salzburger
Nachrichten*; in 1961, he left there to work at Vienna's daily, *Die
Presse*, and stayed there until 1967. He then took five years off to work
as a free-lance writer; from 1972 until his death in 1984 he was in
charge of the TV magazine *teleobjektiv* for Austrian Public Television
(ORF). Gatterer was one of the most prominent and best-known journalists in Austria. Although he spent the most important time of his life not
in South Tyrol but in Austria and from 1956 was an Austrian citizen—or
precisely because of this—he remained to the core a South Tyrolean and
intimately bound to his homeland. The history and fate of his land
concerned him, and he conveyed this to his readers.

The young South Tyrolean journalist Thomas Hanifle presents the
first full-scale biography of Claus Gatterer. Much of the story is drawn
from press-clippings, private letters, Gatterer's diary, and interviews. It
is a good try, well-written and readable, despite the fact that Hanifle
lacks a certain distance towards his "hero," for example, when he
frequently calls Gatterer by his first name, Claus, which sounds very
strange in such a biography.

What, then, do we learn from Hanifle? He makes it abundantly clear
how little a prophet counts in his own country. Gatterer himself said he
was politically "left," and advice from a leftist wasn't worth much in
conservative South Tyrol. Gatterer had a truly critical mind. He fought
in his articles against the continuation of fascist policy, demanded
political autonomy for South Tyrol, and combined this with the call for
internal democracy and a critical examination of South Tyrol's history.
This was the impetus and prerequisite for a new self awareness, which
he considered at the same time requisite for a coexistence of the three
ethnic groups: the German-speaking, the Italian, and the Ladin. What
stood in the way of this, for him, was a lack of historical awareness on
the part of many of his fellow South Tyroleans, who for their part often
viewed him as fouling the nest.

In the period following World War II, among the most interesting
years in South Tyrol were those from 1959 to 1969: bombs in the
beginning, in the end "the package," the basis for a true autonomy.
Gatterer was a pronounced opponent of violence in any form. At the
same time, he was in close contact with Austrian Foreign Minister
Bruno Kreisky. I would have liked to see more information here about
Kreisky's position. Who influenced him? Who knew what about the
bombings and the bombers from the "Night of Fire" in 1961?

We learn, on the other hand, something about the origin of the two most important books Gatterer produced as a free-lance writer: his comprehensive portrayal in 1968 of the struggle of the minorities against Rome and the autobiographical novel in 1969 about his childhood. Gatterer was considered to be an outstanding journalist in Austria, less so in South Tyrol, at least until 1981. In that year, he received the South Tyrolean Press Award from the Bozen Press Association and representatives of the South Tyrolean media. Gatterer was proud of this award, although it was something of a move to keep up appearances. Nonetheless, Gatterer was not one of them, remaining true to himself. In his acceptance speech, he spoke about the "difficulty of being South Tyrolean today," saying, moreover, "The South Tyroleans know their history only in fragments. The complete picture would be disruptive, uncomfortable." At the same time, he criticized the short-term profit mentality, the sell-out and the thoughtless relinquishing of cultural values for economic advantage.

This was surely all true, but the majority did not like it, not at that time—and obviously not today considering the final sentence of the biography, in which Hanifle describes his research in the Claus Gatterer Library in his native Sexten, where he could not help feeling that he was "one of the rare visitors" of that library.

Hans Seidel, *Österreichs Wirtschaft und Wirtschaftspolitik nach dem Zweiten Weltkrieg* (Vienna: Manz-Verlag, 2005)

Dieter Stiefel[*]

Two important trajectories have raised interest in post-World War II European reconstruction in the course of the 1990s: first, the contentious debates over "Holocaust-era assets," namely the issue of expropriation of Jewish properties by the Nazi regime and the restitution efforts after 1945; and second, the "opening of the East" after the end of the Cold War and the transition of Eastern European state-directed economies to market economies. In the case of the first issue, it was a rare instance of a unique historical research effort driving the process of the financial debates over non-restitution of Jewish wealth; in the case of the second issue, the question has been raised whether lessons from postwar Western European reconstruction may be of value for the rebuilding of the formerly communist countries. What can be learned from history?

Discourses on both these trajectories have greatly enriched scholarly investigations of these issues. First, the timeline on critically engaging historical issues in Austria has been shifting. Up until the 1990s, scholars had been researching the interwar era or the Nazi period and World War II; they have only slowly approached the postwar era. It had been symptomatic of Austrian scholarly and public discourse to see the year 1945 as the "zero hour"; continuities with the prewar years were largely ignored. Since the 1990s, the period from the 1930s to the 1950s has been seen as a contiguous era of its own, which opened new perspectives and insights. Second, confronting the "Holocaust-era assets" issue before, during, and after the war, Austrian archives opened their rich holdings for the first time to a small army of researchers. The "Austrian Historians Commission" published more than forty volumes of research on its own; publications on this issue around Europe are so vast that no single historian can master them anymore. Third, with the

---

* Translated from German by Günter Bischof.

post-Cold War transition in Eastern Europe, economists have discovered history. The war economies were planned economies, and postwar reconstruction constituted only a gradual transition to market economies. At the end of the 1980s, Eastern European economies, societies, and legal cultures resembled a state of affairs usually only encountered after long, lost wars. Economists intensely debated the question of whether a "Marshall Plan" was required for the East, but reality soon overtook such scholarly debates. This, however, induced economists to take a closer look at the complex post-1945 reconstruction efforts and to move away from their vision of pristine, undiluted market economies. Hans Seidel's *magnum opus* represents such an archetypical case study of postwar reconstruction.

At the tender age of twenty-four and back from the war and a POW camp, Hans Seidel entered the prestigious Austrian Institute of Economic Research (*Österreichisches Institut für Wirtschaftsforschung*, or WIFO). He is a rare case of being both a witness to and an actor in postwar Austrian economic reconstruction. Later, Seidel was promoted to director of WIFO; in the early 1980s, he also served as the state secretary in the Finance Ministry and as such held a position in Chancellor Bruno Kreisky's last cabinet. From 1984 to 1990, he directed the prestigious Institute for Advanced Studies in Vienna, which since its foundation in the mid-1960s has served as the breeding ground for top economists and social scientists in Austria. Hans Seidel never denied his calling of being an "old school" economist familiar with econometric models but steeped in applied economic policy thinking. Given the Austrian norm of retirees usually spending their time in the *Heurigen* or at golf courses, it is a rather fortuitous event that Seidel, following his retirement, hit the archives for months on end to delve into the primary sources of postwar reconstruction. What he found was quite familiar to the former adviser, who had been involved in the wings with making economic policy. As a seasoned economist with a scholarly bent, he found it easy to interpret it in a comprehensive postwar framework. There is nary an Austrian historian who could have written such a well-informed and superior work of economic history.

What, then, was so unique about Austrian economic reconstruction between 1945 and 1955? From 1938 until 1945, Austria had been absorbed by Adolph Hitler's Third Reich. The balance sheet of Austria's seven-year incorporation into the "1000-Year Reich" turned out to be quite different than what had been anticipated at the time of the 1938 "Anschluss": World War II resulted in 194,000 Austrian deaths and 76,000 people missing; this constituted 4 percent of the population. On top of this fact, 170,000 veterans returned wounded and as permanently disabled "invalids." The Nazis murdered some 100,000 Austrians in their concentration camps, among them 65,000 Jews. Fully 120,000 Austrian Jews were forced to leave the country—only very few of them returned after the war. Records indicate that 488,000 Austrian ended up in prisoner of war camps around the world, some of them for up to ten years. At the end of 1945, some 1.7 million refugees/Displaced Persons (among them 650,000 German speakers) lived on Austrian territory; 236,000 of them chose Austria as their permanent home and stayed. Such enormous human suffering on Austrian territory did not stop with the war's end. In 1945, Vienna's mortality rate was 3.59 percent, the highest among any European city in the modern era.

On top of this vast human tragedy came enormous material losses: 76,000 apartments had been entirely—and another 100,000 partially— destroyed as a result of the war and the Allied bombing raids. Energy supplies were almost totally interrupted after the war, half of the railroad tracks were torn up, and 318 bridges had been destroyed or damaged. Only 40 percent of the locomotives and one-third of the automobiles used in the prewar period were still operable. Compared to 1937, Austrian GDP declined by one-third, and agrarian production by half. At the same time, the currency supply was grossly inflated from 1.2 to 8 billion *Reichsmark*.

The victorious Allies promised to treat Austria as a "liberated" country politically. Yet the actual policy suggested that they saw Austria more like the mirror image of defeated Germany. With Soviet, U.S., British, and French zones of occupation, they levied a quadripartite control regime over the land. Vienna, like Berlin, was also under four-power Allied control, with a quadripartite international sector in the inner city of the First District. Then there was the huge problem of "German assets." Based on Allied agreements written down in the Potsdam summit meeting in July 1945, the Allies laid their hands on German assets in foreign countries for reparation purposes. "German assets" in Austria, however, had been considerably augmented as a result of expropriation under duress following the Anschluss and subsequent Nazi wartime investments. For example, German-held shares in Austrian industrial joint stock companies had increased from 8 percent in 1937 to 57 percent in 1945. In order to shield against the transfer of these shares as "German assets" into foreign hands, the Figl government nationalized seventy-one large industrial combines in 1946, comprising some 20 percent of Austrian industry. On top of this action, in 1947 the top three Austrian banks as well as 85 percent of Austria's electricity industry were nationalized. The three Western powers tolerated with reservations these nationalization decrees; Moscow ignored them and seized all the "German assets" in their zone to organize them in the giant USIA holding company for direct Soviet exploitation for reparations out of current production. For the rest of the occupation period, between 30,000 and 60,000 people were employed by USIA. The Austrian economy suffered enormous losses from it.

The occupation regime also bled the Austrian economy directly, for the Austrian government had to pay for the occupation costs, which during the immediate postwar period (1945-1947) increased from 1 billion to 3 billion Austrian schillings. In 1947, one-third of the Austrian budgetary expenses went to covering occupation costs. In the same year, the United States decided to pay for these costs itself and to reimburse Austria for the previous occupation costs it had incurred. The Soviets followed suit in 1953 and the British and French in 1954, but never reimbursed these costs to Austria.

We also must not ignore that "mastering the World War II past" incurred costs for the economy. Massive "de-Nazification" procedures against half a million former members of the Nazi Party and restitution payments to the numerous victims of the war put a heavy burden on the economy, including legal and administrative costs. Part of the "economic *Vergangenheitsbewältigung*" included the settlement of Austria's prewar national debt, concluded in a special international conference in Rome in 1952. The most challenging problem in this arena was the disentanglement of economic and property issues with the young Federal Republic of Germany; who would shoulder the financial burdens of the National Socialist era? These issues were only resolved as a result of the conclusion of the Austrian State Treaty in 1955 and a special German-Austrian economic assets treaty in 1958.

The expropriation of Austrian property in the succession states of the Habsburg Monarchy that turned Communist constituted an egregious loss of wealth for Austrians. In the territory of the former empire, only South Tyrol/Trentino and Austria were not swept up by Communism. The roundabout expropriations in Czechoslovakia were the most enormous losses to the Austrian economy.

The reconstruction regime also had repercussions in the legal sphere. Postwar Austria made a basic decision to allow for legal continuity with the prewar period: only the laws introduced by National Socialism were purged. Further legal innovations followed subsequently; reconstruction thus offered Austria the opportunity to modernize its entire legal system.

The postwar Austrian political leadership then faced enormous obstacles in reconstruction in 1945 and thereafter. Any historian tackling the postwar era faces the same challenges trying to write a comprehensive study. Seidel is fully up to the task. He first presents both an overview of the structural factors of the economy since the 1930s and the basic options for economic policies after 1945. Then he focuses on reconstruction strategies, namely the competing visions of the Western allies and Austrian leaders. Major chapters also cover the complexities of currency reform, government alimentation, the black market, the state-directed trade regime, and the Marshall Plan. Finally, he concludes with a chapter on economic costs of the State Treaty of 1955 as well as a preview of the economic parameters of the "golden economic age" (E.J. Hobsbawm) of the post-occupation years.

Seidel's most impressive feats are his analysis of Austrian monetary policy and the Marshall Plan. His analysis is based on his mining the rich archives of the Austrian National Bank. He goes into great detail about the planning and the implementation of the entire currency reform schemes—from the Banking and Schilling Law of 1945 (which blocked some assets in bank acounts and cash reserves) to the Currency Law of 1947 (which cancelled these blocked accounts). He zooms in on the brazen credit arrangements extended by the Soviets (*Russen-Kredit*) in 1945. When the Red Army liberated Vienna and Graz, they seized the entire cash holdings of the Austrian National Bank and private banks. When the Provisional Renner Government began operations in May 1945, it had no cash to re-launch governmental operations. The Soviets provided 600 million in seized *Reichsmark* banknotes (Nazi Germany's currency). The Renner government considered this offer as stopgap help and intended to return the *Reichsmark* notes once enough Austrian currency had been printed. However, when new Schilling notes had been printed after the currency reform laws had been passed, Moscow insisted on being repaid in the new Schilling currency and eventually succeeded with this ploy. The seemingly generous Russian "loan," in fact, turned out to be a hidden reparations scheme.

Seidel also covers the reconstitution of the Austrian National Bank (which had never been completely liquidated), the basics of its monetary policy, and its strict currency control regime. He does not shy away from analyzing rampant postwar inflation—up to double digits in 1952—and its ballooning effects on the GDP. The Austrian social partners came up with a traditional, elaborate, corporate economic policy regime to control inflation via five unsatisfactory wage-price agreements. Only a restrictive budgetary spending policy began putting the brakes on inflation. With resulting higher unemployment in the workforce, the political costs were considerable.

The highpoint of Seidel's book is his chapter on the Marshall Plan, the legendary U.S. aid program that was enormously important for Austrian reconstruction. His study could have been even more definitive if he had taken the time to incorporate the U.S. Marshall Plan files, too. However, he chose not to go the Washington archives. Yet mining the rich Austrian Marshall Plan files allows him to analyze the contributions of the European Recovery Program (ERP) in unmatched detail. He summarizes the development of a number of U.S. aid programs and how they helped with both closing the "dollar gap" and providing the domestic investments funds needed to eventually balance Austrian foreign trade and currency reserves. In the first years of the Marshall Plan (1948/49), the ERP paid for half of Austrian imports. Seidel's signal contribution is to stress the *gradualism* of the Marshall Plan and its quiet step-by-step strategy towards building a market economy. It is a precious irony of history that in Austria the lion's share of Marshall Plan counterpart investment funds went to the nationalized, state-owned industries. This is a rare example of the U.S. market economy promoting a state-directed industrial sector.

In the final chapter on the State Treaty, Seidel takes stock of the entire occupation period. Like Günter Bischof (*Austria in the First Cold War*, pp. 87, 102) before him, but in much greater detail, he arrives at the surprising conclusion of a rough equivalency between Western aid (including the Marshall Plan) and "hidden reparations" to the Soviets (for example, occupation costs, industrial removals, the "Soviet loan," current production of the Soviet-controlled USIA businesses, and the transfer costs of the State Treaty). In other words, had Austria been a truly liberated, free country without such a burdensome occupation regime, Austrian economic reconstruction could have been fuelled with its own resources. This would have been even more the case were it not for the Cold War, which interrupted Austria's traditionally intense economic ties with her neighbors Czechoslovakia, Hungary, and Yugoslavia.

Hans Seidel's book, no doubt, provides a rock-solid and lasting scholarly footing for Austrian postwar economic history for the occupation/reconstruction decade. Given the depth of this 600-page monograph, one is tempted to skim over areas that have received inadequate treatment in Seidel's monograph. But this reviewer would be amiss in failing to point out that the entire complex of de-Nazification and restitution has not been addressed. Both, of course, are not only political, but also economic problems. The basic legal framework of the Austrian economic arrangement is not much covered either, among it the origins of mandatory membership in the chambers of commerce. The loss of Austrian foreign assets in Eastern Europe deserves more attention as well, as do demographic developments, for hundreds of thousands of refugees and displaced persons were integrated into the Austrian economy and played a crucial role in the reconstruction effort. Seidel may turn a blind eye to such social and political trajectories because the Austrian Institute of Economic Research habitually trained its students to ignore such factors, too. The advantage of Seidel's perspective, however, aided by his long-standing WIFO affiliation, is the serious interest of the theoretically wise economist in fine points of economic history. Here the regular historian is no match. Given the length and depth of this study, one would have wished for a concluding chapter summarizing the many new insights that he introduces to the scholarly discourse of the occupation decade. But Seidel may want to keep the interested reader waiting for the continuation of his study after 1955. A successor volume is already on its way and will keep us waiting for more. Stay tuned.

Ingrid Böhler, *Dornbirn in Kriegen und Krisen: 1914-1945*, Innsbrucker Forschungen zur Zeitgeschichte 23 (Innsbruck: Studien Verlag, 2005)

Renate Huber, *Identität in Bewegung: Zwischen Zugehörigkeit und Differenz, Vorarlberg 1945-1965* (Innsbruck: Studien Verlag, 2004)

Wolfgang Weber

In Austria, the 1970s saw history becoming a discipline of the social sciences. The 1980s saw history becoming part of a local research movement. The 1990s made it postmodern. Consequently, the first decade of the twenty-first century should see Clio becoming post- structural. The two books reviewed here may give a hint how history as a post-structural discipline could develop. Both investigate local/regional history. Where Ingrid Böhler carried out her research on the history of the small Austrian town Dornbirn in the most western Austrian province of Vorarlberg in the first half of the twentieth century, Renate Huber focuses her study around the history of the entire Vorarlberg province itself from the mid 1940s to the mid-1960s. Postmodernity in both books talks through the titles: the authors decided to include central themes such as "wars and crises" (Böhler), "identity" and "continuity/discontinuity" (Huber) in the book titles. Within their monographs, they group these "big themes" around the "big narratives" in the local (Dornbirn) and regional (Vorarlberg) discourses. Such narratives are constructed through written sources of administrative origin stored in public archives such as the Vorarlberg and the Tyrol Provincial Archives as well as through interviews which both authors have carried out in the course of their research. Therefore, written and oral sources provide the main theoretical framework of both studies.

Böhler's study, based on her dissertation at Leopold Franzens University Innsbruck, consists of three central chapters. Chapter One deals with the political, economic, and social history of Dornbirn during the First World War; Chapter Two deals with the same issues during the interwar period; Chapter Three picks up the political, economic, and social developments in Dornbirn during World War II. Economically speaking, all three époques were characterized by modernization and diversification strategies of the main local employer, the textile industry. In the course of World War I, the local textile factory owners successfully re-arranged their products as well as their markets. With the decline of the Habsburg Empire in the autumn of 1918, Dornbirn's industry lost the main market for its products which has been the eastern half of the old empire. A substitute was found in the Vorarlberg province's neighboring countries of Germany and Switzerland. Wage cuts and shortened hours combined with the a rationalization of the work process and a modernization of the plant enabled the local industry not only to survive the World Economic Crisis of 1929-1931, but also to establish savings and reserves. In 1936/37, approximately 10 percent of goods produced by local weaving mills were produced as reserves. After the Anschluß to Hitler's Germany in 1938, such reserves were dumped on the bigger and depleted German market and offered the local industry good profits. Such profits were reinvested in the companies which then had to be modified to reach the wider German market and to join the German warfare industry. Dornbirn capitalists, especially the textile crowd, had been on good terms with the new Nazi elite, for they traditionally were linked to the German nationalist stratum of the population. Several members of the local industrial elite engaged in nationalist politics during the 1920s und 1930s and had been involved not only in the Dornbirn but also in the Vorarlberg Nazi movement. In her study, Böhler introduces the most influential amongst these political and industrial elite with its prosopographical background. By doing so, she is able to offer a convincing explanation why the Anschluß in Dornbirn and, therefore, in Austria was such an easy business: An astonishing number amongst the old conservative and the new national political elite was related to each other or at least shared a common socialization in the same neighborhood, the same school, the same leisure associations. As simple as this sounds is as simple as it really is. Concerning the social history of the three époques, Böhler concludes that it had been a period of poverty and impoverishment for the majority of the middle and lower classes. The average unemployment rate from the early 1920s to the late 1930s was 20-30 percent. In 1932, a fifth of Dornbirn primary school pupils were classified as suffering from malnutrition. The local history of this small town in the most western Austrian province did not differ from the national histories of Austria or Germany at that time. The big merit of Böhler's study is that she establishes that fact, and by researching the Dornbirn microcosm, she is able to offer insights into the various games of power within politics and economics that may be lost by carrying out a national or universal study. She includes such national and universal aspects in her interpretation and compares the national with the local experience. Therefore, her findings can be generalized at least for Austrian national history and may serve as an example of how National Socialism came to power in the provinces and not only the cities.

Böhler concludes her study by adding two more central (and post-modern) themes to the ones mentioned in the title of her book. Besides "wars and crises" she writes of "continuity and change." These two additional themes characterized Dornbirn history during the two decades under review.

Continuity and change are also two key terms in Renate Huber's book about the development of identity in postwar Austria between 1945 and 1965. The study is based on her dissertation at the European University Institute at Florence (Italy). The Vorarlberg Province and its polity, policy, and politics from the mid-1940s to the mid-1960s serve as the research laboratory for Huber's investigation of one central sociological process, the building of identity. According to Huber, history acts as a main tool within that process. She argues that the central discourse on identity is a discourse on continuity and discontinuity. To exemplify this, she investigates the various statements of the Vorarlberg political elite about Austrian nation building post-1945. Such statements were published in daily newspapers, but are also reflected in the records of the provincial government stored at the Vorarlberg Provincial Archives in Bregenz. Huber's findings are amazing and convincing at the same time.

Picking up several well-known notions describing Austria in the postwar decade, she makes a plea for a multi-layered postmodern approach to the recent past and its description by historians (and politicians). "Resurrection," for example, was and is a common term used to label the early years of the Austrian Second Republic. If a thing is erected again, it excludes issues that existed before the resurrection and at the same time includes issues which must have been there even earlier. In the Austrian case, the National Socialist dictatorship between 1938 and 1945 was the issue to be excluded and the governments before 1938 was the issue to be included, irrespective of whether such governments were democratic, fascist, or royal. The latter was the case regarding Austria before 1938. The Habsburg Monarchy was followed by the First Republic which was followed by the Austro-fascist state. Although the polity in these different époques of Austrian history was completely different, the political elite referred to the three as one single period. Doing so produced a continuum of the Austrian past which never has been there in reality. The public stage on which this continuum was performed in the Vorarlberg province changed during the two decades under research. In 1946, the local politicians celebrated the "resurrection of Austria" together with the French occupation forces. On May Day, they took the salute at a parade in the province's capital, Bregenz. In 1955, the Austrian federal government in Vienna celebrated the State Treaty as Austria's liberation with a big public rally at the Belvedere Castle, whereas in Vorarlberg no public activities were reported. The local governor only delivered a commemorative speech published in local newspapers. In his speech, he was very keen to stress that Vorarlberg's population welcomed neutrality long before "the Austrian politicians" made it an issue of the State Treaty due to the long democratic tradition the province developed since the Medieval Ages (!). According to Huber, the governor's view may be interpreted as a turn away from the national Austrian continuous identity delivered in the 1940s towards a more specified regional Austrian identity—as a result of the then-ended resurrection process.

Besides investigating the discourses about central notions such as "resurrection" amongst the political Vorarlberg establishment from the 1940s to the 1960s, Huber also looks at how "the people" in Vorarlberg experienced these discourses. For that purpose, she carried out several biographical interviews with female *Zeitzeugen*. The analyses of these interviews enlarge Huber's findings with a central category of a (post) modern historiography: the personal dimension. History is not only created by human beings as actors, it is also experienced through the common man or common woman. The historical myths by which we live may exclusively be created by a political establishment, but they are transferred and kept alive through the people. The people's perception of central notions within historical discourses depends on several sociological features such as gender, class, and geographical origin. None of these features are stable. On the contrary, they are in flux. So are the notions. Besides continuity, says Huber, change is another central category of the identity-building process—be it political or personal, national or regional, male or female, self or other.

If history as a research discipline may join the road other social sciences have entered in the late 1990s by defining themselves as post-structural, Böhler and Huber's studies could be used as a role model for the design of such research activities: The objects of research are "big themes" such as change and continuity, reflected in oral and written sources, investigated in local or regional environments, and generalized for a wider national or even universal history. Methodologically, such studies may use descriptive, quantitative, or qualitative methods, depending on the questions of research which ideally have been derived in academic and international contexts.

ANNUAL REVIEW

Austria 2005

2005: 60-50-10
FPÖ – BZÖ
Elections in Styria, Burgenland, and Vienna
Irving and Gudenus
Economic Data

Reinhold Gärtner

2005: 60-50-10

The year 2005 was one of remembrance: sixty years after the liberation from National Socialism (1945), fifty years after the state treaty of Vienna (1955), and ten years membership in the European Union. There were celebrations, exhibitions, more or less thought out performances (for example, the heavily disputed "25 Peaces"), but according to reliable polls, most of the population were not really interested in these events. Consequently, the participation of the population in various activities was not really overwhelming, either. For example, on 15 May—exactly fifty years after the signing of the state treaty of Vienna—the crowd at the Belvedere was relatively small.

FPÖ – BZÖ

In April 2005, Jörg Haider, together with Vice-Chancellor Hubert Gorbach and Minister Ursula Haubner, founded a new party, the *Bündnis Zukunft Österreich* (BZÖ, or Alliance for the Future of Austria; cf. *CAS* vol. 11). Prior to that, the divisions within the FPÖ had become more and more visible, especially between the right wing of the party (centered around Ewald Stadler, Andreas Mölzer, and the future chairman Heinz Christian Strache) and the more moderate FPÖ members of government plus Haider. Another reason for the split was that it seemed to be very likely that at the party convention in April 2005 Strache would run for the office of chairman, thus removing Haider from the center of power within the party. So the BZÖ came into being with the objective of gaining seats in the autumn 2006 national State Diet elections. Most of the FPÖ ministers of parliament changed party affiliation from the FPÖ to the BZÖ, as did some FPÖ country organizations (only to come back to the FPÖ a few months later, as in Upper Austria). The one word to describe the situation would be chaos.

The consequences of the split have been very different for both parties. The FPÖ is on its way back (though it is much less powerful than it was in the 1990s). They lost their seats in the Styrian parliament, but the losses in Vienna were more moderate than expected. The BZÖ, though, is still stumbling around, for it was very unsuccessful in the elections in Styria and Vienna (it did not run for votes in Burgenland). At press time, it seems to be very unlikely that the BZÖ will gain 4 percent in the 2006 elections. The party does have the possibility of gaining a seat on the regional level, but as in the 2002 election when the FPÖ did not win a single seat on the regional level, it is very unlikely that the BZÖ will manage that. To do so, the party would need approximately 25-30 percent of the vote to win a seat in a regional constituency. In April 2005, there were doubts if the FPÖ would survive politically; in April 2006, there seems to be no doubt that it will, but it is not likely that FPÖ will achieve the success that it had at its apex, in 1999 (26.91 percent), in the near future.

Elections in Styria, Burgenland, and Vienna

In October 2005, country elections were held in Styria, Burgenland, and Vienna.

The most interesting case was Styria. First, for the first time since 1945, the ÖVP lost the governorship. Waltraud Klasnic's ÖVP was shaken by inner problems (ESTAG, Gerhard Hirschmann), and the SPÖ took advantage of this to win both the governorship (now occupied by Franz Voves) and the majority of seats. Second, another interesting aspect was the results for the KPÖ (Communist Party). The success of the KPÖ was not due to ideological aspects, but to the former performance of its chairman, Ernst Kaltenegger, in the Graz city government. Third, the BZÖ was seriously beaten.

Table 1: Election Results in Styria, 2005

Party	Percentage 2005	Seats 2005 (+/-)
SPÖ	41.7 (+9.3)	25 (+6)
ÖVP	38.7 (-8.6)	24 (-3)
FPÖ	4.6 (-7.8)	0
Grüne	4.7 (-0.9)	3 (+/- 0)
KPÖ	6.3 (+5.3)	4 (+4)
BZÖ	1.7 (n.c.)	

Source: Interior Ministry, Official Election Results.

The elections in Burgenland were without surprises. The SPÖ managed to increase its number of seats, and the FPÖ at least managed to stay in the state parliament. The BZÖ did not compete.

Table 2: Election Results in Burgenland, 2005

Party	Percentage 2005	Seats 2005 (+/-)
SPÖ	52.2 (+5.6)	19 (+2)
ÖVP	36.4 (+1.1)	13 (+/- 0)
FPÖ	5.8 (-6.9)	2 (-2)
Grüne	5.2 (-0.3)	2 (+/- 0)

Source: Interior Ministry, Official Election Results.

Finally, in Vienna the SPÖ did not win as much as expected, but still maintained a comfortable absolute majority. The losses of the FPÖ were smaller than expected, but it is still far from a consolidation (the State Diet elections in 2006 will reveal if the FPÖ can stop the implosion which started in 2002). The ÖVP could finish as runner up (instead of the FPÖ), and the Grüne party faced a problem familiar to it from many elections: their results usually are not as good as the polls prior to the elections would suggest. The BZÖ did compete, but got a disastrous result with only 1.1 percent of the vote.

Table 3: Election Results in Vienna, 2005

Party	Percentage 2005	Seats 2005 (+/-)
SPÖ	49.1 (+2.2)	55 (+3)
ÖVP	18.8 (+2.4)	18 (+2)
FPÖ	14.8 (-5.4)	13 (-8)
Grüne	14.6 (+2.3)	14 (+3)
BZP	1.1 (n.c.)	Not applicable

Source: Interior Ministry, Official Election Results.

Irving and Gudenus

In autumn 2005, David Irving came to Austria to hold a lecture; he was invited by a right- wing students' association (*Burschenschaft Olympia*). In 1989, Irving had previously traveled in Austria, and at least since then he was known as a denier of the Holocaust (cf. the Lipstedt-Irving trial in London a few years ago). The denial of the Holocaust is against the law in Austria (*Verbotsgesetz*). What followed the lecture was Irving's imprisonment and trial. Ultimately, he was sentenced to serve to three years in prison.

John Gudenus was member of *Bundesrat* (the second chamber of parliament), and in spring 2005, he said, "There were gas chambers. But not in the Third Reich. They were in Poland. This is written down in our schoolbooks." Before making that statement, he had already expressed his doubts about the existence of gas chambers, but this new scandal led to a trial in April 2006. The Irving and Gudenus cases were widely discussed, the main point of the discussion being whether or not Austria still needs *Verbotsgesetz* (the law banning National Socialism).

Economic Data

In 2005, an average of 3,234,600 people were employed, and 252,700 were unemployed (compared to 244,000 in 2004). The rate of unemployment was 7.2 percent (+ 0.1 percent). The GDP was at -246 billion; inflation was at 2.1 percent (as in 2004). According to Maastricht Criteria, the public deficit was 1.5 percent of GDP (compared to 1.3 percent in 2004), and the public debt was 62.9 percent of GDP, or -151.3 billion.

List of Authors

Ingrid Bauer, professor of history, University of Salzburg

Peter Berger, professor of economic history, Vienna University of Economics and Business Administration

Günter Bischof, professor and chair of history at the University of New Orleans; Director, CenterAustria

Matti Bunzl, associate professor of anthropology and history, University of Illinois, Urbana-Champaign

Franz Eder, professor of social history, University of Vienna

Dagmar Herzog, professor of history at the Graduate Center, City University of New York

Renate Huber, historian, lecturer both at the department of contemporary history, University of Innsbruck, and the center for social and intercultural competence, the Johannes Kepler University Linz

Pieter Judson, professor of history, chair of the history department at Swarthmore College and editor of the *Austrian History Yearbook*

David Luft, professor of history, University of California, San Diego

Maria Mesner, historian and executive director, Bruno Kreisky Archives, Vienna

Anton Pelinka, professor emeritus of political science, University of Innsbruck; since fall of 2006 professor of political science, Central European University, Budapest

Jonathan Petropoulos, John V. Croul Professor of European History, Claremont McKenna College

Scott Spector, associate professor of history, University of Michigan, Ann Arbor

Rolf Steininger, professor and chair of contemporary history, University of Innsbruck; senior research fellow, Eisenhower Center for American Studies, University of New Orleans

Dieter Stiefel, professor of history, chair of the department of economic and social history, University of Vienna

Wolfgang Weber, historian and archivist, Vorarlberg provincial archives, Bregenz; lecturer, Institute of Contemporary History, University of Innsbruck

Julia Woesthoff, assistant professor of history, De Paul University, Chicago, Illinois

Contemporary Austrian Studies

Günter Bischof and Anton Pelinka, Editors

Transaction Publishers, New Brunswick (N.J.) and London (U.K)

CPSIA information can be obtained at www.ICGtesting.com
Printed in the USA
LVOW11s1626130814

398968LV00004B/902/P